International College
Information Resource Center
2655 Northbrooke Drive
Naples, Florida USA 34119
www.internationalcollege.edu

# About Pfeiffer

Pfeiffer serves the professional development and hands-on resource needs of training and human resource practitioners and gives them products to do their jobs better. We deliver proven ideas and solutions from experts in HR development and HR management, and we offer effective and customizable tools to improve workplace performance. From novice to seasoned professional, Pfeiffer is the source you can trust to make yourself and your organization more successful.

**Essential Knowledge** Pfeiffer produces insightful, practical, and comprehensive materials on topics that matter the most to training and HR professionals. Our Essential Knowledge resources translate the expertise of seasoned professionals into practical, how-to guidance on critical workplace issues and problems. These resources are supported by case studies, worksheets, and job aids and are frequently supplemented with CD-ROMs, websites, and other means of making the content easier to read, understand, and use.

**Essential Tools** Pfeiffer's Essential Tools resources save time and expense by offering proven, ready-to-use materials—including exercises, activities, games, instruments, and assessments—for use during a training or team-learning event. These resources are frequently offered in loose-leaf or CD-ROM format to facilitate copying and customization of the material.

Pfeiffer also recognizes the remarkable power of new technologies in expanding the reach and effectiveness of training. While e-hype has often created whizbang solutions in search of a problem, we are dedicated to bringing convenience and enhancements to proven training solutions. All our e-tools comply with rigorous functionality standards. The most appropriate technology wrapped around essential content yields the perfect solution for today's on-the-go trainers and human resource professionals.

International College
Information Resource Center
2655 Northbrooke Drive
Naples, Florida USA 34119
www.internationalcollege.edu

**Pfeiffer**
www.pfeiffer.com

*Essential resources for training and HR professionals*

*Best Practices in Leadership Development
and Organization Change*

# Best Practices in Leadership Development and Organization Change

*How the Best Companies Ensure Meaningful Change and Sustainable Leadership*

Louis Carter
David Ulrich
Marshall Goldsmith
Editors

A Wiley Imprint
www.pfeiffer.com

Published by Pfeiffer
An Imprint of Wiley
989 Market Street, San Francisco, CA 94103-1741
www.pfeiffer.com

For additional copies/bulk purchases of this book in the U.S. please contact 800-274-4434.

Pfeiffer books and products are available through most bookstores. To contact Pfeiffer directly call our Customer Care Department within the U.S. at 800-274-4434, outside the U.S. at 317-572-3985, fax 317-572-4002, or visit www.pfeiffer.com.

Pfeiffer also publishes its books in a variety of electronic formats. Some content that appears in print may not be available in electronic books.

ISBN: 0-7879-7625-3

**Library of Congress Cataloging-in-Publication Data**

Best practices in leadership development and organization change: how the best companies ensure meaningful change and sustainable leadership/ [edited by] Louis Carter, David Ulrich, Marshall Goldsmith.
p. cm.
Includes bibliographical references and index.
ISBN 0-7879-7625 3 (alk. paper)
1. Leadership—United States—Case studies. 2. Organizational change—United States—Case studies. I. Carter, Louis. II. Ulrich, David, 1953– III. Goldsmith, Marshall.
HD57.7.B477 2005
658.4'06—dc22

2004021983

Acquiring Editor: Matt Davis
Director of Development: Kathleen Dolan Davies
Developmental Editor: Susan Rachmeler
Production Editor: Rachel Anderson
Editor: Suzanne Copenhagen
Manufacturing Supervisor: Bill Matherly
Editorial Assistant: Laura Reizman
Interior Design: Andrew Ogus
Jacket Design: Adrian Morgan
Printed in the United States of America
Printing   10   9   8   7   6   5   4   3   2   1

# CONTENTS

Acknowledgments    ix

About This Book    xi

How to Use This Book    xiii

Introduction    xv
  *Louis Carter, David Ulrich, Marshall Goldsmith*

 1  Agilent Technologies, Inc.    1

 2  Corning    20

 3  Delnor Hospital    43

 4  Emmis Communications    79

 5  First Consulting Group    120

 6  GE Capital    161

 7  Hewlett-Packard    181

 8  Honeywell Aerospace    195

 9  Intel    213

10  Lockheed Martin    239

11  Mattel   262

12  McDonald's Corporation   282

13  MIT   309

14  Motorola   334

15  Praxair   346

16  St. Luke's Hospital and Health Network   365

17  StorageTek   403

18  Windber Medical Center   423

19  Conclusion: Practitioner Trends and Findings   439

About the Best Practices Institute   453

About the Editors   455

Index   457

# ACKNOWLEDGMENTS

| Best Practices Institute Team | Contributors, by Representative Organization |

## BPI EDITORIAL TEAM

Louis Carter, CEO and Founder

Christine Alemany, Research Assistant

Joanna Centona, Research Assistant

Victoria Nbidia, Research Assistant

Michal Samuel, Research Assistant

Connie Liauw, Research Assistant

Shawn Sawyer, Assistant

### Contributors, by Representative Organization

Diane Anderson, Agilent Technologies, Inc.
Kelly Brookhouse, Motorola
Susan Burnett, Hewlett-Packard
Paula Cowan, First Consulting Group
Susan Curtis, StorageTek
Linda Deering, Delnor Hospital
John Graboski, Praxair
Joseph Grenny, Lockheed Martin
Brian Griffin, Delnor Hospital
Dale Halm, Intel
James Intagliata, McDonald's Corporation
F. Nicholas Jacobs, Windber Medical Center
David Kuehler, Mattel
Jamie M. Lane, Motorola
Craig Livermore, Delnor Hospital
Ruth Neil, Praxair
John Nelson, Emmis Communications
Richard O'Leary, Corning
Jeff Osborne, Honeywell Aerospace
Melany Peacock, Corning
Lawrence Peters, Lockheed Martin
M. Quinn Price, Lockheed Martin
Rich Rardin, Praxair
Ivy Ross, Mattel
Susan Rudolph, Intel
Linda Sharkey, GE Capital
Robert A. Silva, Agilent Technologies, Inc.
David Small, McDonald's Corporation
Janelle Smith, Intel
Andrew Starr, St. Luke's Hospital and Health Network
Brian O. Underhill, Agilent Technologies, Inc.
Karen Walker, Agilent Technolgies, Inc.
Bob Weigand, St. Luke's Hospital and Health Network
Calhoun Wick, Fort Hill Company
Karie Willyerd, Lockheed Martin
Tom Wright, Delnor Hospital
Greg Zlevor, Honeywell Aerospace

# ABOUT THIS BOOK

The purpose of this best practices handbook is to provide you with all of the most current and necessary elements and practical "how-to" advice on how to implement a best practice change or leadership development initiative within your organization. The handbook was created to provide you a current twenty-first century snapshot of the world of leadership development and organizational change today. It serves as a learning ground for organization and social systems of all sizes and types to begin reducing resistance to change and development through more employee and customer-centered programs that emphasize consensus building; self-, group, organizational, and one-on-one awareness and effective communication; clear connections to overall business objectives; and quantifiable business results. Contributing organizations in this book are widely recognized as among the best in organization change and leadership development today. They provide invaluable lessons in succeeding during crisis or growth modes and economies. As best practice organizational champions, they share many attributes, including openness to learning and collaboration, humility, innovation and creativity, integrity, a high regard for people's needs and perspectives, and a passion for change. Most of all, these are the organizations who have invested in human capital, the most important asset inside of organizations today. And these are the organizations that have spent on average $500 thousand on leadership development and change, and an average of $1 million over the course of their programs, with an average rate of return on investment of over $2 million.

Within the forthcoming chapters, you will learn from our world's best organizations in various industries and sizes

- Key elements of leading successful and results-driven change and leadership development
- Tools, models, instruments, and strategies for leading change and development
- Practical "how-to" approaches to diagnosing, assessing, designing, implementing, coaching, following up on, and evaluating change and development
- Critical success factors *and* critical failure factors, among others

Within each case study in this book, you will learn how to

- Analyze the need for the specific leadership development or organization change initiative
- Build a business case for leadership development and organization change
- Identify the audience for the initiative
- Design the initiative
- Implement the design for the initiative
- Evaluate the effectiveness of the initiative

# HOW TO USE THIS BOOK

## PRACTICAL APPLICATION

This book contains step-by-step approaches, tools, instruments, models, and practices for implementing the entire process of leadership development and change. The components of this book can be practically leveraged within your work environment to enable a leadership development or change initiative. The exhibits, forms, and instruments at the back of each chapter may be used within the classroom or by your organization development team or learners.

## WORKSHOPS, SEMINARS, OR ADVANCED DEGREE CLASSES

The case studies, tools, and research within this book are ideal for students of advanced degree courses in management, organization development and behavior, or social and organizational psychology. In addition, this book can be used by any senior vice president, vice president, director, or program manager who is in charge of leadership development and change for his or her organization. Teams of managers—project manager, program managers, organization development (OD) designers, or other program designers and trainers—should use the case studies in this book as starting points and benchmarks for the success of the organization's initiatives.

This book contains a series of distinct case studies that involve various corporate needs and objectives. It is your job as the reader to begin the process of diagnosing your company's unique organizational objectives.

When applying and learning from the case studies and research in this book, ask yourself, your team, and each other the following questions:

- What is our context today?
- What do we (I) want to accomplish? Why?
- In what context am I most passionate about leading change and development? Why?
- What are the issue(s) and concerns we are challenged with?
- Are we asking the right questions?
- Who are the right stakeholders?
- What approaches have worked in the past? Why?
- What approaches have failed in the past? Why?

For more information on Lou Carter's Best Practices Institute's workshops, research, assessments, and models on the most current leadership development and organizational change topics, contact Louis Carter's Best Practices Institute directly, toll free at 888–895–8949 or via e-mail at lcarter@bpinstitute.net.

# INTRODUCTION

In September 2003, Lou Carter's Best Practices Institute performed a research study on trends and practices in leadership development and organization change. BPI asked organizations in a range of industries, sizes, and positions in the business cycle to identify their top methods of achieving strategic change and objectives. The study found that there is a strong demand, in particular, in the following areas of leadership development and organization change (see Table I.1). Our continual research in the area of best practices in leadership development and change strongly support the assumptions and organizational case studies that we profile within this book.

Based on this study, BPI chose the top organizations that are implementing leadership development and organizational change with extraordinary results. BPI found that each organization is unique in its methods of change and development. Each organization has different methods, motives, and objectives that are relevant only to the unique landscape of each of its individual dynamics and designs. Leadership development and organization change, therefore, are mere categories or a common lexicon for describing the way in which "real work" is done within our best organizations. This "real work" is illustrated within every chapter of the book in terms of the business results that are achieved as a result of the practices that were institutionalized within the following organizations (see Table I.2). A majority of our world's best organizations describe leadership development and organization change as "the real work of the organization." In the past few years, we have seen this shift occur in the field of organization

Table I.1. Program Method of Achieving Strategic Change and Objectives with Highest
Level of Demand, in Order of Demand

| OD/HRD Topic | Ranking |
|---|---|
| Leadership development | 1 |
| Performance management | 2 |
| Organization development and change | 3 |
| Innovation and service enhancement | 4 |
| Coaching | 5 |

development or "OD." Organizations are finding that in order to compete, innovate, and become more effective, productive, and profitable in an increasingly global and challenging economy, the tools, techniques, and practices of OD are necessary in order to harness the great power of human capital—both in customers and employees. As you will see in this book, our best practice organizations prove the power of human capital through results-driven best practices in organization development and change.

We have brought you eighteen of our world's best organizations that have used leadership development and organizational change program design and development to achieve their strategic business objectives.

# MAJOR FINDINGS

This year we talked to many organizations from a variety of industries with proven, practical methods for leadership development and organizational change to compile this book. We asked them to share the approaches, tools, and specific methods that made their programs successful. These organizations have a strong financial history, formal human resource management programs that integrate company strategy with its program's objectives, a strong pool of talent, passion for positive change, and proven results from their initiatives. All organizational initiatives were carefully screened through a six-phase diagnosis for an extraordinary leadership and organizational change program (see under A Step-by-Step System to Organization and Human Resources Development, below).

We chose companies that have succeeded in successfully implementing results-driven transformational organization change that achieves positive business results. These are the companies where change is facilitated through

Table I.2. Listing of Best Practice Case Studies by Company, Industry,
Number of Employees, and Gross Revenue

| Company | Industry | Employees | Revenues ($U.S.) |
|---|---|---|---|
| Agilent Technologies, Inc. | Electronics | 36,000 | $6,010.0 M |
| Corning | Communications | 23,300 | $3,164.0 M |
| Delnor Hospital | Health care | 1,382 | $235.1 M |
| Emmis Communications | Media | 3,080 | $533.8 M |
| First Consulting Group | Business services | 1,775 | $282.7 M |
| GE Capital | Finance | 315,000+ | $131.7 B |
| Hewlett-Packard | Computer hardware | 141,000 | $56,588.0 M |
| Honeywell Aeorspace | Technology and manufacturing | 100,000+ | $22,274 M |
| Intel | Manufacturing, electronics | 78,700 | $26,764.0 M |
| Lockheed Martin | Aerospace and defense | 125,000 | $26,578.0 M |
| Mattel | Consumer products | 25,000 | $4,885.3 M |
| McDonald's Corporation | Leisure, restaurant | 413,000 | $15,405.7 M |
| MIT | Education | 9,400 | $1,664.7 M |
| Motorola | Telecommunications | 97,000 | $26,679.0 M |
| Praxair | Chemicals | 25,010 | $5,128.0 M |
| St. Luke's Hospital and Health Network | Health care | 5500 | $424 M |
| StorageTek | Computer hardware | 7,100 | $2,039.6 M |
| Windber Medical Center | Health care | 427 | $54 M |

integrated, multilevel programs that are systemic in nature, connect directly to business objectives and continuous improvement, and include the following shared elements.

## Commitment to Organizational Objectives and Culture

Most of the initiatives we examined made a commitment to the strategic objectives or culture of the organization. Almost all of these initiatives have a message or vision upon which change or development was built. Emmis Communication stressed the following objectives in its change effort to promote better under-standing and agreement on its structure, strategy, and culture: "Great Media, Great People, Great Service." Lockheed Martin designed its cultural change management program around its three core competencies:

- Candid and open communication
- Taking personal action to unblock obstacles that prevent effective performance
- Acting when the need exists rather than ignoring issues

McDonalds's leadership development program for regional managers enabled newly promoted managers to meet expectations while furthering the organization's mission and strategic objectives by building the following competencies:

- Developing a strategic perspective
- Maximizing business performance
- Gaining skills in insightful reasoning, problem solving, innovation, and mental agility

Motorola's leadership development program centered around leadership competencies and behaviors that promoted customer focus and superior performance—envision, energize, edge, and execute—which were later dubbed the "4e's + Always 1."

First Consulting Group (FCG) began by exhibiting one of FCG's primary values: "Firm First." It detailed objectives directing that leadership should

- Eliminate barriers to the achievement of FCG's vision
- Build succession plans; identify, train, and support future generations of FCG leadership
- Create an environment that causes leaders to interact and depend on one another
- Instill Leadership First's program values until they are as ingrained in FCG's culture as its universal personal characteristics.
- Be truly substantive rather than a "touchy-feely philosophical/conceptual" program
- Ensure that the initiative is not a short-term "fad" remedy for current problems but something to be kept alive for a multiyear period

MIT's program is designed around the goal of creating an organization that constructs, operates, serves, and maintains physical space in ways that enhance MIT's mission to advance knowledge and educate students in science, technology, and other areas of scholarship. The program at Corning addressed the need to stress innovation as one of the most important quality programs because it transcends and affects all areas of the organization, thus serving as a common thread throughout the entire organization. StorageTek redefined its organizational objectives and in doing so has made strides toward producing a culture that is more employee-centered. Demonstrating greater commitment to its employees has helped reconnect the company with consumer needs and has resulted in greater productivity and a more optimistic outlook. Hewlett-Packard's Dynamic Leadership was designed to address clear and compelling corporate needs with well-defined outcomes. To translate productivity into a true growth engine, Honeywell has successfully evolved Six Sigma from a process improvement initiative to a fundamental component of its leadership system with the powerful combination of Six Sigma, Lean, and Leadership.

## Changing Behaviors, Cultures, and Perceptions

Sometimes leadership development and change programs transformed perceptions, behaviors, and culture(s) within a company. At MIT, employees have been documented as saying that they find themselves being more authentic in their interactions with coworkers and have the desire to create and be a part of an organization that "anticipates" learning opportunities. Decentralizing the institution and control of resources improved the way that operating divisions, previously functioning in independent silos, were innovating. At Mattel, Project Platypus demonstrated that delivering on the values of trust, communication, respect, and teamwork could literally pay off and that creativity in the process of innovation should be the rule rather than the exception. At Praxair, the new management team had to transform a loose confederation of businesses with different cultures, operating procedures, values, and ways of managing employees into a market leader that combines speed advantages of being small with the scale advantages of being large. HP recognized that in order to compete successfully in new market realities defined by global competition, with high-quality products from Asia and Europe competing for market share in the United States as well as their home markets, required a management culture that was capable of engaging in high-speed collaboration, raising and resolving issues rapidly, and making informed decisions efficiently. At Windber Medical Center, Delnor Hospital, and St. Luke's there was a definitive shift toward patient-centered care and significant improvements in employee and patient morale and satisfaction.

## Competency or Organization Effectiveness Models

Virtually all of these programs have some sort of explicit model, usually using behavioral competencies or organization assessment metrics. These range from General Electric values to the metrics within Motorola's performance management system. Many of the study's programs were specific to the behaviors required of coaches and managers who facilitate the performance management process. First Consulting Group's creation of targeted objectives to assist in achieving the organization's vision through an intensified and streamlined leadership development program, incorporating 360-degree/multi-rater feedback, suggests that leaders previously lacked self-awareness. MIT used adapted models based on the work of Peter Senge, organizational learning capabilities, and W. Warner Burke's key competencies for organizational learning. These models frequently form the basis of multi-rater and other competency-based assessment tools, and often provide a focal point to the systemic design of the program itself.

## Strong Top Management Leadership Support and Passion

Top leaders at the organization must not only budget for the change and leadership development initiative, they must also strongly believe in the initiative and model this behavior throughout the organization. Support from senior management has been identified by 88 percent of the contributors as a critical step in overcoming resistance to change.

GE Capital energized its business leaders by designing its program around its leaders' behaviors and values, a focus that generated buy-in in high levels of the organization, and by having participants work on projects for the office of the CEO. Windber Medical Center's patient empowerment program was driven by its CEO, Nick Jacobs. In his account of Windber's organizational change program and what drove its emphasis for patient-centered care at the hospital, President Jabobs writes, "When a patient walks into the typical hospital, the overwhelming confusing signage, the smell of antiseptics, the curt and often unforgiving attitude of the employees, and the awesome power of the physicians are usually clear indicators that they should leave their dignity at the door." Jacobs is passionate about patient care, and it shows in the programs that he has supported for years.

When Agilent first became an independent entity, its CEO made development of future leaders one of his first priorities. He drew on initiatives already in place to ensure buy-in and then improved on these processes by making them universally applicable. First Consulting Group demonstrated a strong sense of support from top-level executives through its creation of the Leadership Development Committee, which included the CEO, two vice presidents, and an eighteen-member task force of director and vice president-level staff, whose responsibility was to aide in conducting organizational assessment and benchmarking survey data to assist in the development of future organizational leaders. At Praxair, the change team recommended a four-step leadership strategy design process to engage Praxair Distribution, Inc.'s (PDI's) top 175 managers in assessing the current state of the leadership practices and the changes required for PDI employees to become a sustainable source of competitive advantage. Former chairman and CEO of Honeywell Larry Bossidy's zeal for Six Sigma was without a doubt exactly what the company needed to get this initiative off the ground and on the radar screen of every leader and employee. FCG is unique in that the firm's CEO and executive committee serve as facilitators to the Leadership First program sessions, and one member is required to be a sponsor for the participants.

# A STEP-BY-STEP SYSTEM TO ORGANIZATION AND HUMAN RESOURCES DEVELOPMENT

The Best Practices Institute has defined a six-phase system to leadership and organization change, which may be seen in most of the case studies in this book:

1. Business diagnosis

2. Assessment

3. Program design

4. Implementation

5. On-the-job support

6. Evaluation

## Phase One: Business Diagnosis

The first phase is usually a diagnostic step in which the business drivers and rationale for creating the initiative are identified. Critical to this stage is enabling consensus and a sense of urgency regarding the need for the initiative. A future vision that is supported by management is a key factor of success for these programs. All of the systems have some model as a focal point for their work. The best of these models capture the imagination and aspirations of employees and the entire organization. Designing the system also leads to strategic questions, such as those taken from the GE Capital example:

- What are biggest challenges facing the business—what keeps you awake at night?

- If you had one message to future leaders of this business what would it be?

- What will leaders need to do to address the business challenges?

- What is it that you want to be remembered for as a leader?

- What was your greatest defining moment that taught you the most about leadership?

- What excites you most about your current role?

HP conducted a survey on "Reinventing HP." More than seven thousand managers and individual contributors responded. Several themes emerged that underscored the need to accelerate decision making and collaboration. Respondents throughout the organization recognized the need to accelerate decision making and increase accountability for action, thereby reinforcing senior management's call for greater agility.

A well-thought-out diagnostic phase is usually connected to an evaluation of the desired business impacts in Phase Six.

## Phase Two: Assessment

Assessments range from GE Capital's assessment system (in which participants complete a 360-feedback survey that includes a question to describe a particular person at peak performance) to the Myers Briggs Type Indicator (MBTI) to the Leadership Impact Survey (a survey that correlates leader behavior with organization culture and value) to First Consulting Group's system (in which individual participant assessment is conducted with five vehicles: participant self-assessment, 360-degree and multi-rater feedback, external benchmarks, managerial style profile, and behavioral needs profile).

Assessment has become a norm for business. The question is how we use the assessment to drive change in our businesses and ourselves. Agilent used it to develop leadership behavioral profiles based on the company's strategic priorities, core values, and expectations of those in senior leadership roles. StorageTek performed an internal scan to determine what components of transformation were lacking. Praxair conducted the assessment process to prepare the organization for future changes by engaging more than five hundred employees: 175 leaders in the top three levels of management and over 325 employees across all fifteen regional businesses. Organizations such as General Electric, Intel, Motorola, McDonald's, and others use behavioral analysis tools such as the Myers-Briggs Type Indicator or 360-degree assessments. Individual coaching often accompanies this assessment to facilitate behavioral change in participants. This coaching has been extremely successful for firms such as GE Capital, Intel, Agilent, McDonald's, and others.

## Phase Three: Program Design

The following outstanding programs have several unique elements that are worthy of note.

- *Coaching.* Intel's coaching and mentoring system features internal coaches and a support network of program participants and graduates. Emmis Communications used coaching to help managers overcome resistance to cultural change.

- *Selection of participants.* Agilent's coaching program has a results guarantee so employees are required to undergo a qualification process, including an interview before being allowed to participate. Intel uses an application process to screen out apathetic or disinterested candidates. McDonald's selects only high-potential candidates chosen by their division presidents.

- *Action learning.* General Electric, Mattel and McDonald's use action learning as an integral part of their leadership development systems. In particular, General Electric's action learning program focuses on solving real business problems, whereas McDonald's centers around operational innovations. These programs address such questions as

  What is a "doable" project that still expands thinking?

  How do we set senior management's expectations for the business value that the learning will produce?

  How do action teams stay together as learning groups over time?

- *Leveraging multiple tools.* Every organization from Mattel to GE Capital took great care to use a variety of methods to train, develop, and innovate. At Hewlett-Packard (HP), the final design was a fast-paced program that interspersed presentations with small group work, practice, and discussions in order to provide sufficient depth and practice without overwhelming the participants or requiring excessive time out of the office. At Mattel, a small group was recruited to participate in an immersion program that included the use of floor-to-ceiling chalkboards and a twelve-by-forty-foot pushpin wall that acted as living journals, and self-discovery speakers to help each participant discover a renewed sense of self and expressiveness.

- *Use of current practices.* Corning uses past strengths and successes to leverage future success. Through focusing on history and storytelling, Corning is able to increase entrepreneurial behavior. StorageTek was careful to build its organizational changes upon programs and practices that were already in place in order to lend a sense of stability and consistency to its initiatives.

- *Connection to core organizational purpose.* St. Luke's Hospital and Health System embraces some basic concepts that foster a culture of service excellence and form the basis of its models for leadership development such as its management philosophy, vision for patient satisfaction, PCRAFT core values, service excellence standards of performance, and performance improvement plan. These concepts include

  1. Employee satisfaction yields patient satisfaction yields a successful "business" (Build your people . . . they build your business)

2. Employee satisfaction begins and ends with effective leaders who provide vision, clear expectations regarding care and service, development and education, effective communication, role modeling, constructive feedback, and recognition
3. Effective leaders can and need to be developed
4. Leadership development and education is based on educating to change behavior

At Windber Medical Center, there was a clear program built on the following transformational changes. The organization determined that it would focus on patient-centered care as the number-one priority of the organization; provide a loving, nurturing environment to the patients and their families; address all patient and patient family issues quickly and efficiently; and become recognized locally, regionally, and nationally for this new type of commitment to care that did not compromise the patients' dignity.

## Phase Four: Implementation

Almost all of the initiatives have a formalized training and development program or workshops to propel the change or development process into action. The following are components of several noteworthy training and development workshops:

• Lockheed Martin trained leaders to teach new behavioral competencies to their employees in order to overcome their own resistance through public commitment to the behavioral competencies. Lockheed Martin also focused on a group of opinion leaders within the company to influence their peers during the cultural change effort.

• First Consulting Group's program, Leadership First, prides itself on employing a situational approach rather than a more typical subject matter approach by incorporating case studies based on actual FCG work and scenarios. Unlike many other programs that focus on motivation and communication, FCG's program focuses on various skills. For example, when completing a merger case study, the potential leader must focus on a variety of issues: financial, legal, business and revenue implications, emotional, motivational, and communication. FCG is also unique in that the firm's CEO and executive committee serve as facilitators to the sessions, and one member is required to be a sponsor for the participants.

• Mattel's Project Platypus centered on individual development in order to maximize creativity directed toward product innovation. Trust, respect, and communication were all encouraged through the use of storytelling, creative culture speakers, and "face-to-face" connection. Outside experts such as a Jungian Analyst and a Japanese Tea Master helped hone the team's observational skills. Using the concepts of postmodernism and the company as a living system, the original group of twelve brainstormed, bonded, branded, and even researched in nontraditional ways; their efforts resulted in "Ello," a hybrid building toy for girls that is expected to be a $100 million line.

- To ensure that dynamic leadership principles were put into practice, HP implemented a rigorous postcourse management system using a commercial follow-through management tool (*Friday5s®*). In the concluding session of the program, participants were asked to write out two objectives to apply what they had learned to their jobs. The following week, participants were reminded of their goals by e-mail. A copy of each participant's objectives was e-mailed to his or her manager to ensure that managers knew what their direct reports had learned and intended to work on. The system made each participant's goals visible to all the other members of his or her cohort to encourage shared accountability and learning. These were entered into a group-specific *Friday5s®* website. The following week, participants were reminded of their goals by e-mail.

Other companies implemented change-catalyst programs to help prevent systemic dysfunction.

- A key exercise in MIT's transformational program was a visionary exercise that focused on helping developing leaders envision change and see themselves as a part of the whole system. Envisioning the department operating in a healthy and productive way in five years stimulated participants to discuss what they are doing today to help ensure that transformation. Participants became involved in thinking in a new way and realized the impact their decisions had not only for the future of the department, but also on each other.
- At Corning, an innovation task force was established to focus on the company's successes and also identify short-comings—both considered an untapped resource that needed to be made more visible and understood by employees in order to champion and embrace the concept of innovation. Formalized training programs for employees of all levels were set up and became part of the basis for promotion, reviews, and hiring. Corning also instituted a program named Corning Competes, which is designed for continuous improvement of business practices through reengineering.
- StorageTek knew that for its initiatives to be successful they would need to instill a sense of urgency, as well as ensure buy-in at all levels. They partnered with a company specializing in transforming strategic direction through employee dialogue to create a learning map called "Current Reality: The Flood of Information." The map was extremely effective in engaging not only top-level leaders worldwide, but all StorageTek employees in discussion about the company's competitive environment. The next step, which included additional communications and initiatives around achieving a high-performance culture, served to sustain the sense of urgency.

• At Praxair the assessment phase lasted over fifteen months and was far more than a few surveys or focus groups. It was an intensive set of actions, engaging more than five hundred employees and simultaneously laying the foundation for implementation actions endorsed by those whose behaviors were expected to change. Resistance during the implementation phase was virtually nonexistent.

## Phase Five: On-the-Job Support

These benchmark programs reach beyond the boardrooms and classrooms and provide on-the-job reinforcement and support. Work in this phase defines the follow-up support that determines whether change and development will transfer on the job. In several of the programs, the support system outside of training is one of the most salient elements of the organization development–human resources development (OD-HRD) initiative. Motorola installed a performance management system to help transfer the shared goals of the organization to individual behavior. McDonald's integrated program-specific insights with the overall organization's ongoing personal development systems and processes. Emmis Communication celebrated individual achievements during special events and used a balanced scorecard measurement system to incorporate the desired behaviors to measure the company's performance.

Agilent uses a slightly different approach in its coaching system, involving periodic "check-ins" with the participants' constituents throughout the coaching process. The check-in is important in part because the developmental goals addressed by the Accelerated Performance for Executives program often pertain to the relations between managers and their supervisor, peers, and supervisees, and so forth, and also because these constituents are the ones that determine whether or not a participants have been successful in their development. Along similar lines, Mattel increased manager participation in its innovation process so that when employees returned to their original roles after participating in Project Platypus, there was smoother reintegration and improved utilization of new skills.

The coaching and mentoring case studies in this book are specifically designed to provide ongoing support and development for leadership development initiatives. Both the coaching and mentoring case studies, Intel and General Electric, are excellent examples of organizations that provide ongoing support for leadership development and more specifically the organization's strategic business goals and objectives. Other organizations take a more direct approach to providing ongoing support and development for change by installing review processes. First Consulting Group, Motorola, MIT, and Praxair have ongoing review, monitoring, and analysis processes in place to ensure that the new policies and procedures are being followed. Delnor Hospital helped teams stay on track by requiring department heads to develop ninety-day plans that outline specific actions to be taken each quarter in working toward annual goals. This principle is also built into the hospital's review and evaluation system so everyone is held accountable for his or her performance in achieving individual, team, and organizational goals.

## Phase Six: Evaluation

Evaluation is the capstone—the point at which the organization can gain insights on how to revise and strengthen a program, eliminate barriers to its reinforcement and use in the field, and connect the intervention back to the original goals to measure success. Several initiatives deserve noting in this stage:

- McDonald's uses behavioral measurements to assess the participants' performance after the program, including the rate of promotion and performance evaluations.

- Emmis Communication measures revenue per employee, employee survey results, and the rate of undesired turnover to measure the success of the change effort.

- Lockheed Martin used employee surveys to track changes in critical behavior. The results indicated that units that achieved significant improvement in critical behaviors also improved in their financial performance.

- Intel Fab 12's leadership development program measures the effectiveness of its program based upon increased participants' responsibility after graduation, postprogram self-assessments, peer recognition letters, and results of WOW! Projects implemented by participants while in the Leadership Development Forum.

- GE Capital surveys participants about actions taken at the individual, team, and organizational levels to drive change. The surveys follow the original construct of the program around the three levels of leadership after graduation. A mini-360 is conducted around each participant's specific development need; 95 percent of the participants show an improvement as viewed by their original feedback givers. Program evaluations are also conducted to ensure that the design and content remain relevant and adapt to a global audience.

- Agilent used a combination of mini-surveys, telephone check-ins, and face-to-face interviews to determine perceived improvement in a leader's overall leadership effectiveness and specific areas for development. The aggregate results were impressive in that close to 80 percent of respondents felt that the leader rated had been successful in his or her development. That coaching results are guaranteed is another testament to the effectiveness of the program.

# CONCLUSION

Should companies invest in organization and human resource development? Having spent an average of over U.S. $500 thousand and showing a return on investment (ROI) of an average two times their investment in leadership development and organizational change initiatives, most of the organizational contributors in this book would make a strong case for "yes!" Most of the initiatives in this book have made significant impacts on the culture and objectives of the organization. The impacts on the business and transfer on the job may have taken the form of improved global competitiveness, increased profitability, new product sales, increased shareholder value, or hardening of a company for a merger or acquisition. The exact metrics for these transformational impacts need to be continually studied, tracked, and measured.

The future of the field of human resources, organization, and leadership development rests not only in its ability to prove return on investment and measure outcomes on a consistent basis, but is also contingent on several factors that will help sustain its continued growth and development. All eighteen best practice systems share four main factors:

- Implementation and design with a full understanding of the uniqueness of the organizational culture and organizational system within the context of its social system

- Whole-scale organizational excitement and belief in the programs and practices that are provided

- Continual assessment of hard and soft measurements resulting from the program evaluated against costs

- The creation of a profit model for development that is tied to business objectives

Not unlike other major industries, the consulting and development business has become increasingly competitive during the past few years—especially after September 11, 2001, and the Gulf crises in 2003, among several other factors that have contributed to economic instability. Higher unemployment and layoffs within consulting firms have left hundreds of thousands of niche-independent consultants on the market. Organization and leadership development directors within organizations must be more mindful than ever to keep focus on their organizational objectives and needs when dealing with any outside consulting firm. I am reminded of the statement by John Atkinson, "If you don't run your own life, someone else will." It is sage advice to listen to your own needs and instincts for your organization, supported with sound data from all levels of your organization.

Clearly, there are prominently shared views and approaches across the various industries and OD-HRD practices of what is needed to address the challenge of making change. The formula for organization development and change remains an important goal, which companies need to keep as an asset. We look forward to tracking these and other organizations as they continue in their leadership development and change journeys.

*October 2004*                                          Louis Carter
*Waltham, Massachusetts*
David Ulrich
*Ville Mont Royal, Quebec*
Marshall Goldsmith
*Rancho Santa Fe, California*

# CHAPTER ONE

# Agilent Technologies, Inc.

*Agilent Technologies' corporate-wide executive coaching program for high-performing and high-potential senior leaders features a customized 360-degree-feedback leadership profile, an international network of external coaches, and a "pay for results" clause linked to follow-up measurements.*

| | |
|---|---|
| OVERVIEW | 2 |
| BACKGROUND | 2 |
| Early Coaching Efforts | 2 |
| Agilent Global Leadership Profile | 3 |
| DESIGN OF THE APEX PROGRAM | 4 |
| Initial Objectives | 4 |
| Five Coaching Options | 5 |
| Results-Guarantee Clause | 6 |
| Worldwide Coaching Pool | 6 |
| Internal Marketing | 7 |
| ABOUT THE APEX PROCESS | 8 |
| Qualification and Coach Assignment | 8 |
| What Do Coaches and Executives Do in the Program? | 8 |
| Follow-Up with Key Stakeholders | 10 |
| MEASUREMENT: THE MINI-SURVEY PROCESS | 10 |
| RESULTS | 10 |
| Figure 1.1: Aggregate Results for Overall Leadership Effectiveness | 11 |
| Figure 1.2: Aggregate Results for Selected Areas of Development | 12 |
| Figure 1.3: Aggregate Results for Follow-up Versus No Follow-up | 13 |
| KEY INSIGHTS AND LESSONS LEARNED | 13 |
| EXHIBITS | |
| Exhibit 1.1: The Agilent Business Leader Inventory | 15 |
| Exhibit 1.2: The Agilent Global Leadership Profile | 15 |
| Exhibit 1.3: Agilent Sample Mini-Survey | 16 |
| ABOUT THE CONTRIBUTORS | 18 |

# OVERVIEW

As a 47,000-person Silicon Valley "start-up," Agilent Technologies was presented with an opportunity to begin anew. The senior leadership team set out to pursue the company's future strategy and new corporate values. A focused leadership development program aligned with the company's strategic initiatives, including an integrated executive coaching program, quickly became a corporate imperative.

This case study will highlight the development and implementation of Agilent's APEX (Accelerated Performance for Executives) coaching program. APEX has served over one hundred leaders through a sixty-person, worldwide coaching pool over the past two and one-half years. Based on feedback from raters, over 95 percent of the leaders have demonstrated positive improvement in overall leadership effectiveness while participating in the program.

The lessons learned by Agilent Technologies in the implementation of the APEX program serve as valuable insights for any organization committed to the continuing development of key leaders.

# BACKGROUND

In 1999, Hewlett-Packard (HP) announced a strategic realignment to create two companies. One, HP, included all the computing, printing, and imaging businesses. Another, a high-tech "newco," comprised test and measurement components, chemical analysis, and medical businesses. This second company would be named Agilent Technologies.

Agilent became entirely independent on November 18, 1999, while being afforded the NYSE ticker symbol "A" in the largest initial public offering in Silicon Valley history. New corporate headquarters were constructed on the site of HP's first owned and operated research and development (R&D) and manufacturing facility in Palo Alto, California.

At the time of its "birth," Agilent declared three new corporate values to guide its future: speed, focus, and accountability. Agilent also retained the "heritage" HP values: uncompromising integrity, innovation, trust, respect, and teamwork.

With a clear understanding of the need for strong individual leaders to build and sustain the company, an immediate requirement emerged to construct the leadership development strategy. The development of future leaders was and remains one of CEO Ned Barnholt's critical few priorities.

## Early Coaching Efforts

A key piece of the emerging leadership development plan would include executive coaching aimed at further developing key executives who were already recognized as high-potential or high-performing leaders.

Executive coaching had an established track record within HP, but efforts were generally uncoordinated. Coaching hadn't been strategically integrated within the company's leadership development initiatives. Multiple vendors and individual practitioners provided different coaching programs at varied prices. Learning from hindsight, Agilent had a desire to accomplish two early objectives: (1) to create an outstanding "corporate recommended" integrated coaching program and (2) to benefit from a preferred discount rate.

One of Agilent's operating units, the Semiconductor Products Group (SPG), had engaged in a coordinated, "results-guaranteed" coaching program beginning in summer 1999 with Keilty, Goldsmith & Company (later to become Alliance for Strategic Leadership Coaching & Consulting). Over fifty of SPG's senior leaders would receive one-year leadership effectiveness (behavioral) coaching, which included a unique "results guarantee." The effort attracted positive attention in the company and would later form the foundation of the APEX program.

In February 2000, Dianne Anderson, Agilent's global program manager, was charged with designing the corporate coaching solution for the company's senior managers and executives (about 750 people worldwide). She worked with Brian Underhill of Keilty, Goldsmith & Company to collaborate on the design and delivery of the new APEX program, based on the same successful coaching model used within SPG.

## Agilent Global Leadership Profile

At the outset of the APEX program, it was agreed that a critical need centered on the development of a new leadership behavioral profile to clearly and accurately reflect the company's strategic priorities, core values, and expectations of those in senior leadership roles. Although a leadership inventory had been previously custom-designed to begin the SPG divisional coaching effort, at this time it was largely agreed that an Agilent-wide profile would be needed to position the leadership behaviors throughout the whole organization in a consistent fashion.

This next-generation leadership profile was drafted, based upon key strategic imperatives of top management, Agilent's new and heritage core values, and SPG's original profile. After gathering feedback from multiple sources, the Agilent Business Leader Inventory was created in summer 2000. The primary competencies are provided in Exhibit 1.1.

Later, in spring 2001, Agilent decided to update the Agilent Business Leader Inventory and create a set of profiles that would span all management levels from first-level managers through senior business leaders. A multifunctional team of Agilent and A4SL Coaching & Consulting (A4SL C&C) people set out to create the new profiles.

Through a several-month iterative process of document review, internal inputs, and refinements, a scalable and aligned Global Leadership Profile was developed for use throughout the organization. In the end, the midlevel/first-level manager profile turned out to be 80 percent the same as the executive profile, with only slight differences in some of the specific behavioral descriptions for "Leads Strategy & Change" and "Drives for Results" areas.

Finally, both profiles were reviewed by a senior manager in each of Agilent's business units and by representatives of non-U.S. geographies. Feedback from these reviews was incorporated into the final product, and hence the Agilent Global Leadership Profile was ready for consistent application across all divisions and has been in use since summer 2001. The primary competencies are outlined in Exhibit 1.2. Assessment Plus of Atlanta, Georgia, served as APEX's scoring partner throughout the multiple revisions of the profile.

# DESIGN OF THE APEX PROGRAM

## Initial Objectives

During the same time that the design of the initial leadership profile was taking place, the basic components of the new coaching program were being considered and crafted. From the outset, the Agilent viewpoint was a coaching program that could address multiple objectives, including

- *Senior manager and executive focus.* Candidates for APEX participation included vice presidents, corporate officers, business unit leaders, general managers, directors, and functional managers.

- *Global reach.* Agilent is a worldwide organization with facilities in more than sixty countries, including the United States. The APEX program would need to effectively serve leaders with coaches in the local region (as often as possible) or within an hour's flight. The goal was to provide multiple coaching options within each geographic area. Awareness of local cultural nuances would be critical, and local language capability would be highly preferred.

- *Flexible and user-friendly.* APEX needed to be user-friendly from start to finish. To accomplish that a simple menu of options was created, which was suitable for a range of budgets and varying levels of interest in the coaching process. Priority was also placed on creating a program that made it easy to initiate a coaching engagement and easy to administer payment for coaching services.

- *Accountability for results.* APEX needed to provide added value for Agilent. In return for the company's investment in them, participants would need to demonstrate positive, measurable change in leadership effectiveness as seen by direct reports and colleagues.

Several months of design ensued to meet these objectives. The structure of several coaching options was outlined. A general program description was drafted. A global coaching pool was established, emphasizing locations of

Agilent's key global facilities. Certification standards for APEX coaches were determined. Procurement standards were established to smooth the contracting process. Procedures to guide the 360-degree feedback and follow-up survey scoring were created. Finally, pages on the corporate intranet were developed that contained the program description, pricing, coach bios, and contracting information. The APEX groundwork was now in place.

By design, APEX would be a behaviorally based executive coaching approach, focusing on improving leadership behaviors on the job. APEX would not be used for career planning, life planning, strategic planning, or remedial coaching. This distinction was to be made clear throughout the marketing process.

In May 2000 at a corporate Leadership Development Showcase, the Accelerated Performance for Executives program was officially launched. APEX was introduced to human resource (HR) managers and leadership development specialists throughout the organization. The first participants signed up. Although refinements and new services were continually added, the APEX program history now shows two-plus years of delivering results consistent with the original program objectives.

## Five Coaching Options

Based upon an achievement-oriented mountaineering theme implied by the program name, the full APEX offering includes five appropriately named coaching options:

Base Camp. Executive participates in the Agilent Global Leadership Profile and receives a two- to four-hour face-to-face coaching session to review results, select area(s) of development, receive on-the-spot coaching, and create a developmental action plan.

Camp 2. Executive participates in the Agilent Global Leadership Profile and receives six months of face-to-face and telephone coaching and one mini-survey follow-up measurement. Coach conducts telephone "check-in" with key stakeholders. Coaching work is guaranteed for results.

Camp 3. Executive receives six months of face-to-face and telephone coaching and one mini-survey follow-up measurement. Coach conducts up to twelve interviews with key stakeholders and provides write-up of results. Coach conducts telephone "check-in" with key stakeholders. Coaching work is guaranteed for results.

High Camp. Executive participates in the Agilent Global Leadership Profile and receives one year of face-to-face and telephone coaching plus two mini-survey follow-up measurements. Coach conducts telephone "check-in" with key stakeholders. Coaching work is guaranteed for results.

Summit. Executive receives one year of face-to-face and telephone coaching and two mini-survey follow-up measurements. Coach conducts up to twelve interviews with key stakeholders and provides write-up of results. Coach conducts telephone "check-in" with key stakeholders. Coaching work is guaranteed for results.

In addition, several add-on options were made available, including additional interviews, instruments, and team and group-based experiences.

The intention of multiple options was to allow participants maximum flexibility and selection in their coaching experience. Participants in each option were allowed to upgrade or extend into the next higher option without penalty (for example, from six to twelve months). Some line executives have elected to add a team-building objective with intact team participation in APEX. The most commonly selected option has been High Camp.

## Results-Guarantee Clause

Most of the APEX options include a unique offer from A4SL Coaching & Consulting: a results guarantee. *Leaders don't pay until coaching is complete and leaders don't pay unless they improve. Improvement is determined by those working with and rating the leader, not by the leader him- or herself.*

This approach has proven to be popular among Agilent executives. In spite of a challenging market environment, leaders can continue their personal development efforts and delay payment for professional services for up to one year. Plus, leaders know beforehand that they will only pay for demonstrated perceived improvements in their effectiveness as determined via a follow-up mini-survey process.

The results-guarantee clause requires "qualification" of potential participants (more on that below). Leaders leaving the program early or who have been determined to no longer be committed are billed a pro-rated amount for the professional fees.

Further, in establishing a relationship with one coaching vendor, Agilent has been able to negotiate a preferred rate. Coaching fees are set as flat rates for each option. Coaches are encouraged to help achieve measurable change without incentivizing them to spend excessive billable time, wasting money and the leader's valuable time in the process.

## Worldwide Coaching Pool

A recurring challenge during the rollout of the program has been the assurance for the availability of qualified coaching resources on a worldwide basis. As a virtual organization, A4SL Coaching & Consulting contracts with independent coaches to deliver coaching services on a worldwide basis. This means A4SL C&C can add coaches to an Agilent coaching pool without incurring additional expenses.

Coaches had to agree to be compensated in the same manner as the results guarantee—no payment (except expenses) until the conclusion of the coaching program and no payment without successful improvement. Sourcing coaches in the United States was not difficult. However, in Europe and Asia, where executive coaching is less established, quality practitioners have been fewer in number and extremely busy, thus making it difficult to entice them to agree to the results guarantee.

With the wide variance and lack of regulation in the coaching arena in general, it became evident from the outset that a set of coach certification guidelines was needed. Minimum APEX coach requirements were established, which included significant experience working with senior executives, experience as a behavioral coach, multiple years in leadership roles, and an advanced degree. The results guarantee serves as a natural qualifier. That is, generally, the quality coaches believe in their work (and have enough of it), so they can guarantee the results while affording a delay in compensation. Also, coaches agree to participate in company conference calls, remain current in their profession, and abide by a set of ethical guidelines. Coach bios are screened and potential coaches are interviewed in detail.

The coaching pool has grown to over sixty coaches worldwide. Each coach participates in a telephone orientation and receives a sixty-page orientation package. Agilent now hosts quarterly conference calls to keep coaches informed on corporate news, learn about the coaches' challenges in working with Agilent leaders, and provide a forum for peer-to-peer learning.

## Internal Marketing

In that APEX stands as a corporate-developed recommended approach, there has never been a guarantee that any of the decentralized businesses would take advantage of the program. Early on, it was agreed that an internal marketing campaign was necessary to highlight the benefits of the APEX program.

The Leadership Development Showcase served as an appropriate opening for the program. Similar presentations were then conducted in a variety of internal HR and leadership development sessions, both in person and via telephone during summer and fall 2000.

As the program grew, word of mouth became an extremely effective marketing tool. As more leaders participated in the program, word began to spread internally. Some line executives have nominated themselves and entire reporting teams to go through the program together as a unit. Higher-profile leaders have been some early adopters, including multiple corporate officers and vice presidents (VPs). It became apparent that the HR managers were well networked with each other as well. As a result, word of APEX spread through the Agilent HR community.

Finally, a corporate intranet site and supporting documentation were created, allowing for easy distribution of information about the program. Much time was spent crafting crisp, straight-to-the-point documentation to assist business leaders in understanding the program quickly.

# ABOUT THE APEX PROCESS

## Qualification and Coach Assignment

Due to the unique nature of the results guarantee, APEX requires a participant qualification process. Potential participants conduct a brief interview with the A4SL Coaching & Consulting program manager to determine any specific needs and to ensure that APEX will meet their objectives. Participants need to indicate a genuine interest in the program (rather than being "told" to do it), be willing to receive feedback, select areas for development, and follow up with key stakeholders regularly regarding their development goals.

Based on this initial conversation, the program manager sends the participant a set of bios for two to four coaches, based on the participant's needs, style, and location. Participants then telephone interview the coaches, learning more about the coach's style, approach, and background. At the same time, coaches ask questions to determine any unique needs or issues for this individual.

In this fashion, executives have a greater sense of ownership in the process. Encouraging the participant to select a coach greatly reduces mismatches. As a further and final qualifier, leaders are required to fund APEX through their own budgets. (Agilent corporate sponsors the design and ongoing development for APEX but not the individual engagements.)

## What Do Coaches and Executives Do in the Program?

What actually takes place between the A4SL C&C coach and the participating Agilent leader during the delivery of the APEX process? In the broadest terms, the coach's efforts in the delivery of coaching services are directed toward two dimensions:

1. The overall feedback process—guiding the participant through the initial online 360-degree feedback solicitation and one or two mini-surveys, as well as helping the participant both debrief and follow up with feedback raters and providers.

2. Content coaching—helping the participant become more effective in a targeted area (for example, listening skills, influencing without position power, coaching others). For most APEX assignments, the development targets are derived via the administration of Agilent's customized 360-dgree feedback instrument, the Agilent Global Leadership Profile.

APEX coaching assignments have tended to originate in one of two ways. The primary method is through individuals entering the program, generally at the suggestion of a manager or HR manager. In other cases, a senior Agilent executive nominates his or her leadership team to undergo development via the

APEX program. Each individual selects an A4SL C&C coach, and the process is initiated. As individual energies rise within the APEX coaching partnerships, team synergies also grow around the collective personal development efforts. The two objectives of personal development and team development are well served in this model.

On a side note, there is a benefit in the team model particularly with regard to the online collection of the 360-degree feedback data. That is, when full teams are nominated to participate together as a unit, the data collection process happens simultaneously for individual members, and frequently the fact that the whole team is participating creates a greater sense of urgency.

The APEX coaching process includes in-person visits coupled with regular, ongoing telephone or e-mail contact. In practice, coaches visit participating Agilent leaders approximately every six to eight weeks (in any given APEX assignment, the number of visits may be higher or lower). Telephone and e-mail contact during a typical month could range from one to six contacts.

It is interesting that for an extended period spanning most of the APEX program's existence, Agilent has been operating under a restricted travel policy. Although an immediate impact on some APEX assignments was a decrease in travel (particularly internationally), most APEX partnerships continued to benefit through the increased use of telephone and e-mail contact.

This travel restriction was successfully handled, in part, through A4SL C&C's global pool of coaches to supply local coaching resources particularly in key international sites. Also, some coaches have had multiple APEX assignments at a given Agilent site (for example Santa Clara; Denver; and Boeblingen, Germany), thereby making even regular travel more economical, since the cost was shared by multiple participants.

During each individual coaching session, any number of topics may be covered:

- Explore the current business context to determine what may be different or similar since the last coaching session
- Review perceived progress toward the developmental action plan
- Identify resources and tools to support the executive's change efforts
- Review the executive's recent experiences with his or her behavioral goals
- Shadow the Agilent leader and observe first-hand personal leadership tendencies (for example, staff meeting, team meeting, feedback delivery, key presentation)
- Role play (coach and Agilent executive assume roles, do a practice delivery or dry run, and conduct critique and review)
- Prepare for or review follow-up efforts with key stakeholders and feedback providers
- Set action items to complete for next coaching session

### Follow-Up with Key Stakeholders

The APEX program was grounded in the A4SL Coaching & Consulting research regarding the impact of follow-up on perceived leadership effectiveness. In virtually every organization in which A4SL C&C has delivered coaching services, one lesson is universally the same: *regular follow-up with key stakeholders equates with perceived improvement in leadership effectiveness.*

At least some of the Agilent executives who were seen as following up effectively probably informed raters of their development objectives during the initial debrief of the 360-degree results. The initial debriefing is ideally a focused, five- to ten-minute individual meeting held with each respondent immediately after the 360-degree report is received. The follow-up addresses

- Thanking raters for providing anonymous 360-degree input
- Relating the positive feedback
- Disclosing the developmental goal(s)
- Enlisting the rater's help in the participant's developmental efforts

Having conducted this "initial debriefing," APEX participants are encouraged to follow up with raters at regular intervals (quarterly on average) to pursue additional feedback on their improvement. Figure 1.3 provides some compelling data demonstrating the difference in perceived improvement among those APEX participants who followed up and those who did not.

## MEASUREMENT: THE MINI-SURVEY PROCESS

APEX coaching includes up to two online mini-surveys (see Exhibit 1.3). In addition to providing a clear insight into perceptions of behavioral change, these mini-survey results are used to determine improvement for purposes of the results-guarantee clause as well.

Mini-surveys are short, three- to five-item questionnaires completed by a leader's key stakeholders. Raters are asked to measure improvement in the leader's overall leadership effectiveness and specific areas for development. Raters also indicate whether the leader has followed up with them regarding his or her areas for development. Additional written comments are also requested.

Aside from verifying individual improvement, mini-survey data can be aggregated to provide team, group, or corporate-level improvement data.

## RESULTS

APEX results to date (as demonstrated by aggregated mini-survey data) are impressive. Figure 1.1 depicts aggregate results regarding improvements in overall leadership effectiveness. (Data originate from APEX as well as original SPG raters.)

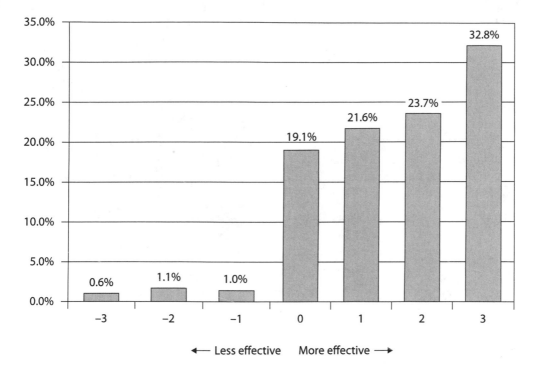

**Figure 1.1** Aggregate Results for Overall Leadership Effectiveness.

*Source:* Data collected and managed by Assessment Plus.

> Question: Has this person become more or less effective as a leader
> since the feedback session?
> Scale: −3 "less effective" to +3 "more effective"
> *N* = 831 raters
> Seventy-three leaders

Nearly 57 percent of respondents felt that APEX leaders had improved in overall leadership effectiveness to a +2 or +3 level. Over 78 percent of respondents felt that APEX leaders had improved to a +1, +2, or +3 level. Nineteen percent of respondents felt that leaders did not change, whereas nearly 3 percent felt that leaders got worse.

Figure 1.2 depicts improvement in participants' selected areas for development. (Once again, the data originate from all APEX as well as original SPG raters.)

> Improvement on specific areas for development selected by leaders
> Scale: −3 "less effective" to +3 "more effective"
> *N* = 2276 raters
> Seventy-three leaders

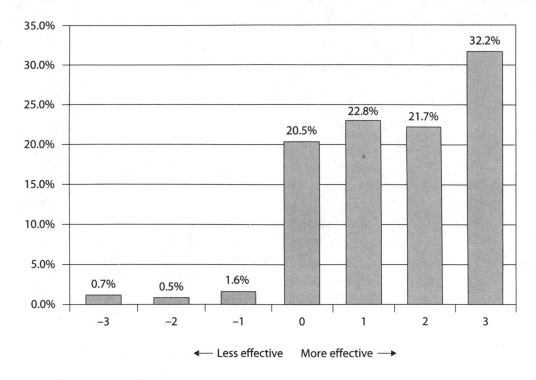

**Figure 1.2** Aggregate Results for Selected Areas of Development.
*Source:* Data collected and managed by Assessment Plus.

Nearly 54 percent of respondents felt leaders improved in their selected developmental goals to a +2 or +3 level. Nearly 77 percent felt leaders improved to a +1, +2, or +3 level. Nearly 21 percent of raters did not perceive any change, whereas 2 percent perceived leaders as getting worse.

**Results for those leaders who followed up versus those who did not
(from APEX and the original SPG groups)**
*N* = 831 raters
**Seventy-three leaders**

Of the 831 raters, 530 (64 percent) believed leaders followed up with them versus 301 (36 percent) who perceived no follow-up. Nearly 67 percent of following-up leaders were seen as improving to a +2 or +3 level, compared to 38 percent for those who did not follow up. More notably, 35 percent of leaders who did not follow up were perceived as staying the same (0) compared to nearly 11 percent who did follow up. Over 5 percent of those who did not follow up were perceived as getting *worse,* compared to 1.2 percent of the follow-up group.

In addition, positive feedback was frequently reported through the qualitative remarks of the mini-surveys.

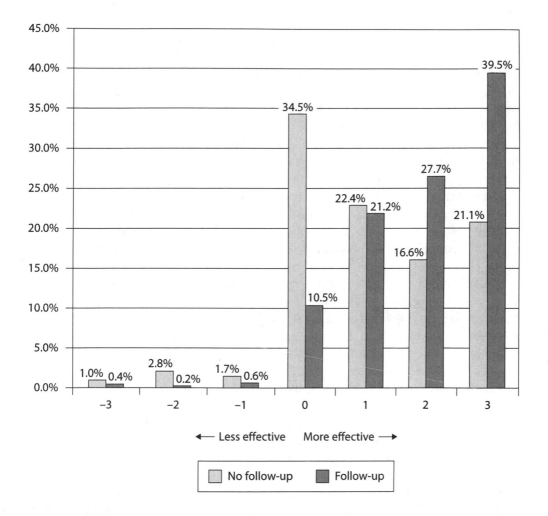

**Figure 1.3** Aggregate Results for Follow-up Versus No Follow-up.
*Source:* Data collected and managed by Assessment Plus.

Overall, APEX results to date have been very encouraging. Leaders are improving in both overall leadership effectiveness and their selected areas for development, as perceived by those working with the leaders.

## KEY INSIGHTS AND LESSONS LEARNED

The following are some key insights and lessons learned from the APEX experience that may enable any organization to more effectively implement an executive coaching program:

- *Senior leadership commitment to APEX.* In the last two years, from 2001 to 2003, the technology sector has suffered its worst downturn in recent history. Agilent's APEX program stands as a visible demonstration by senior leadership of their continuing commitment to developing leaders by sponsoring executive and personal development even in a difficult market climate. Many "high-profile" senior leaders were early APEX adopters, and they inspired many more leaders to enroll in the program.

- *Personal commitment of Agilent leaders.* The majority of APEX participants have displayed a high level of personal commitment to self-development as displayed through their respective individual coaching partnerships. The APEX program has experienced a very low percentage of participants becoming disinterested or dropping out; most participants enjoy favorable feedback from mini-surveys administered at the program's conclusion. The investments being made in personal development pay dividends for most APEX participants over time.

- *Worldwide scope of APEX.* A key challenge in the development of the program was locating and retaining high-level coaches internationally who are willing to work under the results-guarantee clause. Early difficulties have since been overcome in developing an international network of qualified coaches willing to work within the performance-guarantee clause. Prior to this, some coaches traveled internationally to deliver APEX coaching services.

- *APEX target audience.* Since its inception, APEX has been and remains a developmental tool targeting high-performing or high-potential Agilent executives. It is not intended to serve as a remedial process for an underperforming executive or as a performance-assessment program. APEX candidates are first screened by Agilent's Leadership Development Group to ensure that APEX is a good fit.

- *Coach follow-up with feedback raters.* APEX coaches keep in regular contact with a leader's key stakeholders. Coaches want to know whether the leader's new behaviors are being noticed by their raters. The only APEX assignment to go full term without achieving successful results had a coach who was out of touch with the raters and did not recognize their continual dissatisfaction with the leader. Because raters are "customers" in the process, coaches regularly communicate with them.

- *Coach mismatches.* The possibility of coach mismatches appears to have been addressed and minimized. Participants starting in the APEX program receive biographies of up to four A4SL C&C coaches within their geographic area. Executives then contact and screen from this set of prospective coaches, and ultimately select their coach. By allowing executives to largely self-select, the APEX experience has yielded very few mismatches. In those very few instances in which a mismatch has surfaced, alternative coaches have been made available.

Exhibit 1.1. The Agilent Business Leader Inventory

- Delivers superior market-driven performance
    Focuses externally on the customer
    Drives for results
    Models speed
    Models focus
    Models innovation

- Practices active leadership
    Leads people
    Actively manages talent
    Models accountability
    Models trust, respect, and teamwork
    Models uncompromising integrity

- Builds equity in the Agilent brand
    Practices strategic portfolio management
    Promotes a global brand
    Creates a boundaryless organization

Exhibit 1.2. The Agilent Global Leadership Profile

- Delivers high-growth performance
    Focuses externally on the customer
    Drives for results
    Models speed
    Models focus
    Models accountability

- Practices active leadership
    Leads strategy and change
    Actively develops self
    Actively manages talent
    Models uncompromising integrity
    Models innovation

- Acts globally
    Creates a global organization
    Models trust, respect, and teamwork

**Exhibit 1.3. Agilent Sample Mini-Survey**

---

**Agilent Technologies Mini-Survey Follow-up to the 360-Assessment**

Return Information:
You are rating Alison Jerden.
You are in the "PEERS" rater group.
Your Web ID is 434-211667.

You may take this survey online by going to . . .
http://www.assessmentplus.com/survey
or . . .
Fax this survey to 1.413.581.2791
or . . .
Mail this survey via traceable carrier (FedEx, UPS, etc.) to . . .
Assessment Plus
1001 Main Street
Stone Mountain, GA 30083-2922
YOUR FEEDBACK MUST BE RECEIVED BY AUGUST 09, 2000

If you have any questions, please call Alison Jerden at 1.800.536.1470
or email ajerden@assessmentplus.com

Company Items

C1   Since the feedback session, has this person followed-up with you regarding
        how he/she can improve?
   1: No
   2: Yes

C2   Do you feel this person has become more or less effective as a leader since
        the feedback session? (Do not consider environmental factors beyond this
        person's control.)
   −3: Less Effective
   −2:
   −1:
     0: No Change
     1:
     2:
     3: More Effective
     N: No Information

---

Original 360 Survey Items
Please rate the extent to which this individual has increased/decreased in effectiveness in the following areas of development during the past several months.

2.   Distills market knowledge into meaningful trends and patterns
   −3: Less Effective
   −2:
   −1:
     0: No Change
     1:
     2:
     3: More Effective
     N: No Information

2a   Do you feel that change was needed in the area mentioned in the previous
        question?
   1: No
   2: Yes

Exhibit 1.3. (*Continued*)

14  Effectively communicates higher organization's vision
   −3: Less Effective
   −2:
   −1:
    0: No Change
    1:
    2:
    3: More Effective
    N: No Information

14a Do you feel that change was needed in the area mentioned in the previous question?
    1: No
    2: Yes

30  Openly shares information
   −3: Less Effective
   −2:
   −1:
    0: No Change
    1:
    2:
    3: More Effective
    N: No Information

30a Do you feel that change was needed in the area mentioned in the previous question?
    1: No
    2: Yes

You are rating Alison Jerden

Comments
  What has been done in the past several months that you have found to be particularly effective?

  _____
  _____
  _____
  _____
  _____
  _____

  What can this person do to become more effective as a manager in the development areas noted above?

  _____
  _____
  _____
  _____
  _____
  _____

# ABOUT THE CONTRIBUTORS

**Brian O. Underhill** is a senior consultant and coach with Alliance for Strategic Leadership Coaching & Consulting, specializing in leadership development and multi-rater (360 degree) feedback, executive coaching, and organizational culture. Brian designs and implements large-scale, results-guaranteed, executive coaching programs at multiple organizations. His executive coaching work has successfully focused on helping clients achieve positive, measurable, long-term change in leadership behavior. His clients have included Agilent Technologies, AT&T, California Public Employees Retirement System (CalPERS), Federal Aviation Administration (FAA), Johnson & Johnson, Sun Microsystems, and Warner Lambert. Brian has a Ph.D. and a M.S. degree in organizational psychology from the California School of Professional Psychology (Los Angeles).

**Dianne Anderson** is committed to helping individuals and organizations achieve learning, change, and growth. In her current position as global program manager for Agilent Technologies, Inc., she is responsible for all global executive coaching programs, and for learning and organizational effectiveness consulting to one of Agilent's business units. Dianne's career includes leadership positions and operational experience in worldwide marketing for Hewlett-Packard (HP), as well as positions in R&D. Dianne's seventeen-plus years of operating experiences have prepared her to develop the skills, knowledge, and abilities of senior management so they can more effectively compete in the global marketplace. Over her career she has managed complex organizations with multi-million dollar budgets, with experience in line and staff positions at the business unit and corporate levels, and had responsibility for building key marketing and sales capabilities.

**Robert A. Silva,** since January 2002, has served as head of the coaching practice area for A4SL Coaching & Consulting, a consulting group based in San Diego that specializes in leadership development. Prior to his current role, Bob served as one of the seven directors of Keilty, Goldsmith & Company from 1987 to 2001. Bob's business background includes experience in the investment field with Paine, Webber in Boston, and fourteen years in sales management with Minnesota Mining & Manufacturing Company in New England. During his fifteen years as a consultant and coach, Bob has focused on the design and delivery of training to promote leadership development, organizational values, and team effectiveness. Bob's primary emphasis since the mid-1990s has been in the area of executive coaching, helping leading organizations succeed by enhancing the leadership effectiveness of key individuals.

**Karen Walker** is the director of client solutions for Assessment Plus and directs the data services for the Agilent programs. Assessment Plus is an Atlanta-based consulting firm specializing in web-based assessments to maximize results from leadership, team, and organizational effectiveness programs. Karen teaches a 360 Feedback Certification course for Corporate Coach University and a workshop on Best Practices for Implementing 360 Programs through the Cornell University School of Industrial and Labor Relations. Some of Karen's organizational survey clients include Acushnet, Cox Enterprises, Lend Lease, Marsh, Porsche, Vicinity, and Consumer Credit Counseling Services. Karen coaches executives taking part in leadership assessment programs for organizations including the American Cancer Society, Citigroup, Lockheed Martin, Akzo Nobel, BMW, Kodak, and Sun Microsystems. Karen has a degree in Industrial and Systems Engineering from the Georgia Institute of Technology and completed her Ph.D. in Counseling Psychology at the University of Georgia.

# CHAPTER TWO

# Corning

*A change and innovation system that enables best practices in marketing, manufacturing, and product development through Corning's five stage gate process, manufacturing process, innovation pipeline, innovation process, learning coaches and continuous evaluation features.*

OVERVIEW     21

INTRODUCTION     22

DIAGNOSIS: STAY OUT OF OUR HAIR AND FIX IT     22

     Organizational Challenge     23
     Change Objective     23
     Assessment     24
     Approach     24

INTERVENTION: KEY ELEMENTS     25

     Figure 2.1: Five-Stage Stage-Gate™ Model     26
     Turning Point     27
     Critical Success Factors     27
     Figure 2.2: Innovation People!     27
     Innovation in Marketing     28
     Innovation in Manufacturing     29

HIGH-TECH COMPANY     29

     Corning Competes     30
     Innovation Today     30
     Background     31
     Contemporary Success Story: Innovation at Its Best     31
     Figure 2.3: Manufacturing Process     32

ON-THE-JOB SUPPORT: REINFORCING THE REINFORCEMENTS     33

     Innovative Effectiveness     33
     Figure 2.4: Corning Innovation Pipeline     34
     Ideas into Dollars     34

Figure 2.5: Ideas into Dollars   35
Table 2.1: Innovation Delivery   35
Evaluation   36

THE LEARNING MACHINE: DRIVING SUBSTAINABLE VALUE   36
AND GROWTH
Figure 2.6: Innovation Process   36
The Learning Machine: Providing New Angles on Insight   37
Knowledge Management and Organizational Learning   37
Enhancing the Learning Culture: Building Bridges   38
   to Enable Innovation
Figure 2.7: Accelerating Learning by Building Bridges   39
   Across Organizations
Learning Coaches: Establishing a New Core Competency in R&D   39

LESSONS LEARNED   40

POSTLOGUE: CONTINUOUS IMPROVEMENT   41

ABOUT THE CONTRIBUTOR   42

# OVERVIEW

*Many dream of reinventing themselves as nimble technology*
*companies. Corning has actually done it.*
—Charlie Cray, *Wall Street Journal*

For over a century, Corning Incorporated has been a company synonymous with technology-based innovation. Today the spirit of innovation is stronger than ever. This management case study will look at the evolution of the current innovation process practiced at Corning. The case will describe the approach used to successfully create, implement, and grow a world-class, systematic new product innovation process. It will also chronicle those who have championed innovation as a best practice for nearly two decades.

In 1984, then Vice Chairman Tom MacAvoy was asked to "fix" Corning's approach to innovation; the technology cupboard was bare. To get James R. Houghton (Jamie), Corning's chairman & CEO (1983–1996; 2001-current) to bless this effort, MacAvoy stressed the significance of the innovation process as the most important quality program in the company. Learning how to innovate on a systematic basis over a long period, formerly a tacit matter, was now to be formally articulated so that it could be practiced across the company.

Today, the innovation process is alive and well at Corning. In fact, it is clear that the company's expertise in this area is going to play a significant role in positioning Corning for sustainable value and growth. As Corning's current Chief Technology Officer Joe Miller states emphatically, "Innovation will lead the way."

# INTRODUCTION

Corning Incorporated, responsible for at least three life-changing product innovations—the light bulb envelope, TV tube, and optical waveguides—celebrated its 150th anniversary in 2001. Known for shedding old, mature businesses while establishing its leadership in innovative new product lines and process technologies, the company was awarded the National Medal of Technology for innovation in 1993. The drive to remain innovative and reinvent itself is at the crux of Corning's identity and has been since Amory Houghton, Sr. (Jamie's great-great grandfather) founded the company in the 1850s as a small, specialty glass manufacturer.

In the 1870s, Houghton's sons—Amory, Jr., and Charles—established Corning's tradition of scientific inquiry and emphasis on specialty glass products. They believed very strongly in creating unique products for mankind and in staying away from the mundane and the ordinary. They believed, therefore, in innovation and research and development. The next generation, Alanson and Arthur, institutionalized research by bringing under management the company's collective ingenuity. In 1908, they set up one of the earliest corporate research laboratories in the United States, one of four at the time.

Corning's experience since then offers countless examples in which innovative activities aimed at one objective have borne fruit in many arenas. Employees have responded to business challenges by finding new and innovative uses for specialty materials. The company's best business successes have resulted from its ability to tailor specialty materials for particular applications. We will focus on one such example, EAGLE2000™, in some depth later in the case, one that used the innovation process to achieve a great result.

Starting with a semiformal, six-plus-stage process used in the 1960s and early 1970s, Corning's innovation process has evolved through five iterations to its current manifestation as a centralized component of product development.

# DIAGNOSIS: STAY OUT OF OUR HAIR AND FIX IT

As vice chairman with special responsibilities for technology from 1983 to 1986, Tom MacAvoy found himself the target of open resentment expressed by the operating divisions, which seemed to believe that they had been bearing the burdens of an insufficiently productive, centralized technical establishment for far too long. Business leaders were given extremely challenging profit and loss (P&L) targets to meet. They felt the high cost and inefficiencies of research, development, and engineering (RD&E) were a major stumbling block to meeting their numbers. "Stay out of our hair and fix it" was the message MacAvoy was hearing.

## Organizational Challenge

Innovation at Corning, as in U.S. industry more broadly in the 1980s, was a concept that had fallen out of public favor. This did not mean that Jamie Houghton would cut the R&D budget as a percentage of sales; he reasserted his personal commitment to maintain research and development (R&D) spending at 4 to 5 percent at that time. Although this was twice the national average and quite competitive for the glass industry, it was hardly in the ballpark for a "high-tech" company, where 6 to 8 percent was closer to the norm. Today, in 2004, R&D spending is at 10 to 11 percent of sales and expected to stay at that level.

One universal method of "fixing" R&D in the 1980s was to decentralize either the institutions themselves or the control over their funding, or both. At Corning, key managers still believed it was imperative to keep specialty glass and materials research physically centralized, but financial decentralization was a major plank of the profitable growth plan. The centrally located part of the technical community accordingly shrank from a high of 1,400 people in the early 1970s to a core force of 800 people, including central manufacturing and engineering. Today, R&D is a mixture of centralized and decentralized resource allocation. Corning works hard to excel at creating linkages between the technology and the business. In fact, this drive is so strong at Corning that it overrides the natural organizational barriers inherent between the two functions.

## Change Objective

To get Jamie Houghton to bless this significant change effort, MacAvoy had to stress the connection to at least two of the chairman's critical imperatives: performance, that is, 10 percent operating margin (at the time the OM was at 2 percent) and Total Quality Management (TQM). To be sure, Houghton's preoccupation with quality was complete. MacAvoy recalls: "I'd worked out some very simple arithmetic. Let's say we're spending $150 million annually. We're probably wasting about a third of it, we just don't know what third it is. If quality is only about improving manufacturing we can get 5 percent at most improvement in gross margin. The rest has to be about improving the way we innovate. Finally I convinced him that this had to be one of the Total Quality objectives."

The change management mission was clear, and MacAvoy summarized the objective this way: a good research laboratory staffed by good people, skilled at sensing technical trends early; building relationships with OEM (original equipment manufacturer) customers in growing industries; excellent links between scientists and engineers and through sales and marketing groups to customers.

It was also clear that to achieve MacAvoy's vision, innovation would become a key driver for change: Corning's #1 quality process, its #1 vital few. Innovation would challenge the traditional ways of thinking—it would challenge the corporation and its businesses to think differently about what was possible. Innovation would convert ideas into opportunities and those opportunities into sustainable streams of earnings for Corning.

## Assessment

Except for a few key projects protected by top management and a few new products that had come in from the periphery, most other aspects of the RD&E program had fallen into a state of neglect. New product development was insufficient to sustain profitability, declines in new process development had allowed core businesses and acquisitions to become unprofitable, and the manufacturing sciences had deteriorated. There were, to be sure, pockets of promising technology here and there, but they were not strategically integrated even in the desired market-based businesses, end-use and systems-based products.

Corning's defensive moves of the 1970s and early 1980s—to reduce research funding (down 20 percent in real dollar terms over the decade) in favor of development and to confine new investments primarily to low-risk product and process extensions and renewals—had set up a cycle of diminishing returns. Corning's traditional practice of sponsoring exploration and "reach" projects across the board, as well as keeping up a certain level of risk-taking, had had the important side benefit of replenishing the company's "technology till." By the mid-1980s that till was in need of revitalizing—the cupboard was bare.

Further, much of the rest of the company was paying no attention to innovation at all, while low morale in the R&D organization itself was undermining the effectiveness of its projects. Innovations that did occur were based on extreme measures. Efforts to innovate were succeeding by acts of heroism or by fighting the rest of the company.

## Approach

With Houghton's blessing, MacAvoy placed innovation under the umbrella of Total Quality and, with that, was on his way.

The company's innovation process previously had been defined only within the research, product development, and engineering communities, and now the company would work to make this minimalist, yet formal, process the central integrating mechanism across the broader community.

A major part of MacAvoy's effort consisted of a systematic appraisal of Corning's many past innovation successes and failures—its best practices and lessons learned—from which he and his team aimed to develop an explicit, formalized description of Corning's way of innovating: an *innovation process*.

# INTERVENTION: KEY ELEMENTS

*Innovation is possible in every aspect of our work together.*
—Tom MacAvoy

As the first step toward significant change, MacAvoy set up the innovation task force as a quality improvement team to find out why the rest of the company was dissatisfied with RD&E. Members of the team—including recognized Corning innovators—invested months of their time, most of it over early morning breakfast meetings, which became commonly known as the Breakfast of Champions. So as not to ignore outside perspectives, the team retained an outside consultant as part of the program.

The first decision was to focus on Corning's past history of successful innovation as an untapped resource, one that could be crucial to rebuilding morale. They also believed that the understanding of innovation implicit in the company's shared memory needed to be made more visible. MacAvoy proposed a slogan for this effort taken from a well-known saying of Corning veteran Eddie Leibig: *We never dance as well as we know how.*

The group studied hundreds of Corning innovations, mining them for their larger meaning. Many of their generalizations matched those that were coming out in broader studies of innovation across the country: that high-caliber people who were willing to take risks and had good communication and team-building skills were key.

Another factor stood out: Corning's ability to very quickly concentrate maximum strength on a project of major importance, referred to internally as "flexible critical mass." This method enabled Corning to tackle outsized opportunities. In addition, innovation at Corning had never been the sole province of scientists or even technical people. Corning had been good at identifying and developing innovative leaders with the right qualities throughout the company's history, but this kind of leadership had gone by the board in the face of countervailing pressures to specialize, downsize, or reduce the asset base and shifts in balance between the short-term and the long-term. Finally, based on a review of current literature on innovation, the task force identified a five-stage Stage-Gate™ model that could be adapted for Corning's case (Figure 2.1).

The innovation process, although depicted in a linear fashion for teaching purposes, is anything but linear. An iterative process by definition, innovation is one of the most fluid, yet socially complex of business processes. Innovation transcends the entire organization—it is a way of enabling people to learn together; it provides a framework for a common language. Further, Figure 2.1 depicts the concurrency of three functional disciplines—typically organized as cross-functional teams for innovation activity.

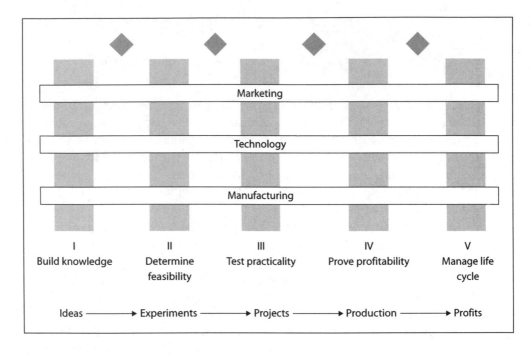

**Figure 2.1** Five-Stage Stage-Gate™ Model.

*Source:* Copyright © Corning Incorporated. Reprinted by permission.

Jim Riesbeck, director of corporate marketing, acting as the marketing member of the Breakfast of Champions, cautioned against doing what many companies were doing at the time, which was to define the process of new product development in such minute detail that it reduced innovation to filling in endless checklists and inhibited creativity instead of enhancing it. The task force adopted a skeletal overview of the essence of a process, grounded in Corning's own unique experience, to be used as an integrative framework. "We are going to make this a marketing document. . . . We are really going to use this thing!" exclaimed Riesbeck.

As a second step toward significant change, MacAvoy orchestrated a two-and-a-half day innovation conference for more than two hundred senior Corning leaders that was intended to focus attention on innovation and re-introduce the innovation process. Moreover, he reminded those in attendance that the conference's subject matter was in fact nothing less than the company's defining activity: "In all cases, technology is involved and is at the heart of what we do. We lead primarily by technical innovation. Translating technology into new products and processes, into new ways to help our customers, into new sources of profit and growth—that's what we're all about as a company."

The task force had not limited its deliberations to celebrating Corning's past achievements. It had also identified the key ways in which Corning had fallen short of innovating effectively. MacAvoy portrayed innovation as one of the top quality problems the company had. He firmly implanted the notion that improving the innovation process by 10 percent a year could cut costs in half. Doubling that rate would be equivalent to doubling the RD&E spending level. It came down to restoring several simple elements: an environment and culture of energy and enthusiasm, entrepreneurial behavior at all levels, the right people in the right places, sound business and technical strategies, improved processes for nurturing ideas, and organizational mechanisms that could support the organization's drive for results.

## Turning Point

The conference was a real turning point. The conceptual marriage of TQM and innovation was far more than simple rhetoric. Although it would be another seven years before quality programs and innovation would work together on the same track, at least they began running on parallel tracks. A full decade would pass before the change in attitude inaugurated at the innovation conference would be reflected in significantly increased RD&E budgets, but a new generation of innovators with the necessary integrative skills was in the making. Today Corning sees a reinvigoration of this marriage between TQM and innovation effectiveness.

## Critical Success Factors

Several enduring success factors emerged from the innovation conference. First, the articulated formal process provided a framework for *training programs* at all levels of the company, becoming part of the structure for *project reviews* and the basis for *hiring and deploying personnel.* One requirement for attending the training was to be part of an established team. Starting with marketing and technology and later spreading to other areas of the company, attention was paid to *fostering innovators and creating integrated technology plans.* According to Charlie Craig, Vice President and COO, Science and Technology, "The graphic we use [three upside-down exclamation marks that resemble people, followed by three right-side-up exclamation points] says it all (see Figure 2.2). The

**Figure 2.2**  Innovation People!

exclamation points represent people, motivation, and the excitement of innovation—the most important ingredients."

The long-term benefit of having the five-stage innovation process and training people across the company in its use was that, in an era when "time to market" became *the* competitive issue for industry at large, Corning had already developed the routine practice of including all major parties in any new process or product innovation as early as possible. Ted Kozlowski, one of Corning's key development managers for many successful products, commented that the relations between people were critical.

Another consequence of the innovation effort was a rise in *internal entrepreneurial behavior.* At Sullivan Park, in particular, technologists were allowed to supplement an essentially flat R&D budget with sales of shelf technology, sales of services in which Corning had particular expertise, and increased government contracting for technologies they wanted to pursue anyway. Those who were willing to expend the effort were given the latitude to form small enterprises.

Yet another success factor was possibly the most unusual for companies at the time: the continuation of a practice of *collective self-examination* that previous Corning generations had also employed. In reviving the practice of *storytelling,* the task force showed that *reinvigorating shared memory* was a powerful way to *build the company's collective ingenuity.* It tied the notion of best practices not solely to the dictates of outside experts or to the examples of other companies, but to the recovery of grounded experience in the company itself.

Additional components were to examine innovation as it impacted marketing and manufacturing.

## Innovation in Marketing

*I never believe it's too early to bring in that marketing expertise . . . it's marketing knowledge, it's customer knowledge . . . where's the product going to be used . . . let's ask someone in that area and see what they think. . . . Once you've got a technology you think you can use for something . . . that's maybe the secret . . . somebody's got to believe . . .*
*"I think it can be useful here."*
—David Howard, Corning Telecommunications

Corning needed to focus on its effectiveness in both approach and deployment of resources to understand current and future customer and market needs—a weak point traditionally. Included in this focus was—and still is—the assessment of current performance, development, and execution of improvement plans. The prescription involved people in all functions and levels collecting data, applying analytical tools, developing insight, and sharing that insight throughout the organization, which today supports "roadmapping," "portfolio," and the five-stage innovation process itself.

## Innovation in Manufacturing

In addition to a renewal of innovation at its R&D centers—the obvious place where creativity matters—manufacturing processes, too, would benefit from a return to Corning's roots. While Corning was working to regain its position at the forefront of innovation by inventing unique materials, processes, and technologies, its manufacturing operations shared some common problems that made it difficult to sustain their lead over competitors. The quality effort was already doing much to improve manufacturing discipline in all of Corning's plants when management asked Roger Ackerman (who, in 1996, succeeded Jamie Houghton as chairman & CEO, until 2001) launched a companywide assessment of its manufacturing operations in 1986.

As the innovation process evolved, the need to develop inherent linkages among technology, marketing, and manufacturing became critical, as each component was an equal leg in the three-legged stool of innovation. Ed Sever, former plant manufacturing engineer, states: "It's as true in plants today as it's ever been—anytime there's a major project, we make sure that there's a plant person assigned to the team . . . who knows they are the receiver, that it's their job to help make this thing happen, and they ought to be pulling equally as hard as they're [R&D] pushing."

# HIGH-TECH COMPANY

*Knowledge, risk, cost, and time to market are critical to*
*successful innovation in a high-technology company.*
—Charlie Craig

By the early 1990s Corning had demonstrated by means of its effective adoption of quality and innovation as complementary disciplines that a future as a high-technology company was a strategic option. Jamie Houghton's address to the Industrial Research Institute in 1993, on the tenth anniversary of his earlier address to that body, was a sign that this was so. Innovation, Houghton declared, was the glue that bound all functions into a cohesive team of inventors, producers, and innovators. Speaking of the obligations of general management leadership in high-technology product development and marketing, he argued that Corning had significantly improved the effectiveness of its RD&E—the quality and rate of its innovation—by applying TQM principles to innovation: "In my view, Innovation is absolutely an integral part of Total Quality; in the mid-1980s, it was the largest single cost of quality problem we had in the company. If we can continue to move forward on this, if we can get another 10–20 percent better in being more effective in linking our technology to the marketplace, we know what a huge opportunity it will be for us."

## Corning Competes

Immediately following Houghton's address to the Industrial Research Institute (1993), Corning launched Corning Competes, a program designed to reengineer its key business processes. Deliberate in its choice to *reengineer* rather than *restructure,* Corning Competes represented a reinvestment in Corning's business processes through continuous improvement of best practices. It also provided the necessary tools for better communication among the technical and business constituencies. The company needed to enhance its capability to compete for present and future business while improving its financial performance.

As the innovation process was the number one cost of quality in the company, the goal of the Corning Competes innovation effectiveness team was to enable Corning to get the most from its innovation investment in product and process technologies. To ensure that the company was well positioned for growth and profitability, the team sought to "reengineer the process by which Corning creates, identifies, evaluates, prioritizes, and executes against market opportunities."

Equally pressing within the technology community was the need to drive *discontinuous improvement*—to instill a "step change" within the continuum of best practice continuous improvement. The company had to manage a culture change that would enable it to strike a balance between continuous improvement and the step changes necessary to deliver breakthrough technologies. Some of Corning's greatest profit-producing technology breakthroughs had come from just that—from achieving that delicate balance between incremental improvements on the one hand and breakthrough invention on the other, thus leading to new product and process commercialization. Going forward, this kind of innovation would be "the ticket" for Corning.

## Innovation Today

The continued focus on innovation at Corning today—with an ever-evolving, dynamic process featuring pronounced cross-functional and cross-disciplinary integration—has allowed the company to make decisions faster and closer to the point of action. Implemented flexibly yet with rigor, the innovation process allows people and projects to overcome both internal and external barriers, to be agile—gaining, sharing, and acting on new information and insights— provide more opportunities to innovate, reduce product development time, and enhance customer relationships. In short, it allows the company to outlearn and lead the competition.

Through generations of change at Corning, innovation is the sustaining thread throughout. "Innovation is in Corning's DNA," says Charlie Craig. It is what allows the company to reinvent itself—most often through the reuse of its technology—which it has done sixteen times in its 151-year history. The company champions and nurtures innovation; it uses innovation as a means to succeed

Here is a current example. One way Corning is dealing with the telecommunications industry collapse, in which an entire market disappeared seemingly overnight, is to repurpose and redirect its investment in intellectual property around optical technologies, clearly into a technology that is non-telecommunications related.

Another use of a core technology resulted in EAGLE[2000TM], a prime example of innovation at Corning today—innovation at its best.

## Background

*Innovation has always been the hallmark of our success.*
—Jamie Houghton

Corning has a long tradition of building on and reusing its existing technology and knowledge bases to innovate and create new business opportunities. An important example is the "fusion process," developed in the early 1960s by Corning engineers. Initially used in combination with a newly developed material, Chemcor (chemically strengthened glass for manufacturing automobile windshields), the fusion process lived on when the windshield market did not materialize for Corning.

During the 1970s, Corning scientists at the company's research facility in Fontainebleau, France, used the fusion process to manufacture sunglass lenses. Long a supplier of tubes to the television industry, Corning began to look for ways to extend its presence in the display markets. Using the fusion process, it began producing flat panel glass for liquid crystal display applications, such as laptop computers.

As the markets for laptops, PDAs (personal digital assistants), flat screen monitors, and flat screen televisions began to grow in the 1990s, Corning scientists and engineers continued to use the innovation process and the Fusion process to meet the demands of its customers. EAGLE[2000TM] is an excellent example of the use of both processes.

## Contemporary Success Story: Innovation at Its Best

*The results for EAGLE[2000TM] have been fantastic. Not only did this project use the Innovation Process to meet the customers' demands for lighter weight displays, it also improved our capacity and profitability as well.*
—Randy Rhoads, project manager

*We had interesting joint sessions very early on. Manufacturing, technology, and marketing worked very, very closely on this—in the first stages with product development, the detailing of the product, and what the customers really required.*
—Dan Nolet, display technologies

With its combination of glass properties and manufacturing technology, Corning EAGLE$^{2000TM}$ flat glass substrates enable active matrix liquid crystal display (AMLCD) manufacturers to make larger, lighter, thinner, and higher-resolution displays for computer monitors and home entertainment. This glass has the industry's lowest thermal expansion, thus decreasing the effects of thermal down shock and breakage, and due to its remarkably low-density composition Corning EAGLE$^{2000TM}$ glass is the lightest AMLCD substrate on the market.

EAGLE$^{2000TM}$ also has improved chemical durability over earlier substrate glasses, which minimizes glass damage during the harsh chemical processes involved with display manufacturing. Corning EAGLE$^{2000TM}$ glass is made using Corning's fusion process. This close-tolerance glass draw process, combined with Corning's patented composition, yields glass with truly remarkable qualities: pristine, near-perfect flat surfaces with improved thickness variations that don't require polishing.

By participating early in the innovation process, the manufacturing group—along with marketing and technology—ensured that the production-delivery process design accommodated all key operational performance requirements. A strong, cross-functional team was established right from the start. This early involvement helped the team avoid many of the later-stage issues that often arise when the manufacturing function is not an active participant in the early innovation stages. In this way, they were able to influence the design so it allows a more robust manufacturing process (see Figure 2.3).

While marketing conducted an extensive study to identify and quantify the customers' requirements, manufacturing defined the performance range of Advanced Display processes, so that technology was able to identify the various compositions that would not only meet customer needs, but would also work within manufacturing's current and expected parameters.

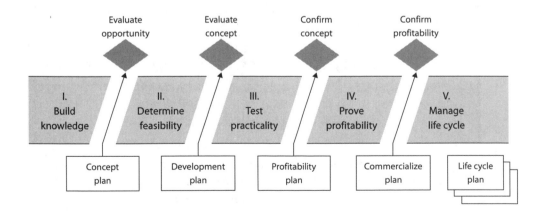

**Figure 2.3** Manufacturing Process.

The EAGLE$^{2000TM}$ product team noted the following additional benefits of using the innovation process:

- The common language and understanding of the five stages made it easier to accommodate the many personnel changes that occurred throughout the project. It also provided the framework to hold their global team together.

- The cross-functional team from the start enabled all functions to actively participate in the development of the project objectives. The shared ownership of the project objectives helped guide the project effectively throughout the five stages

- The team, by proactively using risk management, had the ability to find a balance between market requirements, manufacturing capabilities, and technical competencies. The key for EAGLE$^{2000TM}$ was to find common denominators for all three areas.

- The five-stage suggested activities helped outline the required work and deliverables for their planning process.

# ON-THE-JOB SUPPORT: REINFORCING THE REINFORCEMENTS

*The innovation process has evolved well beyond the rudimentary model we adopted two decades ago . . . and is now embedded in our culture.*
—Joe Miller

On an ongoing and consistent basis, Corning requires employees on project teams to take its innovation training and follow a comprehensive set of guidelines and tools toward product innovation. The company has progressively broadened the training to more teams and functional units, "spreading the language of our business." Corning also renews its innovation process periodically—most recently, for instance, to manage the innovation "pipeline" for new opportunities, g risk assessment, costs, and value added (see Figure 2.4).

## Innovation Effectiveness

*These innovation effectiveness processes are the underpinning for the growth of our company.*
—Charles "Skip" Deneka, CTO, 1996–2001

Innovation effectiveness is the umbrella term for Corning's innovation effort. "Innovation effectiveness encompasses identifying opportunities (roadmapping), selecting opportunities (portfolio decision making), delivering opportunities (innovation project management) in order to realize benefit (dollars), and

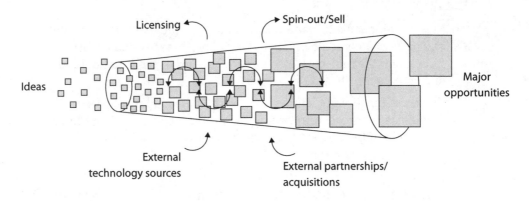

**Figure 2.4**  Corning Innovation Pipeline.

*Source:* Copyright © Corning Incorporated. Reprinted by permission.

staying closely connected to customers and markets" (Bruce Kirk, corporate innovation effectiveness leader).

Innovation effectiveness requires

- Understanding the overall corporate and business strategies
- Developing sound roadmaps based on understanding customers, markets, competitors, and Corning's strengths and weaknesses and estimating resources required for each project submitted to the portfolio management process for funding
- Applying the portfolio management process to evaluate, prioritize, and select projects
- Executing the selected projects well

## Ideas into Dollars

The following list and Figure 2.5 describe Corning's best practice for enabling successful and innovative projects.

- *Roadmapping.* Anticipating and planning for future opportunities. Requires customer focus and forward-looking thinking.
- *Project portfolio.* Selecting the best opportunities, balancing the risks and benefits, and allocating critical resources. Applying process rigor while retaining flexibility to exercise judgment.
- *Innovation project management.* Moving a product, process, or service idea iteratively through the stages of innovation to successful commercialization (dollars). Reduces development time, increases the number of commercially successful products, and cancels the

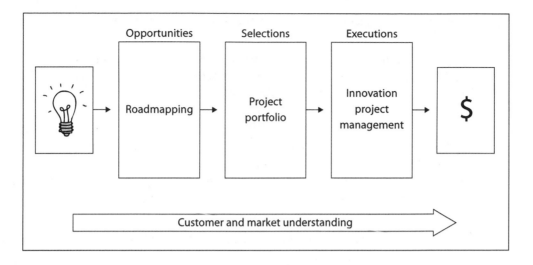

**Figure 2.5** Ideas into Dollars.

*Source:* Copyright © Corning Incorporated. Reprinted by permission.

## Table 2.1. Innovation Delivery

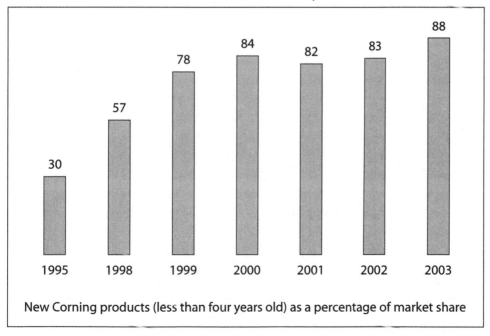

New Corning products (less than four years old) as a percentage of market share

*Source:* Copyright © Corning Incorporated. Reprinted by permission.

less-promising projects earlier. This is the five-stage Stage-Gate™ innovation process, referenced earlier.

- *Customer and market understanding.* Truly understanding customers, markets, competitors, and anticipating their actions and reactions. The underpinning of the other three innovation elements.

## Evaluation

At Corning, a significant measurement of the innovation effectiveness process is the percentage of sales of new products from R&D. Since 1998, Corning has delivered no less than 57 percent of its products to the marketplace within four years. That is a remarkable accomplishment by any corporate standard.

# THE LEARNING MACHINE: DRIVING SUSTAINABLE VALUE AND GROWTH

The innovation process is a learning machine that drives the company's sustainable value and growth (see Figure 2.6). Corning's focus on quality and knowledge-sharing tools and practices provides the "rate-change enablers" that

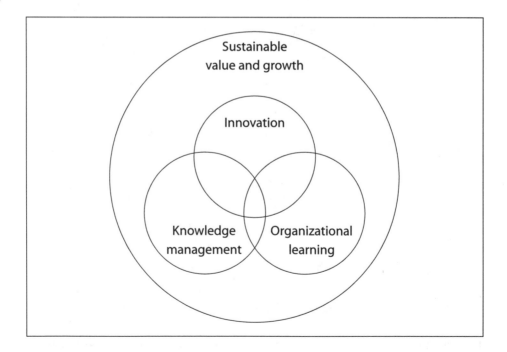

**Figure 2.6** Innovation Process.

*Source:* Copyright © Corning Incorporated. Reprinted by permission.

increase the rate of organizational learning—bringing Corning differential value and competitive advantage—and, in turn, increases the rate of innovation.

## The Learning Machine: Providing New Angles on Insight

Without being overly prescriptive or bureaucratic, Corning encourages sharing of knowledge in the following ways. This has promoted a short cycle "learning machine," which allows colleagues to share and test data and best practices.

- Morning meetings

    A forum to share proprietary research results in progress

    Thirty-minute talk on work or current state of the science or project

    Additional time scheduled for Q&A and discussion

    Audience and speaker exchange ideas and gain insights

- Technical tutorials

    Education on a technology, including orientation, strategy, technical components

    Offered at multiple levels

    Encourages tacit knowledge exchange

- Research reviews

    Enable business leaders and technology community members to stay abreast of rapidly changing technologies and market trends

    Two hours in length, with time for interaction within the technology community, as well as with the business partners

    Begin with opening remarks by the specific project leader, followed by presentations by key project members

- Communities of practice

    Individuals who come together over a common interest, one that could be directly or indirectly related to their current work

    Formal (sanctioned); for example, Centers of Excellence

    Informal (grass roots); for example, software programmers

## Knowledge Management and Organizational Learning

These knowledge-sharing tools and practices are only a few of many examples that have emanated from within the technology community. They demonstrate how innovation is coupled with other ongoing Corning business practices into everyday activities and processes, providing new insights for Corning. Scientists, engineers, technicians, and commercial managers share knowledge, experience, and perspective on a regular basis. In doing so, they optimize, leverage, and *re-use* this key knowledge, experience, and perspective—all critical components of learning—within a technology context. For Corning, this translates into new product and process innovation—ideas into dollars.

A key ongoing goal of Corning's learning machine is to increase its *knowledge re-use quotient.* To do this, the company increases the number of perspectives (people and disciplines) within the organization, improves interdisciplinary sharing (the number of interactions that occur among disciplines), and provides the necessary tools to synthesize all those interactions to reformulate the company's knowledge for re-use. Corning also includes tactical elements such as ergonomics and facilities design to ensure that these interactions occur; for example, secure video conferencing, facilities, and informal meeting areas. Increasing the knowledge re-use quotient means the real-time tapping of institutional knowledge and memory through people in a global culture and in everyday circumstances within the workplace.

Another key element is building the *knowledge (technology) warehouse.* This is basically an archive—a technology cupboard—from which one can research, identify, and access technology for re-use. At Corning, technology investments are never lost: they are either shelved as tangible objects (samples, patents, technical reports, lab notebooks) or accessed through the intangible, tacit corporate memory through storytelling, oral histories, and other everyday means. The company constantly builds its knowledge cache, "packages" it in a complete, relevant form, and trains its employees how to access it for further use—a way to preserve and build upon its core competencies and critical capabilities. The innovation process—an iterative process—is the learning catalyst; it is what ties together both modes of learning into a "learning machine."

### Enhancing the Learning Culture: Building Bridges to Enable Innovation

In order to create and sustain the learning culture to enable innovation, bridges must be built. An example would be a move toward bridging manufacturing effectiveness with innovation effectiveness through process engineering (see Figure 2.7). Another leading example would be the bridging of two traditionally disparate internal initiatives—manufacturing process improvement and the knowledge management and organizational learning effort—focusing on the unifying theme of innovation. Doing so will provide a real-time opportunity to address pressing process technology issues facing Corning today—in short, an opportunity to drive improved profitability now, reinvigorate quality, and be "ready" for the next upturn.

This type of interactive, dynamic collaboration will yield for the company not only the standard cost containment, greater resource availability, and larger internal target audiences, but will also help ensure the company's stability

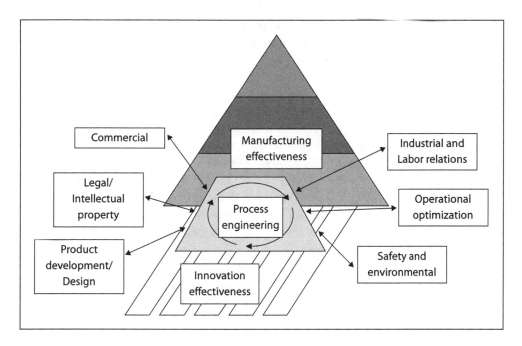

**Figure 2.7** Accelerating Learning by Building Bridges Across Organizations.

*Source:* Copyright © Corning Incorporated. Reprinted by permission.

and growth. It will help rebuild the network, enhance the learning culture, and expand technical know-how through optimizing synergies.

## Learning Coaches: Establishing a New Core Competency in R&D

*The only way to make sure the culture and discipline are*
*sustained is to have an experienced advisor present.*
*Our Learning Coach Center of Excellence will ensure*
*company wide implementation and learning.*
—Charlie Craig

Once the elements of the learning culture are in place, and the organization understands how it learns most effectively, the process is catalyzed with *learning coaches,* similar to Six Sigma black belts. These are individuals whose role it is to become knowledge networking "agents" or learning facilitators within the organization. Part of a Learning Coach "center of excellence" or virtual community of practice, they are trained as innovation project managers and are highly skilled at process excellence around innovation effectiveness and how people learn. These learning coaches join teams and prompt them to share knowledge, cross boundaries, learn together, and become more effective collaborators.

A member of several project teams at once, a learning coach cross-fertilizes the teams with new knowledge on an ongoing basis and provides a learning bridge between projects for sharing best practices and lessons learned. The learning coach also instills "the thrill of a hobby" into the innovation environment, thus stimulating deeper and quicker learning and enabling greater satisfaction through work.

By integrating capabilities and competencies and recycling learning, Corning is constantly optimizing the process. This is a virtuous cycle—it is all about prompting and leveraging change, building knowledge, converting intellectual assets into productive use, and learning better together to innovate better. Corning is thus able to realize in unique ways new opportunities and solutions it never before thought possible—discontinuous improvement and breakthrough invention. It is, in the end, about competitive advantage and setting the pace for innovation.

# LESSONS LEARNED

*Innovation is about flexible management and good judgment.*
—Roger Ackerman

Lessons learned is a shared practice some call *after action review* that takes form to retain organizational memory of important RD&E projects. This practice includes the following actions:

- *Start with a strong, visible, influential champion, one who has a true passion for innovation, who acts as a rallying point and a change agent, and who inspires a cadre of true believers at all levels of the organization.* MacAvoy was able to bring together marketing, manufacturing, technology, and human resources to "fix" the problem. Champions will change over time, but their presence and level of support cannot change. Corning has maintained its innovation champions for two decades; for example, MacAvoy, Deneka, Ackerman, Miller, Craig, Houghton.

- *Establish a strategic link between the initiative and the company's core values and goals.* From the outset, MacAvoy and his team underscored the significant tie to Total Quality Management, profitability, and growth.

- *Establish a progressive, formal yet fluid and iterative process with built-in flexibility.* The process cannot be reduced to the checking-off of boxes, as in a cookbook—that's the fastest way to introduce bureaucracy and stifle creativity.

Today's model emphasizes judgment by the project leader and the sponsor to determine the rigor needed at any specific innovation stage, as opposed to the original model, a linear one, in which the main activity was doing everything that the innovation guide indicated.

- *Encourage cross-functional, cross-disciplinary project teams, in which people openly collaborate, share, cross boundaries, and act on their collective knowledge, experience, and perspective.* By definition, there should be a great degree of communication and "overlap" between project teams.

- *Learn from both best practices and lessons learned.* When Corning effectively uses the innovation process, it allows management to overcome a natural inclination *not* to stop a project that is far down the pipeline due to resource expenditure. Corning is learning that it isn't best practices alone, but also lessons learned that stimulate innovation. (At Corning, investment in technology is never lost; technology is re-used to develop new materials and processes to exploit new markets. For example, a material that failed at its initial target market—sunglasses— has become a steady, profitable business for the semi-conductor industry.)

- *Know who the customer is and what their requirements are.* Never forget that market and customer understanding is the underpinning of the three core elements of innovation effectiveness: roadmapping, portfolio management, and innovation project management.

As Corning reinvents itself for the future, Chairman and CEO Jamie Houghton points out that unlike when he first became chairman in 1983, Corning's technology cupboard is full. He and others attribute this competitive advantage to a rigorous, dynamic, and fluid innovation process. This is all well and good, but the fact of the matter is that Corning, in this time of crisis due to the telecomm debacle, is about to find out, real-time, just how good it is at innovation effectiveness. Given Corning's long history of innovation and reinvention, the attitude of the organization is to step up and welcome the challenge.

## POSTLOGUE: CONTINUOUS IMPROVEMENT

Focus on a few areas that truly influence innovation's process effectiveness:

- Focus on the selection and prioritization of opportunities and projects: what to work on (innovation opportunities) is just as important as how well the innovation work is done (innovation projects).

- Capture and share lessons learned at each diamond decision in the five-stage Stage-Gate (process).

- Ensure senior leadership involvement to drive consistent use of the process.

- Put the right people in the right roles in the critical elements for success:

  Quality of innovation project leadership

  Engaged innovation project sponsors

  Team skills matched to project objective

- Install learning coaches to develop the skills of innovation project sponsors, team leaders, and team members.

## ABOUT THE CONTRIBUTOR

**Richard A. O'Leary** is the director of human resources and diversity for science and technology at Corning Incorporated. He is also responsible for maintaining the strength of the technology community across both the centralized and decentralized organizations. Previously, he was vice president of human resources at Cytometrics, Inc., a biomedical high-technology start-up. He has held director-level human resource positions at the Public Services Electric & Gas Corporation and at Owens-Corning Corporation. He is nationally recognized for his expertise in organizational development and learning. Dr. O'Leary is an adjunct faculty member of the University of New Jersey School of Medicine, a Lt. Col. in the Air National Guard, and serves on the board of directors at Ursuline Academy. Dr. O'Leary was awarded the President's Excellence Award in 2001 and Distinguished Alumni Award from Western Michigan in 2002.

# CHAPTER THREE

# Delnor Hospital

*A cultural change model for achieving excellence in the five pillars of service, people, quality, growth, and financial performance through balanced scorecard, customer service interventions, accountability interventions, and emphasis on measurement of satisfaction for all stakeholders.*

| | |
|---|---|
| OVERVIEW | 44 |
| INTRODUCTION | 45 |
| IT STARTS WITH A TOP-DOWN COMMITMENT TO BECOME THE "BEST OF THE BEST" | 46 |
| Selecting the Right Coach Is Key | 46 |
| Implementing the Right Model for Organizational Change | 47 |
| THE NINE PRINCIPLES | 48 |
| Principle 1: Commit to Excellence | 48 |
| Principle 2: Build a Culture Around Service | 49 |
| Principle 3: Build Accountability | 52 |
| Principle 4: Create and Develop Leaders | 53 |
| Principle 5: Recognize and Reward Success | 55 |
| Principle 6: Focus on Employee Satisfaction | 56 |
| Principle 7: Measure the Important Things | 57 |
| Principle 8: Communicate at All Levels | 59 |
| Principle 9: Align Behaviors with Goals and Values | 59 |
| LESSONS LEARNED | 60 |
| Exhibit 3.1: Structure for Delnor's Customer Service Teams | 62 |
| Exhibit 3.2: Delnor Scripting for Nurses | 63 |
| Exhibit 3.3: Sample of Delnor's Monthly Performance Scorecard | 64 |
| Exhibit 3.4: Sample Agenda for One of the Two-Day Leadership Training Sessions | 65 |
| Exhibit 3.5: Accountability Grid for Best Cost and People, March 2003–May 2003, Delnor-Community Hospital | 69 |
| Exhibit 3.6: Heart Rhythms Before HeartMath "Freeze Frame" Intervention | 70 |

Exhibit 3.7: Heart Rhythms After HeartMath "Freeze Frame"            70
  Intervention
Exhibit 3.8: Best of the Best (a.k.a. "BoB") Award Form            71
Exhibit 3.9: Hospital Employee Satisfaction Results            72
Exhibit 3.10: Dashboard of Indicators            73
Exhibit 3.11: Patient and Physician Satisfaction Surveys            74
Exhibit 3.12: Team Goals            75
Exhibit 3.13: Ninety-Day Work/Action Plan            77

ABOUT THE CONTRIBUTORS            78

# OVERVIEW

This case study describes the key principles and administrative structure used by Delnor-Community Hospital to

- Transform its organizational culture

- Improve internal and external customer service

- Achieve growth in patient volumes and operating margins

- Enhance the quality of patient care

Under the leadership of a visionary senior management team and through the coaching of a leading health care consultant, the hospital has emerged as a national leader in service excellence and patient, employee, and physician satisfaction.

The hospital has also enjoyed significant growth in inpatient admissions and outpatient visits, while improving its operating margin to near record levels. Quality measures have been steadily on the rise, and the entire Delnor culture has been revitalized in ways that many beleaguered hospitals can only hope to achieve in today's challenging health care environment.

How has Delnor done it? By structuring the administration, patient care, and operations of the hospital around the five pillars of service, people, quality, growth, and financial performance, and by integrating the following nine principles into the fabric of the organization:

1. Commit to excellence

2. Build a culture around service

3. Build accountability

4. Create and develop leaders

5. Recognize and reward success

6. Focus on employee satisfaction

7. Measure the important things

8. Communicate at all levels

9. Align behaviors with goals and values

Delnor's experience in implementing these pillars and principles provides a fascinating case study and valuable insights for other health care and non-health care organizations attempting to transform their culture to achieve higher levels of performance.

# INTRODUCTION

It was January 1999, and Delnor-Community Health System President and CEO Craig Livermore knew his hospital had reached a critical point in its history. For years, Delnor had enjoyed a reputation in its service area as a "good" community hospital. Patient satisfaction was good. The quality of patient care was good. Employee relations were good. And the hospital's financial picture was good. The problem was that "good" was no longer good enough.

"Simply put, we made the decision that we wanted to become the 'best of the best,'" recalls Livermore. "As a Board of Directors and senior management team, we committed ourselves to taking Delnor to the next level and becoming one of the top hospitals not just in our region or state, but in the entire United States."

What was the driver for this ambitious goal? "First and foremost," says Livermore, "we felt we had a responsibility to provide our community with not just good, but exceptional patient care and service. That's the heart of our mission and is our fundamental reason for being. But beyond that, we knew that in order to continue to be successful in the future we were going to have to establish the right niche for ourselves in the marketplace—something that would distinguish Delnor from other area hospitals," Livermore said.

After careful deliberation, the senior management team chose "service excellence," and began focusing their energies on improving patient satisfaction throughout the hospital. But as they embarked on their journey, they quickly learned that achieving this goal was going to take much more than implementing quick fixes or a "customer service program."

"The deeper we got into the process, the more clear it became that what we needed to do was far bigger than focusing strictly on how to improve patient satisfaction," recalls Vice President and Chief Nursing Officer Linda Deering. "To become the excellent hospital we were striving to be, we realized that we needed to make major organizational changes that would transform the very culture of the hospital and impact every aspect of patient care and operations. It was a huge challenge, with the future success of the hospital riding on the outcome. But I knew we were up to the challenge and had the determination it would take to get the job done," said Deering.

Over the next three years, Delnor implemented a winning formula for success that propelled the hospital into the spotlight as a national leader in patient, employee, and physician satisfaction. The following case study will provide insight into the key elements of this formula and offer a "how to" approach for implementing "built to last" changes in your organization.

# IT STARTS WITH A TOP-DOWN COMMITMENT TO BECOME THE "BEST OF THE BEST"

When discussing organizational change, many businesses make the mistake of focusing first on finding the right change management model, but at Delnor Hospital leaders found its first key to success was something far more basic and fundamental. Observes Livermore,

> The best system or model in the world isn't going to do your organization a bit of good unless you have a top-down commitment to making it work. To me, that's where it all starts. Your board of directors, CEO, and senior management team have to be firmly and passionately committed to becoming the "best of the best." They set the tone and direction for the entire organization. It's absolutely imperative that they recognize the need for major change and be the catalysts for making it happen. This creates a trickle-down effect throughout the organization. Once mid-level management and line-level employees see top executives leading the way, most of them will begin to support the initiative as well.

"When our CEO and other top administrators began the drive to become the 'best of the best' what most impressed me was their dedication to taking Delnor to the next level," says Hasi Smith, director of information systems. "I think it really showed us, as managers, that they were totally committed to the changes that were being implemented. Their enthusiasm was contagious. Not only did that help us buy-into what was happening, it also helped our staff buy into it as well," Smith says.

## Selecting the Right Coach Is Key

Just as in sports, having the right coach to guide your organization through cultural change is a vital key to success. At Delnor, the administration turned to Quint Studer, who was building a national reputation as a service excellence and change management consultant. Studer, who is president of the Pensacola, Florida-based Studer Group, had helped guide Holy Cross Hospital in Chicago and Baptist Hospital in Pensacola to new heights in patient satisfaction as CEO during the late 1990s.

Studer offered a proven model for change, and, just as important, he brought a dynamic coaching style that made him the right fit for Delnor. "Quint has a real passion for improving health care and patient satisfaction," said Deering. "And that really shines through in his work with clients. He has a motivational way of presenting to groups that really captures their attention and makes his message compelling. That really helped us in rolling our initiative out to hospital leadership and staff and gave credibility to what we were doing."

## Implementing the Right Model for Organizational Change

Delnor's success in achieving cultural change and nationally recognized results can be attributed to the hospital's adoption of Studer's nine key principles and five organizational pillars.

*Nine Principles*

- Commit to excellence
- Build a culture around service
- Build accountability
- Create and develop leaders
- Recognize and reward success
- Focus on employee satisfaction
- Measure the important things
- Communicate at all levels
- Align behaviors with goals and values

*Five Pillars*

- Service
- Quality
- Cost
- People
- Growth

Explains Livermore,

Once you have a top-down commitment and have selected the right coach, the next essential element is implementing the right model, or system, for change. Quint's nine principles and five pillars proved to be the right fit for Delnor. They provided us with the roadmap for improving every aspect of hospital performance and operations. From a communications standpoint, the simplicity of the "principles" and "pillars" helped us in communicating the model to both leaders and staff. It was something everyone could understand, remember, and relate to. And I think that was very important. If the design of your change management system is too complex, your leaders and staff won't "get it," let alone be able to implement it.

# THE NINE PRINCIPLES

## Principle 1: Commit to Excellence

When Studer began working with Delnor, he told hospital leaders that establishing "a championship culture" begins with a commitment to excellence. "When excellence is reached," he said, "employees feel valued, physicians feel an organization is the best, and the patients feel the service is extraordinary."

One of the first things Livermore and the board of directors did to "hard-wire" this first principle into the organization was build a commitment to excellence into the hospital's mission, vision, values, and strategic plan.

*Mission statement:* To provide *excellence* in health care and to promote life-long wellness in the communities we serve.

*Vision statement:* Our community will turn to us first for health care and wellness. We will develop a tradition of service *excellence.* Patients and consumers will experience their care as connected and whole. Physicians will regard us as a trusted partner. Together, we will build a regional reputation for clinical *excellence.*

*Values: Excellence,* service, compassion, respect, and integrity.

*Strategic plan: Service excellence* became one of the eight driving strategies in the hospital's new strategic plan.

"By integrating this principle so deeply into the fabric of the organization, we sent a clear message to leaders and staff that our commitment to excellence was going to be fundamental to the new hospital culture we were building," Livemore said.

To facilitate this process, the administration used a variety of strategies, including

- Employee forums led by the chief executive officer and chief operating officer
- Employee, volunteer, and physician newsletters
- Banners, posters, and flyers
- Presentations to leadership and unit and departmental meetings
- A contest in which employees throughout the hospital were challenged to creatively display the word "excellence" in their departments

"We wanted leaders, staff, volunteers, and physicians to hear and see our commitment to excellence everywhere they went in the hospital. This was the first step in getting them to live the principle and make it a reality in everything they do," Livermore said.

## Principle 2: Build a Culture Around Service

In today's competitive health care environment, most hospitals are offering basically the same menu of services for their patients. So how can a hospital differentiate itself in the marketplace and break ahead of the pack? One of the most effective strategies, according to Studer, is to build a culture around service.

"A nationwide survey of hospital executives a few years ago found that the priorities at the top of most CEOs' 'to do' lists were things like buying more up-to-date technology and improving payer reimbursement rates," says Studer. "What was missing from this list was a very basic and fundamental priority: patient satisfaction."

This revelation struck a chord with leaders at Delnor, and confirmed a strategic direction they had already decided to pursue. "We knew that for our hospital to continue to be successful in the future we had to find the right niche in our local market. And for us, the one that made the most sense and was the most consistent with our mission was service excellence," said Livermore. "So we established an organizational goal to become the best hospital in the area and one of the top hospitals in the country in patient satisfaction."

To achieve this lofty goal, Delnor implemented a service excellence initiative inspired by Studer that comprised five critical elements: (1) creating customer satisfaction teams, (2) scripting "words that work" for employees in their interactions with patients and visitors, (3) rounding by clinical leaders, (4) follow-up calls to discharged patients, and (5) service recovery.

**Creating Customer Satisfaction Teams.**  To put the necessary organizational focus and resources behind the patient satisfaction initiative, Delnor established a series of seven action teams, each charged with addressing a different aspect of the customer experience (see Exhibit 3.1 for a diagram of the structure for Delnor's customer service teams):

- *Behavior standards.* This team established standards of performance that support the mission and values of the hospital and foster excellent customer service. (For more about the behavior standards, see Principle 9: Align Behaviors with Goals and Values.)
- *Removing irritants.* Identifying and addressing barriers to providing exceptional service to hospital patients and visitors is the focus of this team. "So often, there are things—big and small—that we do in the course of providing patient care that are irritants to our customers. But unless an organization has a

means of identifying these and correcting them, nothing gets done about them," says Deering, team chairman. "It makes so much sense to have a team in place whose mission is to look for these barriers and do whatever we can to work with hospital departments to remove them. It's a win, win—it makes the patient's experience at Delnor better, and helps to improve our patient satisfaction scores."

• *Reward and recognition.* Rewarding and recognizing top performers is vital to both encouraging employees to provide excellent service and achieving high levels of employee satisfaction within an organization. At Delnor, this team is responsible for developing and overseeing the hospital's formal reward and recognition programs. (For more information, see Principle 5: Recognize and Reward Success.)

• *Physician satisfaction.* "At Delnor, doctors are viewed as important customers just like patients," says Livermore. "Without our physicians, we wouldn't have any patients. So we felt it was important to establish a team whose sole focus is to enhance the physician experience at Delnor, whether that's making it easier for them to practice medicine here, or recognizing their contributions to patient care and the hospital." To accomplish the former, the team has worked with doctors to identify and address barriers they face at the hospital. To achieve the latter, the team instituted an innovative "Distinguished Physicians Awards" program.

• *Measurement.* To monitor the hospital's progress in improving patient satisfaction, the hospital formed a measurement team that is responsible for administering all patient satisfaction surveys and publishing and interpreting weekly, monthly and quarterly data.

"It's our job to analyze and report the data at a hospitalwide and individual department level," says Michael Kittoe, a vice president and team chairman. "We help hospital leaders and staff understand their surveys and results so they can proactively take action on the data and work on areas that need improvement. We make the whole patient satisfaction survey process very visible throughout the organization. That keeps it top-of-mind for everyone and helps hold leaders and teams accountable for their scores," Kittoe says.

• *Leadership development.* This initiative is led by a steering committee and three subcommittees that are responsible for putting together the training and tools managers need to improve their leadership skills. (For more information, see Principle 4: Create and Develop Leaders.)

**Scripting.** Another key element of building a culture around service is providing staff with scripting, or "words that work," for critical interactions with customers. (See Exhibit 3.2 showing a sample of Delnor scripting for staff.) "The goal is to teach employees how to use the words or phrases with patients, visitors, physicians, and internal customers that are conducive to customer satisfaction," says Deering. "By standardizing how staff interact with customers in certain situations, we're able to provide better service more consistently throughout the organization."

The most widely used example of scripting at Delnor is the phrase, "Is there anything else I can do for you? I have the time." Nurses, aides, housekeepers, and others ask a variation of this question every time they leave a patient room. The phrase has even caught on among employees in administrative departments when dealing with their own internal customers.

**Rounding by Clinical Leaders.** At Delnor, nursing leaders make it a priority every day to visit with patients, families, and staff on their units. "There is no better way for me to stay in touch with what's happening in my area and ensure that patient and family needs are being met than to do regular rounding," says Deborah Dyrek, a nursing manager for one of the hospital's medical floors. "By proactively looking in on patients and asking them and their families how things are going it helps me to address concerns before they become major problems."

Dyrek adds that patients and families are often surprised that a nursing administrator would take the time to stop by their room and talk with them. "This makes a strong impression and says a lot about the importance we place on patient and family satisfaction with the quality of care and service at Delnor."

Just as vital, says Dyrek, is the rounding she does with her staff. "It's important to be visible, to show you care, to provide coaching, and to find out what your team members need to do their jobs to the best of their ability—those are the benefits of rounding for me."

**Patient Call-Backs.** Pretend for a moment that you've just returned home from having outpatient surgery. You're in pain, you're nervous about your recovery, and a dozen questions are running through your head that you wish you would have remembered to ask someone before you left the hospital. Imagine what a comfort and relief it would be if you received a follow-up phone call from your nurse asking you how you're feeling and whether there's anything she can do for you. This scenario is precisely why nursing leadership at Delnor decided to institute patient call-backs to every outpatient and inpatient following their discharge from the hospital.

"It's one more way we can add that personal touch to our patient care," says Deering. "To some, making call-backs may not seem like a big deal. But you wouldn't believe how important it is to the patient to hear from us. Most calls don't last five minutes. But during that time we're able to strengthen our bond with the patient, listen to their concerns, answer their questions, and reassure them that everything is going to be OK. It's an incredibly powerful patient satisfaction tool."

The other important thing to note about patient callbacks, says Deering is that it's good medical practice. "By following-up with our patients, we're able to identify complications that may have developed since they were discharged before they become serious problems. It also provides us with the opportunity to make sure they understood their discharge instructions for self-care, or answer questions they may have about taking their pain medication. From a clinical quality standpoint, it's the right thing to do. There's no question that it helps to lower readmission rates," adds Deering.

**Service Recovery.** "No matter how hard you try, no organization provides perfect customer service," points out Deering. "We're all human and make mistakes. But if those mistakes are handled in the right way, you can quickly turn a negative into a positive and convert unhappy customers into loyal ones by following a service recovery process we call ACT."

ACT is an acronym for apologize, correct, and take action. And at Delnor, it has become the standard process by which staff respond to patient and visitor complaints. When faced with a dissatisfied customer, the first step in service recovery is to apologize for failing to meet his or her expectations. This immediately sets a conciliatory tone and lets the customer know you take the complaint seriously. The next step is to work with the customer to determine how best to correct the situation in an acceptable way. The final step is to move swiftly in taking action to resolve the problem.

"At Delnor, we train our employees to view complaints as a gift," says Deering. "It may sound strange, but customers are actually doing us a favor when they step forward with legitimate complaints. It sends up a red flag that a customer process is broken and needs to be fixed." This becomes even more important, according to Deering, in light of consumer studies indicating that for every customer who complains about a problem, there are nine more who don't complain but simply choose to go elsewhere for service.

"On the positive side, research has also shown that most customers whose complaints are promptly addressed will return to a company or business for service. These statistics really underscore the importance of service recovery. It's amazing how powerful the three simple steps of ACT can be in turning a negative customer experience into a positive one," Deering says.

## Principle 3: Build Accountability

Building a championship culture requires creating an environment of ownership and accountability at every level of the organization. "This principle is absolutely critical," says Livermore. "From top administrators to line-level staff, we needed a team that was going to act like 'owners,' as opposed to 'renters' in their areas. And we needed to put systems in place that would hold everyone accountable for their individual and team performance, as well as the performance of the organization as a whole."

To help foster an environment of ownership, the importance of this principle was communicated extensively throughout the hospital to both leaders and staff in a variety of ways. It also was emphasized in the employee hiring and orientation process.

Greater accountability was integrated into the culture through the development of monthly scorecards monitoring progress in achieving organizational and team goals. (See Exhibit 3.3 showing a sample of Delnor's monthly performance scorecard.) Performance toward these goals was also factored heavily into year-end performance reviews for leadership and staff, and is a key barometer by which the board of directors evaluates the hospital's executive team. Hospitalwide and unit- and department-specific patient satisfaction scores are widely publicized and posted throughout the building, as are the results of internal customer surveys (in which departments rate the service they provide to each other). Leaders and staff are also held accountable for the number of process-improvement and cost-savings ideas they generate annually through the Bright Ideas program.

## Principle 4: Create and Develop Leaders

"In one of our first coaching sessions with Quint Studer," recalls Livermore, "he asked our leadership team how many of them had received formal training to become managers. Very few hands went up. And that was a real eye-opening experience for me.

"I realized that we, like so many hospitals and businesses, often promote people to management roles based on their knowledge, technical skills and past performance in other positions without providing them with tools they need to become great leaders. That's why this fourth principle has become one of the most important factors in creating a new culture at Delnor," Livermore said.

To implement this principal, Delnor followed the Studer Group's model for establishing an in-house leadership institute. The institute's goals are to teach both new and existing managers new skills, competencies, and behaviors that will help them become better leaders and serve as catalysts for organizational change. (See Exhibits 3.4 and 3.5 showing a sample agenda for one of the two-day leadership training sessions, along the "accountability grid" each leader receives as a guide for action steps to take back to their teams to implement.)

The institute is charged with creating customized, quarterly, two-day training sessions for the hospital's leadership team. Each session has a unique theme and is focused on one of the five pillars of growth, service, people, quality, and finance. Presentations are given by a combination of Delnor leaders and professional outside speakers. Program content covers issues such as

- Leading versus managing
- Dealing with poor performers
- Rewarding and recognizing employees

- Recruiting, interviewing, and hiring new staff
- Developing budgeting skills
- Managing conflict
- Giving positive and negative feedback to employees

Following each session, leaders are required to share what they've learned and implement new practices with their teams. In addition to the quarterly meetings, monthly "lunch and learns" are offered to provide leaders with additional training opportunities.

The leadership development initiative is coordinated by a steering committee and a series of subcommittees consisting of a cross-section of Delnor managers. Together, they develop the goals, theme, content, learning materials, and communications for each training session. They also make all of the logistical arrangements.

"We invest heavily in growing and developing our leaders because they're the ones who have the ability to implement and sustain organizational change at the team and individual employee level," says Livermore. "Some executives I've talked to at other hospitals have asked me how we can afford to devote so much time, staffing, and resources to this principle. My response to them is, 'We can't afford not to!'"

Nursing leaders like Katherine Barker testify to the success of the initiative. "I came up through the ranks as a registered nurse," reports Barker. "All of my professional education and training was in patient care. When I was promoted to a nursing management position I had all the clinical knowledge and skills for the position but I had never received any training in how to effectively manage and lead a team. The training I've received at Delnor over the past three years has given me the tools I need to be a confident and effective leader. It has taken me to a whole new level professionally."

While leadership development has played a major role in helping Delnor achieve strong results, hospital administrators have also been sensitive to the added stress the cultural changes have created for the management team. To help leaders achieve optimal performance and emotional balance through these challenging times, the hospital partnered with HeartMath LLC. (See Exhibits 3.6 and 3.7 showing heart rhythms before and after using the HeartMath Freeze Frame technique.)

"We knew that the transformation we were going through—while vitally necessary—was creating stress for our leaders, and we were concerned about that," recalls Tom Wright, chief operating officer. "We began to look for ways to provide them with the support and resources they needed to more effectively cope with change on both a personal and professional level, and HeartMath turned out to be an excellent solution."

HeartMath LLC is a leading-edge performance training and technology company with demonstrated success in creating both personal and organizational health and performance outcomes. HeartMath uses a scientifically validated system of stress intervention techniques and objective biometric feedback.

Science has known for some time that the heart has its own type of intelligence that communicates with and influences the brain through the nervous system, hormonal system, and other pathways. HeartMath's research in neurocardiology shows that when we consciously shift into a positive emotional state, our heart rhythms shift, too. This response in the heart triggers a response in the brain, creating a favorable cascade of neural, hormonal, and biochemical events that actually reverse the effects of stress and improve performance.

HeartMath workshops—which are designed to teach individuals how to better manage stress in the moment, sustain performance under pressure, and maintain a proper work/life balance—have become a vital part of the hospital's leadership training. The results, according to Wright, have been impressive. Among the 422 leaders and employees who participated in HeartMath workshops in fiscal year 2001, turnover was only 5.9 percent, while the hospital's overall turnover rate that year was at 21 percent. "There's no question that the HeartMath workshops have helped our leaders reduce their stress, improve mental clarity and decision making, manage more efficiently, and sustain peak performance. In fact, the program has been so effective that we're now offering it to all hospital employees and physicians," Wright says.

## Principle 5: Recognize and Reward Success

What are the biggest motivators for today's workforce? If you answered pay raises or better company perks, you might be surprised by the results of a study conducted by Dr. Gerald Graham, a management professor at Wichita State University, which found that three of the top four workplace incentives were related to reward and recognition:

- Personal thanks from manager
- Written thanks from manager
- Promotion for performance
- Public praise

"Never let great work go unnoticed," was Quint Studer's advice as he coached hospital managers on the importance of this principle. Rewarding and recognizing employees for excellent performance is not only the right thing to do, it's also a powerful business strategy, says Studer. "When you praise employees, you increase their job satisfaction and create role models for their peers. In addition, studies show that complimented behavior will be repeated. It's truly a win-win situation for staff and the organization."

At Delnor, top management began integrating this principle through leadership training. "We educated our leaders about the importance of praising their staff and taught them skills for how to do it effectively," says Deering. "It sounds simple, but it's amazing how many managers don't take the time to tell their employees they're doing a good job unless you build it into your culture as an expectation."

The hospital also formed a team to develop new reward and recognition programs, including the following (see Exhibit 3.8 showing a Best of the Best, or "BoB," award form):

• *The Best of the Best (BoB) program.* This program involved creating reward certificates that patients, visitors, leaders, coworkers, volunteers, or physicians can fill out to recognize an employee for providing excellent customer service. Staff members receiving the certificates can redeem them with their manager for prizes that include meal passes for the cafeteria or gift cards for local stores and restaurants.

"It's great when someone gives me a 'BoB,'" says Cindy Masa, a registered nurse. "It really makes me feel like I'm appreciated for taking extra time with a patient or doing something nice for a coworker. And the gift certificates are like getting a little bonus. I love it." Masa's comments are representative of the entire staff's response to the program, which has become one of the most successful aspects of Delnor's reward and recognition efforts.

• *Monthly Excellence Awards.* This is the next level of recognition. Employees who go above and beyond what's expected in customer service receive special recognition at a monthly awards ceremony attended by hospital leaders and staff.

• *Annual Excellence Awards.* A select few employees who do something extraordinary for customers or the organization receive these awards, which are given out once a year at an employee recognition banquet. First, second, and third place plaques and cash prizes of up to $1,000 come with this highest level of recognition. As Livermore said, "The awards dinner is our most celebrated employee event and is always one of the highlights of the year at the hospital. It's a tremendous way to recognize the very 'best of the best' at Delnor."

## Principle 6: Focus on Employee Satisfaction

"What we have found is that there is a direct correlation between employee satisfaction and patient and physician satisfaction," says Livermore. "By constantly working to keep our staff satisfied, we have been able to improve morale, while at the same time dramatically increasing our patient satisfaction and physician satisfaction scores. It just stands to reason that happy employees are going to provide better care and service to customers."

At the macro-level, achieving high levels of employee satisfaction depends, in large part, upon an organization's success in integrating the other eight principles described in this chapter. "All these elements must work in concert to create an environment and culture that differentiates you and makes your hospital or business a place where employees feel valued and want to come to work each day," observes Livermore.

At the microlevel, the hospital has taken a number of steps to integrate this principle, including establishing an organizational goal to become the top hospital in Chicago's western suburbs for employee satisfaction. "We built that goal into our strategic plan and formed an Employer of Choice team to serve as a catalyst for helping us get there," says Livermore. Over the past three years, this group has researched and implemented the following successful strategies:

- Developing programs to help staff achieve greater work–life balance
- Enhancing opportunities for career development
- Improving the competitiveness of the hospital's wage and benefits program
- Offering health and wellness opportunities for employees
- Organizing fun activities that build employee spirit

Thanks to these efforts and the hospital's cultural transformation, Delnor recently achieved the highest score for employee morale in a national survey of hospitals and health care organizations conducted by Sperduto & Associates, a national research firm. (See Exhibit 3.9 showing the hospital's employee satisfaction results as documented by Sperduto & Associates.) The hospital was also the 2002 winner of the Institute for Health and Productivity Management's Corporate Health and Productivity Award.

In addition to earning national acclaim, Delnor's "employer of choice" initiatives are also producing bottom-line results for the hospital. Staff turnover has declined from 20.5 percent in FY2001 to 11 percent in FY2002, resulting in a savings of hundreds of thousands of dollars to the hospital in recruitment, training, and other expenses related to hiring new employees.

## Principle 7: Measure the Important Things

"If you set a goal but don't bother to measure your progress along the way, how will you know whether you achieve it?" asks Livermore in underscoring the importance of Principle #7. The keys, he says, are determining the most important and meaningful data elements to measure, and making sure something is done with the information once it's collected. At Delnor, the hospital focuses on measuring data closely related to strategic priorities and organizational goals.

**Dashboard of Indicators.** "We selected key data under the five pillars of service, people, growth, quality, and finance and developed a "dashboard of indicators" to help senior management and the board of directors monitor the hospital's performance," says Gretchen Parker, director of planning. "Each measure is tied to an objective in our strategic plan, such as patient satisfaction, patient volumes, market share, quality of care, financial performance, and so on." (See Exhibit 3.10 showing the hospital's "dashboard of indicators".)

**Customer Satisfaction.** After making "service excellence" a strategic priority and establishing an organizational goal to reach the ninety-ninth percentile in patient satisfaction, Delnor implemented a rigorous system for measuring and reporting patient satisfaction data.

Using Press Ganey, a professional, independent, national research firm, the hospital surveys every type of patient it serves (inpatients, outpatients, emergency department patients, and so on) continuously during the year. Patient satisfaction reports are generated and shared throughout the hospital on a weekly, monthly, quarterly, and annual basis. (See Exhibit 3.11 showing patient and physician satisfaction survey results from national market research firms.)

"Establishing a measurement system this extensive is a huge undertaking that requires considerable staff and financial resources, but we have found it to be well worthwhile," says Michael Kittoe, vice president and chairman of the hospital's Data Measurement Team. "By publishing this data so frequently it really helps our leaders and staff focus on patient satisfaction. What's more, leaders and teams are held accountable for their scores and are expected to utilize the data to identify gaps in patient satisfaction so they can implement process improvements."

Top-scoring teams are recognized and rewarded, creating a celebratory atmosphere that's infectious, says Kittoe. "It creates a healthy competition within the hospital among teams, and constantly challenges them to improve."

Achieving the ninety-ninth percentile (or top 1 percent) in patient satisfaction has become the hospital's rallying cry, and top management emphasizes this goal at every opportunity with both leaders and staff. "Senior management sets the focus and tone for the organization," says Barker. "When we see and hear how passionate they are about this goal it really fires up the rest of us to work hard to achieve it."

In addition to measuring patient satisfaction, the hospital also conducts physician and employee satisfaction surveys and community-based market research. As customer service action plans have been developed and implemented for each of those groups, the hospital has experienced dramatic gains in those scores as well.

"Without a doubt, our achievement of national rankings in patient, employee, and physician satisfaction has coincided with our emphasis on measuring the important things and being committed to taking action on the results," says Livermore.

## Principle 8: Communicate at All Levels

Effective corporate communication is always important, especially during times of major cultural change. "Let's face it, change is uncomfortable, and, at times, even scary," says Livermore. "That's why it's so important for top management to clearly communicate their organization's vision, goals, and strategic direction to leaders and staff. We have an obligation to explain where the organization is headed and why. To fail to do so causes confusion and paralysis."

To achieve this principle at Delnor the administration used a variety of communications tactics, including

- Leadership meetings
- Employee forums
- Memos and e-mails
- The employee newsletter

In addition, team leaders communicated the changes and addressed employee questions at department meetings.

"You can't communicate something as radical as a new vision and strategic direction once and expect leaders and staff to 'get it,'" says Livermore. "Our goal was to get the word out as often and in as many different ways as possible using consistent themes and messages. In situations like this, it's virtually impossible to over-communicate."

In addition to top-down communication, Delnor also employs a technique called "managing-up," in which employees are encouraged to proactively communicate with their supervisor on important issues. "We tell our staff to put themselves in their boss's shoes and ask themselves, 'What does he or she need to know about what I'm doing and how can I help the hospital be more successful?'" says Deering. "Managing-up is also an important way employees can make sure their priorities are in line with their boss's expectations and team and organizational goals."

## Principle 9: Align Behaviors with Goals and Values

"Developing an organizational vision, values, and strategic plan is vital," says Livermore, "but just as important is putting systems in place that integrate them into the daily behaviors, decisions, and activities of leaders and staff." Delnor accomplished this most notably by adopting a series of behavior standards and by tying department and individual goals to organizational objectives.

**Behavior Standards.** To clearly define what's expected of employees, the administration developed a series of behavior standards that emphasize the hospital's values and address issues such as interpersonal communications, commitment to coworkers, personal appearance, and patient privacy.

"At Delnor, we strive to be the 'best of the best' in customer service," says Deering. "This means we must be consistently excellent during every contact with every customer on a daily basis. The behavior standards help us achieve this by making it very clear to employees how we want them to treat our patients, visitors, and coworkers. They set the standard for what we expect."

The behavior standards are spelled out in a manual that's required reading for all new hires. They're also publicized and reviewed monthly with all hospital staff through department meetings, bulletin boards, the employee newsletter, and other means.

**Goal Setting.** "One of the most effective strategies we've employed to achieve the eighth principle is to require every department in the hospital to develop team goals that are aligned with our organizational goals," says Livermore. "Then we take the process one step further by having managers work with each employee to set individual goals that are focused on achieving the team and organizational goals. This ensures that the entire organization is working in concert to accomplish our vision and strategic plan," Livermore says. (See Exhibits 3.12 and 3.13 showing a sample of team goals and the ninety-day action work plan format used by Delnor leaders.)

To help teams stay on track, department heads are required to develop ninety-day plans that outline specific actions to be taken each quarter in working toward annual goals. "These plans are a great tool to help leaders in focusing on goals and measuring their progress during the year," says Livermore.

This principle is also built into the hospital's review-evaluation system so everyone is held accountable for their performance in achieving individual, team, and organizational goals.

# LESSONS LEARNED

Through the journey of creating a championship culture at Delnor, the management team learned many valuable lessons along the way, including

1. Organizational transformation starts with a top-down commitment. The board of directors, CEO, and senior management team set the tone and direction for the organization.

2. A commitment to excellence must be built into the organization's mission, vision, strategic plan, and values.

3. The successful implementation of major organizational change does not happen overnight. It takes time, determination, and a willingness to transform the very culture of your organization.

4. There is no one right formula for becoming the "best of the best." Any model for change and improvement must be customized to fit an organization's unique characteristics, culture, and market conditions.

5. Building a championship culture requires creating an environment of ownership and accountability at every level of the organization.

6. Creating and developing leaders is key to organizational success.

7. Providing training and support in stress management and work–life balance is vital to helping leaders and employees sustain peak performance during time of major organizational change.

8. Never let great work go unnoticed. Recognizing and rewarding top performers is a powerful motivator and a key factor in employee satisfaction.

9. Focus on employee satisfaction. Happy, loyal workers provide better service to customers.

10. Measure the important things. If an organization doesn't track its progress toward reaching goals, how will it know whether it ever achieves them?

11. Be flexible. The implementation of any change management model is a difficult and imperfect process. Be prepared to modify your plans to overcome unanticipated obstacles and adjust to ever-changing conditions.

Exhibit 3.1. Structure for Delnor's Customer Service Teams

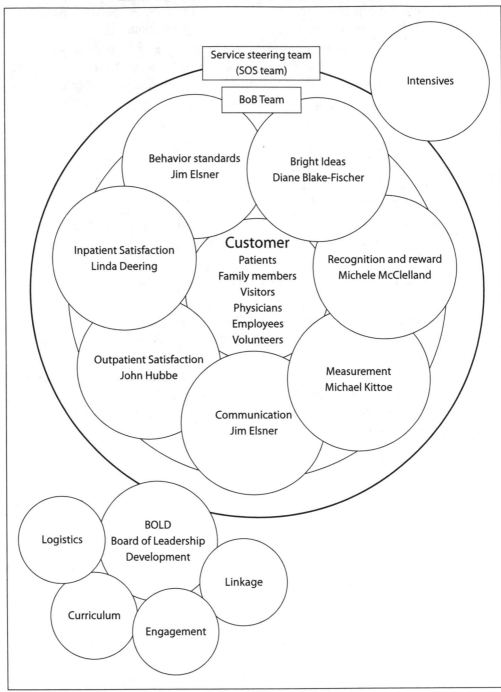

Exhibit 3.2. Delnor Scripting for Nurses

**SITUATION**

If a patient asks you when he or she can expect to see the doctor, please use the following scripting (pick one):

*Scripting*

- "Your doctor usually makes rounds about _____."
- "I am not sure when to expect him but I will call his (or her) office and ask the receptionist as to when you can expect him (her)."
- If the physician's office staff cannot provide a time, ask them to check with the doctor and call you back. Respond to the patient with: "I have left a message with Dr. _____ office and I am awaiting a call back. Is there anything I can do for you in the meantime?"

**SITUATION**

If you need to close a patient's door to ensure their privacy while performing an exam, changing a dressing, giving a bath, or similar procedure, please use the following scripting:

*Scripting*

- "I am closing your door for your privacy. Is there anything else I can do for you? I have the time."

**SITUATION**

To ensure prompt response to patient needs and minimize the use of call lights, please use the following scripting:

*Scripting*

- "This is my phone number. Please call me if you need anything. I will be able to meet your request more quickly if you call me directly. Is there anything I can do for you? I have the time.

**SITUATION**

During high-census periods, patients may become concerned about whether nursing units are adequately staffed to provide excellent care and meet their needs. Should a patient or family member inquire about this, please use the following scripting:

*Scripting*

- "Things are active today, but we have adequate staffing and we have the time to care for you. Feel free to call me at anytime. Is there anything I can do for you now? I have the time."

**SITUATION**

Sometimes patients or families will ask questions that you may not have an immediate answer for. Here's some scripting to help you respond in such situations.

*Scripting*

- "I don't know. That is a good question. Let me check into it and I will get back to you by _____ today with an answer."

## Exhibit 3.3. Sample of Delnor's Monthly Performance Scorecard

Section A.  Hospitalwide performance   As of:_____  Period:_____

| Indicator/Definition | Results |
| --- | --- |
| **Service:** Average percentile ranking of the patient satisfaction surveys for Inpatient, Outpatient/Home health care, Emergency services, and Same day surgery.<br><br>5 = Average equal to or exceeding the 96th percentile<br>4 = Average from 93rd to 95th percentile<br>3 = Average from 90th to 92nd percentile<br>2 = Average from 87th to 89th percentile<br>1 = Average equal to or below 86th percentile | *FY 2004 year-to-date average* |
| **People:** Measured by the employee turnover rate annualized.<br><br>5 = Turnover rate 15.0% or lower<br>4 = Turnover rate of 15.1 – 17.0%<br>3 = Turnover rate of 17.1 – 19.0%<br>2 = Turnover rate of 19.1 – 21.0%<br>1 = Turnover rate greater than 21.0% | *FY 2004 year-to-date* |
| **Quality:** Surgical site infection (SSI) rate performance improvement.<br><br>5 = Implement at least *three* systemwide evidence-based interventions AND a statistically significant reduction in SSI rate<br>4 = Implement at least *three* systemwide evidence-based interventions AND a reduction in SSI rate<br>3 = Implement at least *three* systemwide evidence-based interventions<br>2 = Implement at least *two* systemwide evidence-based interventions<br>1 = Implement *one or more* systemwide evidence-based interventions | *FY 2004 year-to-date* |
| **Financial:** The actual operating income as compared to budget year-to-date.<br><br>5 = Exceeding budgeted income by 10.0% or more<br>4 = 5.0% to 9.9% above budgeted income<br>3 = 0.0% to 4.9% above budgeted income<br>2 = 0.1% to 4.9% below budgeted income<br>1 = Below budgeted income by 5.0% or more | *FY 2004 year-to-date* |
| **Financial:** Measured by the total inpatient and outpatient visits compared to budget year-to-date.<br><br>5 = Exceeding budgeted volume by 3.0% or more<br>4 = 1.5% to 2.9% above budget<br>3 = 0.0% to 1.4% above budget<br>2 = 0.1% to 1.4% below budget<br>1 = Below budgeted volume by 1.5% or greater | *FY 2004 year-to-date* |

Year-to-date average score of Section A:_____

*Note:* 5 (Exceptional), 4 (Exceeds expectations), 3 (Achieves expectations), 2 (Below expectations), or 1 (Needs improvement).

Exhibit 3.4.  Sample Agenda for One of the Two-Day Leadership Training Sessions

## WDCH *Live* from Fox Valley Tri-Cities
## Channel 300 on Your Dial!

Program Guide – Wednesday, March 19th, 2003

MC's – Chad Gilliland & Karin Podolski

| Programming | Listing | Radio & Television Personalities |
|---|---|---|
| Early AM addition | Register to win | |
| Commercial welcome | | Chad Gilliland & Karin Podolski |
| Check your score cards<br>- Review accountability grid (new) | Drama | Chad Gilliland & Karin Podolski |
| Heart Time (Live) | Health Wise | Diane Ball |
| Public Service Announcement | HIPPA | HIPPA Task Force |
| E-learning and Trends | Understanding of Delnor's financial position, current, and future<br>Need for leaders to achieve excellence in financial operations management | Michael Kittoe & Dan Yunker |
| Break | Exercise | |
| Decreasing Cost Through Better Supply<br>Chain management | To increase efficiency<br><br>Refer to 1st item on your Accountability Grid | HFMA |
| Break | Exercise | |
| Substance Abuse in the Workplace<br>Refer to 2nd item on your Accountability Grid | Better knowledge and understanding of substance abuse and work policy | Dr. Woodward |
| Advertisement | HIPPA | HIPPA Task Force |

*(Continued)*

**Exhibit 3.4. Sample Agenda for One of the Two-Day Leadership Training Sessions** (*Continued*)

| | | |
|---|---|---|
| Late Lunch | Eating Enigma | Weight Watchers |
| Would You Believe It! | Making the Year 2002 "Graduation" | All Star Awards |
| To Tell the Truth | Game Show | Audience Participation |
| Managing Labor Costs: Dealing with work force shortages and the need to grow revenues with existing FTE targets. Refer to 3rd & 4th item on your Grid | To improve productivity without increasing resources | HFMA |
| Quick run - the program starts in 5 minutes | Exercise | |
| Station News Flash | HIPPA | HIPPA Task Force |
| Delnor Highlights | News You Can Use | Anchor C. Livermore |
| Coming Attractions | | |

## Exhibit 3.4. (*Continued*)

Program Guide — Thursday, March 20, 2003

| Programming | Listing | Radio & Television Personalities |
|---|---|---|
| Good Morning WDCH | First On Your Dial | Him & Her |
| A Day in the Making | Learn where you are going | Chad & KP |
| Moving Mountains | Increasing confidence and self assuredness when taking emotional risks necessary to forge ahead for significant achievement | Diane Ball |
| Family Feud | Game Show | The Logistics |
| Whether Forecast Yes, whether this or that | Financial Projects through 2006 | Tom & Michael |
| Stretch, Wet, Chew Time | Calories by Pipefitters. Sweet rolls, fruit, bagels coffee, tea or pee | We Fit It to Your Hips |
| Commercial Break | HIPPA | HIPPA Task Force |
| The Gardeners | PCC & Discharge Planners – See how actions speak louder than words in today's episode | M. Schoolfield, L. Pertl, J. Joseph, K. Kalin, L. Adams |
| 6 Secrets to Effective Leadership<br><br>Refer to 5th item on your Accountability Grid! | V- vision<br>O- openness<br>I- influence<br>C- competence<br>E- ethics<br>S- social skills | Brian Smith |

(*Continued*)

**Exhibit 3.4. Sample Agenda for One of the Two-Day Leadership Training Sessions** (*Continued*)

| | | |
|---|---|---|
| Rehab Renegades | OP Rehab – Reality Program | J. Polkow, K. Pennington, D. Hamilton, S. Black |
| Lunching with the Best | Talk Show Variety | |
| The Oldies but Goodies | Delnor Glen – the story BEHIND the story | D. Winecke, P. Faught, L. Spang, D. Sprovieri, C. Duer |
| Public Service Announcement | HIPPA | HIPPA Task Force |
| 6 Secrets to Effective Leadership *continued* | Refer to # 5 on the Accountability Grid | Brian Smith |
| Rolling Three Kidney Stones | 3 North – Talk Show | C. Johnson, B. Nelson, W. Perez |
| Rope Warrior | Thinking Out of the Loop | David Fisher |
| Wright Show - variety | Connect the Dots | Tom Wright |

**Exhibit 3.5. Accountability Grid for Best Cost and People, March 2003–May 2003, Delnor-Community Hospital**

| Who | What | Complete by | Completed Y N | Progress Note |
|---|---|---|---|---|
| Team Leader and Coordinators | Share with your team the challenges related to *non-labor* resources management. Create an action plan with 2–3 interventions. | 04/17/03 | | |
| | Meet with Center Leaders. Identify your personal knowledge/practice changes related to new information on substance abuse. | 05/01/03 | | |
| | Share with your team the challenges related to *labor* resources management. Create an action plan with 2–3 interventions. | 04/17/03 | | |
| | Define a desired 7.5 percent improved productivity or supply chain cost result to be achieved and the related measure of the results. Timeline to be set with your Center Leader within the first 2 weeks. | 04/03/03 | | |
| | Select one of the 3 simple keys, create a personal action plan and share with your Center Leader. | 04/03/03 | | |
| Center Leaders | Meet with your team leaders/coordinators to develop a training goal to ensure proper working knowledge of labor management software. | | | |

**Exhibit 3.6. Heart Rhythms Before HeartMath "Freeze Frame" Intervention**

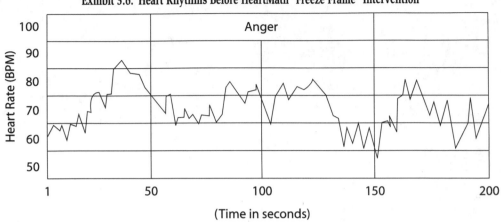

**Exhibit 3.7. Heart Rhythms After HeartMath "Freeze Frame" Intervention**

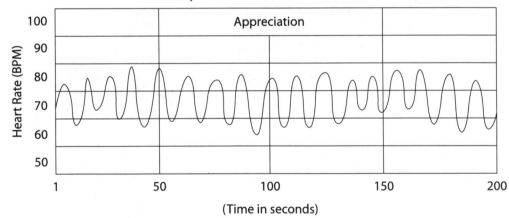

Exhibit 3.8. Best of the Best (a.k.a. "BoB") Award Form

**B**est

**O**f the

**B**est

I commend _____

of Department, _____

for the following reason(s): _____

_____

_____

_____

_____

Your Name: _____

Your Department: _____

☐ Patient  ☐ Staff  ☐ Visitor

Please return this card to your Team Leader, Coordinator or Nursing Supervisor.
Team Leader, etc.: Please send completed card to Maryann Russ, Information Systems

We would like to recognize those individuals
who exceed your expectations.

Leader: _____
Please write in the level of recognition:

_____

Level of Gift

_____
Leader's Inititals

Exhibit 3.9. Hospital Employee Satisfaction Results

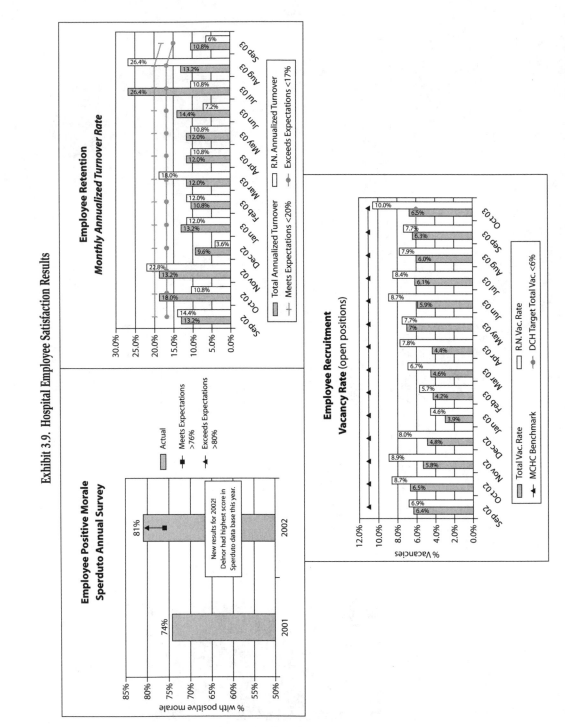

**Exhibit 3.10. Dashboard of Indicators**

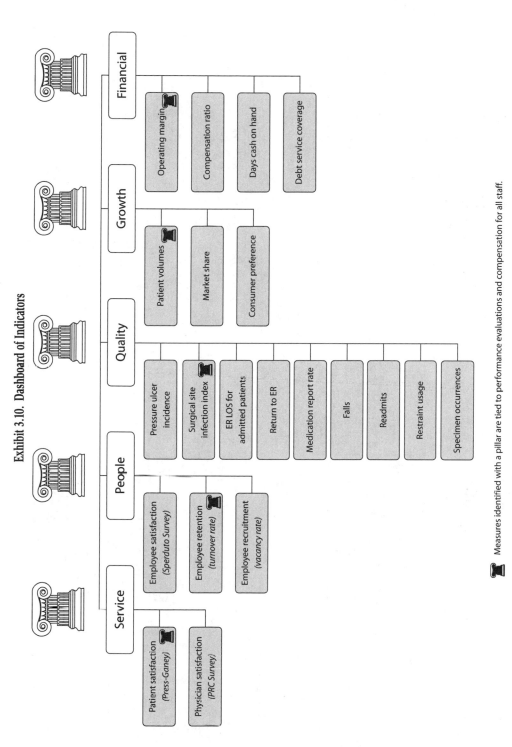

*Note:* Possible scores: At or better than target; Near or trending toward target; Far from target; and Under development.

Exhibit 3.11. Patient and Physician Satisfaction Surveys

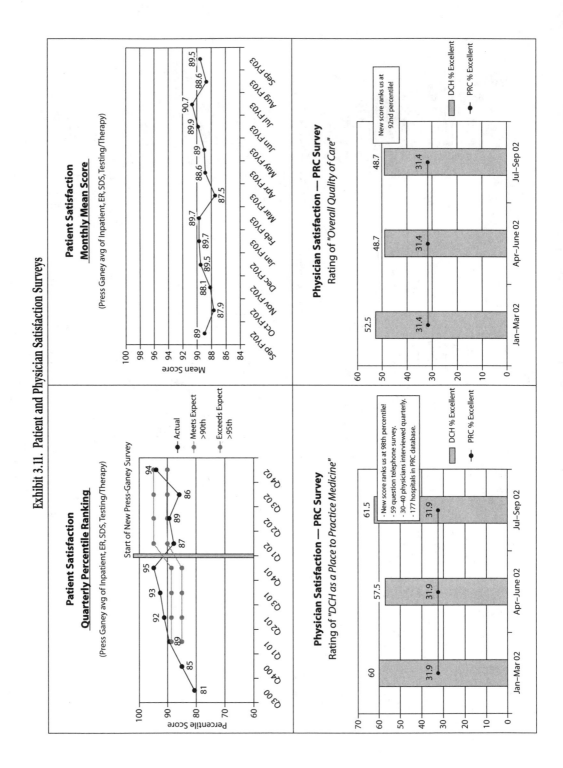

## Exhibit 3.12. Team Goals

*B. TEAM PERFORMANCE.* Team performance can be measured at various levels. For example, it can be measured at the center (division), team (department), or the work unit level. Below are four or more team-based performance objectives and measures that were established by your team in collaboration with the organization's leadership. One of the measures has to be a financial measure of team success. Two or more teams within the same center may share a common measure and each team within the center may have one or more measures unique to their team. A check mark will indicate your team's achievement on each measure.

Your Team Is: Emergency Department _____

*Best Service: Patient satisfaction as measured by average quarterly mean scores for ER.*

[ ]     3 = mean score equal to or greater than 87.8

[ ]     2 = mean score between 86.3–87.7

[ ]     1 = mean score below 86.3

*Best People: Management of turnover as measured by twelve-month average for ER (Current 5 6.1%).*

[ ]     3 = less than 10.0%

[ ]     2 = between 10.0 and 12.0%

[ ]     1 = greater than 12.0%

*Best Quality: Bright Ideas implemented in ER Team. Ideas must be for improvements on the team.*

[ ]     3 = One Bright Idea implemented per FTE on the team ($\geqslant$34)

[ ]     2 = 0.5 FTE Bright Idea implemented per FTE on the team (17–33)

[ ]     1 = Less than 0.5 Bright Idea implemented per FTE on the team (<17)

*Best Quality: Skin Care as measured by time of admission documentation of skin condition for patients being admitted as inpatient.*

[ ]     3 = 90% or greater documented

[ ]     2 = 80–89% documented

[ ]     1 = 79% or less documented

*(Continued)*

Exhibit 3.12. Team Goals (*Continued*)

---

*Best Financial: Management of team financial performance as measured by the Financial Accountability Scorecard (FAS) for ER.*

[ ]     3 = Score of 90 or better

[ ]     2 = Score of 80–89

[ ]     1 = Score of 79 or less

*Best Growth: Increase in volume as measured by number of patient visits.*

[ ]     3 = 3% or greater above budget

[ ]     2 = 0–2% above budget

[ ]     1 = less than budget

*Comments and Goals (Optional):*

Average Score of Section B: _____ (Add each score in this section and divide by the number of measures.)

---

*Note:* 3 (Exceptional), 2 (Achieves expectations), or 1 (Needs improvement).

**Exhibit 3.13. Ninety-Day Work/Action Plan**

| 90 DAY WORK/ACTION PLAN | FY2003 | | Quarter: | | Leader's name: | | Dept: |
|---|---|---|---|---|---|---|---|
| Goal | Action Steps | | % Time* | Priority (1–3)* | Support/ Direction (1–3)* | | 90 Day Result Report |
| Best People | | | | | | | |
| Best Service | | | | | | | |
| Quality | | | | | | | |
| Cost | | | | | | | |
| Growth | | | | | | | |

*Note:* *% Time: Percentage of leader's time to be spent on goal. Priority (1–3): 1 = high; 2 = medium; 3 = low. Support/Direction (1–3): 1 = supervisor approval needed; 2 = supervisor input needed; 3 = move forward on own.

# ABOUT THE CONTRIBUTORS

**Craig A. Livermore** is president and chief executive officer for Delnor-Community Health System and Delnor-Community Hospital in Geneva, Illinois. He earned his B.S. degree in business from Eastern Illinois University and a Master of Hospital and Health Care Administration degree from Saint Louis University. He is past-chairman of the Metropolitan Chicago Healthcare Council Board of Directors and a member of the American College of Healthcare Executives. He is also actively involved in numerous health care and community organizations. Prior to joining Delnor, Mr. Livermore was president and chief executive officer of Augustana Hospital and Health Care Center in Chicago.

**Thomas L. Wright** is chief operating officer for Delnor-Community Health System and Delnor-Community Hospital in Geneva, Illinois. He also serves as chief financial officer of Delnor-Community Health Care Foundation and Delnor-Community Residential Living. He holds a B.S. degree in mathematics and an M.B.A. degree with a concentration in finance from Loyola University of Chicago. He is an advanced member of the Healthcare Financial Management Association, a member and past chairman of the Metropolitan Chicago Healthcare Council Finance Committee, and a Diplomat of the American College of Healthcare Executives. Mr. Wright is also very active in supporting local health care and community organizations.

**Linda Deering** is vice president and chief nursing officer for Delnor-Community Hospital in Geneva, Illinois. She holds a B.A. degree from Northern Illinois University, and an M.S. degree from Northern Illinois University. She is an active member of the American Organization of Nurse Executives, Illinois Organization of Nurse Leaders, and Illinois Coalition for Nursing Resources. In addition to her work at Delnor, she works with other hospitals across the nation to facilitate organizational excellence and culture transformation.

# Emmis Communications

*A change management process is for creating and implementing a distinctive firm brand and fostering a unique employer-of-choice culture while driving performance, accountability and innovation to higher levels. Initiative leverages executive strategic planning and alignment, leadership-development programs, performance-management systems, employee-commitment strategies, targeted organizational communications, and special events and recognition.*

| | |
|---|---|
| OVERVIEW | 80 |
| INTRODUCTION: RAPID GROWTH TO A MEDIA MID-CAP | 81 |
| Distinctive Culture | 82 |
| Internal Growth and Economic Pains | 82 |
| COMPASSIONATE EMPLOYER OF CHOICE | 83 |
| ASSESSMENT: ON THE AIR | 85 |
| DIAGNOSIS: PLUGGED IN? | 86 |
| New Business Realities: Drivers for Change | 87 |
| Change Objective | 88 |
| APPROACH | 88 |
| DESIGN: WHO'S OUR CUSTOMER? | 89 |
| INTERVENTION: GETTING TUNED IN | 89 |
| Executive Alignment | 89 |
| Malicious Compliance | 91 |
| Leading for Results | 91 |
| PROGRAM PROMOTION AND MULTIMEDIA | 92 |
| BUILDING A HIGH-PERFORMANCE DISCIPLINE: CRANKING IT UP! | 94 |
| Balanced Scorecards | 94 |

**Note:** Some information in this case study was taken with permission from Emmis Communications internal and public documents.

Emmis Competency Model                                                        95
Performance and Reward Management                                             95
Employee Training                                                            95

WHAT ABOUT INNOVATION?                                                       96

EVALUATION: MEASURING SIGNAL STRENGTH                                        97

January 12, 2004, Q&A with Emmis Communications CEO                          98
    Jeff Smulyan

LESSONS LEARNED                                                              99

Exhibit 4.1: The Eleven Commandments of Emmis Communications               101
Exhibit 4.2: Dual-Path Results Model                                       102
Exhibit 4.3: Executive Session FAST Agenda                                 103
Exhibit 4.4: Internal Communications Matrix                                105
Exhibit 4.5: Balanced Scorecard Sample                                     108
Exhibit 4.6: Competency Feedback                                           109
Exhibit 4.7: Competency Linkage to Culture                                 110
Exhibit 4.8: Emmis Competency Model                                        116
Exhibit 4.9: Performance Management Insights                               117
Exhibit 4.10: Performance and Reward Management Overview                   118
Exhibit 4.11: Performance and Reward Management                            118
    Implementation Plan

ABOUT THE CONTRIBUTOR                                                       119

# OVERVIEW

*I was certain that we could build a company that would stand for something different. Twenty years ago, radio was an industry characterized by short-term relationships—very few people ever thought of working long-term for one company, and absolutely no thought was given to building careers without moving around. I thought Emmis could create a different atmosphere.*
—Jeff Smulyan, CEO Emmis Communications, excerpt from twenty-year anniversary letter

Emmis Communications is a small entrepreneurial radio company making the leap to being a much larger international company with holdings in various media. This change-management case study describes the systematic approach used by Emmis Communications to successfully create a distinctive firm brand and performance culture while extending the positive employer-of-choice reputation it had earned. Rapid growth required greater corporate structure and strategy clarification. Assimilation of newly acquired businesses required greater alignment and proactive strategies for "Emmisizing" the entire organization.

Under the leadership of a visionary and entrepreneurial CEO, Jeff Smulyan, the organization undertook a process of further defining its strategies, corporate structure, and culture. Using a variety of processes, Emmis drove clarity and focus companywide to drive business results and build the distinctive Emmis Brand and culture. In partnership with Results-Based Leadership, Emmis implemented a cascading and collaborative process of focus, education, communication, and performance accountability. The initiative used many change techniques and focused on a systemwide approach.

The lessons learned at Emmis Communications are important for any organization undergoing a major change initiative that affects the organization's brand, culture, performance, and business results. Companies experiencing rapid growth, overcoming entitlement behaviors, wanting to drive a distinctive culture through the company, building an employer-of-choice reputation, or evolving from a smaller company to a mid-sized company will particularly find these lessons useful.

## INTRODUCTION: RAPID GROWTH TO A MEDIA MID-CAP

Emmis Communications Corporation (Nasdaq: EMMS) is the sixth largest publicly traded radio portfolio in the United States based on total listeners. Emmis owns eighteen FM and three AM radio stations that serve the nation's largest markets of New York, Los Angeles, and Chicago, as well as Phoenix, St. Louis, Indianapolis, and Terre Haute, Indiana. In addition, Emmis owns two radio networks, fifteen television stations, regional and specialty magazines, and ancillary businesses in broadcast sales and publishing.

Founded in 1980, Emmis Communications launched its first radio station, WENS-FM, in July 1981. As Emmis (the Hebrew word for "truth") acquired more radio stations across the nation, it established a reputation for sound operations and emerged as a radio industry leader and innovator. Emmis was the first broadcast company to own top-rated radio stations in both L.A. and New York, and it pioneered such concepts as the Rhythmic Top 40 and all-sports radio formats.

The company launched its magazine division in 1988 with the purchase of *Indianapolis Monthly*, and later acquired magazines such as *Texas Monthly* and *Los Angeles Magazine*. Emmis became a public company in 1994, and moved into the world of international radio in 1997, when it was awarded a license to operate a national radio network in Hungary. In 1998, Emmis expanded into television by buying six television stations in markets throughout the United States. In the last three years, the company has added properties in each of its divisions. In fiscal 2000, the company invested more than $1.5 billion in acquisitions. Annual net revenues have grown from $140 million in fiscal year 1998 to over $562 million in fiscal year 2003. Employee population in that same period grew from under 500 to over 3,100. Emmis maintains its worldwide headquarters in Indianapolis, where the company was founded.

## Distinctive Culture

*While I never could have imagined that Emmis would grow to its current size, I was certain that it could be a company with a culture that separated it from its peers. I believed we could create great radio while treating employees well and letting them profit from our successes. I believed we could draw great ideas from every person in the company, not just the ones at the top. I believed we could win by taking risks. I believed—and this might be the most important thing—that we could have fun and still make a difference. I continue to believe those things. As a result, the approach that made Emmis unique in the media world of twenty years ago makes us even more unusual today.*

—Jeff Smulyan

With its emphasis on sound operations, integrity, community involvement, innovation, and fun, Emmis's culture has been lauded by both its employees and its peers. Trade publications have regularly cited the company's leaders as being among the best in the business. In 2001, *Radio Ink* magazine named CEO Jeff Smulyan its Executive of the Year. Jeff Smulyan has also earned a reputation in professional baseball from his ownership of the Seattle Mariners from 1989 to 1992. He is regularly interviewed by sports and news media about baseball and the economics of the game. In 2001, he appeared as a guest on the Bob Costas Show on HBO, and in 2002, as baseball appeared to be headed for a strike, he was interviewed by a number of media.

The EMMIS culture carries at its heart the belief that in order to succeed, a company must take risks, treat its people well, and give them the tools they need to win. This culture has as its foundation the CEO-authored Emmis Eleven Commandments. (See Exhibit 4.1.) The original Ten Commandments were written as part of a speech CEO Jeff Smulyan delivered at an annual managers' meeting; the Eleventh Commandment, "Admit your mistakes," was added later, after Jeff's experience with owning the Seattle Mariners.

## Internal Growth and Economic Pains

*It's hard to describe what starting the company was like in those days. I was picking all of our music, writing our commercials, buying the equipment, making sales calls . . . in short, being involved in every aspect of the station.*

—Jeff Smulyan

By 2000, Emmis began to feel the pains of its tremendous growth. The company had historically let the divisions and entities run mostly independently, albeit with Jeff's leadership and strong values always being visible and influential. But size and resource-management needs made it prudent to establish greater governance and professionalize corporate functions. Jeff Smulyan believed that the human resource (HR) function especially needed to be professionalized and staffed adequately to help drive the unique culture into all of the newly acquired businesses. This change would require new HR leadership, the establishment of Emmis Learning, and the hiring and budgeting of resources to develop processes and systems to drive the culture into the organization.

As this process of change began, another factor began to draw attention: the economic downturn that developed in 2001, hitting the media industry especially hard. On September 10, 2001, when Jeff Smulyan was with a group of media and advertising executives in New York City, one executive commented that 2001 was the "worst advertising environment he had seen since the 1940s." The historic attacks on New York and Washington, D.C., just one day later, obviously exacerbated the already gloomy situation. Throughout the year and into 2002, the division heads (Radio President Rick Cummings, TV President Randy Bongarten, and Publishing President Gary Thoe) asked their direct reports (general managers for TV and radio, and publishers and editors for magazines) to provide financial reforecasts and aggressively review their cost structures.

In March 2001, the company launched ESAP (Emmis Sales Assault Plan), an initiative designed to increase the size and capability of the sales organizations throughout the company. This required new recruitment, hiring and training, as well as the implementation of performance-and-reward processes. This launch followed closely after the creation of a number of other significant initiatives, including profit improvement, procurement initiatives, IT/systems implementations, sales excellence programs and additional corporate approval-and-reporting requests. As a result of these initiatives and other factors driven by growth, the relationship between Emmis's corporate headquarters and the entities in the field had been gradually changing, with 2001 and 2002 finding some in the field feeling the corporate headquarters was becoming increasingly intrusive.

## COMPASSIONATE EMPLOYER OF CHOICE

Although this case is about the building of a distinctive and higher-performing culture, it easily could have been a case of best practices for building a strong employment brand. You will see, however, that the development and fostering of such a culture could also bring with it some unintended challenges.

Emmis's leadership realized that the development of an employment brand requires much more than slogans or value statements such as the Eleven Commandments. To establish such a strong reputation, the company recognized the need to invest in programs and practices that touch its employees and community in a regular and consistent manner. It would be the leadership's investments, behaviors, and decisions regarding its people that would demonstrate the integrity and genuineness of the organization's values.

The following are some of the factors that have earned Emmis the reputation of a "great place to work":

- Commitment to employee stock ownership programs. The "One Share" program delivers one Emmis stock certificate to every new employee. Annual stock option events are designed to ensure that every employee in good standing gets a meaningful grant of options.

- Employee benefit and welfare programs. Emmis has always had at the core of its HR programs a commitment to being highly competitive in employee health and benefit programs. The goal is to be generally "more generous" than its' peers. Programs are reviewed annually, and visible changes are made based on solicited employee feedback.

- Response to attacks of September 11. While employees at Emmis's strategic radio cluster in New York City were particularly affected by the events of September 11, the company recognized that this was an event that touched every employee in the company. The organization's response to the employee's needs was swift and compassionate. For example, on September 13, Emmis Human Resources introduced an employee assistance program to all employees. Furthermore, Jeff Smulyan sent out an emotional and heartfelt e-mail that reflected on the events and described his personal feelings about how the tragedy touched the business and everyone's life.

- Employment policies and practices. Emmis has had a philosophy that employment policies should allow employees flexibility and freedom in their relationship with the company. It assumes an adult relationship between employee and employer.

- Handling the economic downturn in 2001 and 2002. Emmis was forced to take cost-cutting actions to handle its debt-leverage situation. In total, Emmis had to reduce the workforce by approximately 8 percent—a new experience for Emmis. To address this situation, an enhanced severance package was created and outplacement services were created. Within hours of considerable TV division layoffs, Jeff Smulyan and TV Division President Randy Bongarten participated in a live TV satellite feed to speak about the events, state of the business, and concern for affected employees.

- Maintained investments. Again during this difficult time Emmis executives had to make critical decisions about resources and investments. Two controversial investments were sustained during this difficult time: (1) Emmis Learning's Leadership Development Workshops, and (2) the Annual Emmis Managers Meeting & Emmi Awards Ceremony.

- Annual Employee Survey. Emmis has conducted an annual employee survey since 1986. Not only does it include the standard scaled responses, but it also gathers verbatim comments, all of which are read by Jeff Smulyan. The organization has a formalized Employee Survey Reaction Plan process that ensures review and appropriate accountability for action on areas of concern.

- Creative Stock Compensation Program. Probably most impressive is the innovative stock compensation program created to protect jobs and wages during one of the company's most difficult financial periods. A program was designed to reduce payroll by 10 percent (approximately $14 million), while maintaining employees' monthly net income through a special stock program administered every payroll period.

This is not an exhaustive list of events, programs, practices, and decisions made at Emmis during the recent past, but simply a sample list to provide a sense of the general culture and genuine compassion for the employees of Emmis Communications.

## ASSESSMENT: ON THE AIR

By January of 2001, the HR function was in place and a period of assessment began. Two primary areas were evaluated: (1) the state of the Emmis culture throughout the company, and (2) the presence of appropriate HR process implementations to support the business's strategies and operational needs. The data-gathering period was conducted formally and informally through March 2001.

*Formal Data Collection*

- Employee demographic profiles and turnover trends from HRIS reporting
- Annual employee survey data results and trends
- Focus groups at the Annual Emmis Managers Meeting (March, Las Vegas)
- Aggregated leadership 360 feedback results conducted for all 300 participants at the 2001 Annual Emmis Managers Meeting
- Exit interview data and trends
- Emmis Learning training-needs assessment

*Informal Data Collection*

- HR leadership visits to a large representative group of entities, where discussions and interviews were conducted with general managers, department heads, and key employees; also included all-employee general communication meetings with Q&A sessions

- Interviews and numerous discussions with Jeff Smulyan and executive team members on state of the business and culture and perceived organizational needs

- Review of all prior business plans and strategies

- HR staff identification of morale, employee-relations, and leadership issues and trends

- Review of all current HR processes, policies, and practices.

# DIAGNOSIS: PLUGGED IN?

As hinted to earlier, over a number of years Emmis's paternalistic, employee-friendly culture had created something of an entitlement culture among some employees who did not feel encouraged to perform at higher levels, but instead often felt that if they simply did their jobs consistently and reliably they would be rewarded at increasing levels. Rather than feeling loyal to the company, these employees often felt that the company should be loyal to them regardless of their levels of productivity.

In addition to this observation, some other clear themes emerged. The following is the initial summary of findings that would shape the focus and approach to the organizational change initiative:

- No clear, common, internal strategic planning process existed, making the prioritization of the investments, projects, and initiatives functionally driven and "opportunistic."

- Understanding and integration of the culture throughout the organization was greatly mixed. Most of the newly acquired businesses did not have a working understanding of, or buy-in for, the Eleven Commandments and Emmis culture.

- The executive team had mixed interpretations and beliefs of the business investment priorities, as well as the Emmis culture and Eleven Commandments.

- The divisions and entities preferred to operate as independent bodies, whereas the corporate strategy was increasingly focused on gaining cost advantages and synergies through centralization and business involvement.

- There was general concern about the negative effects of growth (risk of losing small-family company feel) and about the standardization, processes, and formality associated with growth and increased corporate governance.

- Among the corporate and entity groups that had been with the company for many years, elements of entitlement and "job protection" hindered performance, accountability, and innovation.

- Morale and employee commitment was generally lower in the entities that did not understand, or had not been exposed to, the Emmis culture.

- Employees who had had more exposure to, and understanding of, the Emmis culture had high levels of pride.

- Performance management and accountability was underdeveloped, inconsistent, and sometimes nonexistent. Pay decisions were more often based on internal equity and time-in-job than performance.

- Jeff Smulyan was committed to continuing acquisition growth, building higher levels of performance and innovation, and fostering a high-loyalty culture created through the founding values. Not all members of the executive team had appropriate levels of alignment with this vision.

## New Business Realities: Drivers for Change

The economy, competitive pressures, and debt-leverage issues created a necessary and compelling motive to maximize the company's performance. The media industry is undergoing radical changes. Consolidation, acquisitions, and property swapping is redefining the landscape.

This consolidation is being driven in part by new technologies that create opportunities that could be considered conflicts of interest. For example, with recent FCC changes, a media company could easily squelch unfavorable news items about itself in areas where it has market dominance. The larger, more powerful media forces could restrict distribution of a competitor's products. Finally, the big players can cross-promote their products from one platform to another. Not long ago, this would have been considered outrageous. Today it's part of the new business reality—although there is always the chance of FCC intervention until Washington steps in.

These new business realities are forcing Emmis to reinvent itself in radio and TV and develop nontraditional revenue sources while continuing to acquire new properties when feasible. Making this effort more challenging is the company's ongoing desire to complete this transformation and growth while also maintaining the industry-distinguishing Emmis culture.

## Change Objective

To drive business performance, Emmis needed more understanding and agreement on its structure, strategy, and cultural definition, starting at the top of the company. Processes needed to be put into place to drive this new clarity and focus throughout the organization. The company needed increased accountability and a balance between the deployment of strategies, goals, and objectives and the maintenance of the culture, Eleven Commandments and behavioral expectations.

So the hypothesis behind the evolving organizational change initiative was that clear strategy, firm brand, and culture definition with supporting communication and performance systems would result in higher levels of employee productivity and commitment, as well as distinctiveness and value to customers and investors.

# APPROACH

A key principle HR partner, Victor Agruso, was brought in as the strategy, organizational development, and HR effectiveness consultant. With the HR leadership, Agruso helped assess the best way to further clarify and implement Emmis values and strategies, and advise how best for human resources to make a positive contribution. A network of consultants were then appropriately engaged to support the developing change effort. Agruso helped create and implement the blueprint for achieving the external consultant's project goals outlined in this case.

Specific change approaches would include

- An executive team definition of company structure, strategies, and culture
- Strategies for widely communicating the direction of the company
- Performance management systems for driving performance and behavior expectations and accountability
- Communications, forums, and events to extend the unique Emmis culture companywide
- Executive and leadership development programs to build understanding and capability to execute according to the strategy and culture
- Measurement processes to influence performance and behaviors and guide the change initiative
- Programs, symbolic events, and recognition to reinforce direction of the company and accountability

# DESIGN: WHO'S OUR CUSTOMER?

In the media work of radio, TV and publishing, the customers are traditionally considered to be listeners, viewers, and readers. Emmis challenged this paradigm in the course of its organizational alignment process, recognizing the need to define its internal audience and decide how to get its attention, commitment, and energy around the company's "programming." To do this, Emmis needed to take a dual approach to alignment. The model below portrays the definition and translation of the mission/vision and firm brand of Emmis into two parallel *What* and *How* paths to achieving results. The *What* column demonstrates the alignment of strategies, goals, objectives, and results measures; the *How* column demonstrates the alignment of the culture, competencies, and behaviors. The customer in this model is every employee in the company and the supporting systems, or points of influence, are identified in the middle of the *What/How* model.

The model helps create a sequential approach to aligning the organization from the top down. It requires the executive audience to define the "programming" from the top and processes to cascade that programming down to the entire organization. Opportunity exists in the process to get audience feedback to ensure some level of collaboration and listening to the voice of the internal customer. The true "customers" of this change initiative are those who gain value through the success of the initiative: CEO Smulyan, investors, employees, and customers (Emmis's advertisers).

# INTERVENTION: GETTING TUNED IN

How clear, consistent, and strong is the signal about what the company is trying to accomplish, and how will it get there? It was clear that Emmis was an organization full of the industry's best operators—innovating new successful formats and turning around underperforming operations. It was the strength of these operators that allowed the company to permit its divisions to operate so independently. However, it was no longer the same company of just a few years ago. A larger, now international media mix, significant acquisitions, and the development of a corporate structure required new focus and operational definitions. As the company grew, the unique culture was becoming diluted and more difficult to extend to new acquisitions.

## Executive Alignment

With Emmis's partners, Agruso and Results-Based Leadership (RBL), an approach to defining and aligning the executive team and organization was created. Jim Dowling with RBL customized a RBL FAST workshop into an executive two-day, off-site which was then scheduled (Exhibit 4.3). Norm

Smallwood, author of *Results-Based Leadership,* facilitated a session with the company's sixteen top executives, who engaged in a challenging and sometimes emotional process of education, debate, and decision making.

A second, follow-up FAST workshop was scheduled to continue the passionate discussions whereby the company's strategic direction was verified and implications for leaders identified. The FAST workshop set anchor points for how Emmis chooses to conduct business and how it wants its leaders to be seen by their best customers.

Several significant steps where achieved as a result of the workshops:

- Corporate and divisional strategy was further developed
- Allied corporate structure was established, with operational definitions taking shape.
- A new era was defined: *Establishing a new standard for performance and innovation.*
- A firm brand was created: *Great Media, Great People, Great Service.*
- Scorecard development was addressed, and commitment, process, and designated teams established.
- Critical strategic content was created for the next-level RBL leadership program: Leading for Results.
- A need for additional executive development, alignment, and team building was identified.

Worth noting is the conclusion of the company's value chain:

- The customer: the advertiser (in some cases the reader, where subscriber fees exist)
- The product: desirable demographic pool for the advertiser
- The production process: programming and editorial content that builds the product—the attention of desirable watchers, listeners, and readers

The company's firm brand then represents desired distinctiveness in these key areas:

- *Great Media:* driver in production of audiences that are sold to advertisers
- *Great Service:* attention to super-serving the advertisers, the primary customer
- *Great People:* Emmis culture demonstrated through every employee and in their interactions with customers, audiences, investors, and other employees

The new era—*Establishing a new standard of performance and innovation*—represents the company's intention to focus the culture in a way that leverages the positive intended elements of its culture while addressing growing concerns around performance and accountability.

## Malicious Compliance

During the first two-day off-site workshop, signs of executive disagreement and resistance arose in a few key areas: (1) business portfolio makeup and decision making, (2) allied corporate structure versus a holding-company model, and (3) customer definition as the advertiser versus the listeners, watchers, and readers of the content. By the conclusion, the group seemed to be in agreement on the items listed above. After the event, however, there were signs that some key executives and some of their direct reports lacked confidence in their statements of support and communications of the work. This was later labeled "malicious compliance," an effort to support what was decided as an executive team but with reservations and disagreement showing through in their communications. A few chose to continue to behave as though operating in a holding company structure, for example, and taking different courses of action, contradicting the executive team's commitment, and sending mixed messages to the field.

Dr. Jim Intagliata of the Northstar Group was engaged early in the change initiative to provide executive coaching to Smulyan and the executive team. This coaching and assessment work would play a role in shaping future executive team-building and alignment sessions, as well as supporting Smulyan's management of the executives. Intagliata's involvement in the strategy and behavioral work provided the coach tremendous insight to guide the alignment and "malicious compliance" concerns that had evolved. Intagliata was further engaged to conduct a competency modeling process, described later, a key tool in assisting in the focus the executive team.

## Leading for Results

The next level of leadership consisted of seventy-five general managers, publishers, divisional vice presidents, and corporate directors. For consistency, Results-Based Leadership delivered workshops designed to build leadership alignment, commitment, and capabilities. A highly interactive workshop, Leading for Results, was delivered to these next-level leaders to understand Emmis strategy and examine how they will deliver results both individually and through others.

The underlining philosophy was that key organizational leaders would be most influential in driving and extending the Emmis culture to the field locations. To do this, Emmis needed leaders throughout the company that understood the company's strategies, firm brand, and culture intimately. These leaders need also to have the commitment and capabilities to deliver these messages and priorities to their respective staffs with passion. The following is a high-level agenda of the Emmis Leading for Results workshops:

*Day One: Develop Case for Change*

*Opening:* CEO and Executive Team overview and presentation of Emmis strategies, corporate structure, firm brand, and culture

*Focus:* How leaders accelerate change

*Topics covered:*
New Business Realities
Organization Change
Why Quality of Leadership Matters
Leadership Value Proposition
Statement of Leadership Brand

*Day Two: Build Organization Capability*

*Focus:* How leaders get things done

*Topics covered:*
Shared Mindset
Talent
Collaboration
Speed
Accountability
Learning

*Day Three: Individual Leader Implications*

*Focus:* Personal skill and accountability to deliver results

*Topics covered:*
Leader as Coach
Personal Leadership Plan

These participants were also responsible for translating the firm brand, culture, and leadership requirements into a definition of the Emmis leadership brand. The Leadership Brand is a statement of what leaders stand for at Emmis; it is linked to strategy and how Emmis wants to be known by its best customers and provides a focus for leadership development activities. These leaders created the following leadership brand:

**Emmis leaders embody deep customer understanding and quality product focus, communicate well, and turn vision into action.**

## PROGRAM PROMOTION AND MULTIMEDIA

As with Emmis audiences, repetition and mixed media help drive messages and influence buyer behavior. A key strategy for the Emmis change initiative involved using many communication vehicles for building brand awareness and influencing the culture. All corporate communication mediums were identified with appropriate applications and objectives (Exhibit 4.4). These vehicles were strategically identified with timed announcements, stories, and special events.

Emmis's annual managers meeting is the company's largest event, bringing together its top employees for training, networking, and recognition. The 2002 meeting was held in Indianapolis to reduce costs and give the noncorporate managers greater visibility to the Emmis corporate offices and staff. The event was timed to follow up on initial companywide communications (such as the *Emmissary*) regarding the new focus and direction of the company. The theme and agenda for the managers meeting revolved around the new firm brand and era, "Crank It Up! Establishing a New Standard for Performance and Innovation."

The program was structured to communicate the company's strategies, firm brand, and cultural focus. Results-Based Leadership set the tone for the two-day conference. Additional speakers and events followed to reinforce specific elements of the era and culture. The speakers had all been previously introduced, shared program materials, and worked to ensure a common thread throughout their respective presentations. The program was designed to keep all the participants together and networked during the beginning, so all heard the same Emmis messages:

- Jeff's State of the Union—focus on new Emmis "era"
- Norm Smallwood: firm brand, leadership brand, Balanced Scorecards, Emmis competencies, and performance management
- Division head presentations on business strategy
- Mark Williams of the Diversity Channel: great people and diversity awareness
- Robert Spector, author of the *Nordstrom Way:* world-class customer service
- Wall Street perspective from industry analysts and former FCC commissioner

Post-meeting surveys indicated a clearer understanding of Emmis's company strategy and firm brand and that managers could now comfortably communicate this strategy and firm brand to their respective staffs.

The Emmi Awards are Emmis's coveted annual awards for employees and entities to recognize the highest levels of achievement in a number of categories. In 2002, the award categories were altered to better reflect the company's shift to a more performance-based management system and restated objectives. In making nominations, managers were encouraged to consider results more heavily than in the past, and to consider how well the employee met stated objectives. This was a new approach and a significant signal to the organization. The executive team spent hours reviewing the nominations and made objective, fact-based decisions about the winners, which were previously more emotionally based.

The 2002 Annual Report introduced the new firm brand to the investor community. This was another significant step in clearly signaling to the employees that this was the new focus of Emmis and the commitment was strong. Emmis would be known for its *Great Media, Great Service, and Great People.*

# BUILDING A HIGH-PERFORMANCE DISCIPLINE: CRANKING IT UP!

A clear need for a stronger performance and accountability discipline was apparent. From the executive team to front-line employees, opportunities existed to improve clarity about what was expected of them and development of an appropriate level of accountability and recognition. Now that the strategies were in place, the Balanced Scorecards and performance management systems would be developed.

The new performance system would consist of

- Balanced scorecards for

  Corporate

  Corporate functional groups

  Divisions
- Developed competency model that combined strategically needed attributes, behaviors needed to off-set gaps, and Eleven Commandment reinforcement
- New individual performance documents that combine "what" and "how" goals and objectives and behavioral competencies.
- Performance based stock and merit compensation programs.

## Balanced Scorecards

A key process for focusing the strategies and creating accountability would be built through the balanced scorecard. Results-Based Leadership consultants (including balanced scorecard pioneer, Rich Lynch) facilitated a process that built on the work that the executive team had completed. Teams were identified for each scorecard to be developed at corporate and divisional levels. Teams were made up of managers and key contributors within their respective organizations. The makeup of the teams was critical in the change process; competent and influential formal and informal leaders were sought out. The teams spent several days in workshops and participated in a number of follow-up events to define measures to track strategic performance in four key result areas: investor, customer, employee, and organization. The RBL consultants supplemented the data through direct interviews with highly valued customers (Exhibit 4.5).

## Emmis Competency Model

Core to the culture-change process was the development of detailed Emmis behaviors that both helped drive the new strategic direction of the company and supported the extension of the desired Emmis culture and Eleven Commandments. Jim Intagliata led the competency modeling process that became an important element of the performance management process. Since this was such a critical and visible tool companywide, significant involvement of the executive team would be required. One such document during the development process attempted to gather further feedback and participation for key members of the executive team in addition to the interviews and data gathering that they were engaged in (Exhibit 4.6).

Particular attention was given to the integration of the Eleven Commandments into the competency model (Exhibit 4.7). The modeling resulted in eight core competencies for all employees, and five additional leadership competencies (Exhibit 4.8). As a result of the participation from the executives, the draft competencies were utilized almost immediately by a few of the executives with their direct reports.

## Performance and Reward Management

Agruso and Results-Based Leadership conducted interviews, focus groups, and a survey with the executive team that provided current state and preferred results in four areas: design and control principles, planning performance, improving performance, and rewarding performance. In addition, insights were provided relative to the maturity and current state of the process compared to Stage 3 (Disciplined) organizations (Exhibit 4.9). As a result of this involvement and assessment, an annual cycle was designed incorporating compensation systems, organizational development, and talent forecasting (Exhibit 4.10).

The Performance and Reward Management Implementation Plan was created to outline the sequence of all supporting communications and performance management events (Exhibit 4.11). Exhibit 4.11 visually presents the scope of the performance management implementation and the change events that were scheduled in phases to reinforce the overall change agenda.

## Employee Training

In February and March, 100 percent of all employees and managers went through performance management and cultural training. In addition to the traditional performance-management and SMART goal development instruction, some unique, and "Emmis-like" training was delivered: two exercises, one centered on understanding the Eleven Commandments and another focused on building a strong understanding of the new Emmis behaviors. For example, the Eleven Commandments card game was introduced to create an exercise of understanding and dialogue around the Emmis culture. Cards represented various symbols and clip art that were related to a particular commandment. Teams matched the cards to the related value and talked about examples of the values at work in their environments.

The second exercise required innovative exercises around the eight core Emmis behaviors. New teams were formed and each was asked to portray a behavior in one of three mediums that Emmis operates in: visual design (drawings), radio spots, or acted-out commercials. This was an entertaining, fun, and lively learning experience. The other groups would identify the team's portrayal, and there would be some dialogue about their choice and art form. This specific exercise generated meaningful discussions about the new culture, accountability, and leadership. Further, the creative portrayals are certain to improve understanding, retention, and transfer of learning.

## WHAT ABOUT INNOVATION?

"Establishing a new standard for performance and innovation," so where's the innovation? In addition to the Emmis core competency, innovation and agility, additional programs, systems, and events were developed to facilitate organizational emphasis on this important cultural value.

The *Great Ideas Contest* had been in place for several years to help generate creative and innovative business solutions. However, it traditionally did not require actual results or implementation. In many cases the ideas were recognized with stock, but nothing was implemented and nothing was returned to the organization. In some regards the program slowed innovation, because ideas were held for the contest and not shared. The program was changed to encourage group involvement and results. Starting in 2002, in order for ideas to be recognized at the highest levels, efforts must be in the works to implement them or actual results must exist. In addition, teams were recognized for shared development of ideas and implementation. This further drove the message and focus around results and accountability.

A symbolic "think tank" was created at corporate from an old soundproof production studio. The new meeting room was filled with beanbag chairs, toys, costume accessories, games, lava lamps and other bright and creative props. The room was designed for groups to use for brainstorming, team-building, or just to have fun in. It provides a place where employees and teams can step out of the corporate environment and think out of the box.

Additional steps are being taken to use technology to drive information sharing, best practices, and a knowledge network through the intranet, employee portals, or other systems. Technology will provide the organization an advantage in quality and speed of decision making. Ties to the Balanced Scorecard could provide executives and the organization real-time data through an enterprise guidance system.

## EVALUATION: MEASURING SIGNAL STRENGTH

*And so it was that, on July 4, 1981, WENS began to broadcast. I spent my first day as a station owner driving around the city trying to figure if our signal was strong enough to serve the market. It became apparent fairly quickly that we had found a niche in the market, and the station went on to become a big success. When I look back on those days, I realize that what made this company special back then is what makes it special twenty years later: We have always attracted great people with a passion for our business and a passion for the way we operate. If there has been one consistent theme from that first night until today, it has been that EMMIS stands for a different way of doing business.*
—Jeff Smulyan

The question now is whether a "different way of doing business" was integrated throughout the organization. Smulyan had consistently demanded through this process that employees be "all on one page" and "know what is expected of them from their manager." During the development of the corporate and divisional scorecards, three employee result areas consistently emerged:

- Productivity: revenue per employee
- Passionate and committed employees: employee survey results
- Retention of key employees: undesired turnover

Over time these would become the high-level measures of this initiative's impact on the organization.

The survey says? Well, there are telling results on the annual employee survey completed in May 2002. Keeping in mind that the change initiative was not very far into implementation and several of the performance management elements had not yet been developed, the result showed positive signs. The first percentage represents the average employee response to questions on the company's annual employee survey; the second number represents the average score on similar questions for companies listed on the "Fortune 100 Best Companies to Work For."

- I understand the importance of my job and how it relates to our mission/goals: 91 percent, 73 percent
- I have a clear description of my job and I understand what is expected of me: 83 percent, 88 percent
- I really like the people I work with: 86 percent, 84 percent

- I'm not a number here, I'm treated as a whole person with life outside work: 78 percent, 77 percent
- In the past year, I have discussed my performance review with a manager: 76 percent, 78 percent
- My work has special meaning, this is not "just a job": 77 percent, 79 percent
- I'll work for Emmis a year from now: 76 percent, 66 percent
- Taking everything into account, I would say Emmis is a great place to work: 77 percent, 88 percent

The company is continually assessing its annual survey and is considering additional questions that would determine a general employee commitment index score. There are survey questions that the organization would actually expect to decline in some areas as a result of new accountability and employee acceptance of clearly defined standards.

Other measures will begin to track important performance trends on the scorecards. Productivity can be measured by revenue and earning per employee. Undesired turnover, or retention of key employees, will be tracked more effectively after a talent review and succession-planning process is in place. Technology is being developed to effectively measure and present this key performance data.

## January 12, 2004, Q&A with Emmis Communications CEO Jeff Smulyan

Q: When you announced your third quarter earnings, you said the past year was the best in the company's twenty-four-year history. Why?

A: In our early days, as a private company, we succeeded in part because we had that start-up enthusiasm and entrepreneurial spirit. We had some truly great years. What makes this past year even greater is that we turned in a strong performance as a mature company competing against much bigger, tougher competitors in industries that are much more mature. We demonstrated that we can compete in any environment against anybody.

In every area of the business, we're more professionally run than ever before. I'm proud of what's going on in our markets, where our people are finding new ways to succeed, and I'm proud of the services our corporate team provides—our HR, finance, legal, IT, engineering, support staff . . . everybody is contributing. I think there is a genuine feeling that we aspire to be as good as anyone's ever been in these businesses, and I think we're making good on that goal.

# LESSONS LEARNED

*Lesson #1—Study the impact of previous corporate initiatives on this change initiative.* Your change initiative may have to start with damage control of previous initiatives. Be aware of *all* previous corporate initiatives, their successes, failures, and, most important, impact or impression on the operations. Work with all corporate functions to collaborate on the new initiatives, starting with a postmortem of the previous "corporate" initiative list. Full engagement and support of all corporate functions will have to be achieved prior to moving such a key initiative into the field.

*Lesson #2—Constantly monitor and reinforce executive team alignment and involvement in the initiative.* Having CEO support and confidence is not good enough. If any key leadership changes occur, invest a lot of time with the new leader to gain their sponsorship. Incorporate as much of their feedback into the product as possible. Provide enough focus on the business needs and executive input to ensure that it feels like their work. Do not assume that executive alignment will ensure next-level leadership alignment.

*Lesson #3—Leverage technology to drive communications and create constant real-time visibility of key company information, measures, and performance.* Intranet, employee portals, and business intelligence and knowledge management systems should be built and implemented in concert with the change initiative. Make these parallel corporate support systems part of one corporate initiative.

*Lesson #4—Engage in visible beta tests and leverage field executives to drive sponsorships of program initiatives—upward, laterally, and downward.* Gain next-level support through education, such as the Leading for Results workshops but, more important, through involvement in the design and implementation of programs before companywide rollout. Use the field beta tests as examples and utilize the field leadership to communicate to peers and employees their experiences.

*Lesson #5—Monitor and adjust the language, don't scare them away at the onset with "consultant-speak" or "MBA-speak."* Integrate the unique culture of your organization into the new common strategy and performance language you are trying to create. A common language must be created, especially if one does not currently exist around performance and strategy. But be cautious: the mere impression of the language and formality may slow your initiative significantly. Recruit an organizational translator onto your change team, and use him or her at every step of the process.

*Lesson #6—Implement with patience and never take shortcuts.* Utilize the change model and do not shortcut buy-in steps for the sake of speed. Recognize that an effort of this scale will take two to three years to yield measurable and consistent results. Set executive and employee expectations appropriately—undercommit and overdeliver. Credibility will be lost if expectations of a one- or two-year success are established or that success will be easy to achieve. This may be the most difficult process an executive team will ever need to execute; it will be met with resistance to change and will require consistency, tenacity, and visible alignment.

*Lesson #7—Monitor outside events and decisions that might contradict the initiative or dilute leadership's credibility.* Over the course of business, things happen. Decisions have to be made to adapt to the market, economy, and internal factors. It requires courage to portray to management how certain decisions and actions will be interpreted by the rest of the organization. Being the leader of an initiative that some may not be ready for, while also being the voice or messenger regarding contradictions or potential credibility issues, creates a delicate situation at times. Have courage, remind the organization of your role, and prove that it is in the best interest of the whole company and is not just being generated by self-interest.

*Lesson #8—Do not let politics get in the way.* Ensure corporate functions are focused on what is best for the company, not on functional agendas, politics, or leadership egos. Such an initiative must include a strategic and proactive alignment of the corporate functions. It would be prudent to acknowledge and respect the internal pecking order and provide special attention to the internal opinion leaders. The creation of positive corporate results will speak for themselves later in the change initiative. Work to be the example of selfless leadership in the best interest of the corporation.

**Exhibit 4.1. The Eleven Commandments of Emmis Communications**

| XI. | Admit your mistakes. |
|-----|----------------------|
| X. | Be flexible—keep an open mind. |
| IX. | Be rational—look at all the options. |
| VIII. | Have fun—don't take this too seriously. |
| VII. | Never get smug. |
| VI. | Don't underprice yourself or your medium—don't attack the industry, build it up. |
| V. | Believe in yourself—if you think you can make it happen, you will. |
| IV. | Never jeopardize your integrity—we'll win the right way or we won't win at all. |
| III. | Be good to your people—get them into the game and give them a piece of the pie. |
| II. | Be passionate about what you do and compassionate about how you do it. |
| I. | Take care of your audiences and your advertisers—think of them and you'll win. |

### Exhibit 4.2. Dual-Path Results Model

Exhibit 4.3. Executive Session FAST Agenda

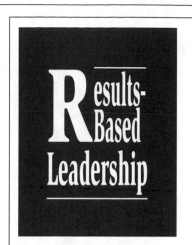

**FAST Workshop**

- *Focusing and Aligning Strategies Together*

***Business & Leadership Agenda***

- ***Strategic direction***

- ***Leadership roles***

- ***Decision-making process***

- ***Accountability***

- ***Measures***

**INTRODUCTION**

**NEW BUSINESS REALITIES**

  Corporate strategy
  Business strategy
  Some organization disablers
  Can we change inside the window of opportunity?

**FAST NOTES & TAKE-AWAYS**

  Role of leadership
  Leadership during transformation
  Desirable outcomes of the workshop
  Change agenda
  What Emmis is about
  New business realities
  Forces acting upon the company
  Norm's inventory of paradoxes
  Leadership value proposition

(*Continued*)

**Exhibit 4.3. Executive Session FAST Agenda (*Continued*)**

Response to environment
Corporate strategy
How an allied model would impact bonus plan deployment
Business strategy
Accountability in an allied business
The intellectual agenda
Types of work
Advantage capabilities
Scorecard
Attributes
Balancing short- & long-term goals
Leadership brand
Enabling systems

**SCORECARDS**
Employee
Organization

**NEXT STEPS**

### Exhibit 4.4. Internal Communications Matrix

| Primary Communication Vehicles, Their Content and Objectives | | |
|---|---|---|
| Vehicle | Medium and Frequency | Objective/Use |
| Emmis Weekly Update | Two-page memo sent to all employees by e-mail every week; it is waiting for them when they arrive on Monday morning | The *Emmis Weekly Update* is used to communicate to employees any information that will help them feel more connected to the company and informed about its operations. It is used for special massages from the CEO and other officers, but also to communicate about company news, media coverage of the company, analysts' views of the company and its industries, and employee benefit news. |
| Emmissary | Two-color newsletter sent to all employees each quarter | The *Emmissary* is used to communicate bigger-picture information about the company to employees. It uses longer stories than would be possible in the *Weekly Update* to deliver strategic messages to employees, provide deeper information about employee benefits and company programs, highlight promotional activities of individual stations and publications, applaud successes, and, through fun features, introduce employees to each other and to their leadership. |

*(Continued)*

**Exhibit 4.4. Internal Communications Matrix (*Continued*)**

| *Primary Communication Vehicles, Their Content and Objectives* | | |
|---|---|---|
| *Vehicle* | *Medium and Frequency* | *Objective/Use* |
| CEO memos | E-mails sent to all employees as needed | CEO Jeff Smulyan occasionally likes to communicate directly with employees through informal e-mail messages to inform them about major company initiatives, comment on company, industry, or national events, or just boost morale. Smulyan also often communicates directly to individuals, individual stations, or specific divisions. |
| "Emmis Announcements" | E-mails sent to all employees as needed | "Emmis Announcements" is the e-mail address for e-mails intended for all employees. "Emmis Announcements" is used only for important communications to employees about company news or benefit information. |
| Division e-mails | E-mails sent to all employees in a single division as needed | To inform employees of a specific division about company news or initiatives |
| Companywide conference calls | Annual (or more frequently if needed) conference call and PowerPoint presentation | For particularly important events or news, the company can host conference calls with all employees and provide them with PowerPoint presentations through the Web. Used only once so far, this was the vehicle for introducing employees to the Stock Compensation Program, which gave all employees a 10 percent cut in pay but at the same time gave all employees a 10 percent stock award. |

Exhibit 4.4. (*Continued*)

| Primary Communication Vehicles, Their Content and Objectives | | |
|---|---|---|
| *Vehicle* | *Medium and Frequency* | *Objective/Use* |
| *News releases* | News releases sent via e-mail as needed | All major news releases, including quarterly financial reports, are e-mailed to all employees along with a short note from CEO Jeff Smulyan. |
| *Annual Report* | Company annual report | Because virtually all employees are shareholders, Emmis views its Annual Report to Shareholders as an employee communication as well as a report to shareholders. |
| *Quarterly conference call with Wall Street* | Quarterly | Because virtually all employees are shareholders, Emmis views its quarterly calls with Wall Street analysts to also be a form of communication to employees and all stakeholders. Employees are specifically invited to listen to the conference calls. |

**Exhibit 4.5. Balanced Scorecard Sample**

*Television Scorecard*

| Measure: Results, dimension, quantity or capacity of a business process output | Operational Definition: How we would define the measure clearly to stakeholders | Formula: How we would calculate the measure | Frequency: When we need to monitor this data | Views: How we would want to slice the data | Data Source: Where can we get the data |
|---|---|---|---|---|---|
| Our measures . . . | Tell us about . . . | Computes as . . . | Reported . . . | Viewable by . . . | Based on data from . . . |
| *Customer* | | | | | |
| Ratings | Percentage of viewers reached based on the universe of market | HUTS share Nielsen formula based on stations' targets PUTS share | • Daily<br>• Quarterly | • Total review all day<br>• News<br>• Show<br>• Syndicated<br>• Network<br>• Time of day | • Nielsen (available electronically) |
| Qualitative demographic research | Profile of viewers who watch programs | Number with decided characteristic divided by total demographic | Two times a year | • Age<br>• Sex<br>• Lifestyle<br>• Behavior<br>• Viewer habits<br>• Consumer habits | • Magid<br>• AR&D<br>• Scarborough<br>• Media Audit<br>• Marshall |
| Demographic hit ratio—reach | Reach of commercial to targeted viewers or the number of target audience reached | Target demographic; GRPs over a specified schedule | Beginning in completion of schedule | By key desired demographic of advertiser | • TV scan<br>• Ad connections |

Exhibit 4.6. Competency Feedback

## EMMIS ATTRIBUTE MODEL

Attached is a draft of the Emmis Attribute model that has been developed based on our work with RBL and the input that you provided individually in your conversations with Jim Intagliata.

To produce this model, Jim has streamlined the standard RBL attribute architecture from twenty-seven attributes down to a more manageable twelve. He has also worked to incorporate all of the Emmis Commandments and Rules for Managers into the proposed model so that it is clear that these values are not being forgotten or discarded as we work to build a more performance-oriented culture (you will see these items *bolded* and noted throughout the text where they fit). Finally, on the initial page of the attachment he has provided a matrix that indicates which roles the attributes apply to and the key reasons these attributes have been incorporated into the model.

As you will see, the proposed model has these key design features:

1. There are eight core attributes that will be expected to be demonstrated by all Emmis employees at all levels, and an additional four attributes that will be expected to be demonstrated by individuals who directly manage other people (managers) and by individuals who manage entire divisions or functions (executives).

2. For each attribute that is in the Emmis model there is a separate set of behavioral indicators, depending on the role the individual is playing in the organization. For example, with regard to Innovation and Agility, what someone is expected to do to demonstrate this attribute varies depending upon whether they are in a position of an individual contributor, a manager, or an executive. The intent of this design is to highlight that the way in which people are expected to add value to the organization changes over time as they grow and advance in their career.

### What We Need From You

In order to refine and finalize this model we would greatly appreciate your input. Please take the time to read through the model and consider the following questions as you do:

- Do you feel that any of the attributes included in the model are unnecessary and add no value?

- Are there any important attributes that you feel are not represented at all in the model and need to be added?

- As you read each attribute, do the differentiation and progression of expectation from individual contributor to manager to executive levels make sense to you?

- Finally, as you review the wording of each competency, do you have any specific suggestions regarding how we might express the same idea but "Emmisize" the language more?

We will be following up shortly to schedule a phone conversation in which we can gather your feedback. The deadline we are working to meet is to have the model finalized by _____ so that the Emmis Attribute model can be introduced as part of the Performance Management System roll-out.

Exhibit 4.7. Competency Linkage to Culture

**KEY ATTRIBUTES FOR EMMIS**

| Behavioral Attributes | Role in Emmis | | | Why Needed? |
|---|---|---|---|---|
| | Individual Contributor | Middle Manager | Senior Executive | |
| **High-Priority Core** | | | | |
| 1. Innovation and flexibility | X | X | X | • To keep up with pace of change in industry and outmaneuver the giants/gorillas<br>• *A new innovation standard* for all aspects of business (not just product/content)<br>• Consistent with "out of the box" element of Emmis culture |
| 2. Passion to reach a higher standard | X | X | X | • To help Emmis compete and get to the next level<br>• Consistent with "never get smug"—"be passionate about what you do" values<br>• Consistent with theme *"Sets a new standard for performance and innovation"* |
| 3. Personal integrity | X | X | X | • Maintain and strengthen a fundamental Emmis principle/commandment<br>• Differentiates Emmis with employees/customers (quality people and service) |
| 4. Informed decision making | X | X | X | • Consistent with Emmis research expertise<br>• Needed to discipline decisions more broadly |

Exhibit 4.7. (Continued)

**KEY ATTRIBUTES FOR EMMIS**

| Behavioral Attributes | Role in Emmis | | | Why Needed? |
| --- | --- | --- | --- | --- |
| | Individual Contributor | Middle Manager | Senior Executive | |
| 5. Accountability for performance | X | X | X | • To improve overall results and deliver for shareholders<br>• To be fair to those who really deliver/add value and attract/retain top performers |
| 6. Teamwork and collaboration | X | X | X | • To support sharing of ideas, practices, people across organizational lines<br>• Consistent with value for treating others with respect/having fun while working |
| 7. Turns vision into action | X | X | X | • Builds on current value of buy-in to shared Emmis vision<br>• Takes it the next step to ensuring it translates into aligned action/execution<br>• Responsive to felt need for sharper focus in the business |
| 8. Delivers the Emmis customer experience | X | X | X | • Create the Emmis customer experience—partner to deliver results/success<br>• *Quality service and people*—differentiates Emmis from competition |

*(Continued)*

Exhibit 4.7. Competency Linkage to Culture (*Continued*)

**KEY ATTRIBUTES FOR EMMIS**

| Behavioral Attributes | Role in Emmis | | | Why Needed? |
|---|---|---|---|---|
| | Individual Contributor | Middle Manager | Senior Executive | |
| **Managerial/Executive** | | | | |
| 9. Motivates and manages individuals | | X | X | • Consistent with values/commandments—"have fun, get people in the game"<br>• Maintain the personal touch emphasis within Emmis culture<br>• Be the employer of choice |
| 10. Builds and leads teams | | X | X | • Creates climate of teamwork and interaction in unit/across units<br>• Leverages people resources effectively—working together vs. lone rangers |
| 11. Recruits, develops, and retains talent | | X | X | • Required for better results and executing allied strategy<br>• Reinforce/strengthen *quality people*—a differentiator for Emmis |
| 12. Manages resources effectively | | X | X | • Contribute to financial vitality of the business<br>• To prioritize and focus use of key resources |
| 13. Strategic perspective | | X | X | • Business-unit heads need to understand their own challenges/opportunities and chart a course for success<br>• Jeff can't be the only visionary |

Exhibit 4.7. (*Continued*)

| | ATTRIBUTE LINKAGE TO EMMIS COMMANDMENTS/RULES FOR MANAGERS | |
|---|---|---|
| *Attribute* | *Emmis Commandments* | *Emmis Manager Rules* |
| Innovation and agility | • Is flexible and keeps an open mind (Commandment #10)<br>• Believes in self and ability to make things happen (Commandment #5) | • Thinks out of the box and fosters creativity in others (Manager Rule #8) |
| Drive to excel | • Is passionate about what he or she does (Commandment #2)<br>• Never gets smug or complacent (Commandment #7) | • Has a passion for everything he or she does (Manager Rule #6) |
| Personal integrity | • Never jeopardizes integrity; insists on winning the right way or not at all. (Commandment #4)<br>• Is able to identify and admit own mistakes (Commandment #11) | • Has a good sense of balance and perspective about what's important in life (Manager Rule #5) |
| Fact-based decision making | • Is rational and looks at all the options (Commandment #9) | |
| Accountability for results | • Values relationships and treats others with dignity and compassion (Commandment #2) | |
| Fosters alignment and collaboration | | • Focuses on doing what it takes to add value to the overall organization, *not on protecting turf or playing politics* (Manager Rule #7) |
| Turns vision to focused action | | • Models personal buy-in and commitment to the Emmis vision/strategy (Manager Rule #1)<br>• Focuses on the work to be managed—*leaves politics to the politicians* (Manager Rule #7) |

(*Continued*)

Exhibit 4.7. Competency Linkage to Culture (*Continued*)

| | ATTRIBUTE LINKAGE TO EMMIS COMMANDMENTS/RULES FOR MANAGERS | |
|---|---|---|
| *Attribute* | *Emmis Commandments* | *Emmis Manager Rules* |
| Delivers the Emmis customer experience | • Knows who his or her customers are, thinks about, and *takes personal responsibility for taking care of them* (Commandment #1)<br>• Doesn't underprice self or medium; builds up the industry in dealing with others (Commandment #6) | • Believes everyday that he/she and Emmis can make a difference (Manager Rule #11)<br>• Is willing to "go the extra mile" for others (Manager Rule #9)<br>• Is able to have fun, laugh at self (Manager Rule #10) |
| Motivates individuals and teams | • Is good to his or her people—gets them "into the game" and ensures they have a piece of the pie (Commandment #3)<br>• Is able to have fun, laugh at self, (Commandment #8) | |
| Recruits, develops, and retains talent | | • Hires energetic people who believe in the Emmis vision and are smarter than himself or herself (Manager Rules #2, 3, and 4) |
| Manages resources effectively | | |
| Strategic Perspective | | |

Exhibit 4.7. (Continued)

### ATTRIBUTE LINKAGE TO KEY RESULT CATEGORIES

| Attribute | Employee | Organization | Customer | Investor |
|---|---|---|---|---|
| *Sets Direction* | | | | |
| 1. Strategic perspective | | | | X |
| 2. Turns vision into focused action | | | | X |
| *Mobilizes Individual Commitment* | | | | |
| 3. Motivates individuals and teams | X | | | |
| 4. Recruits, develops, and retains talent | X | | | |
| *Engenders Organizational Capability* | | | | |
| 5. Holds self and others accountable | | X | | |
| 6. Manages resources effectively | | | | X |
| 7. Delivers the Emmis customer experience | | | X | |
| 8. Fosters alignment and collaboration | | X | | |
| 9. Innovation and agility | | X | | |
| *Demonstrates Personal Character* | | | | |
| 10. Personal integrity | X | X | X | X |
| 11. Drive to excel | X | X | X | X |
| 12. Fact-based decision making | X | X | X | X |

## Exhibit 4.8. Emmis Competency Model

*Core Competencies for All*

1. *Informed decision making.* Approaching situations objectively, gathering the facts and information necessary for clear understanding, and using logic and common-sense to make informed decisions

2. *Innovation and agility.* Working to develop innovative ideas, search for creative approaches and solutions, and adapt to change quickly so that Emmis can continue to excel and be distinctive within the industry

3. *Passion to reach a higher standard.* Being passionate about one's work, never having or accepting an "entitlement" mentality, and consistently expecting more of self, others, and Emmis

4. *Personal integrity.* Demonstrating the fundamental beliefs and values of Emmis in all of one's actions, decisions, and dealings with others

5. *Teamwork and collaboration.* Taking initiative to communicate actively and share resources, ideas, and best practices across organizational boundaries so that Emmis overall benefits

6. *Delivering of the Emmis customer experience.* Knowing who one's customers are, being clear about what they expect and value most, and delivering it

7. *Vision into action.* Being responsible for understanding not only the overall Emmis vision but also what specific actions one individually needs to take to make it a reality

8. *Accountability for performance.* Taking personal responsibility for meeting all commitments, delivering results that meet or exceed one's goals, and identifying and resolving performance issues in a timely manner

*Additional Leadership Competencies*

1. *Strategic perspective.* Being able to take a broad, long-term view of the business and its future and acting in ways that contribute to Emmis's long- as well as short-term success

2. *Motivation and management of individuals.* Managing people in a positive way that "gets them into the game" by sharing responsibility and authority for accomplishing meaningful work and credit for success

3. *Building and leadership of teams.* Assembling teams of individuals with strong and complementary skills and leading them in ways that help them work effectively as a unit

4. *Recruiting, development, and retaining of talent.* Identifying and recruiting only the highest-quality talent for Emmis, coaching people so that they get the most out of their potential, and rewarding people in a way that reflects their level of contribution

5. *Effective resource management.* Planning and organizing work, managing resources efficiently, and understanding what is most important in contributing to growing the revenues and profitability of Emmis.

# Exhibit 4.9. Performance Management Insights

Leadership Brand Insights

## *Performance and Reward Management*

Low process and content ownership for corporate and for divisions. Minimal systems integration and virtually no accountability for execution. Absence of explicit criteria for process excellence. Low correlation between business results and performance evaluation outcomes. No enterprise guidance/knowledge management system capabilities.

Individual performance plans generally not created, thus absent specific measures, attributes, or key projects that link well to business priorities. Very limited training capabilities. No way to differentiate performers via results-based documentation.

Performance coaching occurring more frequently in real time. No dedicated methods for evaluating and developing attributes. Leadership program provides basic training. Extensive multi-rater feeback program; albeit without connections to performance management system. No automated knowledge management capabilities.

Performancce reviews generally do not occur at least once a year. Decisive, constructive action is perceived not to be taken to address problem performance. Low linkages between appraisal outcomes and employment-related actions. Solid use of direct cash variable pay systems with linkages to Corporate/SBU results (vs. individual), and without tight connections to performance management system. Some use of non-cash reward programs for both group and individual performance and reward management.

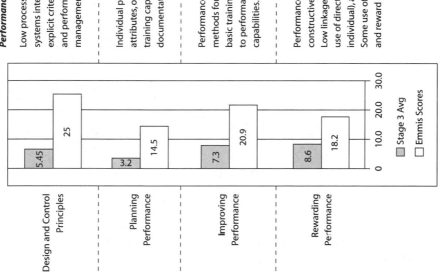

| | Stage 3 Avg | Emmis Scores |
|---|---|---|
| Design and Control Principles | 5.45 | 25 |
| Planning Performance | 3.2 | 14.5 |
| Improving Performance | 7.3 | 20.9 |
| Rewarding Performance | 8.6 | 18.2 |

**Exhibit 4.10. Performance and Reward Management Overview**

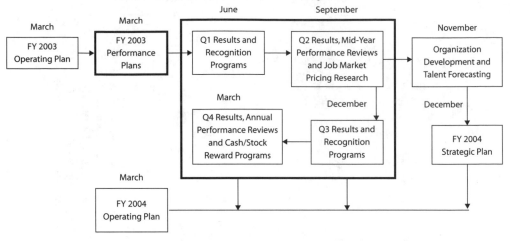

**Exhibit 4.11. Performance and Reward Management Implementation Plan**

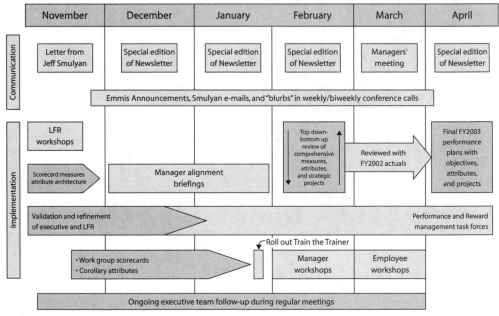

# ABOUT THE CONTRIBUTOR

**John S. Nelson** (jnelson@od-source.com) is president of OD Source Consulting, Inc., which specializes in business and human resource strategy development, culture and change management, performance improvement strategies, and human resource excellence. Prior to this, Nelson was a company officer and vice president of human resources for Emmis Communications, where he was brought in to build strategy and infrastructure, and professionalize the human resource function to manage the significant growth of the corporation and drive the unique culture companywide. Nelson has experience in a variety of entrepreneurial, general management, consulting, and strategic human resource and organizational development roles. He has been a key contributor and a sought out advisor with some of the most respected companies in their industries, such as InterContinental Hotels Group, Honeywell (AlliedSignal), Apple Computer, ARAMARK Business Services, Ceridian Employer Services, Hallmark Cards, HarvestMap Systems, Medtronic, PeopleStrategy, 1.0 & Company, and Results-Based Leadership. Nelson received his bachelor of science degree at Iowa State University in industrial relations and completed graduate studies with honors in industrial relations from the University of Minnesota's Carlson School of Management. For more information visit www.od-source.com.

# CHAPTER FIVE

# First Consulting Group

*This leadership development case study describes the innovative approach used
by First Consulting Group to design and implement a unique skill, knowledge
personal growth program for the firm's mid and senior level executives.*

| | |
|---|---|
| OVERVIEW | 121 |
| INTRODUCTION | 121 |
| DIAGNOSIS: THE CASE FOR LEADERSHIP DEVELOPMENT | 122 |
| Situational Assessment | 123 |
| Program Objectives | 123 |
| Risk-Reward Analysis | 124 |
| Barriers: Anticipating and Addressing Them | 125 |
| ASSESSMENT | 126 |
| Gap Assessment | 126 |
| Participant Assessment | 126 |
| Figure 5.1: Gap Assessment | 127 |
| PROGRAM DESIGN | 128 |
| Design Team | 128 |
| Process, Vision, and Framework | 128 |
| Critical Success Factors | 130 |
| Figure 5.2: Competency Model with Behavioral Indicators | 131 |
| Detailed Design: Key Elements | 132 |
| IMPLEMENTATION | 134 |
| LESSONS LEARNED | 135 |
| Participant Feedback | 135 |
| Facilitator Observations and Insights | 136 |
| BEYOND THE CLASSROOM | 137 |
| EVALUATING LEADERSHIP FIRST | 138 |

EXHIBITS

Exhibit 5.1: Program Overview Schematic   141
Exhibit 5.2: Program Session Outlines   141
Exhibit 5.3: Nomination and Selection Process Schematic   142
Exhibit 5.4: Self-Nomination Form   143
Exhibit 5.5: Sample 360-Degree Feedback Report   145
Exhibit 5.6: Learning Contract   150
Exhibit 5.7: Business Model Exercise   152
Exhibit 5.8: Managing Acquisitions and Mergers Exercise   157
Exhibit 5.9: Effective Communication Exercise   158
Exhibit 5.10: Sample Homework Assignment   159

ABOUT THE CONTRIBUTOR   160

# OVERVIEW

This leadership development case study describes the innovative approach used by First Consulting Group to design and implement a unique skill, knowledge personal growth program for the firm's mid and senior level executives. First Consulting Group is an acknowledged market leader in providing information technology and business transformation solutions to clients in the health care industry.

The Leadership Development Committee (the CEO and two vice presidents) created a task team of vice presidents and directors whose responsibility, with counsel from Warren Bennis, would be to conduct an organizational assessment and a benchmarking survey and to recommend a program design to the firm's executive committee for the accelerated development of current and future leaders.

Incorporating the task force's design recommendations, the Leadership Development Committee created and implemented a highly focused and unique program, based exclusively on their consulting industry environment and FCG's vision, strategy, and culture, and employing extensive in-depth action learning techniques.

Work generated by participants in completing the program's assignments and case problems has exceeded the firm's expectations and contributed to key strategic decisions. The design and implementation process has generated broad support and enthusiasm by the entire organization in less than two years. The approach, process, and design logic and rationale are valuable lessons for any organization.

# INTRODUCTION

Explosive growth over three years had tripled the size of the organization. A very successful, whirlwind initial public offering (IPO) had taken the previously private firm into the public sector, and an acquisition not only doubled the organization but also brought in another culture and another market opportunity. FCG was well positioned, and the future looked exciting.

Then, the untimely loss of the firm's young CEO and founder created overnight the need for second-generation leadership.

Having previously been a private partnership that fostered a highly collegial culture and value system, the team of vice presidents collaborated on what course of action the firm should take going forward and which of their members would lead the organization. Although the founder had expressed longer-term thoughts about who the future leaders might be, succession planning was in the early stages, and each potential CEO possessed certain specific strengths. The question became which particular strengths did the firm need at this particular time.

With the collective good in mind and heart, and with the future of First Consulting Group in the balance, discussions took place that were painfully honest but without malice. After several meetings to generate and evaluate alternatives, consensus was reached and the vice presidents' recommendation was sent to the board. The board concurred with both the action plan and the team's selection of its future CEO, president, and business unit leaders.

The assessment process had been an amazing experience, exhibiting the very best of one of FCG's values: Firm First. But it also elevated developing leaders and creating a strong talent bench to one of the firm's top priorities.

## DIAGNOSIS: THE CASE FOR LEADERSHIP DEVELOPMENT

As a twenty-year-old business in 1998, First Consulting Group found itself facing a number of challenges: the organization had grown from a $25 million firm with 200 associates to a $300 million firm with over 2,000 employees in less than six years; it had evolved from a privately held partnership model into a publicly held entity through a 1997 IPO; and the founder/CEO had passed away suddenly in his mid-forties, leaving a strong vision for the firm but also a leadership team and a succession plan early in their development.

In addition to the internal challenges, a number of external competitive threats were developing as well. The market focus was shifting: the rise of the Internet and the variety of technological advances changed the rules on the playing field and the old consulting model (number of staff × number of hours × billing rate) was no longer enough. Clients were looking for something more creative and more measurable: they were looking for solutions rather than process, and they expected that FCG, as their chosen consultant, would share in the risk-reward opportunity of any consulting engagement.

Further new threats were developing. The advent of e-consultancies and e-vendors and the rise in popularity of partnerships and joint venture agreements was intensifying competition in the market. Clients were demanding the capability to form and manage partnerships, joint ventures, and other innovative relationships and organizational structures as a part of the solution to their issues.

As a technology solutions provider, First Consulting Group's technical skill and knowledge expertise was required to be "state of the art" on a daily basis. Outpacing the technology explosion and understanding where the trends were headed was difficult. Even more difficult was locating, hiring, and retaining talented technology professionals as a fierce competition for high-tech talent raged in the employment market. Although consulting had always been a well-paid profession, it was beginning to lose its former "glamour" appeal. Extensive travel requirements placed on "road warriors" made the lifestyle less appealing and less compatible with the expectations of today's younger technical professionals.

The growth and challenges of managing a larger, more complex organization, increasing competition in the market place, and increasing demands and expectations of clients made it obvious that the current level of leadership skill and knowledge and the numbers of potential future leaders might be adequate for the firm's immediate requirements, but the future demands would prove to be overwhelming if not addressed immediately. Future growth projections anticipated an organization of 5,000 to 7,000 associates, generating the need for over 300 leaders in the coming four-year period. Historically, many leadership hires came from outside the firm, and the cost of projected leadership hires in a short period produced staggering multimillion dollar recruitment-cost projections. It became very clear to FCG's executive committee that failure to develop the requisite leadership bench strength would diminish the firm's ability to grow.

## Situational Assessment

With these issues and challenges well in mind, FCG's executive committee, a three-member leadership development committee and a task force of eighteen director and vice-president-level staff, with the guidance of Warren Bennis, set out to define the skill requirements for future leaders and to build a leadership development program that would provide for the firm's future. The future program was christened Leadership First.

## Program Objectives

Specific objectives were established with the expectation that these objectives would be incorporated not only into the program's design, but also, over time, into the firm's culture and value set (see Exhibit 5.1). The targeted objectives directed that Leadership First should

- Eliminate barriers to the achievement of FCG's Vision 2004 by

    Articulating and propagating a widely understood vision

Creating an enhanced cross-industry awareness

Developing well-rounded leadership traits with self-awareness and self-development support

Making the event a true "leadership celebration," something much more than a training program

- Build succession plans; identify, train, and support future generations of FCG leadership

- Create an environment that causes leaders to interact and depend upon one another

- Instill Leadership First's values until they are as ingrained in FCG's culture as our universal personal characteristics-behavioral characteristics that are in keeping with FCG's culture and values and are common to highly successful employees

- Be truly substantive rather than a "touchy-feely" philosophical or conceptual program

- Ensure that the initiative is not a short-term "fad" remedy for current problems but something to be kept alive for a multiyear period.

## Risk-Reward Analysis

In spite of the firm's name, FCG was not simply a consulting firm: the organization was a public-partnership blend with multiple and constantly evolving business models (consulting, management services, joint ventures, and so on). Historical data reflected that many mid and senior level leaders had advanced largely on the basis of their project-based consulting and "partnership" competencies—a business model that had been established over ten years ago. The organization, the market, and the technology had changed significantly in that period, and it was clear that new and emerging leaders were not prepared to lead and manage the current and future firm. The task force quickly drew two significant observations:

- The firm's changes highlighted FCG's weaknesses, as a leadership group, to articulate a vision and motivate a following.

- The firm's historical underinvestment in developing leadership skills needed immediate correction.

Failing to address the issue and build the leadership and business skills had created substantial risks: loss of market share if the competition moved more quickly in deal-making and responding to the market's demands; inability to generate the sheer number of leaders required to meet the organization's growth estimates; increased risk that good leaders might leave the firm; inability to stimulate excitement in FCG's market valuation; continued reliance on the same names to solve all the problems and meet every opportunity; dilution of FCG's culture and vision if it became necessary to go outside for many key positions; and potentially excessive recruitment costs (potential savings of $16 million over a four-year period by developing 160 leaders internally).

The potential benefits and gains appeared to far outweigh any risks:

- Improved market valuation and customer satisfaction
- Increased ability to navigate and take advantage of the changes being faced
- Ability to scale the organization to meet the challenge
- Succession planning vehicle
- Increased individual (leader) satisfaction
- Improved associate retention via a shared sense of common vision and strong leaders
- Survival of the organization

## Barriers: Anticipating and Addressing Them

The Task Force then anticipated what potential barriers might impede Leadership First's effectiveness, with the intent of removing or at least minimizing them to smooth the program's implementation and success. The lack of a fully shared vision for FCG's future was identified, as was leadership's tendency toward a shorter-term rather than a longer-term perspective. These key considerations would need to be resolved by the executive committee prior to the program's implementation. Although the professional compensation and development system incorporated individual project evaluations, annual evaluation feedback and personal coaching for associates, the absence of instrumentation tools, and a 360-degree feedback process suggested that a general lack of self-awareness probably existed among many of the firm's mid and senior leadership. It was clear that one key design element would have to be the incorporation of comprehensive assessment and feedback for participants. It was also obvious that the vehicles for collecting the feedback data and conducting the assessment did not exist within the current processes and would have to be developed.

Although these largely mechanical items required attention, the larger issue of reward systems seemed a potentially more difficult barrier for the program. Historically, while emphasis was placed on leadership behaviors as they related to FCG's core values, rewards at the senior levels of the firm tended to recognize client performance and revenue generation. It was apparent that reward systems would need to be modified to value the targeted leadership skills and behaviors equally with client and financial performance. The last potential barrier identified was the selection process for participation in the program. The selection of participants and the associated message that might be inadvertently communicated to the firm would be highly sensitive and potentially political. Those who were selected might be seen as the "heirs apparent," whereas deferred or nonselected participants might feel that they had no future with the firm. The selection and communication processes would have to be objectively and carefully managed. Selection criteria would need to be defined and communication to selectees and nonselectees alike would need to be crafted with great sensitivity to ensure proper perspective and encouragement.

# ASSESSMENT

## Gap Assessment

In their efforts to assess the leadership gap, the task force confirmed that the news was not all bad—in fact, good solid leadership skills were being evidenced every day at every level. FCG's professional compensation and development system had a structured progression of skill and competency career path and compensation, and personal coaches provided guidance and mentoring for every associate at every level. The question was, *Would it be enough?*

The task force's summary analysis yielded the following assessment of FCG's current leadership skills and the gap areas to be addressed (Figure 5.1):

## Participant Assessment

FCG's professional compensation and development system (PCADs), a comprehensive skill and career development ladder, served as an excellent foundation for an initial assessment process. Incorporating annual skill evaluation, formal development planning, and the assignment of a personal coach for every associate, the system had provided clear direction and guidance for FCG's associates and also a good perspective on the firm's various strengths and weaknesses.

During 1999, using the insights provided by the PCADs and the counsel of Warren Bennis, the FCG Leadership Development Committee conducted its own assessment of the leadership needs of the firm. Soliciting input from the firm's vice presidents at one of its off-site planning meetings, reviewing the overall strengths and weaknesses of the organization and its senior-level leaders, and then consolidating the internal information for comparison against external benchmark knowledge generated a credible working database. This initial assessment was later refined by the task force's work and input from Warren Bennis. The actual assessment of individual participants in Leadership First was one of the program's design elements but was not used as an input to the structuring of the program. Rather, it was initially administered to participants after they had been selected and immediately before their attendance in the program,

| Current FCG Leadership Skills | Skill Deficiencies for Future Organizational Success |
|---|---|
| • Business and planning skills <br> • Management experience leading alliances, partnerships and joint ventures <br> • Business savvy that translates market opportunity into value creation <br> • Hardcore financial management skills in metrics and reporting <br> • Breadth of perspective about the industry <br> • Ability to build a following and then let go when the time is right <br> • Ability to focus, prioritize, and cut losses quickly when required <br> • Ability and desire to collaborate | • Ability to create and communicate vision <br> • Ability to demonstrate a level of passion that creates and motivates a following <br> • Courage to take risks and create change <br> • Ability to create a team and inspire team play <br> • Ability to develop others and to be seen as a sensei <br> • Understanding of financial intricacies <br> • Broad business acumen <br> • Strength of character, ethics and integrity <br> • Emotional competency |

**Figure 5.1** Gap Assessment.

and was also to be re-administered nine to twelve months following their participation.

Although the PCADs process provided feedback and career and performance coaching to associates, it did not employ any sort of instrumentation or 360-degree assessment. In order to provide maximum self-awareness and insight, a multifaceted assessment process was administered to all participants prior to their attendance in the program. This comprehensive assessment would serve as a "study" focus for participants during Leadership First and also as the foundation for the creation of their formal "learning contract." The assessment package comprised data from five input vehicles:

- *Participant self-assessment* versus the FCG targeted leadership behaviors (a key aspect of the self-nomination process)

- *Participant 360 degree assessment* versus the targeted leadership behaviors by FCG peers, subordinates, and superiors

- *External benchmark*—the participant's behavioral profile versus 600 comparably positioned managerial and professional staff

- *Managerial style profile,* as measured by the Atkins Kacher LIFO

- *Behavioral needs profile,* as measured by the FIRO-B

Consolidated assessment feedback was then provided to each participant, including graphic representation of the data, narrative comments, and discussion of the assessment feedback with a member of the Leadership Development Committee.

As of this writing, six groups of participants (sixty) have completed participation in Leadership First: no assessment trends have become evident as yet based on this limited population. Issues to date have been largely individually focused. Not surprising, typical results indicate subordinate ratings trending higher than participants' self-ratings and those of other assessors. It is interesting, however, that there were very few areas where participants' self-assessments differed significantly from those of their assessors—FCG credits the feedback and coaching aspects of its PCADs for this level of self-awareness.

# PROGRAM DESIGN

## Design Team

Committed effort toward the creation of a leadership development program began with the formation of a three-person Leadership Development Committee of FCG's CEO, the VP of human resources and a key operating vice president who served as chairman of FCG's Quality Initiative. After conducting their assessment of FCG's leadership strengths and weaknesses, the Leadership Development Committee conducted an external benchmarking study of the best practice leadership programs and characteristics being used at several of America's top organizations. The findings yielded twenty commonly identified behaviors and characteristics considered to be key leadership success behaviors. There was little variation in the list of twenty behaviors. What did vary somewhat was the specific order of importance of the items, depending upon the industry and organizational culture.

Armed with the results of their internal assessment and their benchmark analysis, the Leadership Development Committee held several discussions with University of Southern California professor, author, and leadership development guru Warren Bennis. The discussions soon led to collaboration and a more formal strategy for FCG's leadership development initiative.

## Process, Vision, and Framework

The initially critical step in the design process was the education of the executive committee regarding issues associated with the implementation of such a program and to obtain their commitment and ownership for the requisite financial and personal commitments that would be required for the program's success.

FCG had always fostered broad participation in the firm's issues by its associates, and the culture was heavily collegial. Many of the firm's organizational processes, such as the professional compensation and development system and the client satisfaction survey process, had been created by cross-functional, multi disciplinary task teams. It was not unusual, then, that the organization once again elected this process to address the leadership development project.

In June of 2000, the Leadership Development Task Force was formed, made up of eighteen vice president and director-level members. This task force would then work with the Leadership Development Committee and Warren Bennis to more deeply assess the firm's leadership issues and to formulate a program design recommendation. (See Exhibit 5.2.)

With the initial work in hand and the guidance of Warren Bennis, the task force held three, two-day, off-site work sessions, interspersed with individual research and subgroup conference calls, to conduct a comprehensive assessment of the organization's leadership strengths and weaknesses and its future risks, challenges, opportunities, and requirements. The final product was the recommended framework for the Leadership First Program.

The following recommendations for the pilot program were presented to the executive committee for discussion and approval:

- Create a program infrastructure

  Appoint a program steward

  Link leadership attributes to PCADs

  Select 360-degree tools and classroom training

  Immediately begin using leadership attributes in the recruitment process

- Implement leadership succession planning incorporating

  Needs assessment and business unit plans

  Compliance with diversity initiatives

- Structure a nomination and selection process (see Exhibit 5.3)

  Structure nomination process around required FCG leadership behaviors

  Publish program guidelines, timelines, and selection processes and criteria widely

  Allow for self, coach, and business unit nominations (see Exhibit 5.4)

  Select candidates based on a defined set of criteria: ten to twelve VP and director participants for the pilot

- Structure development plans based on assessments

  Employ 360-degree assessment to define participant skills and growth areas (see Exhibit 5.5)

  Provide an objective or external assessment analysis to review feedback reports

Provide assessment feedback training for those who provide assessment input

Include coaches in the assessment process; provide training in understanding results

Build individual development plans involving coaches and incorporating feedback

- Incorporate formal classroom learning

Leadership development classes—internal and external

Executive MBA style using business problem projects

- Utilize Action Learning to supplement the classroom by use of Mentoring

Business projects

Cross training and job rotation

Specific readings

Continuous 360-degree feedback

- Reinforce learning in group and individual programs

Provide a continuous feedback loop via progress assessment, mentoring, 360-feedback, and performance reviews

- Utilize alumni functions, periodic learning activities, and social events for a continued sense of team

## Critical Success Factors

Having established the objectives and framework for Leadership First, the final undertaking of the task force was the definition of FCG's targeted leadership skills and behaviors. Review of external benchmark behaviors, in conjunction with FCG's strategic plan and the members' knowledge of the firm's markets and clients, led to the identification of eleven specific leadership skills and behaviors that would be critical to the firm's future success. These eleven behaviors (in alphabetical order) would form the program agenda for Leadership First (see Figure 5.2).

Following executive committee approval of Leadership First's conceptual design, the Leadership Development Committee embarked on the detailed design of the program. Using the task force's conceptual design, the committee defined parameters that would guide the formal structure and content of the program:

- Active involvement of four executives as training facilitators (CEO; one executive committee member, business unit managing VP; VP of human resources/program administrator; and operating VP, leader of Quality Initiative)

| Targeted FCG Leadership Behavior | FCG Behavior Definition |
|---|---|
| Business acumen | Demonstrates the ability to be a great thinker and business expert who leverages his or her experience, education, connections, and other resources to obtain results; personally demonstrates an unquenchable thirst for knowledge |
| Business development | Demonstrates keen understanding of FCG's industry, competitors, markets, and market trends; leverages that knowledge to develop and close new business to consistently meet annual revenue and profitability targets |
| Citizenship | Demonstrates the ability to evoke trust and respect because he or she embodies the qualities associated with character (integrity, humility, willingness to serve, honesty, and empathy); demonstrates balance in personal, business, and civic responsibilities and is viewed as a model citizen, not just a model businessperson |
| Client relationships | Demonstrates the ability to identify and develop strategic client or vendor relationships; creates excellent relationships with client leadership through delivery of quality service |
| Courage | Demonstrates the ability to be bold and innovative, inspiring trust in associates because their ideas are not necessarily the safest or most logical but because they are ideas which everyone would like to see come to fruition |
| Emotional competency | Demonstrates ability to manage and influence nearly any situation because he or she intuitively senses what others are feeling and understands what makes each player "tick"; demonstrates his or her own self-awareness by constantly evaluating and working with his or her own motivations and drives |
| FCG operations | Demonstrates knowledge of internal FCG business policies and processes such as budgeting, human resources policies, and legal restrictions; applies these guidelines in his or her own decisions and develops understanding and application of them among others |
| Motivation | Demonstrates ability to create passion and excitement, often without being able to articulate anything more than faith and trust, so that people are compelled to follow him or her |
| Sensei | Demonstrates the ability to teach and transfer knowledge by drawing out associates' strengths while paving the way for them to correct weaknesses; people follow this individual with great confidence, not fear, knowing that their development is a mutual goal |
| Team play | Demonstrates the ability to evoke the best from a team by appreciating the responsibilities, dreams, and contributions of each individual in the group; demonstrates the ability to create a team even when such discussions create friction and change |
| Vision | Demonstrates ability to see "the big picture" (the long-term benefit to the team or firm in the next five to ten years of hard work) and is able to communicate this picture to others in a way that generates hope and excitement regardless of their position. |

**Figure 5.2** Competency Model with Behavioral Indicators.

- Maximum group size of twelve; participation restricted to VPs and directors for first two to three sessions to maximize return on investment and gain critical acceptance

- Participants must be immersed in senior-executive level issues and decisions and must be pressed to broaden their thinking and stretch their mental capacity

- Program must be heavily experiential and based on active learning

- Case studies and team exercises must be meaningful in FCG's environment

- Lecture, as a learning methodology, will be minimized during seminars: extensive use of prereadings (contemporary and classic books and articles) will provide the foundation knowledge and conceptual basis for learning and discussion

- Primary learning methodology to be small group break-out case exercises and application problems

- Homework assignments between sessions will require application of concepts, research, and analysis within participant's own business unit

- Program will employ spaced learning: three multiple-day sessions (three days, three days, two days over a five-month period) and attendance in *all* sessions will be mandatory.

## Detailed Design: Key Elements

Having personally participated in various leadership programs during their careers, the Leadership Development Committee felt strongly that to be successful with FCG's intellectually talented and highly motivated associates and to be maximally beneficial for the firm, the program had to be *truly relevant and applicable* to FCG's environment. Case studies and problems based on manufacturing or other industries would not serve and virtually all seminar components would have to be created "from scratch." To achieve this objective, the committee incorporated the following:

- FCG's vision, values, and strategy documents and statements as the basis for case studies and discussions

- Actual FCG business operations situations and decisions for case studies and analysis, including

  FCG business unit competitive situations and market deviations

  FCG service strategies that failed to meet expectations

Potential strategic opportunities for FCG assessment and recommendation

Potential FCG acquisition and merger candidates for evaluation

FCG balance sheet and financials analyses

Hypothetical promotion to business unit head; identification and analysis of business unit issues and board of directors presentation

CEO challenges to be handled—board of directors, public market analysts, and shareholder legal issues

- Selected prereadings to provide the foundation knowledge versus in-session lectures: active learning involvement through participant interaction, facilitator interaction, and case-problem work sessions
- Homework assignments requiring application of concepts to FCG's business unit structure, staffing, and strategies, with individual analysis and recommendations from participants

The ultimate program design incorporated three multiple-day sessions spaced out over a five-month period. The content was sequenced from issues associated with the creation of an organization (vision, mission, structure) to those associated with growing and managing the organization (growing the business, managing financials), and from a broad, conceptual perspective to a highly targeted focus on individual personal leadership style.

In executing this design, the Leadership Development Committee incorporated a variety of vehicles, tools, and techniques.

- *Assessment instruments* were used, including internal self-assessment and 360-degree assessment conducted by participants' colleagues, and the external benchmark assessment conducted by Resource Associates. The administration of the FIRO-B and the Atkins Kacher LIFO completed the assessment.
- *Prereadings* were drawn from *Harvard Business Review* articles and various books on leadership. Internally prepared readings and background materials were distributed to participants thirty days prior to each session to provide a basic conceptual framework for all participants and to minimize in-session time dedicated to lectures.
- *LDC presentations* summarized or targeted discussions of key prereading concepts.
- *Break-out work sessions, FCG-based case studies, and work problems* provided deep participant involvement. After detailed work sessions, participants were required to make LCD projector presentations back to the larger group regarding their analysis and recommendations.

- *Learning contracts* were drafted and discussion of participants' assessment feedback and presentation of their personal learning contract content and goals provided opportunities for mutual support and input (see Exhibit 5.6).

- *Homework assignments* given between sessions drove immediate application of learnings to participants' daily work environment in the form of business problem analysis, the results of which they presented back to their colleagues at the next session.

- *Relationship building* through structured work sessions, homework assignments, learning contract work, and off-site dinners after daily sessions were of key longer-term benefit to the firm in creating internal teamwork.

- *Open, honest discussion and responses* from all facilitators—who committed to reply to issues and questions raised by participants, no matter how challenging, personal, or sensitive—quickly built trust and confidence in facilitators and a genuine level of respect for the firm that it would support and encourage such openness.

# IMPLEMENTATION

While design of the program's actual curriculum was thought provoking and time consuming for the Leadership Development Committee, it was clear that the communication, ownership, and administration of the program would be the critical aspects in the program's success and these aspects would also require considerable time and effort. This awareness led to the creation of a separate implementation strategy and process.

- *Creating ownership and buy-off with the executive committee* was crucial, and significant time was spent with them to ensure their understanding of and comfort with the program, its content, and the commitment of organizational resources that it would require.
- *Visible participation and support of the program* would cement the commitment of the executive committee with the rest of the organization. It was therefore agreed that the program's learning facilitators would be the three members of the Leadership Development Committee (including the full participation of the CEO) plus one member of the executive committee, who would serve as both a facilitator and as the designated sponsor or mentor for that Leadership First group.
- *Creating excitement and interest* among the firm's mid and senior level leadership led to presentations at off-site planning meetings as well as e-mail

and voice mail communiqués from the CEO regarding Leadership First's rationale, development, and importance. Additional marketing by executive committee members to their respective organizations reinforced these messages and demonstrated the commitment of potential participants' superiors.

- *Administrative process clarity and fairness* added to the program's acceptance and credibility. The VPHR was designated as the *program administrator,* who would set the path for the program, finalize processes, administer program mechanics, integrate tools and processes into FCG's infrastructure, schedule program logistics, presentations, and participants, administer the nomination and selection process (in conjunction with the Leadership Development and executive committees), provide verbal and written notification to all selected or deferred applicants, administer assessment tools, consolidate feedback input, prepare assessment feedback reports, and conduct feedback discussion with participants.

- *A self-nomination process* incorporating the completion of documents profiling the nominee's education, background, and experience, along with an explanation of why he or she should be selected over others and a description of what the nominee hoped to gain from participation, was required. Although much of this information was available from FCG files, the self-nomination (which required concurrence from the nominee's business unit head), along with the self-assessment versus the targeted FCG leadership behaviors, provided key information to the Leadership Development Committee about the nominee's self-perception, writing ability, thought processes, and maturity.

- *Selection* of ten to twelve participants for each group was based on a review of all self-nominations and assessments by the Leadership Development Committee, consideration of cross organizational representation, diversity representation, and the immediacy of need for the participant's growth, based on his or her current role. The Committee's final recommendation for participation was then submitted to the FCG Executive Committee for concurrence.

# LESSONS LEARNED

## Participant Feedback

Bearing in mind that the participant population is still very small, input solicited from graduates indicates that they found three particular aspects of Leadership First to have the most impact:

- *The assessment process,* with its breadth and depth of assessment and feedback, was felt to be the single most effective aspect of the program for all participants.

- *Relevant and applicable FCG-based case studies* for analysis was most impressive to participants. Many participants said they had attended development programs of one sort or another but none of those programs had been based on "real world" situations they encounter in their daily work environment and no program had been so closely aligned with their organization as this program.

- *Immersion in and challenge of senior executive and CEO issues, problems, and decisions; role plays of board of directors presentations; and exposure to corporate legal implications* provided by Leadership First afforded participants key insights and understanding of the leadership demands faced by business unit heads and the executive committee at FCG. Such understanding will facilitate readiness to assume similar responsibilities when the time comes and will provide perspective when participants are faced with organizational decisions and initiatives, which they may not have understood, accepted, or supported so quickly prior to attendance in this program.

When queried about which aspects of the program were most memorable and useful for them personally, participants listed the assessment process feedback and the creation of their learning contract, the sharing of concerns and needs with others in the group and learning from them, and the compulsory and demanding analysis and decision making of case studies and business problems.

## Facilitator Observations and Insights

Although the structure and timing of each day of every session had been well formatted by the Leadership Development Committee in the design phase of the program, the facilitators realized that the program would need ongoing refinement as the program and its content "settled in." In particular, the facilitators encountered four challenges that necessitated attention:

- *Managing time.* Beginning with a heavy content agenda to be covered and then encountering tangential interests, questions and issues created a conflict for the facilitators, who had to balance the need to cover the material with the need to help participants develop perspective and deeper understanding. Balancing these two needs at times was costly in terms of time management. Some topics and work sessions were inadvertently cut short due to lack of time, and some discussions, although of value, deviated from the program agenda and had to be curtailed. This conflict generated the addition of another day to the previous format in order to allow for the supplemental discussions without detracting from the time allocated to other important activities and exercises.
- *Assessing and managing group energy levels* throughout the sessions became one of the facilitators' challenges. With daily sessions packed with participation, case problem work, presentations and observation, the participant's

energy levels varied throughout the day. At times, facilitators needed to juggle agenda items slightly or defer certain work sessions for an early morning start rather than continue with a mentally tired group.

- *Balancing motivational levels and capacities of participants* within the group presented a somewhat surprising challenge for the facilitators. Although they were not so naïve to believe that all participants would be equally capable or motivated, there was a feeling that given a group of people at the director and VP levels, most people would fall within a set range on both dimensions. It was surprising to see how each participant actually did perform and respond, given the demands of the situation. Some who were anticipated to excel appeared to lose some of their desire and motivation to master the concepts, and others who were seen as "solid" performers, but who had not previously shown exceptional abilities, were truly challenged by the opportunity and rose to demonstrate their true capacity and potential.

- *Guiding and maximizing case study and break-out group work* necessitated a greater presence from facilitators than was anticipated. Because participants were at times dealing with problems and issues to which they had no previous exposure, there was a need to clarify organizational position and business philosophy, and some input or guidance was required. The value for the facilitators was the insight that the organization really needed to communicate or make clear certain business philosophies so that all the firm's leadership would be fully aligned.

## BEYOND THE CLASSROOM

Aside from the challenges associated with the actual conduct of the sessions, the other major challenge for the facilitators was that of keeping the group together and maintaining the learning process after the formal program sessions were over. In an effort to maintain group identity and reinforce growth and learning, the facilitators had designed vehicles into the framework of Leadership First. A *group sponsor/mentor* (executive committee member and session facilitator) had been identified. The role of the mentor/sponsor was to provide participants with post-session feedback regarding their participation in the program and to work with the group and each individual on learning plans and other issues as requested by the group or individual. Conference calls with all group members on an as-needed, but at least quarterly basis, were incorporated as a means of maintaining the group's identity, as well as perpetuating a support network and mutual problem-solving vehicle and safe environment for sharing and testing progress on individual learning contracts. Last, an annual group reunion was planned as another reinforcement of Leadership First.

Following participation, each individual has been encouraged to *share their learning and personal goals with their respective business unit head*. This coaching process will further serve to link the Leadership First program structure and process into the firm's PCADs process to maximize the value of both programs.

*Continual monitoring* and revision of the participant's individual learning contract is reinforced on an ongoing basis in the follow-up work with the group mentor and the other participants in his or her group, some of whom will have committed to help each other on specific issues, and through the PCADs process itself. To assist in this ongoing development effort, each participant is provided with a Development Resources List of courses, books, and articles as a reference tool. In order to track and evaluate the participant's growth and behavioral progress as observed in the work environment, a *follow-up 360-degree assessment process* is to be conducted nine to twelve months after completion of Leadership First, using the same self-assessment and the same colleagues to provide feedback to the participants.

Providing the structure and vehicles to sustain and reinforce the Leadership First Program's objectives with participants was a critically important aspect of the original program design. The Leadership Development Committee saw the need to incorporate a vehicle to ensure the organization's continued understanding and support. In addition to participant feedback to respective business unit heads and colleagues, continuing communications were to be provided to the FCG organization to keep associates informed about and involved in the program's progress and success. Periodic status reports and feedback were also to be provided to FCG's vice presidents, the executive committee, and the firm's board of directors.

# EVALUATING LEADERSHIP FIRST

In order to monitor feedback and results and to evaluate the effectiveness of Leadership First, the Leadership Development Committee incorporated a number of measurement vehicles and methodologies, including the following:

- Participant assessment ratings and feedback (initial versus post attendance)
- Behavioral changes being observed or reported for participants—both as a result of assessment feedback and skill and knowledge growth
- Feedback from participants' business unit head on participants' behavior and performance improvement
- External benchmark feedback from Warren Bennis on program quality
- Performance effectiveness and advancement of participants (longer term)

- Encouragement of attendance and verbal marketing of program by past participants
- Progress toward achievement of documented personal learning contract measurable goals and time frames

The first six groups (sixty participants) have completed the program. If this limited participant population's feedback and enthusiasm for the program is any reliable measure, the program is extremely successful. Over time, as the participant population grows, the in-place evaluation methodologies incorporated into the program will provide a reliable metric.

Although the relatively short period and small participant population restricts tangible evaluation, the firm has already experienced a number of intangible gains from the program:

- Improved cross-organization communication, an unintended benefit, has been dramatic as a result of the program
- Valuable thought and work in case problems and business unit analysis gave the executive committee additional insights and input for consideration
- Stronger unity of purpose at senior levels has resulted from discussion and ownership of the program and its objectives
- Deeper understanding of values, mission, and strategy (as well as their rationale) and stronger buy-in and commitment to them by program participants
- An increase in the firmwide and strategic perspective of many has been very noticeable
- Deeper appreciation of the stress and demands being faced by senior leaders within FCG
- Sense among most FCG associates that the firm is committed to grow its own, that it has a vision, and that it will have a long and strong future with experienced and trained talent to manage the future organization as a result of Leadership First

Based on internal and external benchmark comparisons and feedback, FCG's Leadership First appears to be a unique program in that its design incorporates actual FCG case studies and problems (see Exhibits 5.7 through 5.10) and it employs a situational approach to leadership training versus the traditional topical or subject matter approach. Unlike many programs that focus on communication or motivation as a learning topic, Leadership First's premise is that various skills are simultaneously required in specific business situations. In handling a merger or acquisition, for example, a leader must assess the financial and legal issues involved, the business and revenue implications, and the emotional, motivational, and communication requirements for employees, and must draw upon a variety of leadership behaviors and skills to address all these various situational needs within the context of the merger. Leadership First approaches the learning process from this perspective.

The program is also unique in that instead of assigning the development task to the training and development staff, it employs active participation of the firm's CEO and executive committee members as facilitators in all sessions and requires one member of the executive committee to serve as the group mentor/sponsor for each group of participants.

Last, the program is tied closely into other FCG processes such as PCADs and the coaching process, and is *totally integrated* with the firm's emphasis on becoming well managed, both financially and in the handling of people.

Evaluating Leadership First in any truly measurable way at this early stage of its administration is difficult. There are, however, a few initial results that merit recognition:

- The disciplines of preparation for the Leadership First sessions are having an immediate impact on practice units' focus and profitability. Because several key members of one practice unit were in the same group, they have been able to make some significant and very different decisions about cutting costs, changing business models, and recruiting people.

- Sharing business unit models and strategy documents with all VPs and directors has made a significant impact on several groups.

- One vice president has changed his approach to his practice unit, resulting in significant improvements in growth.

- Another key practice unit has significantly improved its performance as a result of the attendance of its leader in the program.

The true measure of the program's tangible gains and success, however, will be demonstrated in the coming years through the firm's "bench strength" depth and readiness, and ultimately through FCG's market position, revenue stream, and recognition as an industry leader.

**Exhibit 5.1. Program Overview Schematic**

*Leadership First — Program Overview*

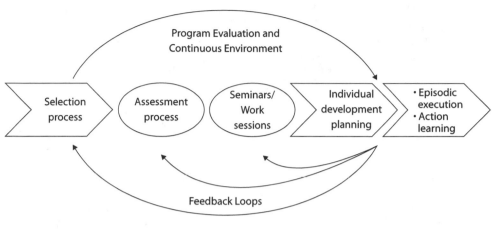

Systematic individual performance and
Progress tracking and monitoring

**Exhibit 5.2. Program Session Outlines**

| Session One (3 days) | Session Two (3 days) | Session Three (2 days) |
|---|---|---|
| • Group expectations<br>• Personal growth and trust<br>• The assessment process and the learning contract<br>• Program mechanics and structure<br>• Creating the organization's vision, mission, and values<br>• Strategy planning—the broad view<br>• Designing the organization structure<br>• Selecting people and creating teams<br>• Business models and their implications<br>• Understanding and managing the balance sheet<br>• Measurements and incentives—performance metrics and reward systems | • Session One recap<br>• Personal learning contracts<br>• Identifying and creating big impact change agendas<br>• Homework presentations—business unit assessment and recommendations<br>• Merger and acquisition management<br>• Understanding public company status<br>• Big game hunting (how to grow the organization) | • Session Two recap<br>• Homework presentations—board presentations on 6-month strategy for their business unit<br>• Communicating effectively—inside and outside the organization<br>• Managing ahead—leading multiple quarters and years ahead<br>• Personal leadership—understanding and developing your style<br>• Revisitation of group expectations<br>• Personal action plans<br>• Going forward—group mentor, group status, and identity; 9–12-month reassessment process |

## Exhibit 5.3. Nomination and Selection Process Schematic

**Leadership First Participant Application Process**

- Self-nomination
- Coach approval
- Business unit head concurrence
- Participant self-nomination and self-assessment forms

**Selection Process—Standardized Yardstick Firmwide**

*10 participants per quarter*
- Group 2—February 7–8–9; April 12–13; June 21–22, 2002
- Initial focus on high impact players for faster results—*restricted to VP and Director levels* (leverage development dollar investment to fullest at start)
- 12 month's minimum service requirement
- Performance requirement
- Diversity consideration
- Business unit leader review/approval
- Selection committee and executive committee review/approval
- Make them feel "special"
- Make them a "class" for identification/networking/collegiality

**Assessment/Individualized Participant Feedback**

- Administration of instrumentation, interpretation, and feedback
- 360 Degree Leadership Assessment, data consolidation, and feedback (Leadership First Assessment Feedback Form) with written report/profile
- Resource Associate Leadership Traits Benchmark assessment report
- Aggregate (for FCG) and individual key strengths and development area profiling
- Pre- and post-360 degree assessment (after 6–9–12 months) for participant progress and feedback
- Emphasis is *development*—not performance—this process is a complement to FCG's existing systems—not a replacement for PCADs

**Action Learning Contract/Process**

- Completion of Learning Contract based on feedback from assessment phase
- Clear goals with measurable results, targets, and time frames
- Most development will/should occur in the participant's *current position/job*
- Largely self-managed vs. structured program
- Consolidated group sessions with case studies, simulations, and lectures by industry leaders and FCG staff—develop "class" identity and address common needs
- Development resource reference list—external programs, distance learning, seminars, university
- Internal resource designation as "Executive Sponsor" for each "group/class" for mentoring and ownership

**Development Contract Execution/Re-Assessment**

- Three meetings of Group 2 as a "class" for group development and feedback on program
- 3/6/9/12-month follow-up with participants
- Reassessment of development needs to assess degree of growth

**Program Evaluation**

- Pre- and post-assessment analysis
- Review/dialog with executive committee on organizational issues (current and future strategy, cultural, organizational, and leadership changes) and development needs
- Individual participant experience evaluation
- Classroom/structured learning experience evaluation

### Exhibit 5.4. Self-Nomination Form

Nominee Information

| Nominee Name: | Current Position: |
|---|---|
| Business Unit: | Hire Date: |

Education Completed/Year/School(s):

Bachelor's ☐ _____ Master's ☐ _____ MBA ☐ _____ Other ☐ _____

| Special Certifications: | Speeches/Articles: |
|---|---|

Briefly describe your experience with international assignments/travel:

Recent Significant Achievements/Contributions

Briefly describe what you believe are your most significant achievements/contributions to FCG during the past twelve to eighteen months.

Nomination Rationale

Briefly explain why you (as opposed to others) should be considered for participation in Leadership First.

(*Continued*)

**Exhibit 5.4. Self-Nomination Form (*Continued*)**

Developmental Value

What particular learnings/value do you believe you will gain from participation in Leadership First? How will these learnings benefit you? How will they benefit FCG?

Career Focus

In what specific capacity/position do you see yourself in the next two years and why that one as opposed to some other? What particular contributions do you feel you can make there (as opposed to someone else)?

Business Unit Head Comments/Concurrence

Briefly describe why you recommend (do not recommend) this person's participation in Leadership First at this time. What capacity/position do you envision this person holding in two years? In five years?

Signatures

Applicant _____(Signature here confirms *your absolute commitment to attend ALL sessions* of Leadership First—if you are not able to make this commitment, you should not apply at this time.)

Business Unit Leader _____ (Your signature here indicates your recommendation, without reservation, for this candidate's participation in Leadership First.)

Participation Disposition (to be completed by Leadership First Selection Committee)

## Exhibit 5.5. Sample 360-Degree Feedback Report

### Leadership Attributes/Behaviors Assessment

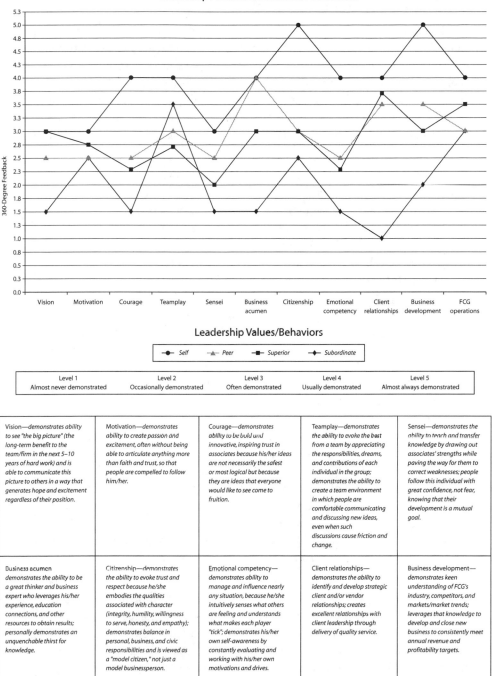

### Leadership Values/Behaviors

● Self ▲ Peer ■ Superior ◆ Subordinate

| Level 1 | Level 2 | Level 3 | Level 4 | Level 5 |
|---|---|---|---|---|
| Almost never demonstrated | Occasionally demonstrated | Often demonstrated | Usually demonstrated | Almost always demonstrated |

| | | | | |
|---|---|---|---|---|
| Vision—*demonstrates ability to see "the big picture" (the long-term benefit to the team/firm in the next 5–10 years of hard work) and is able to communicate this picture to others in a way that generates hope and excitement regardless of their position.* | Motivation—*demonstrates ability to create passion and excitement, often without being able to articulate anything more than faith and trust, so that people are compelled to follow him/her.* | Courage—*demonstrates ability to be bold and innovative, inspiring trust in associates because his/her ideas are not necessarily the safest or most logical but because they are ideas that everyone would like to see come to fruition.* | Teamplay—*demonstrates the ability to evoke the best from a team by appreciating the responsibilities, dreams, and contributions of each individual in the group; demonstrates the ability to create a team environment in which people are comfortable communicating and discussing new ideas, even when such discussions cause friction and change.* | Sensei—*demonstrates the ability to teach and transfer knowledge by drawing out associates' strengths while paving the way for them to correct weaknesses; people follow this individual with great confidence, not fear, knowing that their development is a mutual goal.* |
| Business acumen—*demonstrates the ability to be a great thinker and business expert who leverages his/her experience, education connections, and other resources to obtain results; personally demonstrates an unquenchable thirst for knowledge.* | Citizenship—*demonstrates the ability to evoke trust and respect because he/she embodies the qualities associated with character (integrity, humility, willingness to serve, honesty, and empathy); demonstrates balance in personal, business, and civic responsibilities and is viewed as a "model citizen," not just a model businessperson.* | Emotional competency—*demonstrates ability to manage and influence nearly any situation, because he/she intuitively senses what others are feeling and understands what makes each player "tick"; demonstrates his/her own self-awareness by constantly evaluating and working with his/her own motivations and drives.* | Client relationships—*demonstrates the ability to identify and develop strategic client and/or vendor relationships; creates excellent relationships with client leadership through delivery of quality service.* | Business development—*demonstrates keen understanding of FCG's industry, competitors, and markets/market trends; leverages that knowledge to develop and close new business to consistently meet annual revenue and profitability targets.* |

*(Continued)*

**Exhibit 5.5. Sample 360-Degree Feedback Report (*Continued*)**

*Summary Observations of Assessment Feedback*

Overall, your ratings from all assessors were quite variable and inconsistent in how peers, subordinates, and superiors perceive your leadership behaviors, and there are some significant differences in how your colleagues view your leadership behaviors as compared to how you perceive your own behavior. While you rated yourself at level 4 and level 5 ("Usually Demonstrated" and "Almost Always Demonstrated") in all behaviors except "Vision," "Motivation," and "Sensei," your assessors generally viewed your demonstrated leadership behavior anywhere from 0.5 to 3.0 levels lower than your ratings.

Your subordinates tended to rate you lower than you rated yourself and lower than the ratings of either your peers or your superiors. This pattern is a bit unusual, in that subordinates generally see their boss as more experienced and having more expertise than themselves and as a result they tend to rate the boss much higher than either peers or superiors do. Your subordinates' ratings were mostly in the "level 2—Occasionally Demonstrated" category except in the area of "FCG operations," where they rated your behavior the "level 3—Often Demonstrated." This pattern may suggest that your subordinates are fairly sophisticated in observing leadership behaviors and therefore have some basis for their comparison of your leadership versus their past experience with other managers; or it may suggest that they have not had close enough exposure to you to observe some skills and behaviors in the given settings. Of particular note are areas where your subordinates rated you 2.5 to 3 levels lower than you rated yourself: "Business development" (self-rating 5.0—subordinate rating 2.0); "Citizenship" (self-rating 5.0—subordinate rating 2.5); "Courage" (self-rating 4.0—subordinate rating 1.5); "Business acumen" (self-rating 4.0—subordinate rating 1.5); "Emotional competency" (self-rating 4—subordinate rating 1.5). These differences clearly indicate that there is a significant disconnect between the behavior others are seeing you exhibit and how you perceive yourself. Your demonstration of certain leadership traits seems to be invisible to others at times. It may also be that what you are demonstrating differs from others' definition or expectations of that leadership skill or behavior, but your knowledge and mastery of FCG's leadership behaviors are not as broadly developed or demonstrated as you believe they are.

Your peers' and superiors' perceptions of your leadership skills are more closely related to your own self-perception, but they are also generally lower than your own self-perception of your leadership skills. There is strong consistency around "Vision," where range of ratings varies from 3.0 to 3.5 (your self-rating was 3.0); "Motivation" (peers' and superiors' rating 3.0 and 2.5; your self-rating 3.0) "Client relationships" and "FCG Operations" (peers' and superiors' rating 2.5 and 3.5; your self-rating 4.0).

**Exhibit 5.5.** (*Continued*)

Your peers perceive your greatest strength is "Courage" (rated 4.0) and your weakest area is "Team play" (rated 2.0), while your superiors see your greatest strength as "Client relationships" (rated 3.5) and your biggest weaknesses as "Sensei" (rated 2.0). These data imply that you may be doing a better job of managing upward and laterally than you are in managing downward to your staff. It also suggests that "Team play" and "Sensei" are critical areas for your reflection and focus.

Developmental feedback comments indicate three primary things you may want to start doing: (1) better communication with FCG team and client, (2) invest in your relationship with your team members; spend time with them, nurture them, and help them work through problems so they can learn; assess and give them meaningful and constructive but sensitive and empathetic feedback, and (3) work to make sure the big picture is solidly and consistently presented in our deliverables.

There are many behaviors people want you to continue doing, which indicates that much of your effort and activity is seen as being of value and as a positive contribution. Your thoughtful leadership and calm demeanor are appreciated, along with your enthusiastic attitude and encouragement of others to think out of the box.

People want you to improve your communication skills—(1) improve influencing skills with clients and internally so people can take advantage of the innovative and creative ideas you have, (2) ensure consistent communication so projects don't stray off track, and (3) communicate any billing (or other) problems early on with the appropriate people.

You should compare your own priorities in the START, CONTINUE, and STOP DOING categories with the feedback recommendations from your assessor group to ensure that you have incorporated their input into your developmental planning, and record your priorities and goals on your Personal Learning Contract.

*Developmental Feedback*

| For improved effectiveness, this individual should START doing the following 3 things: | ☐ Accept healthy conflict as exactly that—healthy |
| --- | --- |
| | ☐ Recognize that I can affect a situation |
| | ☐ Be more accepting of my role and level of expertise while using this recognition to build and/or uncover opportunities |
| | ☐ Be more direct and forthright in communications with superiors, especially when it is tough (don't avoid calling it like you see it) |
| | ☐ Find more opportunities to spread your knowledge. Create the next generation of you |
| | ☐ Think in the context of the firm instead of just your business unit or group |

*(Continued)*

Exhibit 5.5. Sample 360-Degree Feedback Report (*Continued*)

|  |  |
|---|---|
|  | ☐ Focus more on managing/coordinating deliverables, and less on contributing to them |
|  | ☐ Update technical skills—stay conversant on new technology, standards, methodologies |
|  | ☐ Spread credit around where it is due for good work |
|  | ☐ Offer solutions to the problem not just stating there are problems and embrace or become a proponent of other and perhaps more appropriate solutions |
|  | ☐ Embrace and manage diversity within a team |
|  | ☐ Sticking on a project from beginning to end |
|  | ☐ Developing better interpersonal skills with the client |
|  | ☐ Develop better speaking skills |
|  | ☐ Become more aware of project financials and their relationship with overall FCG financial performance |
|  | ☐ Be more aware of his ability to influence client/staff—both positively and negatively |
|  | ☐ Finish internal assignments—too often has best intentions to start but seldom finishes |
|  | ☐ Become more active developing literature and publications |
|  | ☐ Focus on long term versus short term |
| For improved effectiveness, this individual should CONTINUE TO DO the following 3 things: | ☐ Maintain current levels of fervor and dedication |
|  | ☐ Build my knowledge base in terms of technical and leadership roles |
|  | ☐ Maintain a healthy work/family balance |
|  | ☐ Broaden influence within his business unit and the firm |
|  | ☐ Look for new ways to contribute and new things to learn |
|  | ☐ Keep calm in the face of crisis or adversity (you are good at this) |
|  | ☐ Allow team members face time with the client |
|  | ☐ Establish client relationships and confidence in FCG's technical capabilities |
|  | ☐ Look for creative ways to involve the client in technical decisions |
|  | ☐ Apply your excellent consulting skills to expand FCG business |
|  | ☐ Network among diverse FCG business units |
|  | ☐ Maintain enthusiastic attitude |
|  | ☐ Encourage the team to think out of the box |

Exhibit 5.5. (*Continued*)

| | |
|---|---|
| | ☐ Develop additional knowledge through industry leadership |
| | ☐ Share and leverage this strong technical skills and vision with other FCG associates |
| | ☐ Demonstrate his creativity and strong work ethic, and commitment to his clients |
| | ☐ Remain willing to do what it takes to get the job done |
| | ☐ Focus on adding value to clients |
| For improved effectiveness, this individual should STOP doing the following 3 things: | ☐ Listening to sniping and griping that is unfocused or destructive |
| | ☐ Focusing on what can happen given the situation, not what could have happened |
| | ☐ Worrying about my longevity with FCG (spend energy on what we can do to ensure this question goes away) |
| | ☐ Thinking of himself as an associate of the firm, instead of a leader of the firm |
| | ☐ Thinking someone else will come up with the answer to the firms/business unit's problems |
| | ☐ Managing in absentia |
| | ☐ Recommending outdated technologies where they don't apply |
| | ☐ Pushing his own agenda, and listen harder to his client's needs and team's suggestions |
| | ☐ Taking issues and problems personally |
| | ☐ Looking for hidden motives which might be causing disruptive behaviors on the team, take the issue head on |
| | ☐ Putting his own interests ahead of the team's |
| | ☐ Avoiding conflicts that may require him to "take a stand" |
| | ☐ Participating in gossip |
| | ☐ Sharing associate confidences with subordinate staff, or venting personal issues he has with senior level FCG associates to subordinate level associates |
| | ☐ Venting to subordinate staff regarding the business/financial issues of the Firm, which creates insecurity among the staff |
| | ☐ Overworking his network to find out how he's doing in the organization |

**Exhibit 5.6. Learning Contract**

*Participant Information*

| Name: | Current Position: | |
|---|---|---|
| Service Line: | Hire Date: | |
| Learning Contract Date: | Participant Initials: | Leadership Steward Initials: |

*Career Advancement Targets*

| | |
|---|---|
| What do I want to achieve? | |
| What obstacles stand in the way? | |
| What am I doing now to get what I want? (focus on continuing what is working and ceasing what isn't) | |
| Is my behavior helping? (Why/why not?) What behaviors need changing? | |

**Exhibit 5.6. (Continued)**

Assessment Feedback Action Plan

| Identified Developmental Need | My Learning Objective | How Will I Gain This Skill/ Knowledge? How Does This Action Address My Development Need? | How Will I Evidence My Growth in This Area | Resource/Help Required | Target Completion Date |
|---|---|---|---|---|---|
| | | | | | |
| | | | | | |
| | | | | | |
| | | | | | |
| | | | | | |
| | | | | | |

**Exhibit 5.7. Business Model Exercise**

*LEADERSHIP FIRST SESSION ONE*

*Team Exercise—Business Models and Their Implications*

You have been provided with information covering the recent history of FCG's Health Delivery Practice. Using this material and drawing upon the information presented and discussed in this afternoon's session:

- Identify the business forces acting on the HD model in late 1999 and early 2000 and determine how it was positioned to either respond or not respond to the changing environment.

- What were the existing business model levers and how were they structured to either respond or not respond to the market changes?

- Which lines of business or services should be reduced or not emphasized?

- Which segments would you invest in and how would you fund those investments?

- How will you increase marketing and marketing effectiveness?

- What key processes and reports must you put in place immediately to manage the business?

- The ultimate goal is to return the unit to profitability over the shortest period possible: within what time frame will you accomplish this?

- How will you position and structure the unit to both deal with the immediate challenges while positioning for a return to acceptable growth rates?

Be prepared to make a twenty-five-minute presentation of your team's analysis and strategy, covering the questions identified above.

Time Frame for Team Exercise: 1 hour 45 minutes

**Exhibit 5.7.** (*Continued*)

| The Health Delivery Business Unit Background Information |
| :--- |

**Background**

Through the year 2000, the Health Delivery Business Unit had been one of the mainstays of FCG's practice. This business unit, and the related service offerings, had its roots in the founding practices of the firm. The portfolio of services comprised two major lines of business: IT consulting services and implementation services. In addition, there was a small process improvement line of business that had a spotty past history in terms of market penetration and success, and had limited internal acceptance within the overall HD group. As shown below, there were sub or component offerings in each of these major lines of business.

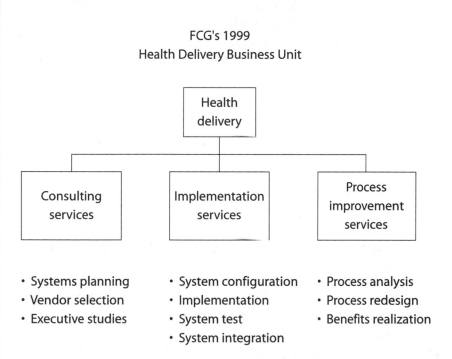

FCG's 1999
Health Delivery Business Unit

In addition to the delivery group, there was an overlay "sales" or go-to-market structure. The regional sales force was made up of geographic-based VPs and several new business directors, whose major responsibility was to sell the full line of the firm's services into the health delivery market (this included not only the core service offerings provided by the HD business unit, but also HD applicable services provided by other business units such as technology and integration services, networking design and implementations, and e-health services). The sales force

(*Continued*)

Exhibit 5.7. Business Model Exercise (*Continued*)

was responsible for identifying and prioritizing "target" accounts, developing marketing and sales strategies, and maintaining "strategic" relationships with key accounts.

The delivery components of the HD business unit were organized on a service-line or service-offering basis and did not have specific assigned geographies or specific account sales responsibilities. Their focus was to support the "sales" process by providing specific functional expertise to support the proposal process, identifying and selling add-on work, managing the quality and economics of the projects, developing additional service offerings or products, managing overall utilization for their groups, and related hiring and HR management issues.

The business unit was designed and structured to capitalize on what had been a twenty-year trend in the HD marketplace:

- Maintain strong relationships at existing or new HD accounts and use the consulting services to drive systems planning and vendor selection services into the client base.

- Use the planning and system selection process to "tee up" subsequent, large-scale, and multimonth or multiyear implementation engagements.

- Sell additional "consulting" services in the areas of process improvement if we had the skills and expertise.

- Repeat the cycle every three to five years at the client when the old systems no longer meet their needs.

*Years 1999 and Early 2000 HD Market Dynamics*

The majority of 1999 continued the successive string of strong quarters for the HD business unit. Buoyed by the tremendous demand fueled by the Y2K problem, almost all the HD organizations began an accelerated cycle of systems replacements. The Y2K phenomenon also created additional demand for "body shop" Y2K testing and remediation support. This demand resulted in the following 1999 revenue and project margin performance *for all services delivered into the HD marketplace.*

Beginning in 1999 and continuing into early 2000, there was an abrupt and precipitous decline in market demand. The factors contributing to this were

- The Balanced Budget Act (BBA) began to seriously erode health delivery organizations' operating margins. BBA went into effect in 1998, and the full impact began to be felt through reduced federal reimbursement in 1999. BBA was a permanent reduction in the level of government reimbursement for health care services.

**Exhibit 5.7.** (*Continued*)

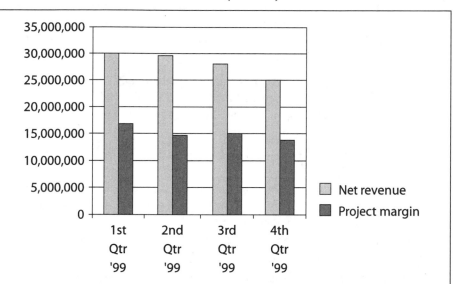

- The overspending in 1998 and 1999 on systems for Y2K readiness shut down capital for IT in 2000.

- Executive management seriously questioned the "value" received for past IT expenditures and the need for future investments.

- All major IT vendors (except Cerner and several smaller firms) experienced significant sales and revenue declines.

As a result, the 1st and 2nd Q FY 2000 operating performance of the HD business unit "tanked." The overall structure, personnel assignments, and reporting formats were realigned starting in FY 2000. However, the relative operating metrics still reflected a significant decline in performance.

*FY 200 HD Operating Metrics*

| Quarter | Revenue | COS | GM | % | Selling | G&A | Op. Inc. | Op. Inc. (%) |
|---------|---------|-----|-----|------|---------|------|----------|--------------|
| Q1 | $13,347 | $8,044 | $5,303 | 39.7% | $1,784 | $1,454 | $2,065 | 15.5% |
| Q2 | $10,914 | $6,955 | $3,959 | 36.3% | $1,617 | $1,574 | $768 | 7.0% |

*Fact Gathering Results*

The leadership of the HD business unit began a series of fact-gathering and analysis exercises beginning in March 2000. This fact gathering focused on garnering input on current and projected market demand, analysis of the operating statistics, review of the services portfolio and offerings, and review of the existing sales and

(*Continued*)

**Exhibit 5.7. Business Model Exercise (*Continued*)**

delivery organization structures. Throughout the process, there was significant debate, conflicting opinion, and contradictory recommendations. A summary of the salient facts and opinions include

- There were no firm data on what the market was currently demanding or likely to demand in the immediate future. Data from the vendors indicated that for the remainder of 2000, and potentially well into 2001, demand for software and new implementation business would be weak. The number of FCG driven systems plans and vendor selections fell to an average of one to two new engagements per month.

- There was a growing "rift" between the HD sales and delivery organizations. The delivery components of the organization felt that the sales side was not effectively pursuing the market opportunities, and the sales side felt that there was limited market demand and the HD service offerings no longer met the market demand they were pursuing.

- Many of the old vendor-based implementation services were no longer "selling" in the marketplace. The demand for McKesson Robbins HBOC software, IDX software, and SMS software was in significant decline. These had been mainstays of the implementation services business.

- Given the falling demand in the marketplace, significant price-cutting began to appear. The vendors and other consulting firm's began to cut rates by 20 to 40 percent in an effort to offset fixed costs.

- The existing measurement and monitoring systems were not strong or sufficient to analyze current or future performance. Specifically:

  The sales forecast process was imperfect and at best showed that future demand was weak or nonexistent.

  There were no clear lines of accountability or measurement of sales and delivery effectiveness.

  There were no tools or practices in place to monitor the controllable cost components of the business unit; e.g. practice development direct expenses, other nonchargeable expenses, sales cost, and time by client type or geography.

  Account plans were nonexistent.

Use the facts, data, and opinions detailed above to support your analyses and recommendations for the exercise.

### Exhibit 5.8. Managing Acquisitions and Mergers Exercise

Drawing upon the assigned prereading materials, the ideas from today's group discussion, and the attached FCG Acquisition Checklists, evaluate the following candidate company as a potential FCG acquisition:

- Identify what potential acquisition strategies may be possible here. Explore with the group not only a wholesale acquisition (if you can make the economics work) but also other forms of acquisition or investment *that meet both organization's goals.*

- Settle on your best option and develop a short, 4–5-page PowerPoint presentation outlining the following:

  The basic structure of the deal

  The strategic advantages and gains for both organizations

  Time frame and economics

  Major "Due Diligence" tasks

  Risks

- If, as a group, you are unable to structure a deal that leads to some form of combining (this can be a viable strategic option), prepare a 4–5-page PowerPoint presentation outlining the following:

  How the two companies will work together—the relationship structure and the leadership structure.

  How you will position the relationship in the marketplace.

  The targeted growth and profitability for the specific ERP practice.

  How you will manage the risks associated with not having a formalized relationship and structure and how you will manage the potential for (company name) selling (company name) to another organization.

  How/where does it fit with FCG's current business strategy and structure?

  What particular advantages/opportunities does it provide for FCG?

  What are the revenue/profitability potentials?

  What is the "culture fit" between the two firms?

  Can a deal be put together? Why or why not?

  What would the deal structure look like?

  How does the staff/skills set fit into FCG? Would we retain everyone or would some have to be released?

  What are the liabilities/risks associated with this acquisition?

  Should FCG buy this company?

Be prepared to make a twenty-minute presentation of your team's analysis and recommendation (be sure to address all the questions above in your presentation).

Time Frame for Team Exercise: 1 hour 30 minutes

**Exhibit 5.9. Effective Communication Exercise**

Effective today, you have been named CEO. You and your management team have gathered to define the communication requirements of the firm and define a communication strategy and plan for the firm.

Drawing upon the assigned prereading materials, the ideas from today's group discussion, and your knowledge of the firm:

- Think about the various constituencies and discuss their particular perspective regarding FCG: What are their key communication issues and need for information? *Spend adequate time in discussing the issues before proceeding to the creation of your plan.*

- Design a communications strategy and plan for your administration: identify how many and specifically which constituencies you will communicate with, regarding what issues, and with what frequency (consider vendors, clients, auditors, attorneys, board, market analysts, executive committee, VPC, VPDC, and any others you think are needed).

- Describe the vehicle(s) you would employ to communicate with those groups/entities and define the manner in which you would evaluate the effectiveness of that communication initiative.

Be prepared to make a twenty-minute presentation of your team's analysis and recommendation (be sure to address all the questions above in your presentation).

Time Frame for Team Exercise: 1 hour 30 minutes

*Source:* © Confidential and Proprietary to First Consulting Group. Reprinted with permission.

## Exhibit 5.10. Sample Homework Assignment

1. Between now and Session Two, interview your business unit leader and prepare an assessment of your business unit. Identify and address the following:

   - Briefly describe the business unit's organizational structure

   - Describe the current business model

   - Identify the current and future key business drivers and market opportunities

   - Identify the unit's relative strengths and weaknesses

   - Describe the unit's skill set strengths and deficiencies

   - Identify the risks, exposures, and opportunities that will exist twelve to twenty-four months in the future

   - Outline how you would accelerate the growth of the unit 50 percent above its current level over the next twelve to eighteen months.

   Be prepared to make a presentation (*no more than 20 minutes in length*) of your analysis to the entire Leadership First group at the next session. *This presentation should be an original-thought, focused analysis of the issues—not merely an academic exercise or a compendium of other presentations that may have been done by members of the business unit.*

2. Using your assessment feedback information as the basis for your personal growth and learning strategy, complete your learning contract, in detail, identifying the key developmental targets you want to set for yourself over the coming six to eight months. Be prepared to share your learning targets and to discuss what progress you have made or are making with your team at Session Two and Session Three.

*Source:* © Confidential and Proprietary to First Consulting Group. Reprinted with permission.

# ABOUT THE CONTRIBUTOR

**Paula Cowan,** SPHR, is vice president of human resources, Emeritus, with First Consulting Group, headquartered in Long Beach, California, retired in 2001. FCG delivers strategic information technology solutions to clients in the health care industry. Joining the firm in 1996, she was the architect of the human resources organization, structuring and staffing the function and designing and implementing many of the organization's HR initiatives. She served as a member of the firm's Operating Committee and the Leadership Development Committee, along with the CEO and the operational vice president, who chaired the firm's Quality Initiative. Before joining First Consulting Group, she held executive leadership positions in the health care, high-tech, and consulting industries. She holds bachelor's and master's degrees from California State University, Long Beach Campus, and the SPHR certification from the Society for Human Resource Management (SHRM). She is a recipient of the American Society for Training and Development's Torch Award and the YWCA's Outstanding Business Woman Award. Her articles have appeared in *HR Magazine, Personnel Journal, HR PC,* and the *Proceedings of the American Society for Training and Development.* She has served as a guest speaker at the Blue Cross Association Conference, PIRA, Los Angeles Compensation and Benefits Association, Pepperdine University, and the Women's Employment Options Conference.

CHAPTER SIX

# GE Capital

*This case study describes a global high-impact leadership development intervention with real business impact that is achieved through a robust diagnostic and assessment process, GE values, the three lenses of leadership, storytelling, futuring, uncovering peak performance, systems thinking, and follow-up forums and evaluation.*

OVERVIEW     162

BUSINESS CASE FOR LEADERSHIP DEVELOPMENT     162

GETTING STARTED     163

    Figure 6.1: Anchoring the Initiative     165

BUILDING THE OPERATING PHILOSOPHY     166

    Figure 6.2: Three Lenses of Leadership     166
    Design, Tools, and Techniques     167
    Organization Analysis Model     171
    Figure 6.3: Organizational Culture     171

FOLLOW-UP AND RESULTS     172

FINAL OBSERVATIONS     173

EXHIBITS

    Exhibit 6.1: Executive Leadership Development Symposium:
      Personal Challenges     174
    Exhibit 6.2: Executive Leadership Development Symposium:
      Organizational Challenges     175
    Exhibit 6.3: Executive Leadership Development Symposium:
      Additional Personal Challenges     176
    Exhibit 6.4: Sample Agenda: ELDS Program at a Glance     177

REFERENCES     179

ABOUT THE CONTRIBUTOR     179

# OVERVIEW

Too many leadership interventions are fashioned in ways that do not engage the business leaders themselves in the design and delivery of the interventions. As a result, the intervention at times feels more like a training exercise than an opportunity to improve from an organizational and personal perspective. We know from studying leadership development interventions that leaders learn the most from experiences that are rooted in what they do every day (Bass, 1990; Argyris, 1976; Clark, Clark, and Campbell, 1992) and that have direct applicability to their job. Too few interventions are tracked to determine the real impact they have on the performance of the organization and the participating individual.

This case study will provide a "soup to nuts" process for designing, delivering, and evaluating leadership development initiatives that can be implemented in your organization. It lays out a process used globally in the financial services business of the GE Company. The process is proven to work in varying cultures and business types, not just financial organizations but also in industrial businesses and across functions as well. Proven methods are outlined for engaging the business leaders in the process—a powerful ingredient for success.

# BUSINESS CASE FOR LEADERSHIP DEVELOPMENT

GE Capital, as it was then known, the financial services arm of the GE Company, was experiencing tremendous business expansion. It was one of the fastest growing financial services organizations in the world, going from a U.S.-based organization in the early 1990s to a global organization in the mid to late 1990s. One of the hallmarks of GE is driving a culture of knowing its key leadership talent and ensuring that the talent reflects the strong values that underscore the company. With rapid global expansion, it was feared that GE would lose this competitive advantage if we did not act quickly to maintain strong ties to our new and emerging leaders. And as the company expanded globally, maintaining the culture became increasingly important.

Leadership plays a significant role in modeling and reinforcing the culture of the organization, and, as the literature underscored, leaders who do not reflect the cultural values of the organization can have a disastrous impact on the bottom line (Finkelstein and Hambrick, 1996). Historically, GE is known for its ability to shape and develop strong leaders, so it was only natural that with the fast expansion of GE Capital that the business would focus on developing leaders. The question was exactly how we were going to go about growing leaders in a cost-effective and effective way.

# GETTING STARTED

The temptation for developing leadership interventions is to go to those who have experience doing them within the organization. Although they are a great resource for institutional history, these "insiders" often can perpetuate their own beliefs and myths about leadership development and training, thus creating their own blinders for "out of the box thinking." The real people who know the issues and what is missing in the leadership equation are the leaders themselves. Also, it is important to build a critical mass of support for an effort to uncover the focal points for significant change and to connect with the leadership community on what they believe is important about leadership.

Contrary to some advice, I embarked on a massive effort to interview all the business leaders about their views on business and leadership challenges. I also interviewed a cross-section of potential users of the system to get a read on their appetite for change and personal development. This was a very useful and enlightening exercise. Not only were the business issues identified but also the business leaders' teachable points of view on effective leadership were uncovered (Tichy and Cohen, 1997). The benefit was two-fold: learning that there was considerable consensus about the business challenges ahead (always good news); and that the leaders themselves could be a critical part of the development effort, since they indeed had strong views about leadership and what it takes to be a good leader. They clearly had their teachable points of view—their "defining moments" when they learned their greatest lessons—and they were excited to talk about them. Potential participants had a strong desire to learn and be on the cutting edge. They had a thirst for understanding the bigger context of the organization, improving themselves, and continuing to motivate those they led.

The same series of questions were asked of both business leaders and potential participants. The interview approach was open-ended, using the following questions:

- What are biggest challenges facing the business; what keeps you awake at night?
- If you had one message to future leaders of this business, what would it be?
- What will leaders need to do to address the business challenges?
- What is it that you want to be remembered for as a leader?
- What was your greatest defining moment that taught you the most about leadership?
- What excites you most about your current role?

- Is focusing on leadership development important? If yes, why? And if no, why not?
- If we were to launch an effort, would you be willing to be part of the faculty?

Although these questions may seem self-evident, they led to some very interesting discussions. You will note that I never asked the obvious question—*What skills do you think leaders need?* That would have been too easy and would have provided the typical answers not necessarily rooted in the business need. The questions were also future focused. This was important because we were not debating, justifying, or trying to rectify what happened in the past. We were thinking proactively about what the business and leaders would need to be successful going forward. The interviewees also had a chance to be reflective about themselves and their business—an enjoyable luxury in today's fast-paced world.

I walked out of these interviews knowing a great deal about the business challenges, leadership lessons from potential teachers, and the leadership needs from potential participants. The group's energy to be involved and engaged in the initiative was building. The time spent in this activity was well worth the effort, as it allowed us to design something reflective of the business environment. A key outcome of this step was to understand what aspects of leadership about which the business leaders were passionate. Each business leader had a particular area of focus that would prove invaluable going forward. A great deal of group excitement was also built for the next steps through this interview process.

*Lesson One: Engage the leaders early in the process. In looking back, I definitely would not skip this step as the first. It laid the foundation and cornerstone of the effort that created great momentum and buy-in. It also helped us see that there was tremendous enthusiasm for developing the next generation of senior leaders.*

With the macro business issues defined, leadership needs determined, and leadership lessons articulated, it was time to get more granular. Now we needed to delve into the world of competencies. If we started with competencies we would have lost leaders pressured by business concerns, in OD and HR jargon (which, by the way, I would avoid at all costs).

Driving to the micro issues became an easier task because the macro issues were understood. The Workout™ process, a GE problem-solving technique, was used to define what the specific macro characteristics looked like when they were being successfully exhibited. The Workout™ was high-energy and fun. Teams of business leaders agreed on the definitions of the characteristics and then drilled the characteristics down into behavioral terms. There was considerable consensus about what constituted successful future leadership. Through

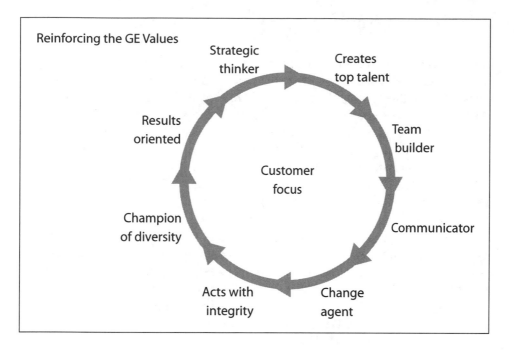

**Figure 6.1** Anchoring the Initiative.

this exercise the leadership development framework in Figure 6.1 and related behaviors were defined.

The framework was sent to all the business leaders for final validation. Once endorsed it became the behavioral underpinning of the intervention to come.

*Lesson Two: Build your own framework. It would have been easier and quicker to research the literature and come up with the framework and competencies, present them to the leadership, and ask for their endorsement, which they probably would have done. Or worse yet have an outside consultant develop it for us. But there would have been no ownership for the behaviors, and the framework would not have had the same weight with the participants as one that was developed and owned by their business leaders. The intervention was not based upon an off-the-shelf set of behaviors but behaviors that we firmly believed in as a business.*

An interesting point to note is that the framework tracked very closely with the major studies relative to leadership characteristics for success (Andersen Consulting, 1999). From a literature and research perspective it was a very defensible, valid document. Ultimately it became the basis for a 360-survey feedback instrument to be used in the intervention. Now we were ready for the design work to begin.

# BUILDING THE OPERATING PHILOSOPHY

Many leadership development efforts are solely designed around leader behaviors and follower reactions. However, a more contemporary view is that leaders are responsible at three levels: their personal behaviors that reflect their values; how they interact, engage their followers, and model their values; and how they build strong, healthy organizations that are sustainable over time. Specifically, leaders build organizations that provide benefit to employees, shareholders, customers, and the communities in which they reside. Keeping organization integrity and ethics in the forefront of leaders' minds, while a hallmark for GE leaders, would become timely in the post-Enron era. The organizing principles that would drive the design would be the interrelationship of these three levels of leadership.

GE is a values-based organization and the GE values needed to be reflected. Values are much more important to true leadership than behavior and style (Clawson, 1999). In fact, as we now know leaders have many different styles but what truly differentiates a leader from others is strongly held values that guide day-to-day work. Many leadership gurus agree on this point (Clawson, 1999; Deal and Kennedy, 1982). Therefore, the program design focused on helping participants undercover their underlying values and see how those values manifest themselves in their behaviors. We wanted to help participants make the link between their values and assumptions and their behaviors so they could be aligned. The idea was to create consistent behavior congruent with their beliefs. Also, there would be a reflective nature to the initiative. Since fairly senior leaders would be attending, we did not want to assume that they did not already have a personal theory of leadership; rather, we wanted to bring that theory to the conscious level to ensure they really understood what drove them personally. We wanted participants to define their guiding principles,

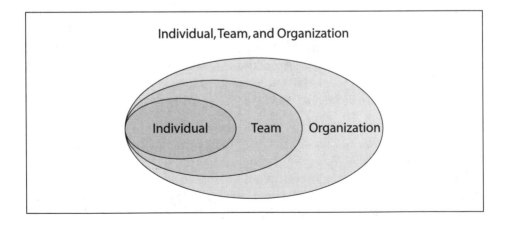

**Figure 6.2** Three Lenses of Leadership.

understand why they were important to them, and share these principles so leaders could learn from each other.

It was also important that the program fit squarely within the GE culture of Action Learning through business-based experience. Thus, Action Learning became the general development principle, whereby participants would take action, reflect, and reframe based upon the experience (Argyris, 1976). In addition to these concepts, we also would employ the following:

- Storytelling. Stories lend themselves to greater retention, and we wanted leaders to learn how to use storytelling in their own environments (Conger, 1993).

- Futuring. One has to change in the context of the future, which is much more energizing than trying to change the mistakes of the past (Goldsmith, 2001). The common OD approach to diagnose the past as a starting point for future planning was abandoned.

- Uncovering peak performance. Everyone is a leader at some point, and reflecting on when you are at your best helps you see that in fact you do have the capacity to demonstrate great leadership. But you must apply those peak experiences to every day (Cooperrider, 1997–1998).

- Systems thinking. Every leader must have a systematic way of viewing the whole organization from a strategic perspective so that he or she can drive organizational alignment and systematic change (Senge, 1990).

*Lesson Three: Defining your conceptual framework, such as the three levels of leadership, is critical because the framework provides the glue that holds the program together. Be sure you have determined your design philosophy and assumptions and that they are consistent with the culture of the organization before you set out to map content and determine tools and techniques to be used. A framework and operating assumptions provide the logic for the initiative, and the participants will be able to feel the congruency adding to the power of the program. A clearly articulated philosophy proved to be essential.*

With this groundwork in place it was time to develop the actual materials (both pre- and post-), the sequence of events, and faculty.

## Design, Tools, and Techniques

The approach needed to be flexible enough to adapt to the constant changing business environment yet be structured enough to be reliable and repeatable with consistent high-quality results. The main components would be pre-work consisting of interviews and personal surveys, a week-long symposium including personal coaches, post-program survey follow-up, and intensive one- or two-day specific topic events to focus on a targeted development need.

The pre-work included the following:

- Interviews to help with the reflective process and to set the targets for their individual development needs. Interviews were conducted with participants' boss, several peers, subordinates, and customers to get a perspective on the challenges facing the business and what leaders of the future needed to do to address these challenges (Exhibit 6.1).

- Personal analysis of peak performance experience. Specifically, what was the event, who was involved, and what were they doing that made it peak (Exhibit 6.2).

- Completion of three survey instruments: a 360-feedback survey, which included a question to describe this person at peak performance, the Myers Briggs Type Indicator (MBTI), and the Leadership Impact (L/I) Survey developed by Human Synergistics, a survey that correlates leader behavior with organization culture and values.

In addition, we personally called each participant to set expectations and explain the design principles and philosophy so they understood what they were going to experience. We wanted to be sure that people were well versed before they attended and understood that the primary focus was leadership.

*Lesson Four: Carefully constructed pre-work helped set the tone for the program and signal that this was not going to be a typical experience. It also helped build excitement for what partipants were to experience. The individual calls proved invaluable, as participants knew what to expect and felt respected as customers of the event.*

The program itself begins with a story from *Killer Angels,* a historical novel about the Civil War by Michael Shaara. The story about Colonel Chamberlain, excerpted from the book, highlighted the three levels of leadership and underscored the notion that real leadership is based upon a moral foundation and a set of principles, not behaviors. The story depicts a defining moment in leadership in which Chamberlain had exactly three minutes to capture the hearts and minds of men to follow him into a key battle. This segment was directly extracted from work done by Jim Clawson, a professor at the Darden School of Business at the University of Virginia. Jim was kind enough to do this segment for us, and it set an extremely powerful tone for what the week ahead was to be like. It caused people to really think about what their guiding principles would be going forward as they expand their leadership roles. The afternoon of the first day is spent debriefing the interviews from the pre-work to help provide the context of what leaders will be called upon in the future to do, given the business challenges ahead.

With the future leadership imperatives defined, it was then time to provide the 360-feedback results so that participants could see what they might need to work on to continue to grow as leaders. This is an important but subtle shift in thinking. It helps people look ahead, not back, and puts leadership in the context of the business world. Not surprising, participants love the discussion because it helps them learn that their business challenges are not unique, others are in the same boat, and that we can all learn ways to improve from each other. It takes the threat out of the 360-degree processes because we are not looking at what they did wrong in the past but what they need to do going forward. At the end of the first day participants signed up for one-on-one coaching time with their personal coach to review their individual feedback instruments and discuss action plans. Each coach would work with a team of six to seven people and provide individual and team coaching throughout the remainder of the week.

As a note, the original design called for outside coaches, but as the program progressed we switched to using internal senior human resource managers. This was a vital switch because the internal coaches understood the context of the business and the values and culture of the company. They gave much more valuable coaching because they could help frame the issues in relationship to the current business realities. In addition, the internal people loved being used as executive coaches, and the coaching relationships often lasted long beyond the actual program, another added benefit.

The first day ended (as does each day) with a "fireside chat" with a business leader who discusses his or her views on leadership: personal defining moment and lessons learned. The fireside chats were structured to be informal dialogues so that everyone could engage in a good discussion and learn from each other's perspective. As noted, borrowing from Noel Tichy's teachable points of view, business leaders would do presentations throughout the program on topics relevant to that day's discussion. Typically, there are about ten to twelve leaders who participate as faculty.

*Lesson Five: Using internal people as teachers and coaches sets a unique tone. It helps people see the various business leaders in a different light. The business leader participation also shows a tremendous level of support that can only help provide credibility and build the success of the effort. Plus internal coaches add tremendous contextual value.*

Day two continues to focus on the individual aspects of leadership by exploring the MBTI and debriefing the Leadership Impact (L/I) Survey that is also 360-degree in nature. The three surveys closely correlate (360, MBTI, and L/I) and provide multiple data points to help people identify what they need to work on to continue to be successful. Also, they see what is said about them at peak performance and what they have said at peak performance, which tends to be closely aligned. It is interesting that peak performance showed up at times of crisis when real focus was needed. Another interesting note about peak performance is that what participants do at their peak-performance level is consistently what they also need to do more of on a day-to-day basis. This reinforces the point that leaders can demonstrate excellence when they have to but also need to pay attention to what they do during normal times, when they tend to fall back into old habits.

*Lesson Six: Pick your instruments carefully and be sure to have enough data points to support change. Surveys need to closely align with the overall construct of the program. In this case the three surveys and peak performance analysis reinforced the three levels of leaderships both from the moral foundation perspective and from the individual, team, and organizational perspective. Also, be sure the instruments can correlate so they reinforce what leaders may need to work on, and don't allow leaders to walk away from the real issues.*

Day two closes with Marshall Goldsmith's coaching model that we have adapted (Goldsmith, 2001). At this point participants have enough data to select one item that they want to work on, and we apply Marshall's coaching model so that they can get ideas about how they can improve from their colleagues. This is a great end to the experiential part of the day because the participants learn that they all have similar issues that they are working on and that they can get very practical suggestions from each other for how they can improve. Marshall's model is very user friendly and easy to implement with busy executives. There is an added benefit, as this sets the tone for peer coaching that will go on for the rest of the week. Participants not only get individual one-on-one coaching but also an environment is created in which they are coaching and helping each other improve. These relationships have lasted well beyond the program; teams often follow up with each and have "improvement calls" with each other. In addition, many have used this model with their own staff to build more teamwork when they return to work.

Days three and four focus on the leader-follower relationships and learning an Organization Analysis (OA) model—a systems thinking model for organizations that helps drive strategy. The OA model is a tool used to analyze a business case specifically selected for the program that is typically around a new change initiative or a contemporary problem that needs to be addressed. The case is not a Harvard Case Study but rather a statement of facts written relative to the Organization Analysis (OA) model—a type of organizational 360. The model builds on Six Sigma and enables a business leader or leadership team to diagnosis a business situation and determine the areas they will need to work on to improve the organization. (See Chapter Seven for more information about the Six Sigma program.)

Participants are also put into intact teams to work on the case. They contract with each other around the team behaviors and process to be used, and the coach plays the role of process observer and team feedback provider. The coach is empowered to point out when dysfunctional behavior or process is occurring, thus enabling the team to learn and self-correct. Team behaviors tend to come out strongly because the teams are given a real business case to work on. This provides another significant level of learning by doing.

## Organization Analysis Model

The case is typically twenty-five to thirty pages long and presents facts on each aspect of the OA model. It provides sufficient data for a team to make reasoned judgments about the issues. In addition, the business owner of the case attends the program and answers any questions that the teams may have about the case. Associated with the OA are a series of questions that assist the teams in determining the component of the model they will have to attack first if they are to drive sustainable improvements. Their recommendations are reported on the final day of the program to the business owner and to someone from the office of the CEO. The teams learn the model and apply it to a real issue. This approach helps them conceptualize how to drive change relative to a serious business concern that can be applied to their own organization.

*Lesson Seven: Driving team behavior and learning change is most effective around a real, pressing business issue. This is not a game or group exercise but something that is important to the success of the company. Also, team behaviors tend to come out in a more pronounced way when people are working on issues they really care about. The lessons of how they affect others and potentially affect followers are even more poignant. They can take a look at their values and see how their behavior in action is or is not consistent with the values that they profess—another very significant learning point. They get a bird's eye view of the impact they have on their followers.*

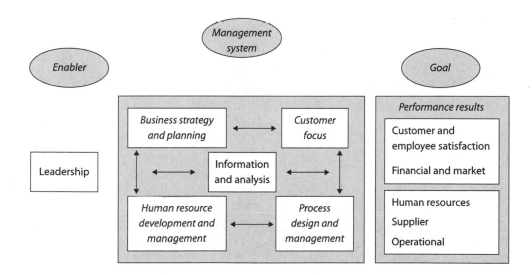

**Figure 6.3** Organizational Culture.

The program ends on day five with pulling all the experiences together into a cohesive whole. Participants finalize their personal development plans and their group recommendations on the business issue, and do one last round of team coaching to determine what could they have done better as a team and as individual team players. They also define their leadership lessons learned. The program concludes with a report and dialogue conducted with typically the president or CEO or someone very senior from the office of the CEO. The concluding reports are significant in that they lay the groundwork for what recommendations will be adopted by the organization going forward. For the record, many of the suggestions have gone on to be implemented within the company with great success. A week at a glance is provided so the readers can get a flavor of the actual flow of the program (Exhibit 6.4).

# FOLLOW-UP AND RESULTS

Even though the formal program ends, there is considerable follow-up that takes place. Participants are surveyed for actions they have taken at the individual, team, and organizational levels to drive change—following the original construct of the program around the three levels of leadership. By all accounts significant improvements have been noted. Also, participants are queried relative to additional support they might need in order to continue to grow as leaders. These data are used as the basis for one-day follow-up sessions around specific leadership issues. These "Best Practice" forums are events for which we bring in experts on specific key topics. Marshall Goldsmith did an intensive session on coaching, and Jay Conger did an in-depth session on strategic communication, to name just two. This keeps the learning going.

Three months and six months after the initial program we also conduct a mini-360 around each person's specific development need. We have found that in 95 percent of the situations participants have improved on the job as viewed by their original feedback givers. This is a very important statistic. We know for a fact that the program has significant impact because the business has been changed as a result of the participants' recommendations, and participants themselves have noted significant personal change, but most important the people they deal with have seen sustained change. We think the results speak for themselves.

Of course we do program evaluations to make sure that the design and content remain relevant and adapt to a global audience. The program consistently gets a 4 out of 4 rating, indicating that we have perfected an approach that is repeatable and reliable no matter where it is conducted. The real proof of success, though, is in the quantifiable results that come from the effort.

*Lesson Eight: Follow-up is absolutely key to demonstrating improvement and change. An intervention without follow-up is just another intervention that cannot document real business impact beyond the smile sheets.*

## FINAL OBSERVATIONS

Constructing powerful leadership interventions with lasting impact requires a lot of planning up front. Of particular importance is a thorough understanding of the business challenges going forward. This provides the context for leadership development that is essential. Leadership development is not about skill building; it is about getting in touch with your values and principles and acting in ways that are consistent with those values and principles.

In constructing global leadership development, understand that organization culture and leadership values are different from country cultures and values (Hofestede, 1997). At the leadership and organization level, we discovered that there was remarkable consistency relative to the organization cultures and personal values that leaders and their teams felt were optimum for excellent business performance. The data collected from around the world support this assertion.

**Exhibit 6.1. Executive Leadership Development Symposium: Personal Challenges**

Reflect upon the following questions about your personal leadership challenges and bring your written responses to the Symposium.

What has been your greatest leadership challenge?

1. What was the situation?

2. What made it a challenge?

3. How did you handle the situation?

4. What did you learn?

**Exhibit 6.2. Executive Leadership Development Symposium: Organizational Challenges**

1. What do you see as the biggest strategic challenge facing the company in the next two or three years?

2. What leadership skills and capabilities do you consider to be key development priorities for me in order to meet these challenges?

**Exhibit 6.3. Executive Leadership Development Symposium: Additional Personal Challenges**

Reflect upon the following questions about your personal leadership challenges and bring your written responses to the symposium.

When you look at your career, what do you see as the critical decision points? How do you feel about the choices you've made over the years?

What were your critical success factors?

Describe a time when you were at your best as a leader.

1. What was the situation?

2. What were you doing that made this a defining moment?

3. What do you value most from this experience?

4. What characteristics of effective leadership did you demonstrate?

**Exhibit 6.4. Sample Agenda: ELDS Program at a Glance**

| | Monday, September 30 | Tuesday, October 1 | Wednesday, October 2 | Thursday, October 3 | Friday, October 4 |
|---|---|---|---|---|---|
| Morning | 9:30–10:30 A.M. Opening & Framework for the Program<br><br>10:30–12:15 P.M. Foundation of Leadership | 8:30–8:45 A.M. Morning Pulse Check<br><br>8:45–10:15 A.M. The Challenges of Leading a New Business<br><br>10:30–12:00 P.M. Leadership Behavior & Organizational Performance: A Cause & Effect Relationship | 7:30–8:30 A.M. Coaching Breakfasts<br><br>8:30–8:45 A.M. Morning Pulse Check<br><br>8:45–9:45 A.M. Introduction to the OA Model and Individual Analysis of GEC<br><br>9:45–12:15 P.M. Initial Team Discussion of Analysis of GEC | 7:30–8:30 A.M. Coaching Breakfasts<br><br>8:30–8:45 A.M. Morning Pulse Check<br><br>8:45–10:00 A.M. Q&A with Business Case Owner<br><br>10:15–12:00 P.M. Team Meetings: Analysis of Case | 7:30–8:30 A.M. Coaching Breakfasts<br><br>8:30–8:45 A.M. Morning Pulse Check<br><br>8:45–9:45 A.M. Challenge Rounds: Organizing for Final Recommendations<br><br>9:45–12:00 P.M. Prepare for Final Report:<br>— Business Case<br>— GE Capital<br>— Leadership Lessons Learned |

*(Continued)*

**Exhibit 6.4. Sample Agenda: ELDS Program at a Glance** (*Continued*)

| | Monday, September 30 | Tuesday, October 1 | Wednesday, October 2 | Thursday, October 3 | Friday, October 4 |
|---|---|---|---|---|---|
| Lunch | 12:30–4:30 P.M. Building the GE Brand in Europe | 12:00–1:45 P.M. First Impressions Exercise | 12:30–2:00 P.M. Leadership Challenges | 12:15–2:00 P.M. Leadership Discussion: Driving Growth | 12:00–1:30 P.M. Final Team Feedback |
| Afternoon | 2:15–4:30 P.M. Discussion: Business Challenges & Leader of the Future Requirements<br><br>4:30–5:30 P.M. 360° Feedback Introduction of Executive Coaches | 2:00–4:00 P.M. MBTI—Leadership & Team Performance & Decision Making<br><br>4:15–6:00 P.M. Luxor Case & Behavioral Coaching Model/Action Plans Started | 2:15–3:00 P.M. Prepare for Report on GEC<br><br>3:00–3:45 P.M. Reports<br><br>4:00–5:00 P.M. Team Huddle to Discuss Business Case/Questions Determined to Ask Case Owner<br><br>5:00–6:00 P.M. Coaching Meetings | 2:00–5:30 P.M. Business Case (cont.)<br><br>5:30–6:30 P.M. Coaching Meetings | 1:30–2:00 P.M. Rehearsal<br><br>2:15–4:00 P.M. Report & Dialogue<br><br>4:00–4:30 P.M. Group Photo and Program Evaluation |
| Evening | 6:00–7:30 P.M. Fireside Chat: Building a Career in GE & the Leader's Responsibility in Attracting and Retaining the Best<br><br>7:30 P.M. Dinner | 6:30–8:00 P.M. Dinner, Coach Meetings<br><br>9:00–10:00 P.M. Coaching Meetings | 6:00–9:00 P.M. Offsite Dinner on Pescatori Island, Fireside Chat | 6:30–8:00 P.M. Fireside Chat: The Leader's Role in Driving Six Sigma<br><br>8:00 P.M. Dinner/Coaching Meetings<br><br>9:00–10:00 P.M. Coaching Meetings | |

Last, but perhaps most important, involve your business leaders directly in your effort. Make them your partner in the design, delivery, and follow-up. This is how you all win in the end.

# REFERENCES

Andersen Consulting. (1999). The Evolving Role of Executive Leadership. Wellesley, Mass.: Andersen Consulting Institute for Strategic Change.

Argyris, C. (1976). *Increasing Leadership Effectiveness.* New York: Wiley.

Bass, B. M. (1990). *Bass and Stoghill's Handbook of Leadership: A Survey of Theory and Research.* New York: Free Press.

Clark, K. E., Clark, M. B., and Campbell, D. P. (1992). *Impact of Leadership.* Greensboro, N.C.: Center for Creative Leadership.

Clawson, J. (1999). *Level Three Leadership.* Upper Saddle River, N.J.: Prentice Hall.

Conger, J. A. (1993). "The Brave New World of Leadership Training." *Organizational Dynamics, 21* (3), 46–58.

Cooperrider, D. L. (1997–1998). "Appreciative Inquiry." (Class lecture: Benedictine University Ph.D. program, Lisle, Ill.)

Deal, T. E., and Kennedy, A. A. (1982). *Corporate Cultures: The Rites and Rituals of Corporate Life.* Reading, Mass.: Addison Wesley.

Finkelstein, S., and Hambrick, D. C. (1996). *Strategic Leadership: Top Executives and Their Effects on Organizations.* St. Paul, Minn.: West.

Goldsmith, M. (2001). "Helping Successful People Get Even Better." *Leading for Innovation.* San Francisco: Jossey-Bass.

Hofestede, G. (1997). *Cultures and Organizations.* New York: McGraw Hill.

Senge, P. M. (1990). *The Fifth Discipline: The Art and Practice of the Learning Organization.* New York: Doubleday.

Tichy, N., and Cohen, E. (1997). *Leadership Engine.* San Francisco: Jossey-Bass.

# ABOUT THE CONTRIBUTOR

**Linda Sharkey** is currently vice president of organization development and staffing (O&S) for GE Commercial Equipment Finance (CEF), a billion-dollar net income business, part of GE Commercial Finance. In this role Linda is responsible for the identification, development, and succession planning of CEF's leadership talent and leads the Session C and performance management processes. She also spearheads CEF's strategic staffing initiatives and works closely with the leadership team on organizational design, restructuring, and acquisition integration. Linda joined CEF from GE Equity, where she served as senior vice president of human resources. Previously, she held the position of manager, global executive development for GE Capital. In this role, she spearheaded the Executive Leadership Development Symposium (ELDS), a successful program aimed at developing senior leaders. Before beginning her GE career in 1998 as part of GE Capital's Leadership Development team, Linda held various human resource roles with Paine Webber, Chemical/Chase Bank, and several government-related offices in New York and Washington, D.C. Linda holds a bachelor of arts from Nazareth College, a masters of public administration from Russell Sage College, and a Ph.D. in organizational development from Benedictine University.

# CHAPTER SEVEN

# Hewlett-Packard

*This case study describes the dynamic transformation process of HP sanctioned by the CEO in which over 8,000 managers throughout the world were developed through key principles of accelerating high performance and alignment and executing with accountability. The program's most successful key features of on-the-job support, continuous evaluation, coaching, business mapping, and rapid decision making enabled the program to show value of fifteen times its cost, as well as contribute to the success of the merger with Compaq.*

OVERVIEW     182

DIAGNOSIS AND ASSESSMENT     182

PROGRAM DESIGN     183

PROGRAM IMPLEMENTATION     185

ON-THE-JOB SUPPORT     186

EVALUATION     187
    Immediate Post-Program Evaluations     187
    Thematic Analysis of Follow-Through     187
    Three-Month Post-Program Financial Analysis     189

CONCLUSION     191
    Exhibit 7.1: The Follow-Through Process for Dynamic Leadership     191
    Exhibit 7.2: Distribution of Follow-Through Objectives in Dynamic
       Leadership Programs     192
    Exhibit 7.3: Distribution of Most Valued Aspects of Dynamic
       Leadership Programs     193

ENDNOTES     193

ABOUT THE CONTRIBUTORS     194

# OVERVIEW

In late 1999, Carly Fiorina, the then recently appointed CEO at Hewlett-Packard, launched a campaign to "Reinvent HP." This chapter describes Dynamic Leadership—an ambitious worldwide program to support the rejuvenation of HP by helping managers excel in an accelerating pace of change. More than 8,000 managers were trained in the first year. The return on investment was outstanding and generated savings and new revenue more than fifteen times the cost, as well as contributing to the merger with Compaq.

The success of Dynamic Leadership resulted from six key elements: (1) Dynamic Leadership addressed clear and compelling company needs with well-defined outcomes; (2) implementation was led jointly by internal line leaders and external "certified" experts; (3) rapid experimentation and ongoing assessment were used to ensure continuous improvement; (4) an aggressive roll-out schedule with the full support of HP's executive committee created a critical mass of managers who shared common terminology and methodology; (5) an innovative post-course follow-through system assured application, practice, coaching, and support; (6) rigorous measurement was designed into the program from the outset.

# DIAGNOSIS AND ASSESSMENT

Hewlett-Packard has enjoyed an exceptional record of innovation and growth for more than sixty years. Sustaining that record has required the company to continually reinvent itself in order to capitalize on new technologies and address the changing needs of the market. Throughout the twentieth century, 80 percent of HP revenues were generated from products it had produced in the last three years.

The 1990s witnessed unprecedented changes in the technology sector. The pace of change—already rapid—accelerated further. Product life cycles became shorter and shorter even as their technologic sophistication and integration needs became increasingly complex. Competition became global, with high-quality products from Asia and Europe competing for market share in the United States as well as their home markets. Prices declined precipitously.

Hewlett-Packard, long one of the most admired companies in the world, was showing signs of deceleration. Its growth curve flattened, decision making slowed, and lack of alignment and shared purpose led to wasted opportunities and resources. To reinvigorate the company, HP's board of directors named Carly Fiorina, the brilliant architect of Lucent Technology's early success, as HP's new CEO in July 1999. Later that year, Carly announced that "The company of Bill Hewlett and Dave Packard is being reinvented. The original start-up will act like one again."

Carly and the executive team of HP recognized that competing successfully in the new market realities required a management culture capable of engaging in high-speed collaboration, raising and resolving issues rapidly, and making informed cross-boundary decisions efficiently and effectively. In 2000, a reinvention survey was launched for employees at all levels to assess progress. The results showed a real understanding of the company's strategy and reinvention imperatives. Employees agreed that reinvention was necessary, particularly faster and better decision making across the boundaries of the organization. They wanted increased accountability for measurable results and greater focus on the customer.

To meet these needs, HP's Workforce Development and Organization Effectiveness (WD&OE) Group designed and implemented Dynamic Leadership—an intensive development process specifically designed to accelerate alignment to senior purpose, improve collaboration across boundaries, accelerate raising and resolving issues, and improve decision making. The program includes two full days of instruction and working in groups followed by nine weeks of on-the-job application and follow through. To date, more than 8,000 managers have completed Dynamic Leadership and are using the tools and methods. This case study reports the results of the initiative, its return on investment for HP, and the factors critical to the success of such an ambitious undertaking.

## PROGRAM DESIGN

Since the reinvention survey indicated the common needs across business units, functions, and geographies, HP decided that the development process had to be global in scope, focused on the issues of the day, and deliverable effectively in the 157 countries in which HP operates. The program had to deliver substantive results in the first year, since it was launched within a month of the proposed merger announcement with Compaq. A solid value proposition was essential, otherwise HP managers would be too distracted by the impending merger, the proxy battle, and the continued deterioration of the economy, all factors competing for their most precious resource—time. To maximize the return on investment, HP decided to focus on a limited number of objectives that would have the greatest immediate impact. Specifically, Dynamic Leadership was designed to improve HP managers' ability "to produce rapid time-to-value for HP customers first, shareholders, and employees."[1]

The program focused on two key areas[2]:

1. Accelerating high-performance collaboration and alignment

   Working from a shared view of "value"

   Using conversation technology to gain alignment to purpose and rapidly raise and resolve issues

2. Executing with accountability

   Using rapid decision process to make effective and efficient decisions

   Designing accountability for actions

   Learning and adjusting

Given the need for credibility and rapid global rollout, HP elected to use a blended approach of external providers and internal facilitators. Conversant Solutions, LLC, of Boulder, Colorado, was already a partner with HP in other areas and was selected to cocreate the solution. They also provided the lead consultants and facilitators. In particular, their concepts of how to achieve higher value through more effective conversations had already proven valuable to senior management.[3] It was particularly well suited to the goals of Dynamic Leadership and formed the core components of the program.

The final design owed as much to rapid prototyping and experimentation as it did to a formal design process. Given the tight time lines and the need for action, we used Carly Fiorina's "Perfect Enough" principle to go to launch. Several small pilot programs were run; the most effective ideas and approaches were incorporated into the ultimate design. As the rollout got under way, further adjustments were made based on feedback from participants and monthly teleconferences among facilitators.

The final program design was an intensive two-day experience, followed by action planning and nine week follow-through. Two days of in-person dialogue was chosen in order to provide sufficient depth and practice without overwhelming the participants or requiring excessive time away from their work. The in-person portion of Dynamic Leadership is a fast-paced program that intersperses presentations of concepts and tools with small group work, practice, and discussions of current issues facing the business. The number of topics is intentionally limited to ensure adequate time for explanation and mastery.

Topics include

- Context setting through business mapping
- Laws of conversations
- Conversations model
- Rapid decision making
- RACI Model for decision making
- Authentically raising and resolving of issues

The designers selected a live group format as the most effective way to introduce and illustrate the targeted skills and concepts. Participants are provided a learning journal that includes the key concepts and ample room for personal notes. The program continues after supper on the first day, when participants must practice what they have learned to create an "evening of value." The next morning is a feedback and coaching session on how they did—the heart of the experience and often an intervention.

An important part of the design is accountability for action—the idea that development does not end on the last day of class but only when participants put what they have learned into action. As part of the design, participants must commit, in writing, to their goals for applying Dynamic Leadership. These goals are shared with their managers (see below) to underscore accountability and management support. HP didn't require managers who had attended the program to follow up with their reports. They counted on the HP culture of high-participation and management support, and it worked. When they received a copy of a participant's objectives and action plan, most managers responded to affirm and recognize or redirect their work.

## PROGRAM IMPLEMENTATION

The Dynamic Leadership program is presented either on-site or at a local hotel to minimize travel time and expense. Group size is limited to a maximum of thirty to ensure individual participation and practice. The VP of workforce development's executive advisory team for the program decided to offer both open enrollment and intact team sessions. The senior advisors believed that intact team participation was the best, because it institutionalized a new way of operating in a team, but limiting Dynamic Leadership to intact teams was a slower and more expensive way to build these skills and accelerate reinvention of the organization. Reinventing HP was all about increasing the velocity of change and decreasing time to valuable action. Moreover, at the time of launch (December 2001), HP was in a travel freeze in some countries and businesses; the open enrollment option ensured that people who could not travel could still participate.

To ensure the program was immediately relevant, each session was taught by a pair of facilitators—one external and one HP role model line leader who could bring the concepts to life with current business examples. In order to conduct the hundreds of sessions required to achieve the rollout targets, facilitators from more than a dozen firms were recruited. External facilitators trained together with the line managers in in-person train-the-trainer sessions. Training was reinforced and ideas for continuous improvement shared through ongoing virtual (simultaneous Internet and telephone) conferences. Whenever possible, new facilitators were paired with experienced ones for their first few sessions. Outside the United States, local bilingual facilitators were recruited and trained to lead the program. To ensure quality and continuous improvement, participants complete an evaluation form at the end of each session (see evaluation below). In 2002, more than four hundred sessions were held in more than fifty countries. Altogether, over 8,000 managers participated in Dynamic Leadership programs in its first full year.

# ON-THE-JOB SUPPORT

A unique aspect of the Dynamic Leadership program was a system for managing the post-course application (follow-through) period. Work by Goldsmith and others had shown a direct correlation between the degree of follow-up and the increase in leadership effectiveness.[4] Adult learning studies have shown the importance of immediate application of new skills. To ensure that Dynamic Leadership principles were put into practice, HP implemented a rigorous post-course management system using a commercial, web-based follow-through management tool called *Friday5s®*.[5]

In the concluding session of the program, participants were asked to write out two objectives to apply what they had learned to their jobs. These were entered into a group-specific *Friday5s®* website. The following week, participants were reminded of their goals by e-mail. A copy of each participant's objectives was e-mailed to his or her manager to ensure that managers knew what their direct reports had learned and intended to work on. Each participant's goals are visible to the members of his or her cohort to encourage shared accountability and learning.

The follow-through process is illustrated in Exhibit 7.1. On five occasions following the course (weeks 1, 3, 5, 7, and 9), participants were sent a link to the group's website and asked to update their progress by answering the following questions:

- What have you done to make progress on this goal?

- How much progress did you make?

- What are you going to do next?

- What has been your most important lesson learned?

The purpose was to encourage participants to continue to practice what they had learned, reflect on the experience, and continue group learning by sharing insights with one another. In addition, program participants could send a link to their update to a manager or coach for feedback and counsel. On the last update, participants were asked to describe the business impact of working on the goal and, based on their two months' experience since the program, what had proved most valuable.

Program learning was also reinforced through an on-line feature called GuideMe™ that provided practical suggestions for action based on course materials.

# EVALUATION

Three types of evaluation were used to continuously improve the program, measure its impact, and calculate the return on investment:

- Immediate post-program evaluations
- Analysis of follow-through reports
- Three-month post-program financial impact analysis

## Immediate Post-Program Evaluations

At the conclusion of each two-day program, participants were asked to complete an anonymous evaluation that included questions about both the content and presenters. These were forwarded to the program office, where they were reviewed by the program staff. Presenters with poor ratings were coached. If they were unable to improve their ratings in subsequent programs, they were replaced.

Feedback from these evaluations was also used to improve the program materials; the train-the-trainer and learning journal were both revised based on participants' input. Aspects of the presentation and emphasis were modified in order to clarify areas that participants indicated were unclear or more difficult to understand. As a result of these continuous improvement efforts, the overall program evaluations increased over time and now consistently exceed four on a five-point scale.

## Thematic Analysis of Follow-Through

Kirkpatrick proposed that rigorous evaluation of training programs should include documenting behavioral change (level 3) and measuring business results (level 4), in addition to measuring the participant's reaction to the program itself.[6] Dynamic Leadership included both level 3 and 4 analyses.

Because all of the participants' goals were entered into a database, it was possible to evaluate the distribution of planned post-course objectives (Exhibit 7.2). As the program design team intended, more than three quarters of all goals focused on improved alignment, more effective (authentic) conversation, and accelerated decision making.

The ability to efficiently review post-program goals provided assurance that the program was emphasizing the topics of greatest importance and that participants were receiving the desired message. The post-program objectives illustrated that the participants planned to apply their learning in ways that would have practical benefit for HP:

> Obtain clear accountability for all initiatives on cost plan; define roles of cost team; create process for reporting status and measuring deviation.

Reduce by 25 percent the time it takes to process a customer order.

Strive to understand the main purpose of all participating team members to find the common ground upon which decisions can be rapidly made.

In my next project meeting I will make a note to ask, "Is this adding value?" Explain definition of value to team.

Use conversation [meter] to draw out all the facts and senior purposes of my peer group . . . in order to make faster-decisions measurement, reduction of revisits on business issues.

Decrease the time of meetings on projects by always involving the right person, with a purpose described and shared. Document a measured decrease of 25 percent time spent.

Use the RACI model to improve Time-to-Value for the customer regarding Action Items and take-always during an upcoming customer review.

HP recognized that such goals are necessary but not sufficient. Level 3 analysis requires demonstrating *changed behavior:* that learners took new, different, and better action as a result of the program. There are two clear lines of evidence that this was achieved in Dynamic Leadership: (1) the real-time self-reports of the participants themselves, and (2) the independent observations by their managers and coaches. Participants' biweekly *Friday5s*® reports indicated that they not only absorbed the content of the program but also translated their learning experience into actions that benefited their teams and the company as a whole. Sample actions:

Reviewed "value" concept with staff. . . . Assigned people to come to next staff with (1) how they believe their own job adds value to the customer, (2) identify areas to increase percentage of value added activity.

Shared the principles from the class regarding the conversation meter, and the appropriate use of accuracy and authenticity (versus pretense and sincerity).

I introduced the concept of "Value" versus "Waste" from the customer's perspective and facilitated an eye-opening brainstorm session on what customer value my group really provides.

I introduced the conversation meter by way of a real-time dialog example with my team at our group meeting. The example could not have been better to explain the "Sincerity" type.

Used the process to map out my approach to working with my co-managers to agree on our combined group charter.

The team learned how the use of the RACI methodology led us to finish not only the process definition as planned but also the development of a web tool.

The effects of the Dynamic Leadership training and the efforts made by the participants also were apparent to their managers and coaches, as evidenced by their feedback:

Dear P___, First I want to thank you for investing time in your continued development. It is often one of those things that we let fall by the wayside . . .

Dear J___, Good job on streamlining the Project Review process. Can you also ensure that the linkages with our review process are clearly defined? This will also help to gain alignment all around . . .

Dear D___, I appreciate the facilitation of the decision process discussion. It was amazing the number of subprocesses that require decisions. . . . I have a much higher level of confidence about our ability to get to a good decision through the use of this model.

Dear B____, I think you are doing terrific work here, but don't let it stop at this. Transformational leadership is about visioning a compelling future, modeling that future, and gaining followers.

Dear G___, You made important progress in sharing the tools with your teams and key people! I believe that after you obtain the measures you are planning to do, you will find other opportunities for reducing the time spent in meetings . . .

In the tenth week following the program, participants were asked what they had found most useful from the program. Over half of all comments mentioned the conversations tools and the closely related concepts of shared purpose and intersections (Exhibit 7.3).

## Three-Month Post-Program Financial Analysis

Although the follow-through process provided ample anecdotal evidence that the program was having a positive impact at HP, it did not provide the quantitative data necessary to prove the return on investment with the rigor needed to satisfy HP's discerning financial managers. To quantify the impact of the program, HP worked with the Fort Hill Company (Wilmington, Delaware) to design an analysis system that could be administered after each participant had sufficient on-the-job experience with Dynamic Leadership tools to have produced results.

Three months after attending the Dynamic Leadership program, participants were asked to indicate how frequently (if at all) they had used the Dynamic Leadership tools. They also were asked to describe, if possible, a specific example in which this created value for HP and to provide details of quantifiable benefits, such as hours saved, new revenue generated, or costs avoided. In evaluating the program's financial impact, only specific examples for which there was good documentation and a sound basis for determining worth were included. No attempt was made to ascribe value to important, but difficult-to-quantify benefits such as increased morale, better quality, or enhanced customer satisfaction. Hence, this analysis underestimates the total return from the program.

The value generated by the program was calculated by multiplying the median value of reported events by the number of reported uses of program material, then discounting (75 percent) for positive reporting bias. The median value of reported events (rather than the average) was used in the analysis to avoid undue influence of a small number of very high-value instances. The return on investment (ROI) was calculated by comparing the value generated to the full cost of delivering the program, including the per hour cost of the attendees' time.

The results overwhelmingly supported the value of HP's investment. Key findings reported to the board of directors included

- *The training was practical and useful on the job.* Ninety-four percent of participants reported that they had used the Dynamic Leadership tools to advantage in the first three months after training. The average participant used the tools 9.5 times during the follow-through period.

- *The program produces a significant return on investment.* The median value per single reported application was $3,800—50 percent more than the fully-loaded cost. On an annual basis, the return on investment is 15 times cost.

- *Most of the immediate benefits were attributable to time saved in reaching decisions and gaining alignment.* Perhaps most remarkable, these results were achieved in the midst of the disruption of one of the largest reorganizations in corporate history: the HP-Compaq merger.

HP's executive council took the bold decision to push forward with Dynamic Leadership despite the inevitable uncertainty and turmoil that would accompany the HP-Compaq merger. Their vision has been rewarded not only in financial terms but also by frequent mention of many real but not readily quantified benefits, including improved customer service, higher quality, and better morale. Especially rewarding are the comments shared by participants during the wrap-up session. Many expressed the feeling that this program has helped restore their faith in HP and their commitment to the company. One manager wrote, "It has renewed my strong interest in team development. I have volunteered to become a coach and use my background in TQC and process improvement again." Similar sentiments were echoed in two feedback sessions held with core line managers; they reported a renewed sense of optimism and commitment among attendees. Dynamic Leadership provided a common language that colleagues from both parent companies could share.

# CONCLUSION

The case reported here—the introduction of Dynamic Leadership methodology at HP—demonstrates that a well-designed and well-executed learning program with strong senior leadership support can produce significant and measurable results. The positive ROI for the Dynamic Leadership program reflects its practical focus, thorough planning, well-managed implementation, rigorous post-program follow-through, and ongoing assessment. Further opportunities to create value include extending the program to additional managers and developing complementary programs focused on other key management skills.

Exhibit 7.1. The Follow-Through Process for Dynamic Leadership

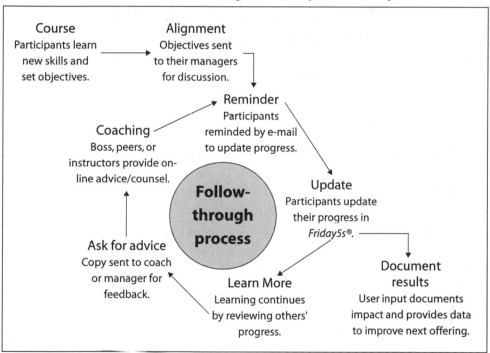

*Note:* At the conclusion of the program, participants set goals to apply what they had learned. These were sent to their managers. Then on five occassions following the program, participants were asked to update their progress, share insights with others, and continue their learning.

Exhibit 7.2. Distribution of Follow-Through Objectives in Dynamic Leadership Programs

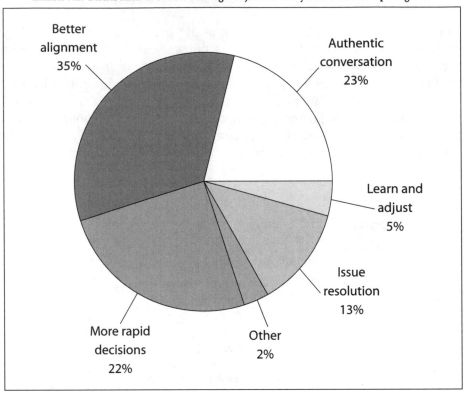

*Note:* Distribution of 13,720 DL Objectives; the distribution of goals matches the design objectives.

Exhibit 7.3. Distribution of Most Valued Aspects of Dynamic Leadership Programs

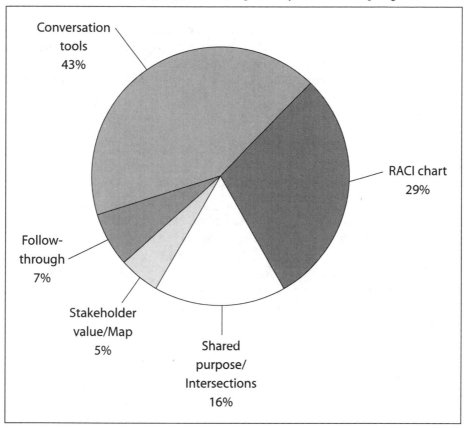

*Note:* Distribution of 400 Responses to the Question: "What Have You Found Most Valuable from the Dynamic Leadership Program?" (after ten weeks).

# ENDNOTES

1. Hewlett-Packard, Inc., *Dynamic Leadership Learning Journal,* 2002.

2. Hewlett-Packard, Inc., *Dynamic Leadership Learning Journal,* 2002.

3. Connolly, M., and Rianoshek, R. *The Communication Catalyst.* Chicago, Ill.: Dearborn Trade Publishing, 2002.

4. Goldsmith, M. "Ask, Learn, Follow Up, and Grow." In *The Leader of the Future.* San Francisco: Jossey-Bass, 1996, pp. 227–240.

5. *Friday5s®*, Fort Hill Company, Montchanin, Dela. www.ifollowthrough.com

6. Kirkpatrick, D. L. *Evaluation of Training Programs,* 2nd ed. San Francisco: Berrett-Koehler, 1998.

# ABOUT THE CONTRIBUTORS

**Susan Burnett** leads workforce development for Hewlett-Packard. The organization's mission is to develop the most competitive and committed workforce in the world as determined by its customers. Most recently, she served as Hewlett-Packard's director of enterprise workforce development, the first integrated training capability for HP that brought together over seventy decentralized training organizations in five businesses, seventeen product categories, four regions, and ten functions. Prior to this role, Susan was the director of Global Learning, an organization that developed and delivered employee, management, and executive development. Before moving into her corporate roles, Susan was the manager of organization effectiveness for the Business PC organization of HP, where she led the management team's process for creating a new go-to-market model and organization design. Susan also served as staff to the CEO and executive committee of HP, facilitating the cultural, management, and leadership changes needed for HP to continue value-creating growth. Susan's twenty-year HP career also has included seven years in line management positions in global marketing and sales support. She was an elected member to the ASTD board of directors from 1997 to 1999, an officer of the board from 1999 to 2000, and the chairwoman of the board in 2001. Susan has a B.A. from Simmons College and a master's in education technology from Columbia University.

**Calhoun Wick,** founder and chairman of Fort Hill Company, has spent over two decades studying how managers develop and businesses learn new capabilities. His research led to the development of *Friday5s*®, a unique web-based solution that helps companies motivate follow-through action from learning and development events and measure results. Cal is a nationally recognized expert in turning corporate education into improved business results and has published a book on the subject. Cal earned a masters of science degree as an Alfred P. Sloan Fellow at MIT's Sloan School of Management. He graduated as a Rockefeller Fellow from Trinity College in Hartford, Connecticut.

# CHAPTER EIGHT

# Honeywell Aerospace

*The following case study will examine the path of Honeywell's successful Aerospace businesses in leveraging Six Sigma as the core productivity strategy that will fuel its aggressive growth plans. It examines how Honeywell has successfully evolved Six Sigma from a process improvement initiative to a fundamental component of its leadership system. Honeywell is achieving this end-state with the powerful combination of Six Sigma, lean, and leadership. Throughout the chapter there will be practical points to highlight key areas and issues.*

OVERVIEW                                                                                      196

INITIATIVE DU JOUR: ANOTHER ATTEMPT
AT SEATBACK MANAGEMENT                                                                        196

THE JOURNEY OF CHANGE                                                                         198
    A New Family Member                                                   198
    Bringing Them into the Fold                                           199
    Another Merger Attempt: The Burning Platform                          199
    The Missing Ingredient                                                200
    Figure 8.1: Divergent Expectations                                   201

SIX SIGMA: AN ENCORE PERFORMANCE                                                              202
    The Vision                                                            205
    Figure 8.2: Business Y Model                                          207
    Figure 8.3: Project Selection Model                                   209
    Selecting Talent                                                      209

CHANGING THE DNA AT ALL LEVELS                                                                210
    Exhibit 8.1: Changing the DNA at All Levels                           211

ABOUT THE CONTRIBUTORS                                                                        212

# OVERVIEW

In the aggressive world of Fortune 500 firms there are certain associations that are assigned to a company after a substantial period. As time passes the company earns a reputation with their customers, industry peers, and Wall Street. Honeywell International, Inc. over the past decade has gained a clear reputation for having a culture of execution and productivity. This legacy has the distinct fingerprint of its former chairman and CEO, Larry Bossidy. The challenge that faces this industrial giant today is how to translate that productivity into a true growth engine that will perpetuate Honeywell to an even greater level of performance. This is one of the greatest challenges that faces the current chairman and CEO, Dave Cote.

Honeywell International Inc., is a diversified technology and manufacturing company, serving customers worldwide with aerospace products and services, control technologies for buildings, homes, and industry, automotive products, specialty chemicals, fibers, plastics, and electronic and advanced materials. This well-known industrial company has a rich heritage of successful aerospace companies in its pedigree, including Sperry Flight Systems, Garrett Turbine Engines, Air Research, AlliedSignal, and now Honeywell.

In the mid 1990s Larry Bossidy brought a new way of thinking to what was at that time AlliedSignal. Looking back, business has never been the same for this company since Bossidy breathed life into the Six Sigma initiative and created a healthy passion for productivity. Since that time AlliedSignal and the companies it has acquired have continued to gain momentum at a rate much greater than the majority of their industrial peers. Today, after a successful merger combination, Honeywell has positioned itself as one of the leading Six Sigma companies in the marketplace. It is well positioned to take advantage of this discriminating core competency to attract new customers and new talent and drive profitable growth.

# INITIATIVE DU JOUR: ANOTHER ATTEMPT AT SEATBACK MANAGEMENT

When Larry Bossidy decided Six Sigma was going to be the new initiative that would create unlimited opportunities for improved quality, on-time delivery, and productivity, you can only imagine the groans from the audience: "Great, another seatback initiative." A seatback initiative is what happens when the CEO reads a magazine from the airplane seatback in front of him on a trip and decides he wants to try a little experiment on the business when he gets back to the office. Well, it didn't take too long for the employees to realize this initiative had much more staying power than most people would have imagined.

As always, launching a large-scale change initiative is difficult at best, particularly if the organization has already launched several "false starts" with a similar look and feel. Total Quality was the rave of the 1980s, and this Six Sigma program sounded curiously like a similar game with a different name. As expected, when Bossidy first began the implementation of Six Sigma it was driven with a typical Bossidy fashion and aggressive deployment. Failure was not an option and resistance futile. Bossidy's zeal for Six Sigma was without a doubt exactly what the company needed to get this initiative off the ground and on the radar screen of every leader and employee.

*Practical Point One: All change encounters resistance. The more people are pushed to change, the more they will push back. People don't mind change as much as they mind being changed. Zeal and a strong business case are essential ingredients for effective change. Resistance needs reason. People need to see why the change is important for the company and themselves. Are we clear why the change is needed? Are we communicating the reason in a clear, simple, and compelling message and format? Do we have the commitment needed to make the change despite the resistance? What do we need to do better?*

What commonly follows the rollout of initiatives with such strong senior management support is a sudden but veiled adoption of the initiative evidenced by the inclusion of the initiative in every leader's annual goals and objectives. In addition, you now begin to see the Six Sigma language appearing throughout presentations and reports across the business. *Wonderful,* you might think. I have what most initiatives would die for, senior management support. What else could I possibly ask for after achieving this milestone? True acceptance would be one key component that comes to mind! Not too many leaders would be so bold as to stand up to the chairman and tell him or her that they do not accept Six Sigma as a critical element to achieving their aggressive business objectives. No one would make such a career-limiting decision—at least not openly. While many stood up and cheered for Six Sigma on the outside, they were sitting down on the inside and hoping this, too, would pass.

*Practical Point Two: Once the business case is understood and the vision is clear, the next and more difficult challenge of effective change is forging agreement on the new behaviors. New visions require new behaviors. In order to build lasting change, behaviors must change. What will we do differently to create our vision? What is our agreement? Once behaviors are agreed upon it becomes evident who is on board and who is not. Without behavior agreements, it is easy to feign compliance.*

# THE JOURNEY OF CHANGE

So the change journey began. Although many leaders were less than completely on-board with Six Sigma, vast operational improvements and excellent productivity resulted from this new methodology. Six Sigma was added to the operational excellence toolkit and didn't appear to be leaving any time soon. From 1995 to 1999 AlliedSignal, Motorola, and GE became the three large industrial firms to implement Six Sigma across their companies. During this time AlliedSignal began to create an excellent Six Sigma technical training program that was second to none. It continued to grow in its breadth and depth of Six Sigma knowledge, experience, and personnel. Once Bossidy saw significant improvements in the manufacturing area, he began creating an urgency to drive Six Sigma into all aspects of the business: "It's time to stop paying lip service to moving Six Sigma beyond the factory floor and simply do it—the potential here is huge."

## A New Family Member

The year 2000 would prove to be a great challenge for Honeywell Aerospace. The Aerospace business nearly doubled in size with the completion of the AlliedSignal-Honeywell merger. Now the Aerospace leadership team needed to bring the former Honeywell Aerospace employees up to speed with Six Sigma and how it would be used to drive productivity and help the company realize the merger synergies and cost savings they promised to the Street. The former Honeywell Aerospace business was not new to process improvement, it was, however, new to Six Sigma. Honeywell had used the Malcolm Baldrige model as its framework for continuous improvement and for the most part had made significant improvements in many areas of its business. In an attempt to combine the best of both worlds, a team was put together to understand whether there was room for both improvement initiatives to live under one roof. The team determined that a marriage between Six Sigma and Baldrige was plausible. It was clear that if you properly deployed the Baldrige model as the assessment tool to diagnose where your business needed improvement and then used the Six Sigma methodology to generate the process solutions, you would have a winning combination. As you can imagine the personal biases and emotional energy around the two sides of the tug-of-war line were *huge*. This was a hill that people were, in fact, willing to die on. It was seen by many as dilutive to focus on two improvement initiatives. As often happens in large industrial mergers, initiatives that are viewed as competing will ultimately end with someone losing and someone winning. This was no different, once the determination was made that Six Sigma would be the overarching improvement initiative and the Baldrige model "could" be used as one of many supporting tools in the toolbox, the proverbial writing was on the wall. Several pilots were conducted to determine the practicality of combining both initiatives into one synergistic program. Although the two could have complemented one another and made a reasonable marriage, it was seen as a distraction to most of the Six Sigma saints and an uphill battle to the Baldrige believers. Six Sigma was the clear choice for the go-forward improvement strategy.

*Practical Point Three: Usually the fight is not about the fight. Usually the fight is about power, politics, the fear of change, or some related matter. Consequently, it is necessary to deal with emotional matters first. A series of town meetings to air concerns, a process of dialogues to discuss competing points, or informal lunch gatherings to raise questions can help sort through these issues. It is most effective when these sessions are led by leaders who are open to comments, can hear competing points of views without becoming defensive, and have the courage to say what they know and what they don't know. When these sessions are facilitated in a spirit of openness and honesty, the emotional issues are allowed to dissipate. This dissipation permits the possibility of a true merger, mutual cooperation, and integration. It opens the way to a brighter future. Otherwise, it is more like a takeover with winners and losers.*

## Bringing Them into the Fold

Now it was time to focus on bringing Six Sigma into the former Honeywell businesses and maximize productivity across the combined bigger and better Honeywell Aerospace business. It was very evident within six months of the merger combination that former Honeywell and former AlliedSignal had a lot to offer in terms of their experience in deploying successful initiatives. Both companies understood the importance of having a standard approach and, even more important, a consistent deployment of that approach. They began by ensuring that all of the new Aerospace leaders had fundamental Six Sigma training. Many companies call this Champion training. The objective is to teach leaders the fundamentals so they can effectively influence the deployment throughout the organization. Black Belt and Lean Expert waves were initiated in 2000, and best practices were being shared across former company boundaries. Progress was beginning to take place, and customers and employees could begin to see the potential benefits of the newly combined company.

## Another Merger Attempt: The Burning Platform

By now, Larry Bossidy had fulfilled his obligation as chairman and CEO and handed the reins over to former Honeywell CEO Michael Bonsignore. Bonsignore saw the clear benefit of the Six Sigma methodology and what it could do for bottom-line performance, but before he had much opportunity to help or hurt the cause the newly formed business had underperformed in its first several quarters. Wall Street and the Honeywell board of directors did not have the luxury to see whether the situation would improve. After an attempt to attract United Technologies as a potential suitor to help bring Honeywell out of this quagmire, GE's Jack Welch stepped in and made a last-minute purchase offer that the Honeywell board of directors could not refuse.

It appeared unavoidable that another large-scale merger was on the horizon for Honeywell, albeit this one had a bit more of the acquisition-takeover mentality than that of the previous Honeywell-AlliedSignal experience. One bright spot for those who lived in the world of Six Sigma and continuous improvement was that GE had taken Larry Bossidy's advice from the mid 1990s and implemented their own very successful Six Sigma program. What GE found when analyzing Honeywell's Six Sigma program was not quite what it had expected. It found a company with dozens of highly trained Masters, hundreds of technical Black Belts, and thousands of working-level Green Belts who were all trained in the Six Sigma tools and methodologies—but something was missing.

## The Missing Ingredient

It was the leadership component. *Wait a minute . . . I thought you said Honeywell had the full support of senior management.* It did in fact have the full support of management but it did not have a leadership-driven Six Sigma model ensuring that the disciplines and behaviors of this powerful change tool permeated the business. No one would argue that Honeywell Aerospace had a very solid Six Sigma program, but it was clear that the time was right to move from a good program to a great program. It was time to exploit Six Sigma in all areas of the business, including leadership. We needed to move the leadership team from sitting in the bleachers to participating out on the field. Six Sigma has never been and will never be a spectator sport. It is all about alignment and engagement of leadership. Let's be honest, senior management cares primarily about three things—business performance, business performance, and finally business performance! And that is exactly what they should care about. Honeywell Six Sigma champions found themselves in the all-familiar trap that often accompanies large-scale change initiatives. Senior management understood and embraced the value Six Sigma brought to the table, and conversely the Six Sigma team saw a solid effort on the part of management to support the initiative. Yet often the owner of the initiative has an unrealistic expectation of management. It is often expected that management will virtually maintain a singular focus on that particular initiative. It is a huge failure mode to expect management to be consumed with the perpetuation of the Six Sigma initiative, or any initiative for that matter. There is a big difference between genuine support of Six Sigma and asking leadership to create an organization that is Six Sigma–centric. There are countless examples of the initiative having moved from being an enabler to drive improved business performance to becoming an end in itself. The Six Sigma zealots believed so strongly in Six Sigma as a measurement system, a methodology, and a strategy that they often found themselves upset at management because they were not able to recite the Six Sigma pledge or perform the secret handshake.

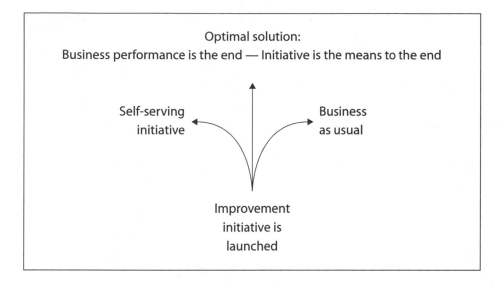

**Figure 8.1** Divergent Expectations.

Now of course you would be hard-pressed to find an initiative owner to actu-ally verbalize this approach as the actual strategy or goal, but the behaviors exhibited from the individuals driving the initiative often speak the loudest (Figure 8.1).

In some instances the exhibited behavior is asking that we rearrange or mod-ify the business model to fit within the Six Sigma model versus the correct approach, which is modifying Six Sigma as appropriate to fit within the model of the business. At Honeywell there was evidence that some forms of this behav-ior were alive and well. For example, a Black Belt would get certified and then get assigned the task to go out into the organization and find a million dollars worth of savings. What transpired would be a very excited and well-trained process expert beginning the hunt for savings. Like a bloodhound in search of its quarry, the very-well intentioned Black Belt discovers an excessive pile of inventory sitting in a particular manufacturing cell. The Black Belt then begins to hone in and lock on this as "their" million-dollar project. The Black Belt confronts the manufacturing manager and informs him or her that the inventory in the manager's area is targeted for removal. Subsequent to the dis-cussion, the Black Belt begins explaining the cadre of tools that would be used to take out the inventory enemy. Of course the manufacturing manager resists being changed. This initial meeting marks the beginning of the organizational brick wall that will be quickly built to keep out these renegade Black Belts. It is not that the manufacturing manager does not want to eliminate inventory and improve the performance of the his or her area, it is just that there is a signifi-cant disconnect in goal alignment. This misalignment causes the key stakeholder of the potential project to reject the potential benefits because it was perceived as a scud missile from out of nowhere.

Although this type of project misalignment was not an every day occurrence, it happened enough to create a cultural barrier at Honeywell that caused the Six Sigma initiative to plateau and in many regards even decline. It was perceived by many to be a self-serving initiative. One that was so focused on doing what was "right" for the business that it did not consider the most important element of a change initiative, absolute stakeholder acceptance.

*Practical Point Four: The most critical key to any initiative is building healthy coalitions. Without acceptance and coalitions there will be no successful implementation. Who are the stakeholders? Who are the people providing resources to this initiative? Who can block or veto this process? Who needs to implement it? Who will be affected? Every team needs to carefully consider the stakeholders. List the stakeholders and get to know them. It is the leader's role to make it as easy as possible for the stakeholders to say yes. If the leader does not respect the stakeholder's views, why would the stakeholder consider the leader's? First things first. Consider the stakeholders and they are more likely to consider you. Lead with the stakeholders' agenda.*

This common approach of overzealous deployment did not keep Honeywell from making countless improvements and generating very respectable productivity goals, but Six Sigma found itself slipping into the abyss of "been there, done that," nothing new or exciting here.

Now we had come full circle. The father of the Six Sigma initiative at Honeywell, Larry Bossidy, was returning to the scene. Bossidy was asked by the Honeywell board of directors to come out of retirement and help get the struggling corporation back on its feet. As Larry returned to his comfortable position of leading the ship, he quickly saw the companywide distraction that had occurred due to the GE merger attempt and the removal of CEO Michael Bosignore. Larry knew Honeywell needed an injection of energy around the struggling Six Sigma initiative. It was obvious the merger activities had a dilutive effect on Six Sigma. It was time to recharge the troops.

## SIX SIGMA: AN ENCORE PERFORMANCE

Not being new to the Six Sigma initiatives proved to be one of Honeywell's greatest strengths and one of its biggest challenges. In order for Honeywell to be successful in its revitalization of Six Sigma, it desperately needed to leverage the past years of technical knowledge and expertise while significantly beefing up the leadership component of the program. How this took shape at Honeywell's Engines, Systems, and Services business was with the renewed vigor of President and CEO Steve Loranger. Loranger was convinced that without Six Sigma becoming a game-changing strategy across his nearly $5 billion business, he would be unsuccessful in executing the aggressive strategies he had outlined for the next 2–3 years. One of the defining questions that needed to be answered was, *Is this a face-lift to Six Sigma, or is this a complete new game plan?* This was precisely the question that was asked by Jeff Osborne before he agreed to accept the challenge of leading the effort to revitalize Six Sigma at Honeywell's Engines, Systems, and Services Aerospace business. Loranger answered the question with clarity and simplicity. *We must take Six Sigma to a greater level of impact if we are to be successful in today's challenging Aerospace climate.* The mission was clear, change the game and take Six Sigma to a new level. This would not be a tweak to the current program but rather a completely different approach to how it deployed, utilized, and reinforced Six Sigma. Now that Loranger and Osborne were aligned, how would they convince over 16,000 employees that this all too familiar program was really going to be different? As the new vice president of Six Sigma, Jeff Osborne had to quickly figure out how to make sure the organization knew it was not business as usual for Six Sigma. The good news for Osborne was that this business within Honeywell was relatively agile and had the ability to make change happen at an aggressive pace. In addition, the organization was well down the Six Sigma journey and had done many things well in driving the initiative into the business.

As with any restart or revitalization program, you have to carefully assess what you did well and what you need to change. You must balance the temptation to hold on to past sacred cows with throwing out the baby with the bath water. These are the some of the clear strengths the Engines, Systems, and Services business had within its organization:

*Strengths*

- Senior executive support of Six Sigma
- Excellent technical capability
- Solid training curriculum and learning program
- Dozens of Master Black Belts (advanced practitioners) and Lean Masters
- Hundreds of certified Black Belts and Lean Experts
- Thousands of certified Green Belts
- Common Six Sigma language and terminology across the business

Many companies would be envious of this staring point. In fact, most companies invest several years and millions of dollars just to arrive at this so-called beginning. Of course the task at hand was not to initiate a Six Sigma program but to take the current one from good to great. Osborne made an interesting observation. Most of the key ingredients for a successful Six Sigma program were in place. Why was it then that the recipe was not generating the desired outcome: an unquenchable drive for continuous improvement and a demonstrated capability to sustain the improvement gains? As you probably have experienced in your own attempts at cooking, there is typically no margin for error. If you leave out even one key ingredient, the dish is compromised. Consequently, all ingredients are required to have a healthy and vibrant Six Sigma program. Beyond simply having all of the necessary components there is a bit of leadership magic required to properly bring the components together to create a compelling vision that will generate the desired end-state. So let's look at what challenges Osborne faced as he began the journey to rebuild Six Sigma at Engines, Systems, and Services.

*Challenges*

- Leadership saw Six Sigma primarily as a group of process consultants
- Training and certification had become a checkmark for most employees
- Tools were often taken to an extreme and became more important than the business issue trying to be solved
- Talent level within the Six Sigma organization had become mostly average
- Many certified Six Sigma Masters and Black Belts were leaving the company for attractive outside offers
- Projects were often self-selected by the Six Sigma resource versus business leaders
- Six Sigma in many ways had become the end-state versus the means to the end

Six Sigma momentum had waned at best. Osborne realized that at Engines, Systems, and Services the Six Sigma initiative had become way too focused on the initiative itself. Osborne's rally cry became, "It is time to take Six Sigma from being about Six Sigma activity to being about business performance." No longer would they give teams credit for simply training other teams and consulting them on how to use the tools. Now it was time for Six Sigma to rally the Honeywell leadership team and take them to a new level of performance. If there was one concept Osborne understood it was, *Leadership rallies around business performance not initiatives.*

*Practical Point Five: The only reason for a business to exist is to provide service to customers and clients. It is to create value in the marketplace. As a result, the only reason for a business to change is the customer. What does the customer need that we are not providing? How does this initiative provide more value to the customer? How can we apply the tools of Six Sigma to improve our value in the marketplace? This is the only legitimate starting point for any initiative. Everyone must "see" the customer.*

## The Vision

The process to create a new and compelling vision began by gathering data from sources inside and outside the Six Sigma organization. To do this the Six Sigma leadership team utilized the Six Sigma tools and methodology to look at the failure modes and successes of the prior Six Sigma program. Once Osborne had a good understanding of where they were (baseline), he created a clear and simple vision statement that described what he wanted from the Six Sigma efforts: "Six Sigma a core business value . . . the way we think, act, and execute." You may say to yourself, *OK, clear and simple but not overly unique.* Many vision exercises have a propensity to end up on a plaque on the wall or a poster in a building, never to be bothered with again—just one more thing checked off and put on the list of completed actions. That would not be the story in this case. Far from it—this was only the beginning, but a significant beginning it would turn out to be. The Six Sigma leadership team formulated what key components made up the desired end-state and what it would look like if they really got there. After many discussions with leaders and employees they created a clear description of where it was they were headed. It was now imperative that they define a set of clear strategies that would take them to that end-state. Also needed was a set of goals and objectives that would align with these strategies and vision. It was imperative that the overall end-game for Six Sigma was precisely that of the Engines, Systems, and Services executive team. The path to get to that end-state is where Six Sigma would make all the difference.

In order to get to the new end-state with momentum and speed, there were several key perspectives and behaviors that would create the success criteria for the new Six Sigma model.

*Success Criteria*

- Six Sigma is a mindset, not a quality program
- Six Sigma vision and strategies will be a subset of business vision and strategies
- Six Sigma organization must align directly to business and functional organizations
- Project selection must be top-down versus bottom-up
- Focus will be on application of Six Sigma tools versus certification
- Measure business results not Six Sigma activity
- Six Sigma resources should be full-time and dedicated
- Six Sigma resources must be business leaders not statisticians

- Never overstate Six Sigma benefits; math wins every time
- Six Sigma serves the business—the business does not serve Six Sigma

In order for Engines, Systems, and Services to get to a place where Six Sigma was serving the business, several factors had to be considered:

- Management will never buy into a program or initiative that is self-serving; make the objective clear and unquestionable.
- Six Sigma is the means to the end, not the end itself; avoid focusing on metrics and systems that reward the "behavior of the checkmark." For example, *Management told me I had to take this Six Sigma training class, so I will do it, get my checkmark, and they will leave me alone.*
- Speak the language of the business—language should be focused on business impact, not the perpetuation of a particular tool or methodology.
- Create business leaders, not Six Sigma leaders.
- Business *always* takes the priority over the initiative; if it is unclear to leaders and employees where the priority lies, you have already lost.
- Let your results be the compelling "why" when someone asks, *Why are we doing this Six Sigma thing anyway?* The *why* is always more compelling than the *what.*

And finally, to ensure there was full and complete leadership buy-in across the board, it was essential for leadership to have the correct perception of Six Sigma. It was determined that there were three key perceptions that Osborne wanted the executive staff to have regarding Six Sigma.

- *Six Sigma must be seen as an entrée not a side-dish.* Leadership must consider Six Sigma as a primary strategy to generate and sustain business productivity, not as an afterthought. So when teams are being formed, products are being transitioned from suppliers, and new products are being designed, Six Sigma skills and resources need to be a core component of the team design. The idea that there is a time and place for Six Sigma is a bad idea. This is why at Honeywell Six Sigma is not subordinated under quality or manufacturing. This would only limit its impact to those important but by no means exclusive functions within the business. Six Sigma has a time and a place already; the time is now and the place is every crack and crevice of the business.

- *Six Sigma must be an accelerator not an anchor.* There was a common perception within many elements of the Engines, Systems, and Services business that if you include a Black Belt in the problem you are trying to solve it will greatly slow down the process. This perception did not evolve without reason. There were many times when the Black Belt was so adamant about using each tool to the fullest degree that he or she lost sight of the need for the team to analyze the problem quickly, make a decision, and move forward. If the tools and methodologies of Six Sigma are seen as devices to hold back, hinder, or slow down the pace at which decisions must be made, it will fail in the minds of business leaders.

• *Six Sigma maturity is a marathon not a sprint.* As with any significant cultural change initiative, you can't rush the change process. You would be hard-pressed to find any professional or consultant who would suggest systemic culture change can happen in a matter of months. Since you cannot change culture but you can change behaviors, which greatly influence the culture, you can expect it to take anywhere from three to seven years to have a lasting effect on your organization. Many of us in executive leadership positions love to challenge and often short-circuit this principle. In doing so we often pay the price and end up at best with several false starts and at worst a completely failed deployment. Six Sigma must be seen as a journey that will transcend several years and often several rounds of senior leadership. We must operate with speed and agility but coupled with realistic expectations of what can be done in a year or less.

Now with this calibration, Engines, Systems, and Services was ready to drive through the rest of the rebuilding process. The process began by getting the executive leadership to agree on what the top improvement areas were that we wanted Six Sigma to address. At Engines, Systems, and Services they called these the Business Ys (Figure 8.2). Where the foundational equation for Six Sigma is $Y = f(x)$, expressed as $y$ is a function of $x$. This means that the output ($y$) that you are trying to achieve is really a function of many inputs ($x$). The premise here is that if you understand the inputs and how they affect the

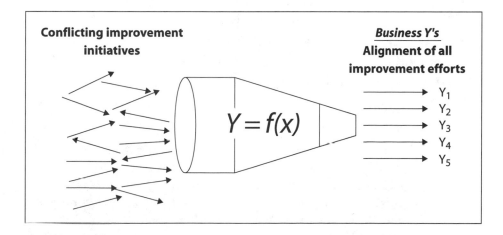

**Figure 8.2** Business Y Model.

output, you can drive an improvement in the output by focusing on the most critical inputs. The executive team agreed on a half dozen Business Ys that would be the focus for the Six Sigma organization. One of the many benefits in selecting a handful of focus areas such as the Business Ys is that you create a natural alignment for your improvement efforts. This approach allowed Honeywell to ensure that improvement efforts were not suboptimized by Six Sigma projects being performed in parallel at various locations across their global business. An executive owner was assigned to each of these Business Ys, as well as an accompanying Six Sigma leader. This ensured ownership, accountability, and congruency.

This approach proved very effective for Honeywell. It was able to align its large-scale improvement projects to these Business Ys, as well as the hundreds of Green Belt projects being performed at any point in time. The Six Sigma leader and the associated executive champion could drive improvement priorities and synthesize the organization's activities through this model. One of the common pitfalls companies run across when deploying a Six Sigma initiative is once there are a large number of Masters, Black Belts, and Green Belts across the organization, project selection is driven from the bottom up. Where this often becomes a problem is when the Six Sigma resource is driving an improvement effort that is not on the radar screen of the business leader. This is when misalignment results. Now that Honeywell had a Business Y model in place, it was able to effectively ensure that all Six Sigma improvement projects were aligned to one of the Business Ys and subsequently approved by the Business Y champions (Figure 8.3).

Helpful questions that Six Sigma leaders asked when deciding what projects to select were

- Is the project tied directly to the objective of the business general managers and functional vice presidents?
- Will the customers see the benefits if we execute this project?
- Does this project fit within current business initiatives?
- What are the consequences of *not* doing this project?
- Assuming the project is aligned to the critical business objectives, is the timing right to execute this project right now?

*Practical Point Six: The leader and executive's job is to be effective through the efforts of others. This requires making people's strengths a priority. It demands a robust system that encourages and creates a discipline of rational action. First and foremost this means a leader's job is to create a discipline of decision making and alignment. All rational action starts with a sound decision. What are we going to focus on? How are we going to measure it? What difference will this make to the customer? How can we align our resources and energies to have the*

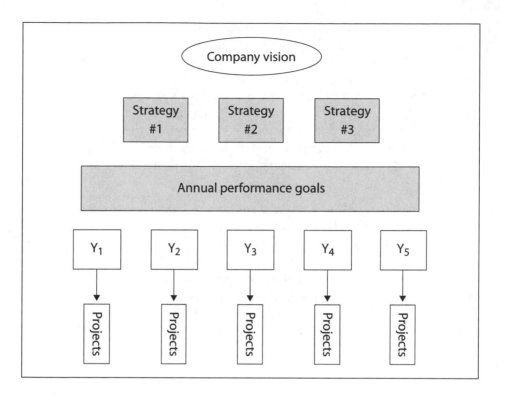

**Figure 8.3** Project Selection Model.

*greatest impact? Effective leadership begins with pertinent questions that surface relevant data and criteria. This information is the path to a sound decision and rational action.*

## Selecting Talent

Even with the best vision, strategies, and aligned projects we must not forget the most crucial piece to the puzzle. Top talent. Honeywell knew if it was going to take this initiative over the top it must recruit and develop the best talent within its business. Leadership creates vision and sets the strategy and direction. Six Sigma provides a tremendously powerful set of analytical tools and skills to create data-driven decisions. Top talent within an organization creates energy and a culture of getting things done: execution. When all three of these elements are combined, you have an amazing outcome . . .

### Leadership + Six Sigma + Top Talent = Power!

When Engines, Systems, and Services began the rebuilding process for its Six Sigma organization, it went after the best of the best. It now only brings in its top talent to fill Six Sigma positions. Whether it be Six Sigma leaders, Master

Black Belts, Lean Masters, Black Belts, or Lean Experts, Honeywell makes it an imperative that these individuals have the capability and desire to hold key leadership positions within the organization once their Six Sigma tour of duty is complete. Although many companies claim this as their mantra, Engines, Systems, and Services actually made this a reality. It spent 2001 and the first half of 2002 building a team of talent that would meet this criteria. Six Sigma Vice President Jeff Osborne puts it this way, "Many companies hire Black Belts and try to teach them leadership, we are hiring leaders and teaching them Black Belt skills." This subtle but distinct difference has made all the difference for Honeywell.

*Practical Point Seven: The most talented leaders serve with passion, commitment, and enthusiasm. They thrive on the experience of using their talents and abilities. They love being challenged. For this reason, talented people require challenging jobs. If the job does not demand their full energy, they get bored. On the other hand, no one has the talent for all challenges. Each challenge is unique. Place talented people in the wrong job and they quickly experience burnout and frustration. Consequently, talented people need the right challenge in the right job.*

# CHANGING THE DNA AT ALL LEVELS

As Engines, Systems, and Services set out to change the basic makeup of Six Sigma across its diverse global organization, it was necessary to target three employee groups. The masses would be trained and equipped via a whole-scale Green Belt program that included all salary-exempt employees—over 6,500 people. Within this population were nearly 3,000 engineers who would need a specific flavor of Green Belt training called Design for Six Sigma. This step would ensure that all engineers and supporting personnel involved in the design of a product, process, or service would use the fundamental principles of Six Sigma from the genesis of all designs. To address the unique needs of the sales and marketing and customer-facing employees, a Green Belt program was created titled Growth Green Belt, which focuses on how to use the Six Sigma skills to understand customer needs and requirements. To transform primarily the middle-level management within the business, the centralized Six Sigma organization of nearly 200 dedicated and full-time resources would be the mechanism. As these Masters, Black Belts, and Lean Experts fulfilled their twenty-four-month commitment to the Six Sigma program, they would repatriate back into other business or functional roles at the middle- to upper-middle management level. Finally, they needed to address the several hundred folks who were already in upper-management positions and would never realistically take a detour in their career to partake in one of the full-time Black Belt roles. For these individuals the Leadership Black Belt program was established. This intense program consists of the very same Black Belt and Lean tools that Honeywell's experts learn. At the end of the four-month training program and another four- to six-month project application, these executives end up with an actual Black Belt certification. This comprehensive learning program ensures that all aspects of the Engines, Systems, and Services culture is affected with the Six Sigma methodology and analytical skills necessary to achieve premier business results (Exhibit 8.1).

The best litmus test of course is whether or not a company is able to translate all of this activity around organization alignment, culture change, leadership development, and training and mentoring into tangible business improvements. For Engines, Systems, and Services the results were unquestionably positive. In the year 2002 it restructured its Six Sigma organization to align directly with the business while creating a tremendous pull from leadership to use and embrace Six Sigma resources and tools. In addition, Six Sigma organizational talent was upgraded to consist of the best and brightest Engines, Systems, and Services has to offer. The businesswide Green Belt, Growth Green Belt, and Design for Six Sigma programs have now trained nearly 6,500 employees. Over one hundred executives from the business completed the Leadership Black Belt program, and the real business benefits, including cash, operating income, and sales, far exceeded management's expectations and positioned the

**Exhibit 8.1. Changing the DNA at All Levels**

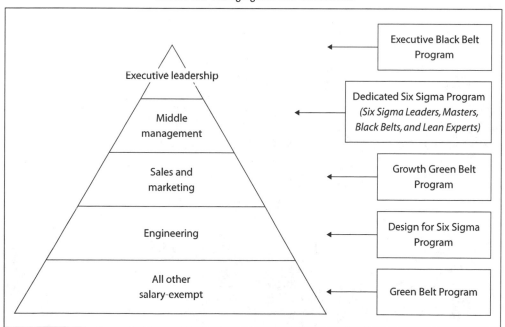

Six Sigma team well for the upcoming year. All these efforts resulted in alignment, focus, and accountability that will only continue to increase as Honeywell's Engines, Systems, and Services continues on the journey of continuous improvement.

# ABOUT THE CONTRIBUTORS

**Greg Zlevor** is the founder of Westwood International, a company dedicated to executive education, consulting, coaching, and cultural improvement, and the founder of the Leadership Project at Boston College for undergraduate students. Recent clients include Intel, Volvo, Honeywell, Johnson & Johnson, the federal government, and GE. He has published several articles and was recently published in the *Change Champion's Field Guide.*

**Jeff Osborne** has been a leader in the Honeywell Aerospace business for since 1988. During that time he has held leadership positions in Honeywell's Avionics and Engines, Systems, and Services business. Jeff has held positions in engineering, customer and product support, operations, program management, Six Sigma, and general management. Jeff is a certified Black Belt and is currently the vice president of Business Aviation, a $700 million jet engine business. Jeff holds a Bachelor of science degree in electrical engineering from Arizona State University.

CHAPTER NINE

# Intel

*This case study describes the systematic approach employed by Intel Corporation's Fab 12 Organization Development Team (ODT) to successfully launch an innovative, nontraditional way of developing leaders.[1] The ODT works at the manufacturing-site level (not corporate), responding to specific challenges at Fab 12. Applying a rapid prototype design strategy, the ODT delivered an in-depth leadership development program, the Leadership Development Forum (LDF), using self-reflection and Action Learning as its primary learning methods.*

| | |
|---|---|
| OVERVIEW | 214 |
| INTRODUCTION | 215 |
| Purpose | 215 |
| Objectives | 216 |
| APPROACH | 217 |
| PROGRAM DESCRIPTION | 219 |
| PROGRAM EXAMPLE: SESSION BY SESSION | 221 |
| Prep Session | 221 |
| Session 1: Orientation | 221 |
| Session 2: The Leadership Challenge™ | 222 |
| Session 3: Challenging the Process | 222 |
| Session 4: Building Trust | 222 |
| Session 5: Encouraging the Heart | 223 |
| Session 6: Enabling Others to Act | 223 |
| Session 7: The Vortex | 224 |
| Session 8: Inspiring a Shared Vision | 224 |
| Planning for Session 9 | 224 |
| Session 9: Modeling the Way | 225 |
| IMPACT AND RESULTS | 225 |
| Overall Results | 225 |
| Evaluation Results | 226 |

Table 9.1: Self-Assessment Results,   226
   by LDF Composite Evaluation Results
WOW! Projects™: Examples   227
Personal Testimonials   228

LESSONS LEARNED   229

CONCLUSION   230
Exhibit 9.1: Four Stages of WOW! Projects™   231
Exhibit 9.2: Leadership Action Plan   232
Exhibit 9.3: Leadership Autobiography   233

ENDNOTES   237

ACKNOWLEDGMENTS   238

ABOUT THE CONTRIBUTORS   238

# OVERVIEW

The Leadership Development Forum (LDF) was first delivered in 1998 and received an overwhelmingly positive response from participants. Every LDF since the pilot has generated a "wait list" of employees interested in improving their leadership skills. Participants of the fourth LDF program made an impassioned plea to Fab 12's senior staff requesting that the *staff* attend LDF and model the way for the factory. As a result, the entire twenty-two-member senior staff attended LDF in 2000. Since its inception, eleven LDF programs have been delivered at Fab 12 to a total of 204 middle (group leaders) and senior (department manager) level factory managers.

Although the first LDF was delivered to Fab 12 leaders only, subsequent programs have included participants from other Intel business groups in an effort to proliferate LDF throughout the company. In 2002, LDF was first piloted outside of Fab 12 to Intel's Supplier Group and Corporate Quality Group. The participants' feedback about the program resulted in an expanded pilot to proliferate LDF on a large scale. LDF is now being offered to other Intel business groups across the United States and in Asia.

In 2000, the LDF program was highlighted at the corporate Intel Manufacturing Excellence Conference (IMEC). IMEC, an annual event attended by a worldwide audience of five hundred selected Intel employees, shares papers, presentations, and exhibits to proliferate "best known methods" across the company. A rigorous selection process ensues to select the exhibits and presentations (only eighty of 1,100 are selected). The focus of IMEC is primarily technical; however, due to LDF's unique design and success it was selected for the conference. The LDF program philosophy, key components, and results were shared in a presentation following the conference's keynote speaker, Intel's vice president of manufacturing. IMEC established LDF as the premier leadership development program throughout Intel.

The lessons learned are important for anyone in any organization coping with the daunting challenge of how to develop their management's leadership abilities.

# INTRODUCTION

Throughout 1997, Fab 12's senior staff engaged in a series of work sessions and off-site meetings to clarify operational priorities and plan for the long-term success of the factory. Within the staff, this process became known as the Journey. As the Journey progressed, leadership emerged as a key concern. The majority of Fab 12's middle level managers at that time had been employed by Intel for less than three years and had very little experience leading people.

How would Fab 12 provide the necessary leadership to meet aggressive technology ramps and high-volume manufacturing demands? A corporate process to develop Fab 12's leadership potential did not exist. The only courses in existence at the time were (1) a Survey of Management Practices ©, a 360 assessment customized for Intel by the Booth Company,[2] and (2) Intel's corporate off-site, forty-hour management training program, Managing Through People, offered to middle and front line managers. Both of these courses focused solely on management practices, not leadership practices.

In March 1998, Fab 12's plant manager challenged the ODT to design and deliver a factory-specific leadership development program by Q3, 1998. One month later, the ODT proposed delivering the Leadership Development Forum twice a year to middle and senior level managers on a voluntary basis. LDF, a five-month program, would utilize and expand on leadership content and activities experienced in the Journey.

## Purpose

The overall purpose of LDF is to provide a learning process, not a training program, whereby participants' assumptions about leadership are challenged and their ability to affect change and meet factory performance goals is significantly improved.

LDF focuses exclusively on leadership. It makes the distinction, as noted by John Kotter, professor of management at the Harvard Business School, that leadership is about setting direction, aligning constituents, and inspiring others versus the fundamental management skills of planning, budgeting, staffing, and problem solving.

According to Warren Bennis, renowned author and professor of business at the University of Southern California, "One of the problems with standard leadership courses is that they focus exclusively on skills and produce managers rather than leaders, if they produce anything at all. Leadership is the ability to meet each situation armed not with a battery of techniques but with openness that permits a genuine response."[3]

LDF was formulated on the premise that leadership is just as much about *who we are* as it is about *what we do.* By incorporating fundamental principles of leadership experts John Kotter, Warren Bennis, Terry Pearce, Boyd Clarke, Ron Crossland, Tom Peters, Ben Zander, Joel Barker, James Kouzes, and Barry Posner into the program's design, LDF serves as an "inquiry" into leadership versus a prescription on how to lead others. The premise of LDF is that leadership is a "generative process" best described in a *Harvard Business Review* article by Tracy Gross:"During our thirty-five years of research and consulting for U.S. and multi-national corporations, we have found in senior executives, an unwillingness to think rigorously about themselves or their thinking. It is not surprising that so many executives decline the invitation to reinvent themselves. There is another choice, but it requires a serious inquiry into oneself as a leader. This is not a psychological process of fixing something that is wrong, but an inquiry that reveals the context from which we make decisions."[4]

LDF participants focus on what they are *doing* (applying leadership practices, leading breakthrough projects) and how they are *being* (shifting paradigms, focusing on relationships, stepping out of comfort zones). Participants are asked to let go of looking good and being right, and instead operate from an orientation of *leaders are learners* who are vulnerable and take a stand for what is possible. The ultimate purpose of LDF is for participants to improve themselves, their circumstances, and the lives of those around them.

## Objectives

The ODT established four primary program objectives and a firm set of expectations:

1. Participants' assumptions about leadership are challenged by defining leadership as *who you are* and *what you do,* identifying leaders as learners versus someone who knows, and demonstrating that leadership results from authenticity and self-expression.

2. Participants deeply reflect on and complete a one-page leadership autobiography describing their purpose at work, their personal values, their vision for their organization, and the legacy they wish to leave behind.

3. Participants develop and implement a leadership action plan, enabling them to apply the five practices of Kouzes and Posner's Leadership Model on a current breakthrough project and their day-to-day work.[5]

4. Participants build a strong cross-functional network among themselves.

Participants are held accountable to uphold the following set of expectations to ensure their total participation in LDF:

- Attend 100 percent of all sessions. (Participants must attend each session for the entire session, and are expected to be on time at the beginning of each session and after breaks.)

- Complete all homework assignments. (Read articles, watch videos, complete assignments.)

- Provide specific feedback to other participants and program facilitators.

- Be willing to take risks. (Try new things, don't be afraid to make mistakes, get out of your comfort zone, challenge each other.)

- Participate fully during LDF sessions and one-on-one coaching sessions.

- Listen from empty. (Come with questions versus answers, let go of showing other participants how effective you are and how much you know about leadership.)

- Speak up. (Many participants demonstrate weak public speaking abilities or are overly soft spoken; leaders speak up and are conscious of how their communication affects others.)

Though seemingly trivial, much of the success of LDF can be linked to the rigorous adherence to the program objectives and expectations. Participants who do not comply with the expectations are asked to leave the program. When people are held accountable to honor their commitments, leadership shows up. During an LDF prep session, these expectations are made explicitly clear to participants setting the stage for the tenacious work of self-reflection and leadership development.

# APPROACH

To develop LDF, the ODT adopted the following seven design strategies.

1. *Anchor LDF on the principle that leadership is a self-discovery process.* As the ODT conducted research on leadership, a consistent theme emerged: one is not taught leadership; leadership is learned. According to author and international executive coach Kevin Cashman,

"Leadership is not something people do, it comes from somewhere inside us, it is a process, an expression of who we are. It is our being in action."[6]

2. *Focus on a small number of broad leadership practices versus a long list of competencies.* A study of other Intel manufacturing sites and external programs revealed that as many as twenty-four competencies were identified as key to leadership development. Which ones would Fab 12 focus on? The ODT determined that the five leadership practices of Kouzes and Posner, which embody effective "ways of being," offered a simpler, more powerful framework for leadership than a long list of competencies.

3. *Design or modify LDF "just-in-time" session by session.* The ODT developed a shared vision that identified a high-level program schedule and key learning concepts. This allowed the team to let go of the need to have the entire program designed before the first pilot session. At the completion of each session, feedback is reviewed and inputs are incorporated into the design of upcoming sessions. This just-in-time approach allows students to benefit from sessions that are specifically tailored to meet their needs.

4. *Offer LDF as a volunteer program.* Each Fab 12 department is allocated "volunteer slots." Managers are responsible for reviewing the program with their group leaders and providing the ODT with a list of interested candidates. This process fosters real commitment; only group leaders and managers truly interested in developing their leadership abilities participate in LDF.

5. *Apply Warren Bennis's Innovative Learning Methods to the design of LDF.*[7] This method advocates that learning is most effective when it is active and imaginative. Listening to others and shaping events, rather than being shaped by them, are the cornerstones of self-knowledge. Real understanding comes from reflecting on experience. This approach was adopted as the premise for all design decisions. Each session was designed to allow time for dialogue and feedback in order to allow the students to learn from one another. All sessions include action learning, whereby students get to practice what they are learning, and end with the sharing of how they will apply their new learnings on the job.

6. *Deliver LDF on-site over an extended period.* Attending a program on-site is convenient, is cost effective, and builds peer relationships across factory departments. Ninety percent of LDF is delivered on-site. One-time events inundate participants with theory; seldom do they allow participants the opportunity to practice new behaviors over an

extended period. Leadership development has the most impact when it is embedded into the day-to-day lives of managers. Thus, LDF is delivered weekly over a five-month period, allowing new leadership behaviors to become habit and have lasting impact.

7. *Have ODT members serve as facilitators and coaches.* As facilitators, the ODT provides a process and environment for learning. As coaches, the ODT serve as sounding boards for participants, rather then act as job content experts. As coaches, the ODT's role is to help participants see things differently, say what they're going to do, then do what they say. Coaches get participants to self-reflect and solve their own problems by asking questions, providing feedback, and giving assignments that open their minds to new possibilities.

# PROGRAM DESCRIPTION

Program materials are updated and delivered at the start of each session. Participants are given a binder that provides an archival system for program materials, software, leadership articles, schedules, and evaluations. Participants are placed in cross-functional "learning groups." Typically, eighteen participants are divided into three learning groups (six participants per group). Participants remain in these learning groups throughout the duration of the program.

Each learning group is assigned an ODT facilitator or coach. This coach conducts four to six meetings with each learning group participant throughout the program to provide coaching, feedback, resources (that is, books, articles, and videos), encouragement, support, and advice specific to their leadership development needs. In the LDF prep session, the coaching role is explained, and coaches ask the participants for their permission to "press in" and challenge their thinking. Each coaching relationship is built on mutual trust and respect and a willingness to be vulnerable and self-expressed. Coaches offer 100 percent confidentiality in all their interactions with the participants. Since the beginning of LDF, the coaching sessions have been described by participants as the most valuable part of the program. Frequently, students request that the coaching sessions continue long after the LDF program has ended.

To foster accountability, LDF sessions begin by having each participant briefly update their learning group on what they have done (the *doing* of leadership) and how they have conducted themselves (the *being* of leadership) between sessions. How have they led, influenced, or moved their projects or teams forward? How have they shifted their thinking? What risks have they taken? What mistakes have they made? What relationships have they built? What personal breakthroughs have they experienced?

Based on these discussions, participants vote (secret ballot) to identify one winner from their learning group to receive the Leadership Breakthrough Award (LBA), an eighteen-inch trophy with pillars depicting the five leadership practices. The learning group winners share their stories with the entire class and display the trophy on their desks until the next session, where the process is repeated. At the conclusion of LDF, each learning group selects one person who, throughout the entire program, has developed the most as a leader, and that person is awarded the LBA permanently.

Participants complete a self-assessment at the end of the program. The assessment measures participants' ability to apply the five leadership practices of Kouzes and Posner in their day-to-day work. A chart is posted with a matrix listing the five leadership practices and a six-point rating scale (1 = beginning, 6 = mastery). Participants score themselves "publicly" against the leadership practices and then discuss the results.

Participants use three key tools throughout the program.

1. WOW! Projects[TM] [8] (Exhibit 9.1). Participants identify a specific project they will complete during LDF that links to operational goals and requires participants to *lead* and enroll others to take action. WOW! Projects[TM] need to be audacious in scope, have measurable results, have huge impact, and demand a personal breakthrough for success. WOW! Project[TM] efforts are discussed regularly in class and during coaching sessions. Participants hold each other accountable on actions with regard to WOW! Projects[TM] and offer advice and support to members of their learning groups.

2. Leadership Action Plan (LAP) (Exhibit 9.2). The LAP is a one-page planning document referred to and updated by participants throughout LDF. As participants learn, reflect, and commit to actions or new behaviors, the LAP acts as a tracking and accountability system. Action plans for each leadership practice are recorded on the LAP and participants are held accountable to complete their plans. At the beginning of each session, participants share actions they have taken on their LAPs with their learning groups while obtaining feedback and encouragement. LAPs are also discussed with facilitators in coaching sessions and are used as a coaching tool.

3. Leadership Autobiography (Exhibit 9.3). The leadership autobiography is a one-page self-reflection tool that participants complete over the duration of LDF. Key questions prompt the participants to clarify their values, what they stand for as a leader, experiences that influenced who they are, the vision they have for the organization they manage, and the leadership legacy they intend to leave behind.

The ODT delivers 80 percent of the program's content and utilizes consultants to deliver the remaining 20 percent. The ODT develops strong partnerships with consultants and contracts up front with them to ensure that materials and learning processes can be adapted to best fit the needs of the participants. This ensures that external consultants will be well received by the participants, and that LDF program objectives are met.

On average, a 20 percent redesign has been completed for each program offered. To manage the redesign process in an effective manner, the ODT adopted the following method. First, storyboards are used to build conceptual maps of the overall process and content for each session. Second, a detailed session agenda is developed, including a materials checklist and room designs. Third, the OD team conducts a detailed "dry run" prior to each session.

# PROGRAM EXAMPLE: SESSION BY SESSION

## Prep Session (3 Hours)

The ODT and participants introduce themselves, a video is shown highlighting the LDF experience, program objectives and expectations are reviewed, and an overview of LDF is presented. Participants are informed that they will complete a WOW! Project™, use action plans, write a leadership autobiography, and complete a Leadership Practices Inventory (LPI).[9] The facilitator's role as coach is explained in detail, and participants are made aware that they will be going on an overnight camping trip where activities will be "challenge by choice." Past graduates share the impact LDF has had on them, discuss how to get the most out of LDF, and answer participants' questions. Participants are encouraged to rethink their commitment to the program, and let the ODT know if they choose not to go forward so interested candidates on a waiting list can attend the program in their place.

## Session 1: Orientation (4.5 Hours)

Fab 12's plant manager welcomes participants, and learning groups complete inclusion activities. A presentation is delivered making the distinction between leadership versus management, emphasizing that LDF will focus exclusively on leadership. Participants share their WOW Projects™ ideas, challenge each other against the criteria, and advise each other on how to make their projects successful. In learning groups, participants are videotaped responding to questions regarding their leadership. Without prior knowledge of the questions, participants are asked (1) *What is your vision for the organization you lead?* and (2) *If your title and authority were taken away, why, specifically, would anyone want to be led by you?* After videotaping, the groups discuss the importance of vision and their reactions to their own and other's vision statements. Participants are expected to view the video before the next session, using it as a feedback tool.

## Session 2: The Leadership Challenge™
## (9 Hours, Split Over 2 Half Days)

A guest speaker from the Tom Peters Company[10] presents an overview of the Leadership Model of Kouzes and Posner. In learning groups, participants share personal stories describing their best leadership efforts. Leadership Practices Inventory results are explained and delivered (group profile and individual reports). One-hour modules are delivered on each leadership practice: enabling others to act, challenging the process, inspiring a shared vision, encouraging the heart, and modeling the way. These modules include video case studies, dynamic learning activities and simulations, dialogue, self-reflection, and action planning. Participants review video footage taken of them presenting their visions in Session 1, and then provide each other feedback on the impact of their visions. Participants observe their direct reports in a focus group discussing the type of leadership they feel is needed at Fab 12. Afterward, participants and their direct reports meet individually to review their initial leadership action plans and get feedback.

## Session 3: Challenging the Process (8 Hours)

WOW! Projects™ are introduced as a powerful method for challenging the process. Tom Peters' WOW! Projects™ concepts are shown via the Internet from selected video segments from the Ninth House® Network Innovation: WOW! Projects™ Course.[11] Participants transform current work into WOW! Projects™ by applying four key elements: create, sell, execute, and move on. Participants create a "quick prototype" of their project and develop a "pitch" to enlist sponsor support. Participants practice "selling" this pitch in triads, receive feedback, and incorporate the feedback into a new "pitch." Progress on WOW! Projects™ is discussed in subsequent LDF sessions and in coaching sessions with facilitators.

## Session 4: Building Trust
## (1.5 Days Plus Overnight Camping Trip)

This session is co-facilitated by the ODT and Venture Up.[12] Participants depart from Fab 12 and caravan to a remote campsite. Learning groups travel together, one group per van, to foster team building. Upon arrival, participants are blindfolded and told to erect tents in an activity led by a group member who is not blindfolded. Participants debrief the tent activity, have dinner, then assemble at learning group campfires to discuss "what will success look like" for the following day. Personal values and leadership legacies are also shared at the campfires. On day two, Venture Up conducts a "high ropes safety orientation," and participants caravan to a rock-climbing location. In learning groups, participants rappel down and climb up rock formations as team members coach and support each other on rope systems. Lunch is served, and participants discuss trust as a key element of leadership. A celebration is held where groups share key learnings, then learning groups return to Fab 12.

## Session 5: Encouraging the Heart (4.5 Hours)

The impact of encouragement is discussed and a Fab 12 produced video is shown highlighting the difference in perceptions that managers and subordinates have regarding encouragement. Participants read excerpts from *Encouraging the Heart, a Leader's Guide to Rewarding and Recognizing Others,*[13] emphasizing that encouragement means being authentic, expressing our emotions, and being sincere. Participants discuss what kinds of encouragement they have received and the impact the encouragement has had on them. A video case study (Tom Melohn, North American Tool and Die)[14] is presented that identifies seven key essentials for encouraging the heart: set clear standards, expect the best, pay attention, personalize recognition, tell the story, celebrate together, and set the example. Participants write letters of encouragement to coworkers, share them within their learning groups, and are given the assignment to deliver the letters and observe what happens as a result. In learning groups, participants encourage each other and acknowledge the contributions each other has made to the group by presenting certificates containing individual rock-climbing photos taken during Session 4.

## Session 6: Enabling Others to Act
## (11.5 Hours, Split over 2 Days)

During this session, participants explore ways to enable others through developmental conversations. Career Systems International's[15] "5 L Model of Developmental Coaching" is introduced, including Listen (to the desires of the employee), Level (give feedback and reflect on development needs), Look Ahead (discuss how future trends affect the employee), Leverage (analyze options and contingency plans for enrichment), and Link (provide networking opportunities). Participants receive tools from Career Systems International, which include a coaching survey, motivational survey, interest cards, conversation cue cards, and a networking map. The session focuses on utilizing these tools to discuss employee interests and development. Participants use the tools to practice having developmental conversations with each other. Each participant develops a plan for a developmental meeting with one of their direct reports during the session, as well as a plan for their own developmental conversation with their manager. On the second day, direct reports (invited previously) join the participants for a fifty-five-minute individual development conversation; then they participate in a debriefing about the effectiveness of the those meetings. The session then switches from an individual focus to a team focus. The remainder of the session is devoted to enabling teams. Participants view *The Unified Team*[16] video and have a discussion about the concepts presented. They self-reflect about their own team's performance and, using a team survey, they create and share action plans to better enable their own teams.

## Session 7: The Vortex (8 Hours)

Participants improve their ability to work effectively across individual, group and organizational boundaries, through a simulation experience. The ODT facilitates the Vortex Simulation™,[17] where participants are assigned roles in a new organization, called the Vortex. Participants are divided into departments of leaders, marketers, designers, analyzers, and builders. To succeed in this new organization, participants must interact effectively with the other departments in the organization, create and share an organizational strategy, gain an understanding of the "big picture" environment (instead of departmental focus), and create a feedback system. Throughout the simulation, more complexity is introduced by giving selected departments new market data, changes in demand, and changes in direction for the company. At specified intervals, debriefings are held, new models for organizational effectiveness are introduced, and participants make leadership recommendations to improve the effectiveness of the simulated organization. Participants complete "reflection logs" requiring them to be introspective about how this experience relates to their work at Intel. A final debriefing is held in learning groups to discuss key learnings and develop action plans for applying their insights as leaders at Fab 12.

## Session 8: Inspiring a Shared Vision (6 Hours)

Inspiration is discussed as a key component of an effectively communicated vision and is generated by a leader being authentic in his or her communication. The ODT introduces participants to a collection of articles and readings that pose the question: *How authentic are you?* Participants view video clips and movie scenes to assess the impact that passion, authenticity, and vulnerability have on leading others. Participants define the barriers that stop them from voicing their true convictions at work and discuss ways to overcome these barriers. Participants practice communicating authentically, and are videotaped sharing their visions with their learning groups. Participants model how they would inspire others around their vision and provide feedback to each other on the impact of their message.

## Planning for Session 9 (4 Hours, 2 2-Hour Lunches)

Participants meet without the ODT to plan their presentations for Session 9.

### Session 9: Modeling the Way (4 Hours)

Participants invite their managers, peers, and direct reports to an open forum, where they deliver a presentation that describes their LDF journey, results they achieved both operational and personal, and what they are committed to as leaders. A question-and-answer session between the attendees and participants is conducted, and then participants move to a separate room for a celebration. A Ben Zander video is shown, *Leadership, an Art of Possibility*,[18] emphasizing that leadership is about creating "possibility" in others. In learning groups, participants share their key learnings and the results they have produced as a result of LDF. One person is selected by secret ballot from each learning group as the person most deserving of the Leadership Breakthrough Award. Learning groups conduct a roundtable process whereby participants receive recognition and encouragement from each other. Participants receive a framed copy of their leadership autobiography, a book called *Flight of the Buffalo*,[19] and a LDF watch with the words *inspire, challenge, model, encourage,* and *enable* inscribed on the watch face.

## IMPACT AND RESULTS

Although it is always difficult to measure the results of any leadership development program, the ODT believes the following measures are indicative of the program's impact both to the organization and individual participants. The ODT uses one of Albert Einstein's famous lines as a guide to measurement: "Not everything that counts can be counted, and not everything that can be counted counts."

### Overall Results

- Forty-seven percent of participants who have completed LDF have new positions of greater responsibility.

- Self-assessment composite results show a 68 percent improvement in participants' ability to apply the five leadership practices to their work.

- Eighty-nine percent of LDF participants report a stronger and expanded network of interdepartmental peers.

- One hundred percent of LDF participants report that LDF has improved their ability to lead.

- Benchmark: when compared to nine member companies at the Q3, 1999 SEMATECH[20] Manufacturing Council meeting, Fab 12's LDF program was recognized as the most innovative, results-oriented leadership program reviewed.

- The ODT is always being asked how it measures the impact of LDF. It is interesting that when the ODT asked whether LDF should be continued, 100 percent of participants who completed LDF said that it should continue in an environment of numerous operational priorities.

## Evaluation Results

Each program is evaluated in three ways (see Table 9.1). First, upon the conclusion of each program, self-assessment results are calculated representing a percentage improvement of how effectively participants are applying the five leadership practices. Second, each LDF session (content, process, materials, facilitation) is evaluated and a composite score is calculated using a six-point rating scale (1 = low value added, 6 = high value added). Third, the ODT asks peers, managers, and direct reports of LDF participants to write letters to participants recognizing changes they have witnessed in participants' leadership abilities. Often the ODT receives copies of these testimonials that publicly acknowledge the positive impact participants have had as a result of their LDF experience.

### Table 9.1. Self-Assessment Results, by LDF Composite Evaluation Results

| LDF Self-Assessment Results (percentage improvement in participant's ability to apply 5 leadership practices over a 5-month period) | LDF Composite Evaluation Results (out of 6.0) |
|---|---|
| Q1/2 2004, Program 11 = In progress | In progress |
| Q3/4 2003, Program 10 = 64% | 5.5 |
| Q1/2 2003, Program 9 = 53% | 5.6 |
| Q1/2 2002, Program 8 = 100% | 5.3 |
| Q3/4 2001, Program 7 = 58% | 5.5 |
| Q1/2 2001, Program 6 = 54% | 5.8 |
| Q3/4 2000, Program 5 = 38% | 4.4 |
| Q1/2 2000, Program 4 = 71% | 5.6 |
| Q3/4 1999, Program 3 = 56% | 5.0 |
| Q1/2 1999, Program 2 = 109% | 4.7 |
| Q3/4 1998, Program 1 = 73% | 4.9 |

The following is a recognition letter written to a LDF participant from his manager.

Cory,

I have really noticed your growth and positive change over the past couple of months. The main differences I have noticed are an increase in the passion around your work as well as your willingness to encourage the heart of those you work with. You are continuing to stretch your capabilities and are now being viewed as an expert across many factories. I really appreciate your contributions to our staff. Your leadership from within continues to make us a stronger team and is a great role model for your peers.

Best regards, Bruce.

# WOW! Projects™: Examples

## Example 1: Facilities Department Manager

- *WOW! Project™ Description.* For the past eighteen months, Arizona Facilities Operations has worked to achieve three utility systems through SEMATECH's Total Productive Maintenance program. We must rapidly accelerate our pace to complete thirty utility systems within the next three months. By channeling significantly more effort into this program we will reduce injuries, increase utility reliability, and decrease the time consumed in utility system maintenance. We will lead this implementation effort for all Corporate Services Organizations.
- *WOW! Project™ Results.* Facilities productivity doubled in three years and 2001 cost reduction goals were achieved. Factory reliability has improved by allowing 86 percent fewer "impacts" to manufacturing. As a result, Arizona Facilities Operation won Intel's Technology Manufacturing 2001 Excellence Award.

## Example 2: Finance Department Manager

- *WOW! Project™ Description.* My WOW! Project™ entailed inventing a new way to analyze and optimize the way we allocate manufacturing equipment to product lines in order to maximize Intel profitability. To help solve this problem, we created a financial model to evaluate scenarios involving complex assumptions coming from multiple Intel organizations.
- *WOW! Project™ Results.* Once we had the data needed to convince others that a change was required, we met with several key stakeholders in each organization to "sell" our hypothesis and convince them that a problem (and solution) existed. We then modified our modeling and approach based on feedback we heard from various perspectives (factories, marketing, and divisions). We suggested that we review these decisions at the product taskforce meeting with appropriate decision-makers present all at once. As a result, we've proposed new alternative supply strategies that increased Intel margin by $59 million in Q4 2000.

### Example 3: Site Material Manager

- *WOW! Project*™ *Description.* Reduce delivery time and associated costs for manufacturing equipment spare parts.
- *WOW! Project*™ *Results.* We attribute the success of the Integrated Spares Solutions (ISS) program to our involvement in LDF. As a result, we now have a reduced supply chain and have eliminated Purchasing, Receiving & Stores from the tactical procurement chain. ISS introduced an "integrated distributor" to take requirements from Field Service Engineers and deliver parts back within 60 minutes versus 15 days. Contracts currently in place project estimated savings of $20 million. LDF enabled us to challenge current methods, use a shared vision to gain multiple factory acceptances, and provide leadership, which encouraged employees to overcome seemingly impossible obstacles.

## Personal Testimonials

*I have really changed my daily focus. My focus is now on building relationships with my group versus focusing always on deliverables. This has made me a more balanced leader as evidenced by improved scores on my 360 management assessment.*
—SORT group leader

*Efforts of the Phoenix Clean Air Initiative Team (PCAIT) which I lead resulted in the Phoenix Metropolitan Area achieving three consecutive years of zero days of unhealthy ozone readings. This ensures that Fab 12 is in attainment with the Federal Ozone 1-Hour Standard, enabling the factory to make rapid equipment and process changes without additional regulatory restrictions. The PCAIT was my LDF project. The key to its success was my application of the five leadership practices.*
—Safety manager

*I found the LDF program to be more powerful than my State University's Leadership Scholarship Program. Nothing I have ever participated in has had the impact on me that LDF has. Its structure, content, facilitation, and pacing all combine to provide a thoroughly inspiring experience. As a result, I have been much more effective handling operational issues, and I am more aware of how I interact with others.*
—Materials group leader

*LDF has helped me understand the value of inspiring others. For too long, we've been losing sight of the human element in the factory. People have become a consumable resource. It's been my goal to make people feel valued by practicing techniques demonstrated in LDF.*
—Engineering group leader

*LDF is a choice you make about how effective you want to be. I have been able to shift from an overwhelming goal-pressured micro-manager needing all the details to a trusting, encouraging, and inspiring contributor.*
—Manufacturing shift manager

*LDF reinforced the difference between management and leadership. Participating in the program enabled me to see that being vulnerable is acceptable and that learning from my peers is invaluable.*
—Training manager

# LESSONS LEARNED

• *Lesson #1. Don't wait for corporate.* In a large company, there are often corporate initiatives focused on how to develop leaders. These efforts can be significant and can provide consistency while eliminating duplication. However, corporate programs can take a "one size fits all" approach, not tailored to meet the needs of its customers. At the factory level, the need to develop managers is urgent. A small team of competent individuals who understand their immediate customers' needs can move faster than corporate efforts to creatively design and implement a leadership development process. Don't wait for corporate, develop your program then share it with corporate, build it on the inside, share it with the outside. Be bold. Experts are people who started before you did.

• *Lesson #2. Continuously redesign and update your program.* LDF is successful because the ODT continuously asks, *How can we make it better? How can we enhance participants learning?* No two LDF programs have ever been the same. Sessions, content, materials, and learning processes are constantly being revised, updated, added, or deleted. If the ODT observes that participants are disengaged or resistant, he or she modifies subsequent sessions or programs to address those issues. The mantra for success is: *Design, deliver, redesign, and never stop seeking to enrich your audience's learning experience.*

• *Lesson #3. Leadership development equals self-reflection.* Is LDF about leadership or personal development? It's about both. Every aspect of your program needs to be designed around managers examining what they are doing and how they are being as leaders. Provide a variety of ways for them to see themselves (videotaping, assessments, focus groups, one-on-one coaching) and experience challenges whereby they can apply new learnings. Leadership programs need to provide numerous opportunities for authentic self-expression of vulnerabilities: that's how participants learn, and that's how participants grow. Development is not about being comfortable. Forget competency models. You can't put the art of leadership into someone. True leadership comes from the inside out.

- *Lesson #4. Three must haves:* (1) Risk—Innovate, do what's never been done at your site, take a stand for implementing a program, be relentless. (2) Support—Do whatever it takes to get key stakeholders on board (sell senior and grassroots supporters, use data to identify development needs). Don't get locked into the mindset that top management has to attend your program first—they just need to support it. Ensure key stakeholders "hear" from participants what value they are receiving. (3) Passion and knowledge—Implementing an effective leadership program requires dedicated, full-time resources. To succeed, these people must have knowledge of leadership theories, be innovative program developers aligned with the design principles discussed in this case study, and most important, demonstrate a passion for building leaders.

# CONCLUSION

Fab 12's LDF Program offers an innovative, comprehensive leadership development process utilizing unique learning methods over a five-month period. Participants embark on a journey of intense self-reflection, action learning, and coaching sessions whereby they are held accountable to apply new leadership behaviors on the job. Several participants report that they experience LDF as a personal transformation.

A rigorous redesign process based on participant feedback and the ODT's relentless effort to deliver the best learning experience of participants' careers has resulted in the continuous delivery of LDF regardless of changes in operational priorities, factory ramps, and intense cost-cutting initiatives. The ODT has achieved this while honoring the fundamental design principles and objectives on which the program was founded. LDF has provided a leadership development program that has enabled Fab 12 to meet and exceed demanding factory output goals.

**Exhibit 9.1. Four Stages of WOW! Projects™**

| 1. | Create | Find projects that make a difference!<br>Reframe projects to be memorable and have impact for your team and the organization! |
|----|--------|---------------------------------------------------------------------|
| 2. | Sell | Sell your vision to gain support!<br>Create quick prototypes, reframe your project based on your customers' needs. Get buy-in! |
| 3. | Execute | Develop and implement a plan and ensure accountability.<br>Transform barriers into opportunities. |
| 4. | Celebrate and move on | Recognize those who contributed to the project.<br>Publish your team's results.<br>Hand off your project to a steward who will carry it forward. |

*Note:* WOW! Projects™ is a trademark of Tom Peters Company.

**Exhibit 9.2. Leadership Action Plan**

Name:

WOW Project Description:

| Challenging the Process | Enabling Others to Act | Encouraging the Heart | Inspiring a Shared Vision | Modeling the Way |
|---|---|---|---|---|
| I will challenge the current situation (think outside the box) to create breakthroughs by: | I will enable others to accomplish great things by: | I will encourage others by: | I will inspire and enroll others by: | I will "model" the following actions/ behaviors to ensure success by: |

Exhibit 9.3. Leadership Autobiography

| Name | Leadership Stand |
|---|---|
| Insert Picture Here<br><br>Who I am: 8 words or less "brand" | Think about your current role at work for a moment and assume you are here to make a unique contribution. What are you here to do? What REALLY matters to you? Consider:<br><br>• Why do you come to work?<br><br>• What is your purpose at work?<br><br>• What are you passionate about at work?<br><br>• What are your convictions toward your work?<br><br>• Why are you committed to this? |
| *Personal Values* | *Personal Experience* |
| What value(s) serve as the foundation of your stand? Consider the following:<br><br>• Guiding principles that you live by<br><br>• Values you want to proliferate in the organization<br><br>• Values you hold to be so fundamental that you would keep them regardless of whether they are rewarded—they would stand the test of time and would not change | Reflect back on experiences in your life. What experiences helped shape the importance of these values for you? What experiences could you share that would convey your expertise and, at the same time, acknowledge your limitations? Consider:<br><br>• Experiences that convey your "humanness"<br><br>• Experiences that you use to engage, energize, teach, and lead others<br><br>• A story that describes what makes you tick and how you became the person you are |

*(Continued)*

Exhibit 9.3. Leadership Autobiography (*Continued*)

| *Group/Team Vision* |
| --- |
| Your vision of the future state of your group or team must give people a sense of four things: <br><br> • Why you feel things must change (your case for change) <br><br> • Where your group/team is going (a clear and powerful image of a future state that is ideal, unique, and establishes a common purpose) <br><br> • How you will get there (your business philosophy/strategy, your ideas to make the group/team successful) <br><br> • What it will take from followers, and what the payoff will be when you arrive |
| *Leadership Legacy* |
| Your "Leadership Legacy" is what you will leave behind. It is what you want to be known and remembered for. Some personal insights to consider: <br><br> • What you want to achieve at work <br><br> • Success you hope to realize <br><br> • Impact you would like to have on others <br><br> • The business/operational results you want to be known for |

**Exhibit 9.3.** (*Continued*)

| Name<br><br>Insert Picture Here<br><br><br>Who I am: | Leadership Stand |
|---|---|
| **Personal Values** | **Personal Experience** |
| | |

(*Continued*)

**Exhibit 9.3. Leadership Autobiography (*Continued*)**

| Group/Team Vision |
|---|
|  |

| Leadership Legacy |
|---|
|  |

# ENDNOTES

1. A "fab" is a semiconductor factory. Intel uses a number to designate each fab (i.e., Fab 8, Fab 11, Fab 12). Fab 12 is located in Chandler, Arizona, and employs 2,100 personnel.

2. Since 1972, the Booth Company (www.720Feedback.com) has provided a full series of role-specific management and leadership surveys.

3. Bennis, Warren. *On Becoming a Leader.* (New York: Addison-Wesley), 1994, p. 73.

4. Gross, Tracy, and others. "The Reinvention Roller Coaster." *Harvard Business Review,* November 1992.

5. Kouzes, James, and Posner, Barry. *The Leadership Challenge.* (San Francisco: Jossey-Bass), 1995. Kouzes and Posners' Leadership Model encompasses five practices: challenging the process, inspiring a shared vision, enabling others to act, modeling the way, and encouraging the heart.

6. Cashman, Kevin. *Leadership from the Inside Out.* (Utah: Executive Excellence Publishing), 1998, p. 18.

7. Bennis, Warren. *On Becoming a Leader.* (New York: Addison-Wesley), 1994, pp. 76–79.

8. WOW! Projects™ is a registered trademark of the Tom Peters Company; WOW! Projects Seminar is a copyrighted workshop (www.tompeters.com).

9. LPI (Leadership Practices Inventory), a thirty-question, 360 leadership assessment by James Kouzes and Barry Posner, assesses five leadership practices: challenging the process, inspiring a shared vision, enabling others to act, modeling the way, and encouraging the heart. LPI is a product of and published by Jossey-Bass, Pfeiffer (www.pfeiffer.com).

10. Tom Peters Company (www.tompeters.com) offers global consulting services and in-house training.

11. Ninth House and Instant Advice are trademarks of Ninth House, Inc. Innovation: WOW! Projects™ (and Capturing Brand You™ are trademarks of Tom Peters Company.

12. Venture Up (www.ventureup.com) provides interactive and outdoor adventure team-building events, Phoenix, Arizona, since 1983.

13. Kouzes, James, and Posner, Barry. *Encouraging the Heart: A Leader's Guide to Rewarding and Recognizing Others.* (San Francisco: Jossey-Bass), 1999.

14. The "Tom Melohn Case Study" is featured on *In Search of Excellence with Tom Peters* training video (BusinessTrainingMedia.com).

15. Career Systems International (www.careersystemsintl), a Beverly Kaye company, provides career development, mentoring, and talent retention tools and programs, Scranton, Pennsylvania.

16. *The Unified Team Video* highlights a leader's plan for promoting team unity, covering the need to achieve, belong, and contribute (Media Partners Corporation), Seattle, Washington. Founded 1993.

17. The Vortex Simulation designed and produced by 3D Learning, LLC (www.3Dlearning.com), an organizational development consulting service specializing in simulations since 1996.

18. *Leadership, an Art of Possibility* video features Ben Zander, conductor of the Boston Philharmonic Orchestra, who seeks to lead in order to make others powerful (www.provantmedia.com).

19. Balasco, James, and Stayer, Ralph. *Flight of the Buffalo* (New York: Warner Books), 1993.

20. SEMATECH (www.Sematch.com), located in Austin, Texas, is the world's premiere semiconductor research consortium, since 1986. Member companies such as Hewlett-Packard, IBM, Intel, Motorola, and Texas Instruments cooperate precompetitively to accelerate the development of advanced semiconductor manufacturing technologies.

# ACKNOWLEDGMENTS

We'd like to thank the people who have continued to develop the LDF program throughout other business groups at Intel: Steve Thomas, Dorothy Lingren, Brian Schwarz, Lori Emerick, Dina Sotto, Elisa Abalajon, and Mariann Pike. They have managed to transfer the LDF program in its entirety without sacrificing its quality or integrity. Other Intel employees who have facilitated the LDF Program at Fab 12 include Laurel Henkel, Paul Denham, Dennis Danielson, Louise Williams, and Tom Eucker.

# ABOUT THE CONTRIBUTORS

**Dale Halm,** a twenty-year veteran of Intel Corporation, is currently the manager of Organizational & Leadership Development for Intel's Fab 12 microprocessor factory in Chandler, Arizona. Dale holds a M.A. and B.A. in Speech Communications from Northern Illinois University.

**Janelle Smith** is the LDF Program manager with nine years' Intel experience. Prior to Intel, she was a captain in the U.S. Air Force, with a B.S. in industrial engineering from the University of Arkansas.

**Susan Rudolph,** an organizational development specialist with seven years' Intel experience, holds a B.S. in business management and psychology & social sciences from Kansas State University.

Together, Janelle, Susan, and Dale leverage their passion and commitment to personal transformation to build the leadership capabilities of Intel's managers.

CHAPTER TEN

# Lockheed Martin

*Big change, fast—that was the demand made on Lockheed Martin's tactical jet business. The alternative to meeting this change challenge was not only to lose the largest defense contract in history, but also to become a second-tier subcontractor at best, or be put out of business at worst. This is the story of how the company met this challenge. It offers readers best practices for approaching "big change, fast" when the stakes are high . . . and when the alternative might be going out of business.*

| | |
|---|---|
| OVERVIEW | 240 |
| BACKGROUND | 241 |
| A RAY OF HOPE? | 242 |
| A CULTURE OF RESISTANCE | 243 |
| SHAPING THE FULCRUM BY DEFINING CRITICAL BEHAVIORS | 244 |
| POSITIONING THE FULCRUM BY CLARIFYING ACCOUNTABILITY | 245 |
| A HOPEFUL BEGINNING | 245 |
| LEVER #1: FORMAL LEADERS BECOME TEACHERS | 246 |
| LEVER #2: INFORMAL LEADERS BECOME PARTNERS | 247 |
| CAVEATS | 249 |
| THE IMPACT? | 251 |
| YOU CHANGED THE CULTURE. SO WHAT? | 252 |
| SUMMARY AND BEST PRACTICES | 253 |
| APPENDIX | 254 |
|    Everett Rogers: Lessons from Known Studies of Diffusion | 254 |
|    Survey Details | 255 |
| EXHIBITS | |
|    Exhibit 10.1: Crucial Conversations in Six Sigma | 256 |

Exhibit 10.2: Potential Opinion Leaders' Roles in Culture Change     257

Exhibit 10.3: Survey Results     258

Exhibit 10.4: Significant Correlations Between Specific Critical
Behavior Items and Three Performance Metrics     259

BIBLIOGRAPHY     260

ABOUT THE CONTRIBUTORS     260

# OVERVIEW

What's beyond "white water?" That was the term used to characterize the competitive challenges faced by companies a decade ago. Today, the rapids are shallower, the holes deeper, the boulders bigger, and the current faster. Not only is winning in this environment harder, but losing puts a company at greater risk of making a spectacular crash. This was never more clear than in the defense industry, where the end of the cold war challenged defense contractors to win in fewer contract opportunities (for fewer dollars) . . . or leave the scene. The industry consolidation of the 1990s made the white water froth. "Win or die" wasn't a saying—it was a reality.

For a company like Lockheed Martin Tactical Aircraft Systems (LMTAS), that meant winning competitive contracts in world markets for F-16 fighter jet sales against some of the best competition worldwide. As if that wasn't enough, in 1997 the defense department announced that LMTAS was one of the two finalists in competition for what was expected to be the last manned fighter jet contract the U.S. government would give—a *$200 billion dollar contract* with a thirty-year life . . . and it was going to be a *winner-take-all* contract. This was the Joint Strike Fighter (JSF) contract competition, and the competition was not only winner-take-all, but *loser-leave-the-stage.* For LMTAS, losing this contract would put a horizon on the company's very existence—even if it won F-16 sales in world markets, F-16 sales were not a growth business, as the JSF would eventually become the product of choice on world markets.

This case study reports how Dain Hancock, president of LMTAS, recognized and responded to those challenges by gaining rapid support for change in what for decades had been a fiercely rigid organization. His leadership not only positioned the company to win worldwide F-16 sales, but more important, to win the JSF contract—assuring the survival and prosperity of the company long into the twenty-first century.

We'll use the metaphor of a fulcrum and lever to describe the strategy that Hancock eventually used. His first challenge was to shape the fulcrum—to give relevance and focus to necessary behavior change. He needed to make a clear, succinct, and compelling business case for behavior change. That case needed to articulate the behaviors that were critical to business survival—and it had to do so in a way that defied contradiction.

As we will see, the fulcrum was not enough. Although Hancock did all the right things to demonstrate the absolute relevance of behavior change, nothing happened. What he still lacked was a *lever*. The lever is what extends the influence of a handful of senior leaders throughout to organization to influence day-to-day behavior change. In the algebra of organizations, leaders represent the numerator while all others combined form the denominator. In this configuration, change can look like a mathematical impossibility. Discouraged leaders can wonder what a relative few vision-bearers can do to drive change in an organization that outnumbers them a thousand to one—or more.

The senior leaders at Lockheed Martin produced no real change until two things occurred. First, they articulated a concrete role for both formal and informal leaders (as teachers and as partners, respectively) in influencing change. This turned out to be an important change lever. And second, they implemented a method for holding themselves accountable. Only when senior leaders clarified their accountability in tangible ways and grasped these two levers did they gain traction against overwhelming organizational inertia and begin to produce real change. Note that by holding themselves measurably accountable for results and implementing these two change levers, they accelerated changes that often take the better part of a decade to occur in large companies. Evidence reported in this case shows their impact within three years, and, what is important, this success was among the factors that enabled LMTAS to win the largest contract in their industry's history—and to remain a force in the aeronautics industry.

## BACKGROUND

When Dain Hancock was named company president in 1995, it appeared he was assuming the catbird seat. The company had a large worldwide sales backlog for F-16s. In the previous two years, they had dramatically reduced costs at the same time that base production was decreasing, a first in the industry. The major customers were enthusiastic about the company's record of quality improvements, and—perhaps most important—the facility had proven itself to be a remarkable "cash cow" for Lockheed Martin.

But looks can be deceiving. As the former vice president of the company's largest product line, Hancock was aware of a far different reality: the voluminous business backlog was shrinking rapidly, with a three-year lead time for new orders and no F-16 production scheduled on the books after 1999. The factory was still limping along with 1970s vintage manufacturing technology—not surprising, since the plant had suffered from a lack of capital investment for several years. During the tenuous early 1990s in the defense industry, the previous owners' corporate strategy had become "milk the backlog and spend as little as possible." In addition, the workforce was aging, with most of the younger engineers having fallen victim to mass layoffs earlier in the 1990s and with no new hiring at the facility for almost eight years. In short, the business horizon looked bleak.

# A RAY OF HOPE?

The major product line for the company—the F-16 Fighter Jet—was also beginning to age. Consolidation and post-Cold-War contraction of the industry left little room for aging products. For this company, the message of the marketplace was clear: win the next major fighter program . . . or die. Shortly before Hancock assumed the president's office, a competition was announced for the Joint Strike Fighter—a major program with pre-purchase commitments from the U.S. Air Force, Marines, and Navy, as well as the U.K.'s Royal Air Force and Navy. Securities analysts hailed the announcement as a harbinger of which of the key companies in this industry would survive into the twenty-first century. Hancock knew that if the company failed to win this competition, all he would preside over was, at best, becoming a subcontractor to the winning company or, at worst, the organization's demise. Since the contest was announced as winner-take-all, the latter seemed like the more likely outcome.

As Hancock considered what it would take to develop a bold new product against world-class competitors, he quickly concluded that the company's 12,000 employees faced another tough tradeoff: *change or lose.* Past mindsets would run up against aggressive affordability goals and the necessity of creating the complex product for a wide range of domestic and international customers through long-distance partnerships with a host of other companies. It was clear that old ways of thinking and doing business would not suffice.

In the coming months, the president and his senior staff would try to sell a message to the workforce that changing the culture was a survival-level issue. In a straight-talking address, Hancock told the workforce, "It may not be clear to many folks, but our company damn near died last year . . . and the primary reason was our culture! We have been so inwardly focused and have inhibited new ideas to the point that we were headed down and out."

A blunt statement by Darleen Druyan, the Air Force's acquisition chief, helped Hancock put a sharp point on his message. After thousands of F-16 purchases, it might have been easy for the Fort Worth crew to assume the Air Force was in their corner. Druyan made it clear that even the Air Force wondered about whether Lockheed Martin could compete in this new kind of program when she said, "This competition is not about an airplane. It's about a management team."

# A CULTURE OF RESISTANCE

Hancock knew the culture well. He had worked his way up through the ranks under various owners of the facility. Over time he had watched as good ideas, whether incremental or monumental, were smothered while birthing. As president, he found his schedule filled with appointments with passionate agents of change who used him as a sort of bodyguard to keep from being taken out by those who were threatened by their ideas.

For example, Hancock initiated a Six Sigma—or "lean manufacturing"—effort to help drive major improvement in manufacturing processes, which had changed little since the mid-1970s. He also hoped to show the JSF decision makers by this effort that Lockheed Martin could rival their competitor, Boeing, in innovative management practices that would lead to world-class quality, on-time delivery, and low cost production. The Six Sigma effort was a critical way of demonstrating that capability.

And yet, a year into the effort there was little to show beyond a few colorful displays and a couple of pilot projects. Although the uninitiated would think that the president's approval would be sufficient aid and comfort to sustain a strategically critical program like this one, the culture had perfected a strategy to deal with just such contingencies: *slow rolling.* When authority was lacking to kill something outright, lower-level managers found ways to deliver death in the same way an alligator kills its prey: it embraces it—after a fashion. In fact, it drags it under water and slowly rolls it, over and over, until it drowns. Managers at Lockheed Martin responded to Six Sigma the same way. They openly applauded the new ideas, dragged them back to their departments, then starved them of attention, hoping senior leaders would eventually lose interest in the failed initiative and move onto the next *program du jour.*

In spite of Hancock's endorsement, little initiative was taken to implement Six-Sigma ideas. Most managers gave only lip service to Six-Sigma goals. If they did assign staff to special projects, it was not their best and brightest, but rather their "surplus." And breakthrough recommendations arising from training sessions gathered dust in in-boxes while the "real work" got done.

Month by month, the senior staff would write articles for the company newsletter, speak at the beginning of another training session, or gather all the managers and deliver another speech about the importance of the effort. In short, Hancock and his staff would find some way to apply brute force to breathe a little more life into the program.

Through this and dozens of other experiences, Hancock became convinced that for every innovative effort he fought to rescue, there were a hundred promising ideas that must be dying before they left the drawing board.

## SHAPING THE FULCRUM BY DEFINING CRITICAL BEHAVIORS

Hancock began attacking the problem of changing this culture like any good engineer. He clearly defined the kinds of behaviors that would cut away the webs of resistance that were choking innovation. We (the authors) were engaged by Hancock as consultants and advisors. Over a period of months, with our help, he and his senior staff went through a process of interviewing employees, documenting stories, and writing papers that helped them see how their culture affected their ability to meet their business challenges.

Our goal was to identify *critical behaviors*. These, in our view, were the two or three behaviors that would first, have an obvious positive impact on business performance; and second, produce a domino effect by influencing many other behaviors to change. We reasoned that the typical approach to culture change—long lists of abstract values or dozens of desirable behaviors—would lead to failure. Hancock's objective was to pick a *critical few* that could clearly be shown to drive business performance—and focus all of leadership's energy on those. The trick was to pick the right few.

After conducting focus group interviews with over six hundred employees, the senior staff began to discern patterns in the success and failure stories they heard. They began to see that a handful of negative behaviors were at the nexus of every painful story of stifled change and choked creativity. In addition, in the areas of the company where innovation thrived, a few key behaviors were universally present. For example, interviews with the few Six Sigma "pockets of excellence" turned up a few behaviors that *always* differentiated these areas from the rest of the organization. Most of these behaviors were *crucial conversations* that enabled Six Sigma progress when they were handled well, or stalled it when they were either avoided or handled poorly (see Exhibit 10.1).

Through this study process, senior leaders came to conclude that candid and open communication about specific high stakes subjects was a *critical behavior.* They concluded that if they could positively influence the quality of these crucial conversations, these conversations would have a "pulling effect" on other, nonproductive behaviors. Thus, open communication about these crucial topics became a major part of the fulcrum of the change effort.

In addition to *open communication,* two other critical behaviors emerged from this process. The first was called *personal engagement* and referred to "taking personal action to unblock obstacles that prevented effective performance." The third was called *sense of urgency,* and, as implied, was about "acting when the need existed rather than ignoring issues that needed to be addressed or escalating those issues to others who would have to address them."

# POSITIONING THE FULCRUM BY CLARIFYING ACCOUNTABILITY

Hancock's experience with the culture led him to conclude that if culture change was to be taken seriously he needed a credible way of holding senior leaders accountable. He was doubtful of the traditional "activity" measures associated with soft change efforts. For example, leaders were perfectly capable of "slow-rolling" the Six Sigma effort because they were measured only for things such as the number of people trained and the number of pilot projects implemented.

In this case they began with the end in mind. Since what Hancock wanted was real behavior change, he would hold senior managers accountable for that and that only. A brief survey was developed to measure the perceptions of change in the critical behaviors across the organization. A 10 percent goal was set and the top two levels of leadership were given eighteen months to influence change. Incentive compensation was linked directly to meeting this measurable goal, and, not surprising, change was on the radar screen for senior leaders.

# A HOPEFUL BEGINNING

We had the senior staff begin their journey by asking themselves, "What drives old behavior?" and "What will it take to foster the new behaviors?" As a result, they put in place a number of change initiatives. These initiatives included changing the values embedded in the existing appraisal system, improving dysfunctional aspects of the organization design, and expanding the leadership feedback to reflect the critical behaviors.

By early 1998, the senior staff had a clear and measurable goal, a sound way of measuring change, incentive pay tied to executive-team success, and a robust plan. After months of deliberating, Hancock announced the formal beginning of what came to be called "Workforce Vitality."

And nothing happened.

Well, actually, teams were formed to study and make recommendations to move these initiatives forward, lots of meetings were held, presentations were made, surveys were conducted, and easy, low-impact, employee-friendly changes were made. But survey scores and anecdotal evidence showed that nothing of substance was changing. That is, if one didn't count an increase in cynicism. Hancock began to conclude that Workforce Vitality, like other innovations, was being "slow-rolled."

In the beginning, Hancock used the traditional top-down approach of getting things done, and he made an enormous effort to communicate the need for change and the change strategy to the three levels immediately below the senior staff in monthly "briefings." He demanded progress reports, held review meetings, and even promised to remove those who weren't on board. Unfortunately, the president spent most of his time on the road in a high-level sales role—promoting F-16 purchases all across the globe. That left a lot of time for nothing to happen. As it became painfully clear that there was a lack of grassroots support for the change effort, he came to believe that irrespective of those institutional changes he could use brute force to implement, behavior would not change without a core of support from the ranks. The prior culture was deeply entrenched, and the hierarchical "cascade" approach to driving change was met with perfunctory compliance that whipped the masses up into little more than a yawn.

Nothing happened until leaders began to look for leverage in an entirely different way. Rather than ratcheting up the direct efforts of senior leaders to plead for change from the masses—an impossible influence challenge given the sheer number of people in the organization—we encouraged them to work instead to *influence the influencers*. To do so, they engaged two groups with irresistible day-to-day social influence throughout the organization: first, they defined a clear change leadership role for the formal chain of command; and second, they identified and involved informal leaders—the *opinion leaders* from throughout the organization.

## LEVER #1: FORMAL LEADERS BECOME TEACHERS

On our advice, Hancock and his team stopped diffusing all of their attention on the 12,000-person organization. Instead, they were encouraged to spend 40 percent of their Workforce Vitality attention on influencing the formal chain of command to engage in fostering the critical behaviors.

To begin with, senior managers ensured that their direct reports all understood the absolute necessity of changing behavior as an enabler of a JSF win. Then they gave them a specific method for influencing behavior in their own direct report teams. They would become teachers.

Over the next few months every leader in the organization held biweekly training classes with their direct reports. During these Single Point Lessons, they would teach concepts and skills for improving the quality of the conversations identified in the Workforce Vitality critical behaviors. Every two weeks, senior managers would teach a new concept to their direct reports. These students would then become teachers. After they taught the concepts to their direct reports, the cascade continued until everyone in the organization was taught.

The initial response from the chain of command to the idea of teaching ranged from stunned silence to open revolt. Managers and supervisors were appalled that they were being asked to teach. They cited two common reasons for this concern. First, they thought teaching should be the job of professionals—not engineers or plane-builders. Second, many asserted that people would widely dismiss the new skills as unrealistic because their teacher (that is, their boss) was a raging example of the *opposite* behavior.

Time turned both of these concerns on their heads. For example, research into areas that showed significant improvement in critical behaviors demonstrated that there was almost no relationship between the skill of the teacher and the degree of change that resulted from the instruction. The best predictor of change was not what happened in the training, but the dozens of spontaneous conversations that happened *between* training sessions, where leaders encouraged their direct reports to use the skills they had learned earlier and where direct reports reminded leaders of their need to use those same skills as well. By becoming teachers, leaders had placed themselves in an advocacy role for the critical behaviors. As a result, they naturally seized opportunities to coach people in day-to-day interactions that they would never have recognized had they been relieved of this role by professional trainers. So while the quality of training may not have always been stellar, the quantity of change that resulted from having leaders teach was far beyond what typically occurs when outside professionals are responsible for instruction.

The second concern—that leaders who taught one thing but exemplified another would undermine the effort—likewise proved a false concern. In fact, the areas that experienced the greatest degree of change were those where the leaders themselves had to change the most. As leaders taught, their most attentive students were themselves. In the process of preparing to teach, many became more convinced of the relevance of the new behaviors. As they came to believe the behaviors were important, those who were the worst offenders found themselves in a sticky situation. They felt excruciating dissonance when they taught one thing but modeled another. Thus, many of the "worst offenders" were the ones most likely to use the training forum to acknowledge their own mistakes. They were also some of the first to make visible attempts to improve. And with these leaders, even small adjustments to align their words and their deeds were immediately noticeable by their direct reports. A spillover benefit was that employees who saw even modest changes in their boss saw the entire culture change initiative more favorably, thus encouraging them to make changes in themselves.

## LEVER #2: INFORMAL LEADERS BECOME PARTNERS

In addition to engaging the management chain, we advised senior leaders to engage informal leaders—people whom students of change call *opinion leaders*. Opinion leaders are those whose words and actions carry great weight in the minds of their colleagues. To coin a phrase, when they speak, people listen. Hancock's team was hopeful that this strategy would invert the ratio that had augured against them. Research on how change diffuses encouraged them to think of this subset of the population (representing from 5 to 10 percent) as their primary target for influence. Consultants to the company suggested that these five hundred or so people, if convinced and engaged, were the key to gaining more rapid support of the remaining 11,000+ employees. To the senior staff this was a breakthrough idea. Influencing five hundred people seemed a much more doable task than over 12,000 had been. From this point forward, senior leaders would spend 40 percent of their Workforce Vitality efforts with this powerful group—hoping that they would in turn bring influence to bear with others (see boxed text on Everett Rogers).

We identified opinion leaders in a rather straightforward way—by asking survey respondents to identify up to three people whose opinions they most respected. A list of persons whose names were mentioned frequently was created. This proved to be an easy and reliable identification method. The names were given to willing vice presidents who agreed to pilot an "opinion leader engagement strategy."

One such person, Bill Anderson, the successor to the president's previous job as vice-president of the F-16 program, was one of the first to engage opinion leaders. Since the primary theme of the critical behaviors was candid dialogue about crucial subjects, he reasoned that engaging regularly with this influential group in a way that demonstrated they could dialogue about anything would send a powerful message to the rest of the organization. So he brought them together in groups of fifty to a hundred and laid his cards on the table.

His first step was to help them understand the role they already played as informal leaders. Anderson met with the groups of opinion leaders in two-hour orientation sessions. During these two hours Anderson worked to sell his business case for change. He helped opinion leaders see how past behavior had cost—and in the future could kill—the company. He told the opinion leaders how their peers had identified them (a tremendous compliment) and described potential roles they could play in supporting the change. Anderson made it clear that their involvement was voluntary, and that opinion leaders were not meant to become management cronies, but independent partners in change. He pledged to support of their efforts and offered to be available for dialogue on any topic of importance to them. At the conclusion of each session, he asked for interested persons to volunteer to attend an opinion leader summit, where they would work together to define ways to create change in the organization.

The follow-up summit allowed opinion leaders to dialogue with their senior leader about the need for cultural change, develop skills for positively influencing others, and identify issues that most needed to be attacked. Opinion leaders initially served as advisors to Anderson's senior staff in reviewing culture change strategies, and as conduits of meaning and intent to the rest of the organization by helping others understand more than any official communication could ever explain about these strategies.

For example, senior leaders decided to change pay policies to reflect a market-based, broad-banding model. As rumors of the changes leaked out, employee reaction was quick and negative. In the midst of the reaction, Anderson began meeting with groups of his opinion leaders for extensive conversations on the subject. In these sessions executives shared the business problems, the proposed solutions, and the inevitable tradeoffs they faced in any solution set. These dialogues created change all around the table. Based on input from opinion leaders, executives modified plans. Opinion leaders, by seeing the positive intent of leaders and appreciating the complexity of the issues, changed their opinions. While the company emerged with a better plan, it also emerged with a hundred or so highly credible "in-the-trenches" leaders who helped explain reasons and issues more deeply than the senior staff could ever hope to in an audience of over ten thousand cynical people. The leadership lever seemed to be working.

Although all opinion leaders began in this advisor-conduit role, many seized even larger leadership opportunities. Some helped formal leaders teach dialogue skills to their peers that supported the goal of creating a culture based on the critical behaviors. Others helped lead improvement efforts through Six Sigma events. Yet others took key roles in designing new performance appraisal, organization design, and hiring and selection processes that would help improve Workforce Vitality (see Exhibit 10.2 for more opinion leader roles).

This leadership strategy was proving so useful that Anderson began to meet monthly with a large group of opinion leaders. These meetings included candid dialogue about the state of the enterprise, progress of companywide improvement teams, and identification of barriers that needed to be addressed.

## CAVEATS

Most innovations have a host of unexpected consequences. The company opinion leader strategy was no exception. Once word got out that formal leaders were engaging a special group called Opinion Leaders, some managers responded with defensiveness. Early rumors pegged opinion leaders as more promotable; others saw a conflict between opinion leaders' work and the management chain. Yet others saw a lack of coordination between opinion leader groups. Because of a matrix-like organizational design (for example, engineers were both members of the engineering core and deployed to a business program), some opinion leaders were on the list for multiple vice presidents and would be invited to what appeared to be redundant events. Others wondered whether opinion leaders were like union committeemen—people whom employees could take their gripes to and who, in turn, would be expected to be their voice with management.

Formal leaders dealt with initial resistance by downplaying the opinion leader list, citing the fact that it was not a perfect process and that involvement of opinion leaders is only one way to create change. Senior managers pointed out that half of the opinion leaders were also managers. They also reminded them that the list came directly from employee input, not from them. Coordination conflicts were worked out by the opinion leaders themselves; they chose the events or issues that they felt were appropriate for them to participate in.

Our intention from the beginning was to have opinion leader involvement slightly lag involvement of the chain of command. This is important for two reasons: first, because it is the formal leaders' job to lead change—and engaging opinion leaders too soon absolves them of that responsibility. And second, because giving opinion leaders advance information about change provokes jealousy—and therefore resistance—from members of the chain of command. But good intentions don't always fit reality. Reality at Lockheed Martin was that many of the senior leaders dragged their feet month after month in implementing actions to involve the chain of command. So here we sat with a few willing executives like Bill Andersen ready to roll with their opinion leaders while chain-of-command strategies were caught in a traffic jam. We decided to ignore our better judgment and get opinion leaders moving. In retrospect we're not sure what would have been best. Change got rolling. Some formal leaders got their feathers ruffled. And in some ways preemptively involving opinion leaders put pressure on lagging executives to get the chain-of-command strategies off dead center. Whatever we *should* have done—we clearly advocate that the chain of command should get significant attention prior to involving opinion leaders.

As we've worked with opinion leaders we've found them to be very sensitive to the possibility of being manipulated. Trust and credibility are essential currency in this relationship. With these, opinion leaders become powerful allies that help move the rest of the organization toward productive change. Without trust and credibility, we believe that any time spent with opinion leaders just makes them more credible opponents to change efforts. Since the rest of the organization will know that formal leaders have attempted to influence them, their opinions about the relevance and desirability of change will carry even more weight. It is important, therefore, to realize that opinion leaders might walk away from an exchange more negative and cynical, and, if so, they will carry *that message* to the rest of the organization.

In the case of Hancock's company, the challenge of building trust with opinion leaders was particularly vexing. What Hancock wanted to see change was *behavior.* Opinion leaders, in response, made it clear that unless and until they saw that their formal leaders were willing to change themselves, they would be less willing to spend their credibility helping to influence others. As senior leaders learned to work with opinion leaders, a virtuous cycle was created in which leaders demonstrated more openness and trust while opinion leaders practiced greater directness and candor.

## THE IMPACT?

The most important impact of opinion leaders is not in the headlines, it's in the cafeteria lines. Opinion leaders reach into every conversation, every meeting, and every decision made in an organization. The question is: *Are they influencing these interactions positively or negatively?* Although survey results dramatically improved after the leader-as-teacher and opinion leader engagements took hold, we believe the best way to understand *how* opinion leaders drive change is through specific anecdotes.

A classic example of how opinion leaders exert influence led to a companywide acceptance of the president's leader-as-teacher concept. Initially, his senior staff was ambivalent about this approach and began to slow-roll, the idea. Many below them, however, were more vocal in their concern. One detractor summed up what others felt when he said: "We're managers, not trainers!"

While executives deliberated, the operations area moved ahead to pilot the concept. As it turned out, the most frequently nominated opinion leader in the company was in the first operations pilot. He came away convinced that the training was crucial but that the leader-as-teacher concept was deeply flawed. After receiving the preparatory training, he reluctantly began to train others. As he did, his attitude changed, as did his remarks about the leader-as-teacher approach. In fact, he became such a vocal advocate that he even offered to substitute for his peers when they needed coverage. While his journey from opposition to zealot was encouraging, what was more important was the influence it exerted on the dozens of others who witnessed it.

Although we expected this peer effect, what surprised us was the influence he wielded *upward.* In one session in which the senior staff deliberated, once again, on whether to make a companywide commitment to leader-as-teacher, Russ Ford, the vice president of operations, described this man's journey. At the first mention of his name, those who had been shuffling papers and holding side conversations stopped. Executives also respected him, and they knew he was no pushover. As the VP told the story, previously skeptical staff members began asking genuine questions. At the conclusion, opinions had changed. Although not even present during the discussion, this opinion leader had exerted powerful influence.

Beyond anecdotes, it is always hard to disentangle cause-and-effect in large-scale organizational change efforts. This case is no different. A large number of discrete change initiatives were implemented in cascading and overlapping ways throughout the organization. However, it is possible to examine data that speak to all change efforts to see whether results are consistent with the timing of particular interventions. In this case, the regular survey results provide some insight into the impact of the change effort (see Exhibit 10.3 for survey findings). Survey results over the first year and half of the change initiative (measured in April and September of 1998 and February and June of 1999) indicated no meaningful change in the critical behaviors. This changed on the December 1999 survey, where statistically significant ($p < .001$) and meaningful shifts in those results were observed companywide.

Although the first opinion leader engagement began in the late spring of 1999, it was during the last six-month period that most activities involving opinion leaders and leader-teacher efforts were carried out. We believe this is more than coincidence.

Other evidence also pointed to change efforts having their desired impact. The surveys provided employees with an opportunity to write about recent changes they noticed at work. These comments did not show evidence of change consistent with the Workforce Vitality initiative until the leader-as-teacher and opinion leader efforts were under way. A shift in the tone and number of positive-change comments started to occur on the fourth survey. Even more positive changes were noted on the last survey, but this time, they were specifically attributed to the Workforce Vitality effort. Thus, the timing of employees' reports of change matched the changes in the numerical survey results.

## YOU CHANGED THE CULTURE. SO WHAT?

Although it's always nice to succeed at what you set out to do, sometimes success isn't worth the cost. So, the ultimate question should not be merely, *Did what you do actually change the culture?* Unless changing the culture also made a clear business difference, scarce resources should probably have been put elsewhere. After all, Hancock wasn't pursuing culture change for philosophical or intrinsic reasons. He was convinced that critical behaviors *had* to change for the company to survive—to both win the JSF contract and be able to deliver on that contract. From this perspective, the key questions are both *Did the behavior change?* and *Did the changed behaviors lead to improved business performance?*

With good engineering discipline, Hancock arranged from the beginning for good research to help answer these questions. The culture change survey was administered approximately every five months. This survey tracked changes in the critical behaviors. Movement on this metric was an indicator that the culture had started to shift.

We were able to address the second key question by following changes in performance in each of eighteen F-16 production units. In this case, we were able to see whether improvement in these performance metrics was associated with greater success in holding the targeted crucial conversations (see Exhibit 10.4). These results indicate that units that are seen as better able to engage in crucial conversations are more efficient and productive, and produce higher-quality work.

Although statistical methods can never finally answer the questions about causality (that is, did improved performance lead to behavior change or did behavior change lead to improved performance?), the story here is pretty compelling. First of all, leaders announced an intention to influence specific critical behaviors. Second, they implemented interventions designed to influence these behaviors. Measurable behavior change followed the implementation of these interventions. And performance improvement *followed* change in behavior. In fact, research with follow-up focus groups indicated that *there were no examples of performance improvement in any unit studied where there was not also significant improvement in the critical behaviors.*

An interesting anecdote: as the evidence of culture change was becoming clear, LMTAS was going through an assessment for the coveted Shingo prize for manufacturing excellence. In the end, not only did LMTAS win that prize, but in awarding the prize, evaluators specifically applauded the breakthrough approaches to increasing employee involvement described in this chapter.

Did culture change help with the JSF win? There is no concrete way of answering that question. Did winning the Shingo Prize, *Industry Week*'s Plant of the Year award, and most important, demonstrating the ability to lead and influence an organization toward measurably improved performance help? It's hard to think it didn't.

## SUMMARY AND BEST PRACTICES

It is a daunting challenge to attempt to change widely held and deeply entrenched patterns of behavior across a large and complex organization. And yet there are times when it is the only path to significantly improved performance. New strategies or processes are worthless if poorly implemented— and behavior is the key to effective implementation. Such was the challenge facing Lockheed Martin.

A few best practices emerge from Lockheed Martin's successful effort to change its culture in its successful pursuit of the Joint Strike Fighter contract.

The major lesson is that a handful of committed leaders *can* positively influence thousands of others with the appropriate leverage.

Dain Hancock and his staff prepared themselves for effective influence by

1. Identifying a few *critical behaviors* that were easy to tie to improved performance
2. Setting a specific and measurable improvement goal
3. Holding the top two levels of leaders accountable *not* for supporting culture change activities, but instead for achieving measurable changes in critical behaviors

Lockheed Martin leaders gained leverage for influencing 12,000 others by

1. Enabling formal leaders to take responsibility for influencing new behaviors by having them assume the role of "teacher"
2. Enlisting informal opinion leaders in leading change by identifying them, listening to them, and involving them in strategic ways

# APPENDIX

## EVERETT ROGERS
## Lessons from Known Studies of Diffusion

Everett Rogers is well known for his systematic study of how new ideas and behaviors catch on in large and complex populations. There is evidence of his influence in words he helped introduced into business usage such as "early adopters" and "laggards." What is less known is that he began his academic interest after a summer job in which, as a county agent, he utterly failed to induce Midwest farmers to accept free advice on what were irrefutably better ways of farming. He was stunned.

Through this and similar experiences, Rogers began a systematic exploration into what came to be known as the *diffusion of innovations.* He looked at every kind of new behavior one could try to foster. He examined what encourages doctors to begin using new drugs, what inspires farmers to begin using better farming techniques, what motivates people to buy a VCR for the first time, how new management techniques are adopted, how passing fads become popular, and so on. He examined 3,085 behavior-change studies, and concluded that 84 percent of the population is unlikely to change its behavior based solely on arguments of merit, scientific proof, great training, or jazzy media campaigns. The majority of those who try new behaviors do so because of the influence of a respected peer.

Rogers came to this realization in an interesting way. In reviewing these 3,000+ studies, he noticed that in every one of them, change followed an S-shaped curve. Change begins slowly and progresses grudgingly at first. Gradually a few converts are won over. As more of the "right" converts amass, the process accelerates. That's where the S-curve becomes steep. Later, as most of those who are easy to moderately difficult to engage adopt the innovation, the curve levels back out, finishing off the S. Progress past this point slows again, requiring great effort.

Consider a common challenge, such as attempting to introduce the use of quality tools, like fishbone diagrams, process mapping, and Pareto analyses. Many reports suggest that this innovation follows the S-curve precisely. Some people buy in fairly quickly, creating a false sense of momentum. The true picture emerges when the initial euphoria wears off and leaders realize that, behind the few faithful who are giddy about these new tools, no one else is standing in line. A few influential managers later begin using the ideas in meetings and advocating process-mapping in some of their less-effective departments. These few gain pockets of support. The adoption curve climbs slowly for about eighteen months. This is the stretch of road where many leaders just quit pushing, declaring the effort an unofficial failure.

If the top leaders persist, they might enjoy the rewards of the steeper part of the curve—that is, if those who are persuaded before the curve points upward are the right people. The people living at this elbow are the key to everyone else. At first Rogers and his colleagues called this group "early adopters." After discovering their relationship with everyone to their right on the curve, they began calling them "opinion leaders."

What these scholars found was that opinion leaders tend to adopt new behaviors for reasons different from those who show up later. Opinion leaders tend to listen to various arguments, read objective sources, and carefully weigh options. Other characteristics of this group distinguish them, too: they are seen by their peers as smarter, better connected, more widely read, and more influential. Whereas opinion leaders often try new things because they've studied it, *other groups more often adopt because opinion leaders did.*

The good news in all of this is that leaders trying to pound through the layers of clay in their organizations can accelerate their progress if they take the time to identify and engage this smaller group of very influential people. Opinion leaders are the key to accelerating the S-curve. If leaders miss with these people, they risk missing completely.

## SURVEY DETAILS

Surveys were administered five times from April 1998 to December 1999, approximately five months apart. Surveys were administered electronically to all white-collar employees. Represented employees who did not have access to the Internet took a paper-and-pencil survey administered in the company auditorium.

Each survey contained thirty-two items, eight of which were designed to assess the three critical behaviors. All scales were found to have acceptable reliability (Cronbach's alpha > .70, on each administration). Means for each critical behavior, at each survey administration, are depicted in Exhibit 10.3.

For the first four surveys, random samples were drawn representing from 30 to 40 percent of the workforce. Response rates ranged from 33 to 51 percent. For the final survey, a census was drawn. The response rate for this survey was 44 percent. All participation was voluntary and anonymous. Analyses were conducted to ensure that each survey was representative of the demographics of the company, in terms of functional area, organizational level, and union representation. These proportions were consistent across survey administrations and consistent with the proportions for these variables within the company. Finally, results from represented and nonrepresented sectors of the workforce paralleled each other, and indicated significant changes only on the December 1999 administration of the survey.

### Exhibit 10.1. Critical Conversations in Six Sigma

- People spoke up when they saw wasteful or unproductive practices.
- When supervisors were slow in responding to employee needs, employees spoke up in a way that got results.
- When upper management needed to pay attention to problems, employees and supervisors gave candid feedback up the chain of command to the appropriate person.

**Exhibit 10.2. Potential Opinion Leaders' Roles in Culture Change**

*Information Conduit*—Attend briefings; convey information to others based on your understanding of company efforts.

*Advisor*—When solicited, give feedback on proposals and ideas for improving vitality in the organization.

*Model*—Model the critical behaviors of open communication, personal commitment, and sense of urgency.

*Data Collector*—Interview others, run focus groups to discover root issues, and help formal leaders improve vitality.

*Participant, Improvement Event*—Participate in a focused improvement event, such as a Kaizen event or large-group problem-solving meeting.

*Facilitator*—Notice unproductive patterns in groups and among senior managers; candidly share observations with others and gain commitment for more effective strategies.

*Teacher*—Facilitate single-point lessons aimed at improving communication and teaming skills.

*Improvement Event Leader*—Facilitate or lead an improvement event, such as a Kaizen event or large-group problem-solving meeting.

*Improvement Project Leader*—Lead or support specific improvement projects to remove barriers to cultural vitality.

*Coach Formal Leaders*—Give behavioral feedback to leaders from interviews or personal experience to promote openness and change.

**Exhibit 10.3. Survey Results**

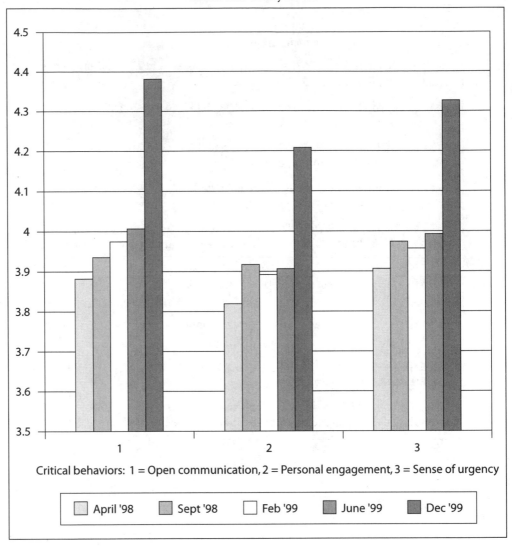

Critical behaviors: 1 = Open communication, 2 = Personal engagement, 3 = Sense of urgency

April '98    Sept '98    Feb '99    June '99    Dec '99

Exhibit 10.4. Significant Correlations Between Specific Critical Behavior Items
and Three Performance Metrics

| | Efficiency* | Productivity | Quality |
|---|---|---|---|
| People challenged coworkers when they saw wasteful or unproductive practices. | | .50 | .42 |
| When supervisors were slow in responding to employee needs, employees spoke up in a way that got results. | .53 | .52 | .49 |
| When upper management needed to pay attention to problems, employees and supervisors gave candid feedback up the chain of command to the appropriate person. | | .68 | .43 |

*Efficiency is a measure of time per unit, standardized by size of unit. Productivity reflects the percentage of possible work actually accomplished. Quality is measured by amount of rework required, standardized by size of unit.

Note: Only statistically significant correlations are reported.

# BIBLIOGRAPHY

A good source for background information is *The Balancing Act: Mastering the Competing Demands of Leadership* by K. Patterson, J. Grenny, R. McMillan, and A. Switzler (Cincinnati, Ohio: Thompson Executive Press, 1996). This book points out that no matter how large or compelling the vision, change leaders need to focus on specific behaviors as targets for change. The authors develop an understanding of what supports existing behavior and what needs to change for new behavior to replace it. The book includes a chapter on how to gain leverage through social influence by working with opinion leaders.

Also see *Crucial Conversations: Tools for Talking When Stakes are High* (New York: McGraw-Hill, 2002) by the same authors. This book describes the pivotal role that certain common but challenging conversations play in accelerating or impeding change—and the skills for succeeding at them. The book outlines the principles referred to in this chapter that were taught by leaders at Lockheed Martin.

Everett Rogers' *Diffusion of Innovations* (New York: Free Press, 1983) is a seminal work on leading change and the foundation for the opinion leader intervention described in this chapter. Rogers describes the challenges faced in the diffusion of any new idea, whether a new behavior or new medicine, and outlines best practices from ongoing meta-research into the hundreds of available studies of change.

In *The Leadership Engine: How Winning Companies Build Leaders at Every Level* (New York: Harper Trade, 1997), Eli Cohen and Noel Tichy conclude that winning companies have leaders who "nurture the development of other leaders at all levels of the organization." They explain that top leaders must develop a teachable point of view on business ideas and values, and they must have a personal vision that can be codified, embodied as a story, and communicated throughout the organization. In short, they argue that leaders are teachers, regardless of their level or role.

*The Tipping Point: How Little Things Can Make a Big Difference* (New York: Little Brown and Company, 2000), by Malcolm Gladwell, describes various roles played by informal influencers. Gladwell describes Connectors, Mavens, and Salesmen—three kinds of informal leaders—and their pivotal role in the rapid diffusion of new ideas.

# ABOUT THE CONTRIBUTORS

**Joseph Grenny** is a founding partner in VitalSmarts, Inc., a management consulting and training company located in Orem, Utah. Prior to starting his own company, he spent six years as an executive with the Covey Leadership Center. In over fifteen years of organization development consulting, he has worked with senior leaders in Fortune 100 and government organizations to bring about clear and measurable culture change. He has authored or co-authored numerous articles in the areas of personal and organizational effectiveness, and co-authored *The Balancing Act: Mastering the Competing Demands of Leadership* and *Crucial Conversations: Tools for Talking When Stakes Are High*.

The latter book is currently on the *New York Times* and *Wall Street Journal* best-seller lists. He has designed and delivered major culture-change initiatives for AT&T, Coregis Insurance, IBM, the State of California, and Lockheed Martin, among others. Contact: Joseph@VitalSmarts.com.

**Lawrence Peters** is professor of management at the Neeley School of Business at Texas Christian University and president of Leadership Solutions. He has published over fifty articles in leading journals and books, has written two case-books, and is senior editor of the *Encyclopedic Dictionary of Human Resource Management*. He has been the recipient of college and university teaching awards, and specializes in the area of leadership. He currently teaches leadership courses at the undergraduate, M.B.A., and Executive M.B.A. levels. He consults with private and public organizations in a variety of areas associated with change efforts. In the past three years, he has consulted with Bell Helicopter, Chubb Insurance, Ford Motor Company, The Hartford Insurance Company, Lockheed Martin, Sprint PCS, and Verizon Communications. Contact: L.Peters@TCU.edu.

**M. Quinn Price** is a senior manager in the Organizational Effectiveness Group at AT&T Wireless. His expertise includes leading cultural transformations, designing responsive organizations, and managing large-scale change. His clients have included Microsoft, Safeway, S.C. Johnson, and Lockheed Martin, among others. His work has been featured in the *International HR Journal* and *HR Magazine.* Contact: quinn.price@attws.com.

**Karie Willyerd** is the chief talent officer for Solectron Corporation, an electronics manufacturing services company. She previously worked at both H. J. Heinz and Lockheed Martin, where she was director of People and Organization Development. Currently she is on the board of the International Athena Foundation and is a former board member of ASTD. She holds a master's degree in industrial and performance technology from Boise State University and bachelor's degrees in English and journalism from Texas Christian University. She is a 2003 candidate for an Executive Doctorate in Management from Case Western Reserve University. Contact: KarieWillyerd@ca.slr.com.

**Change Champions**—Collectively, this group has served as internal and external consultants to a number of major corporations, government agencies, and nonprofit organizations that were attempting to make significant changes (see individual bios). These client companies have helped us better understand the change levers reported in this chapter—some by not embracing them, others by actively doing so. The difference was dramatic and helped shape our thinking. We are thankful to clients with whom we have worked and know our understanding reflects what we learned together about creating successful transformations.

CHAPTER ELEVEN

# Mattel

*This case study describes Mattel's Project Platypus—a dynamic change and innovation process for bringing out human potential in an organization through the synthesis of collaborative, action-, and results-oriented experiences, resulting in new business opportunities and high-performance products.*

OVERVIEW                                                                      263

INTRODUCTION                                                                  263
   Postmodernism                                              264
   Company as Living System                                    264
   Figure 11.1: Platypus                                       265

THE INITIATIVE                                                               265
   The Living Stage                                            266
   The Theater                                                 266

PROJECT PLATYPUS: THE PROCESS                                               267
   Scene 1: Immersion                                          267
   Exhibit 11.1: Project Platypus: Organization of People, Ideas,
     and Experiences                                  268
   Exhibit 11.2: Elements of Story                             269
   Scene 2: Expression                                         269
   Exhibit 11.3: Bonds and Membrane Form                       270
   Figure 11.2: Person, Obstacle, Want/Need                    270
   Scene 3: Alignment                                          271
   Figure 11.3: Bonds Strengthen                               272
   Scene 4: Alignment                                          273
   Figure 11.4: Realignment                                    273
   Scene 5: Alignment                                          274
   Figure 11.5: Impulses and Chaos                             275
   Scene 6: Evolution                                          276
   Figure 11.6: Impulse and Coherence                          276
   Scene 7: Communication                                      278
   Figure 11.7: Interaction with Exterior Systems              278

RESULTS AND IMPACT                                                    279

    Figure 11.8: Comments from Platypi                     280

ABOUT THE CONTRIBUTORS                                        280

# OVERVIEW

This case study describes the unique approach used by the Girls Division at Mattel to successfully reinvent how the world's number one toy company innovates. This is an originative prototype that demonstrates how companies can leverage their human assets through new ways to collaborate.

The organization initiated a re-occurring product development process involving employees from all areas of the company, which is centered on the concept of living systems within a theatrical model. It promotes collaboration, self-organization, self-generation, and self-correction. The division has established a ground-breaking methodology that capitalizes on human potential, creating new brand opportunities for growth.

The lessons learned by Mattel, Girls Division are important for any company or community seeking new ways to ensure a healthy, sustainable, and innovative future.

# INTRODUCTION

It's the year 2001. Mattel, the world's largest toy company, had survived its first annual loss in more than a decade due to the 1999 acquisition of the Learning Company. CEO Robert Eckert, formerly Kraft Foods president, had been in place for a little over a year. During this time, the focus had been primarily on cost cutting and supply chain improvement. Mattel had become an efficient machine. It created over three thousand new toys annually between each of its three divisions: Boys, Girls, and Fisher-Price.

Ivy Ross, senior vice president of design and development for the Girls Division, had been at the company for about three and a half years. She had witnessed and participated in many reengineering processes. Mattel already dominated most of the traditional toy categories. It was clear that in order to keep growing, Mattel needed to start looking for new opportunities. This meant exploring emerging patterns in the marketplace or creating new ones.

Based on known realities of Mattel's processes, Ross's instinct told her that a new process to innovation had to be developed. It was important that the new process leverage all the human assets that Mattel had. As Margaret Wheatley puts it, "If we want to succeed with knowledge management, we must attend to human needs and dynamics. . . . Knowledge [is not] the asset or capital. People are." The key to innovation lies in creating a community where everyone feels valued, with passion and trust at it's core. The end result must be something greater than any one person could have created by themselves. The process must be as innovative as the brands it would produce. It must mirror society from both a cultural and humanistic point of view.

What follows is a description of the research that influenced the approach and methodology that has become known as "Project Platypus."

## Postmodernism

Postmodernism is a term first used in architecture during the 1960s, when architects started to reject the unique architecture of modernism, expressing instead a desire for the more classical forms of the past. They began incorporating elements of the past forms onto modern designs. The result was somewhat of a hybrid or collage approach that used several styles in one structure. This created a certain playfulness of architecture, where there were no boundaries and no rules, another trait of postmodernism. Art is seen as process performance, where the artist shares identity with the audience, as opposed to art being made in isolation and then validated by the audience. There is a movement toward improvisation with an emphasis on what is emergent or what is being created at the moment, not what is scripted. Postmodernism calls for an end to the dominance of an overarching belief in scientific rationality, because it denies the existence of any ultimate principle. Nothing can explain everything for all groups, cultures, traditions, or race. Postmodernism focuses on the relative truth for each person. Interpretation is everything; reality is merely our interpretation of what the world means to us. There is a rejection of the autonomous individual with an emphasis upon the collective unconscious experience. There is a merging of subject and object, self and other, and a loss of centralized control, with more politics at the local level, due to a plurality of viewpoints.

## Company as Living System

What is a living system? It is a body that has the capacity to self-organize, self-generate, self-correct, and self-regulate. It cannot be controlled, only contained or perturbed by sending impulses rather than instructions. A living system thrives on feedback, and it is known to produce a spontaneous emergence of order at critical points of instability. It seeks relationships and connections that lead to more complex systems and relationships. It is alive and life enhancing.

There is no reason that we shouldn't think of a company in the same way. Most of the assets in a company are human beings. Unfortunately, an assembly-line machine mentality has become etched into our corporate thinking. Social sustainability theorist Fritjof Capra notes, "Seeing a company as a machine also implies that it will eventually run down, unless it is periodically serviced and

**Figure 11.1** Platypus.

> **Plat-y-pus** (plat e pes) n, pl. nes. 1. A semi-aquatic, web-footed, egg-laying mammal with a duck's bill. 2. An animal made up of two *different* species. 3. *An uncommon mix.* 4. A whole *new* kind of animal. 5. An accidental creature. 6. An animal that never should have existed. 7. *Unexpected,* yet oddly understandable.

rebuilt by management. It cannot change by itself; all changes need to be designed by someone else." A living system, however, contains all the generative attributes that a company needs to survive and flourish. Some of these attributes are the constant generation of novelty, partnership through relationship, and a strong sense of community around a common set of values. Living systems continually create, or re-create themselves by transforming or replacing their components. Companies, in contrast, have a very hard time changing. In fact, they often have to be "reengineered" instead of naturally evolving.

Therefore, it was determined that the Mattel process should embrace the known tenants of postmodernism: ambiguity, hybridity, improvisation, performance, and fun. It should embody the attributes of a living system as well: openness, regeneration, inclusiveness, chaos, and coherence.

The stage was set. Ross was the playwright and she needed a director. She hired David Kuehler to lead the project. Project Platypus was born!

## THE INITIATIVE

Project Platypus was launched in 2001 as a way of creating new opportunities for Mattel. The deliverables include a new brand that can deliver at least $100 million in revenue by the third year in the marketplace. The final presentation includes tested products, packaging, merchandising ideas, and a full financial analysis.

This was accomplished by choosing twelve Mattel employees from different areas of the business unit. They vacated their existing jobs for twelve weeks and shed their titles and their hierarchical way of working. They worked in the Project Platypus space as part of a living system in a postmodern way. Alumni were released back into the system, where they utilized their newly acquired skills to share the process with their managers and colleagues. Each session would be unique. The participants and the *vision,* or business opportunity that need to be explored, would change with each session.

Finally, Ross and Kuehler needed a model to embody this kind of thinking. They found it in the theater.

## The Living Stage

*Immerse people in universal and extreme situations which leave them only a couple of ways out, arrange things so that in choosing the way out they choose themselves, and you've won—the play is good.*
—Jean-Paul Sartre, *Sartre on Theater*[1]

In theater, people from a variety of disciplines converge in one place and serve a common vision, the play. It's a process of openness, collaboration, and wholeness. The group defines a working methodology that allows for personal and group expression—a living system. The group's process must embody "real life" so they can create a believable fantasy life on stage.

Although plays, and the play itself, change from production to production, there is an innate process and language that is carried inside each member of the community. It allows members to align themselves to a common vision, the play, yet remains flexible and open enough for creativity to emerge organically.

## The Theater

A new process required a new theater, a place that would inspire collaboration, play, and creative thinking. Space was located across the parking lot from the Design Center. Grass-green flooring was installed, and skylights were punched into the roof, providing bright sunlight. "It feels like a meadow," said one of the construction crew. The furniture consisted of beanbag chairs, ergonomically designed office seating, and large rubber balls to sit and bounce on. All of the desks were on wheels so they could be moved around to create a variety of group configurations. Many of the possessions taken for granted in traditional offices would be shared, such as computers, telephones, and office supplies. Adjacent to the great room were two smaller rooms. The first, a library and lounge for reading and off-line socializing, and the second, a sound room that contained a sound chair, developed by Dr. Jeff Thompson, that would encourage maximum creativity by aligning the right and left halves of the brain by using music embedded with binary beats. Finally, a twelve-by-forty-foot pushpin wall was installed, as well as floor-to-ceiling chalkboards. These would serve as living journals to document the processes to come.

# PROJECT PLATYPUS: THE PROCESS

Exhibit 11.1 captures how people, ideas, and shared experiences aligned themselves during a twelve-week session. Three independent, yet related, variables were charted over time: the wall (ideas contained on ten- by forty-foot wall), the people (cellular alignment of living systems), and the scenes (experiences and events the group shared).

## Scene 1: Immersion (Weeks 1 & 2)

Immersion set the field for a unique culture to organically unfold. Speakers, participants, and experiences were programmed with great detail. There was no specific formula. We set the vision and served it (see Exhibit 11.2). Not the process of work. The solutions evolved organically as a result of what we did to discover it.

First, the leaders shared the project vision with the group to give them a sense of mission. Second, they planted the seedlings of culture by providing the group with a collection of shared experiences that personified the core values of immersion: shared experience, shared knowledge, and self-discovery.

**The Wall.** The vision was posted on the wall as a way for the group to visualize and hold the overall objective in their minds.

**The People.** Speakers and outside experts were invited in to promote the core values of immersion.

*Knowledge speakers* provided the group with a 360-degree view of the vision. If you're trying to design a car, you don't just look at other cars. You look for knowledge and inspiration in out-of-the-way places. We consulted with a Jungian analyst, a Ph.D. in child development, and a Japanese tea master to hone the team's observational skills. The collection of speakers provided the group with the information and context they needed to approach the project with fresh eyes.

*Self-discovery speakers* helped each Platypus rediscover his or her dreams and individuality. A participant said, "This process helped me find a way back to myself." Some of the speakers included a practitioner in collaborative living systems and a researcher in music and brainwave activity. Members were encouraged to spend time in a sound chair to stimulate creativity. The

### Exhibit 11.1. Project Platypus: Organization of People, Ideas, and Experiences

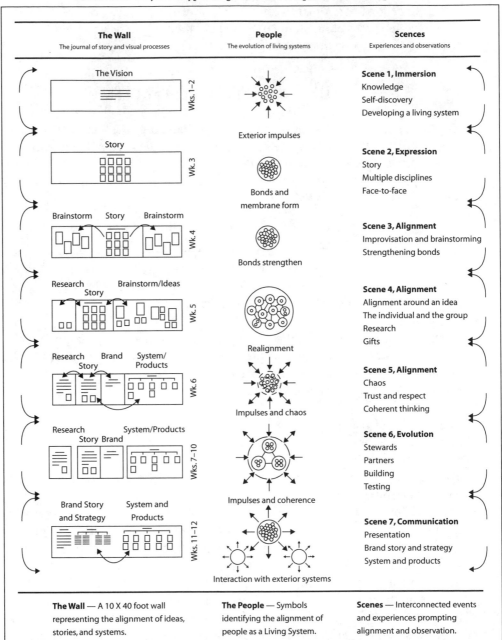

**The Wall** — A 10 X 40 foot wall representing the alignment of ideas, stories, and systems.

**The People** — Symbols identifying the alignment of people as a Living System.

**Scenes** — Interconnected events and experiences prompting alignment and observation.

### Exhibit 11.2. Elements of Story

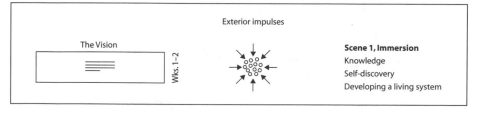

*Source:* Exhibit created by Bill Idelson.

objective was to help each participant discover a renewed sense of self and expressiveness.

*Creative culture speakers* set the groundwork for a productive living system. A cultural mythologist discussed the significance of archetypes in story and culture, and an improvisation artist led the group in a variety of theatrical games to teach participants the fundamentals of group storytelling and brainstorming. One of the most important rules of improvisational theater is to respond to an idea by saying, "yes, and . . ." which sets the stage for acknowledgment and acceptance of ideas.

By the end of immersion, the change in many of the individuals was noticeable. People began to dress differently; they laughed more. Relationships were forming, and people were more comfortable expressing their feelings and ideas. This is often referred to as the "inclusion phase" of a living system. The culture was beginning to emerge.

**Lessons Learned.**  Time. The group was given time to "graze," to learn, and to develop meaningful relationships. Many organizations don't allow employees the time they need to prepare for an initiative. The process is often mechanical and impersonal. "Here's the objective and the deadline. You, you, and you work together." Imagine the innovative ideas that are lost because people become slaves to a process.

## Scene 2: Expression (Week 3)

The intent of expression was to allow individuals to express their interpretation of the vision by using their learnings from the first two weeks while continuing to develop community (Exhibit 11.3).

The group was made up of people from multiple disciplines. Some expressed their ideas visually, others through words or technology. A common "language" was required—story. What does a person want or need? And what is keeping them from getting it? The diagram below is the foundation of all stories. Whether it is "Little Red Riding Hood," *War and Peace,* or a brand story, it all starts here.

**Exhibit 11.3. Bonds and Membrane Form**

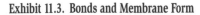

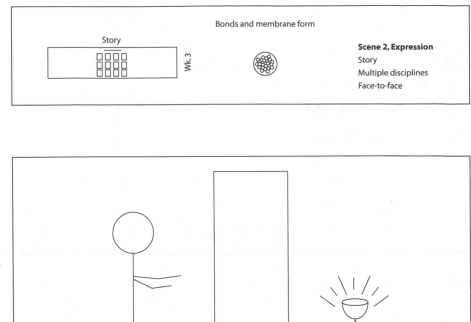

**Figure 11.2** Person, Obstacle, Want/Need.

Person    Obstacle    Want/Need

**The Wall.** Subjective and objective storytelling exercises were performed and placed on the wall.

*Subjective*—Find your passion in the vision. Create a story about what this initiative means to you in a very personal way. Platypi were asked to participate in an exercise called "What If?" For example, "What if we could create a brand that helped children understand their emotions?"

*Objective*—Tell a story based on something you have observed. Platypi were sent into the field to perform observational research. They created stories by watching children play. They identified the physical, mental, and emotional aspects of what was taking place.

Platypi shared their stories with the rest of the group, then posted them on the wall. They analyzed them and looked for emergent patterns. The patterns provided the sparks of the emerging brand story.

**The People.** Although people were working individually they still needed to stay connected. A check-in called "Face-to-Face" was implemented. Each morning the group met in the center of the room, formed a circle of chairs, and simply connected with each other, as humans, before the day and the work commenced.

**Face-to-Face.**

> *Any human service where the one who is served should be loved in the process*
> *requires community, a face-to-face grouping which the liability of each for the*
> *other and all for one is unlimited, or as close to it as it is possible to get.*
> *Trust and respect are highest in this circumstance and an accepted ethic*
> *that gives strength to all is reinforced.*
> —Robert K. Greenleaf, *Servant Leadership*[2]

Face-to-face served three purposes. The first two are explained here, and the third will be explained later. One, it provided people with a forum to connect with each other, and to be "in relationship." It was important for them to understand their mutual involvement. They discussed topics that were related to the project, or sometimes, they talked about completely unrelated matters. The idea was to look each other in the eye, connect, and renew their relationships on a daily basis.

Two, it allowed people to name and resolve conflict. Someone once said, spouses should never go to bed angry. The team's motto was, never go through the day in conflict. When people are "in relationship" conflict isn't a bad thing. In fact, it's necessary for a living system to survive. Face-to-face gave people the opportunity to name their differences and seek resolution within a healthy and respectful community.

At the end of the expression phase the Platypi seemed fulfilled. They created meaningful stories that they felt passionate about, and by committing their stories to the wall they "announced themselves" to the community. In an uncomplicated way, they were beginning to build trust and respect for each other.

**Lessons Learned.** Vulnerability = creativity. The group connected on a daily basis, which held them in relationships of trust and respect. When people are vulnerable, they are the most open—free to create. Traditionally, employees have been told, "leave your feelings at home. This is business." When organizations strip humanness from the workplace they strip away human potential and creativity as well.

## Scene 3: Alignment (Week 4)

This was the first of three scenes of alignment. It was designed to build on the stories that the team had created and strengthen the bonds between individuals (Figure 11.3). A renowned product development firm and an improvisational artist

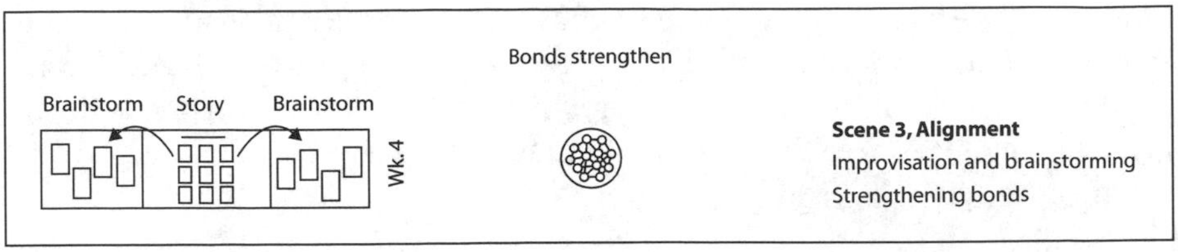

**Figure 11.3** Bonds Strengthen.

were brought in to lead the group in Creation workshops. The combination of improvisational theater and product development brainstorming techniques helped the group create the tools they needed to define their own ideation process.

**The Wall.** There were twelve stories on the wall, which did they work on first? They voted. Each Platypi was given three Post-it notes, and they picked the stories they felt served the vision. The stories with the most votes were the ones they brainstormed.

The wall evolved into two sections with the original twelve stories in the center and the more refined stories to either side.

**The People.**

> *Group participation and agreement remove all the imposed tensions and exhaustions of the competitiveness and open the way for harmony.*
> —Viola Spolin, *Improvisation for the Theater*[3]

Individuals gathered into small brainstorming groups and aligned themselves around the stories they felt most passionate about. One person facilitated and acted as the scribe, while the rest of the group added ideas and built on those of others. A playful atmosphere, mutual respect, trust, openness, and ownership took center stage. Competitiveness and egos were set aside.

The group defined their own rules for brainstorming: No judgment, go for quantity of ideas, build on the ideas of others, there are no bad ideas, no editing, don't think too much, stay connected, and pass the pen (rotate scribes during the brainstorm).

This scene put everything the group had learned to the test. They

- Applied their individual and collective knowledge
- Saw how play could enable spontaneity
- Felt what it was like to surrender their ideas to serve the story
- Discovered the intelligence of twelve is far greater than the intelligence of one

**Lessons Learned.** The group experienced the power and fulfillment of creating something together through play. It strengthened the bonds between individuals, and competitiveness slipped away.

Organizations often rely on competition to act as a catalyst for innovation. Employees are left feeling unfulfilled, burnt out, and isolated.

> *Imposed competition makes harmony impossible; for it destroys the basic nature*
> *of playing by occluding self and by separating player from player.*
> —Viola Spolin, *Improvisation for the Theater*[4]

## Scene 4: Alignment (Week 5)

In this scene Platypi began to express themselves through the stories they felt passionate about, while still honoring the vison (Figure 11.4). They aligned themselves around narratives in groups of one or two, and they used the wall to develop their work, which created a visual representation of the process. A practice called "Gift Giving" emerged.

**The Wall.** The Platypi continued to develop the stories here. Some achieved this through research, drawings, or style boards and others through the written word or product concepts. Everything hit the wall with the vision at its center. Each of these manifestations informed each other. A living, breathing brand began to coalesce.

At one of the open houses we noticed a guest walk to each corner of the room. He would stop, look at the wall, and then move on. We asked him what he was doing, and he said, "I can see that wall from every corner of the room. No matter where I stand, I can see where you are in the process."

**Gifts.**
> *We live in a gift-giving economy. Once you create a gift and give it*
> *away you are empty, and free to create again.*
> —Sam Hamill, NPR Radio interview[5]

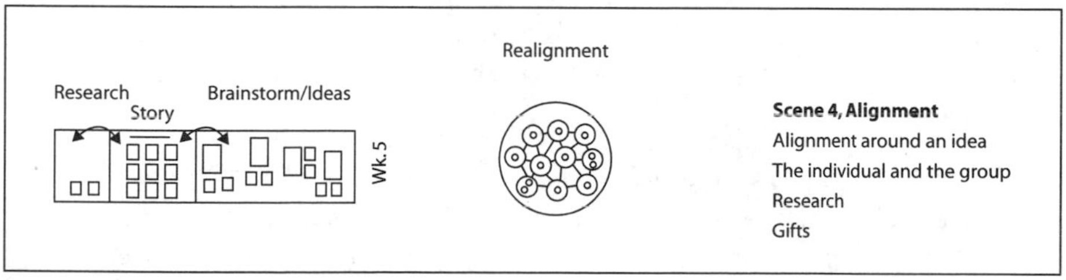

**Figure 11.4** Realignment.

Participants began to give each other "gifts." If someone created an idea that seemed right for another person or group, they would draw or write it and pin it next to their work on the wall. Since everyone felt a sense of ownership over the process there was very little competition. Gifts were given away freely.

**The People.** People aligned themselves around ideas they felt passionate about. We never said, "You, you, and you will work together on this." This was the opportunity for individuals to express themselves. So much of their future work would be centered on the group. This was the time for a person's voice to come forward. Some people chose to work together. The alliances formed organically around an idea.

For some, this part of the process was threatening. They were used to working in an environment where they would have a meeting, disappear into their cubes, and emerge only when they had a solution. "My idea is ready now!" Their process was isolated and invisible. At first it was very difficult for some members of the group to commit their idea to the wall because they knew that it meant giving it away. Face-to-face became very meaningful at this stage. Members of the group were able to reconnect each morning before they began their individual work.

At first the group didn't want to relinquish the comfort and security of the group to work alone. However, they knew they were an organic whole of the living system. They had the support and trust of the group, which allowed them to open up and create freely.

**Lessons Learned.** A system of trust, respect, and support freed members to create ideas for one another and give them away as gifts. It made sense. They were all telling the same story. In some companies, the brand story is held by a chosen few. They consider it their property. But if all employees have a stake in the story, they will be more willing to share ideas and promote it.

## Scene 5: Alignment (Week 6)

The final scene of alignment was meant to bring the brand story into view. The stories, research, and product concepts were orbiting on the wall. The group searched for patterns and tried to bring coherence to the story. The wall and living system had entered a new, yet necessary, phase of development—chaos (see Figure 11.5).

> *Chaos theory proposes that when repetitive dynamics begin to interact with themselves they become so complex that they defy definition. Yet from these "complex dynamics" there eventually emerge new patterns that are based loosely on the old. In other words, while chaotic systems break down order, they also reconstitute it in new forms.*
> —John R. Van Eenwyk, *Archetypes and Strange Attractors*[6]

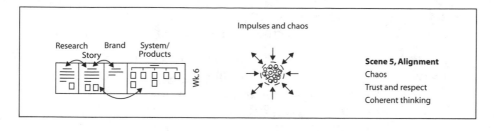

**Figure 11.5** Impulses and Chaos.

**The Wall.** Like "strange attractors" the research, brand, story, and product were orbiting on the wall. The group looked back upon their experience and compared the patterns of knowledge they acquired earlier to the learnings and macro-patterns on the wall. They were close, but they couldn't make sense of it. Two days later, a Platypus "gifted" the wall with the skeleton of a unique system. Then someone else added an idea, then another. Then without warning, order emerged.

**The People.** This was a difficult time for the group. They remained connected; however, their frustration with themselves and each other was obvious. They moved from *inclusion* to *conflict* to *coherence* and back again. They were looking for meaning, and they couldn't find it.

In the theater, every production reaches a point when the performers become stagnant and frustrated. Actors are unable to move to the next level of performance. The director sends them impulses, hoping that if they spark one actor the others will respond and rise to the occasion. Unfortunately, this happens in its own time. The group finds its own syncopation. Inevitably, an individual will raise his or her game and, like magic, the rest of the group will synchronize. This transformation often happens in the blink of an eye. When you look back and try to identify that liminal moment, you can't remember when and how it happened. It just did. A similar experience happened at Platypus. One day they were in a state of chaos, where it seemed nothing made sense, and a couple of days later—coherence. The new brand unfolded before their eyes.

At this pivotal scene in the process the group experienced frustration and disorder; they were trying to make sense of their efforts. They could see the light at the end of the tunnel, but they couldn't get there. The leaders remained supportive, trusting the people and the work. They, too, had to surrender to the chaos; it was necessary and essential to the process.

**Lessons Learned.** Organizations often experience chaotic moments on the path to innovation. Rather than support the emergence, they become nervous. They switch to Plan B, the "tried and true" process. Who knows what could have emerged if they had only remained supportive and committed to the process.

> *The experience of the critical instability that precedes the emergence of novelty may involve uncertainty, fear, confusion, or self-doubt. Experienced leaders recognize these emotions as integral parts of the whole dynamic and create a climate of trust and mutual support.*
> —Fritjof Capra, *The Hidden Connections*[7]

## Scene 6: Evolution (Weeks 7–10)

The brand story and system were coherent (Figure 11.6). The group needed to access its relevance to the consumer. This was structured in three phases: partnering, building, and testing. The face-to-face meetings became an essential part of their project planning, and the concept of "stewarding" was implemented.

**The Wall.** The wall was segmented into three sections: research, story and brand, and system and products.

**The People.** The group realigned themselves into small teams around the segmented wall. Individuals volunteered to act as the point person between the group and their partners.

- *Stewards.* A steward was someone who guided the development of a specific product, process, or system of thinking. This person may have been but was not necessarily the individual who came up with the idea. Once again, people aligned themselves around ideas they felt passionate about. Someone may have conceived the original idea, gifted it, and then moved on. The steward didn't own the idea, the group did. The steward guided the idea to its next evolution.
- *Partners.* Partnership development was two-fold. First, as part of the bigger mission of Platypus, it was important to include people from other areas of

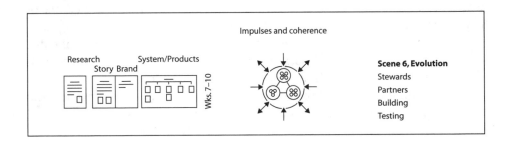

**Figure 11.6** Impulse and Coherence.

the company in the process. Second, the team couldn't do it alone. To bring the brand to life, it was essential for them to find and work with partners that held the expertise they needed.

Each person that walked through the doors of Platypus was considered a partner in the process—from Bob Eckert, the CEO, to the service man who changed the toner in the printer. The Platypus room was a field of creativity. Everyone who entered was part of the field. Each guest was asked to leave a gift on the wall before they departed, such as an inspirational saying or drawing to record their participation in the larger story.

- *Building.* The team partnered with engineers to help them cost products and build prototypes. In the spirit of Platypus they sat down with each partner and communicated the story. It was important for them to understand that their input was essential to the evolution of the product. They were not there just to cost the product and tell the team whether it could work or not. They were there to serve the vision and tell the story and to make each product better from the spark of the idea to the delivery to the consumer.

- *Testing.* As part of the overarching mission of Platypus, products from each new brand went through two rounds of focus testing with consumers. Each test was a milestone for the project; it permitted the team to check in and see whether their ideas were resonating with the consumer.

Focus Test 1: Testing of the brand thinking

Focus Test 2: Brand system, fourteen product concepts in 2-D

Focus Test 3: Brand system, six product models, 3-D.

- *Face-to-face.* As mentioned earlier, the third component of face-to-face was planning. It allowed the Platypi to define the process as they went. There was an overall project schedule, but the schedule and planning for each day happened in face-to-face. Every day was valuable. If a focus test didn't go well the night before, they had to rethink the product the next morning—they couldn't wait a day or two. The group had to think, plan, and reach consensus quickly. When twelve people are connected and "their point of concentration" is on the same thing, the combined intelligence and ability to solve complex problems is remarkable. The fluidity of the face-to-face allowed them to realign the process and create customized solutions to suit the need.

The group had to look both inward and outward to further the development of the project. Communication was an essential component this phase. The small groups, the larger body, and their partners needed to stay in relationship to ensure success.

Communication, trust, and relationships were crucial at this phase. Multiple processes were happening concurrently. Stewards had the trust and support of the rest of the group to guide the micro-processes. They relied on face-to-face to bring the larger group up to speed and to

- Adjust daily planning if necessary
- Ensure that all of the processes were "on brand"
- Use the group intelligence to help overcome obstacles and reach solutions

**Lessons Learned.** It wasn't necessary for one or two people to carry the weight of the project on their shoulders. The responsibilities spread out naturally. Stewards had the trust and support of the larger body, and most important, every Platypus "owned" the story. They didn't have to constantly check-in to make sure they were making the right decisions. How often do corporate managers feel like they have to micro-manage a process? If employees feel like they're part of the big picture, and feel trusted, they are much more likely to own their processes as well.

## Scene 7: Communication (Weeks 11–12)

The team's findings were presented in the final week to senior management to attain buy-in (Figure 11.7). Shortly thereafter, the strategy for the next phase of design development was initiated. The presentation consisted of the process, research, brand strategy, products, and recommendations for a three-year business plan.

**The Wall.** The wall became more refined. It evolved into a communication tool, a journal of twelve brains. As the team's understanding of the initiative became more coherent, so did the wall. Anyone could "walk the wall" and understand the entire development process from start to finish.

**The People.** The team had reached an elevated level of interconnectedness. They were all striving for the same goal. They were working individually or in small groups, yet they were able to shift their thinking and tasking swiftly if

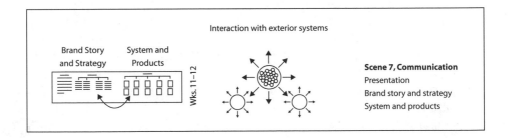

**Figure 11.7** Interaction with Exterior Systems.

necessary. They operated inside and outside of the living system with relative ease.

> *In a group, when members reach a certain level of high interconnection, they form a similar web or matrix. The resources, talents and expertise of each member become available to the whole group. Inclusion, then, allows the group to shift from working as parts of a system to working as a whole system.*
> —Mukara Meredith, MatrixWorks Inc.[8]

The final presentation was a performance. It was a chronology of the process, content, and methodology. In some instances the members gave testimonials of their personal and work-related transformations. They felt it was vital for the audience to understand the complex journey that the individual, the group, and their ideas had taken.

# RESULTS AND IMPACT

The results of Project Platypus have gone beyond our expectations. The first group produced a hybrid building-toy brand for girls called "Ello," which went into full distribution in Spring 2003. According to Mattel first quarter financial reports, "Ello™ brands were up 7 percent for the quarter." *The Akron Beacon Journal* reported on Thursday, October 16 that, "Strong sales of Flavas, Polly Pocket, and Ello toys led a 15 percent increase in sales for other girls brands." "It blew me away," said Chris Blyme, a long-time industry analyst and a contributing editor at *Toy Report and Toy Wishes.* "You rarely see something original any more in this industry. Usually, everybody copies everybody else's ideas."

The next two brands (currently in development) are equally original. Besides providing Mattel with growth opportunities, Project Platypus will influence the culture of the company more and more as each group of employees is released back into the system. They become creative catalysts, bringing new ways of being, doing, and creating back to their previous jobs. There have been sightings of cubicle walls being taken down, dialogues replacing meetings, stories being told, and gifts being given every day. The appreciation of intuition and the ability to read patterns in the field suggest "future possibilities" and "imagination" as qualities of observation. Designers and marketers are collaborating in a different way. There is a level of intimacy and freedom of expression among those who have participated in the Platypus experience.

Most important, there are a growing number of people in the division who have experienced the magic that can transpire when they come to work as who they really are, give all they can give, have fun, and be inspired at the same time. As one Platypus said, "All our truth is welcome here."

When asked what makes Platypus unique, the team responded with the comments in Figure 11.8.

**Figure 11.8** Comments from Platypi.

## ENDNOTES

1. Sartre, John Paul. *Sartre on Theater.* New York: Pantheon Books, 1976.

2. Greenleaf, Robert K. *Servant Leadership: A Journey into the Nature of Legitimate Power and Greatness.* New York: Paulist Press, 1977, p. 38.

3. Spolin, Viola. *Improvisation for the Theater.* Evanston, Ill.: Northwestern University Press, 1963, p. 10.

4. Spolin, Viola. *Improvisation for the Theater.* Evanston, Ill.: Northwestern University Press, 1963, p. 10.

5. Sam Hamill, editor of Copper Mountain Press. (Radio interview). NPR/KCRW, Los Angeles, Calif.

6. Van Eenwyk, John R. *Archetypes and Strange Attractors.* Toronto: Inner City Books, 1997. p. 43.

7. Capra, Fritjof. *The Hidden Connections.* New York: Doubleday, 2002, p. 123.

8. Meredith, Mukara. (Interview). MatrixWorks Inc., November 22, 2002.

## ABOUT THE CONTRIBUTORS

**Ivy Ross** is currently the senior vice president of design and development in the Girls Division of Mattel, Inc. She oversees the design and development of all products and packaging for girls, including Barbie dolls, accessories, Diva Stars,

What's Her Face, Ello, Polly Pocket and six other unique brands, with total sales of approximately $2 billion. In addition, Ross is in charge of the model shop, sound lab, chemistry lab, and sculpting functions for all Mattel products. Ross's education was in design and psychology and included time at the Harvard Business School. Her high-level background in fashion and design spans more than two decades. She came to Mattel from Calvin Klein, where she led a turnaround in men's accessories. Prior to Calvin Klein, Ross served as vice president of product design and development for Coach, the maker of high-end leather goods and accessories. She also held positions at Liz Claiborne, Bausch & Lomb, and Swatch Watch. In addition, Ross was a founding partner of two independent design firms and a retail store. She has a proven ability as a design leader and also possesses a strong sense of business management. A world-renowned artist, Ross's innovative metal work in jewelry is in the permanent collection of twelve international museums, including the Smithsonian in Washington D.C., the Victoria and Albert Museum in London, and the Cooper Hewitt Museum in New York City, among others. A winner of the prestigious National Endowment for the Arts grant, Ross has also received the Women in Design Award and Diamond International award for her creative designs. She has served as a juror, teacher, and critic in a wide range of product categories.

**David Kuehler** is the director of Project Platypus, an innovative product development initiative within the Girls Division of Mattel, Inc. Kuehler's background encompasses over fifteen years in the design and entertainment fields. His education is in design, engineering, and theater. Before joining Mattel, Kuehler was director, creative development and programming for Robert Redford's Sundance Film Centers. At the Walt Disney Company, Kuehler was instrumental in the design development and rollout of Club Disney, a location-based entertainment concept. He produced initiatives for Walt Disney Imagineering, R&D, Disney Online, and ESPN Zone. As an instructor and speaker at Art Center College of Design, he taught spatial graphics and successfully led students in a project sponsored by Intel Corporation, creating user interfaces and products for the next generation of wireless, personal computers. A versatile thinker with a unique ability to both conceive and implement innovative ideas, Kuehler cofounded an entertainment design and production company. He has developed shows for Nelvana Communications and the Sundance Channel. He is currently cocreating children's programming with Britt Allcroft, best known for her popular *Thomas the Tank Engine* series.

# CHAPTER TWELVE

# McDonald's Corporation

*A leadership development program designed specifically to help participants prepare for success in meeting the increased challenges and demands of one of the roles most critical to success of the business.*

| | |
|---|---|
| OVERVIEW | 283 |
| Business Context and Need for the Leadership Program | 283 |
| Objectives of the Leadership Development Experience | 285 |
| ASSESSMENT OF PARTICIPANTS | 285 |
| The Role of Assessment | 285 |
| Process and Approach | 286 |
| Insights Emerging from the Assessment Results | 287 |
| Initial Feedback and Coaching | 287 |
| THE PROGRAM | 288 |
| Designing the Leadership Development Experience | 288 |
| Content of the Program | 289 |
| Tools, Instruments, and Training Materials | 290 |
| Reinforcing and Building on Learning | 291 |
| EVALUATION | 291 |
| Methods and Measure | 291 |
| Program Outcomes | 292 |
| Critical Success Factors | 293 |
| Lessons Learned and Opportunities for Improvement | 293 |
| Additional Benefits and Impacts Realized After Initial Program Completion | 294 |
| ENHANCED PROGRAM LAUNCH | 295 |
| SUMMARY | 296 |
| EXHIBITS | |
| Exhibit 12.1: Regional Manager Success Profile | 297 |
| Exhibit 12.2: Team Charter—Sample Format | 298 |

Exhibit 12.3: Team Metrics                                              299
Exhibit 12.4: Team Process Check                                        300
Exhibit 12.5: Pros and Cons of Data Collection Methods                 301
Exhibit 12.6: Force-Field Analysis                                     303
Exhibit 12.7: Project Review Checklist                                 304
Exhibit 12.8: Business Improvement Recommendation Process              306

ABOUT THE CONTRIBUTORS                                                 308

# OVERVIEW

## Business Context and Need for the Leadership Program

In early 2001, the HR Design Center for McDonald's Corporation initiated the development of a special leadership development program for a select number of high-potential managers identified as candidates for possible promotion into a key role in its system, that of regional manager (RM). The program developed was entitled the McDonald's Leadership Development Experience. This chapter will describe what differentiated this program from other leadership development activities that had previously been offered within the company, what program elements worked particularly well (and which didn't), and how this program has helped influence both the training methodology and substantive content of current and future planned leadership training initiatives at McDonald's.

There were a number of factors that led the company to support this initiative. First, the regional manager role was a very significant one within the overall operations structure of the business. At the time of this initiative, individuals in the regional manager positions were responsible for managing regions that comprised 300 to 400 stores that generated $480—$640 million in revenue. The regional manager position was not only considered a significant business responsibility but also a key stepping stone for many individuals who were thought to be capable of advancing to the senior executive level of the company. Another factor that helped create a felt need for developing a special leadership development program focusing on future candidates for the regional manager role was the fact that the expectations and challenges for this position had shifted significantly over the previous five to ten years as a result of both changes in the marketplace and within McDonald's. These changes included heightened competition, the increased challenge of growing market share, RMs being given more autonomy as the organization became more decentralized and moved decision making closer to the market and customer, and the growing expectation for RMs to act strategically as well as tactically. Given this evolution in the role, it was decided to develop an accelerated leadership development experience that could assist potential future RMs to be better prepared to meet these new expectations and challenges.

A final factor that helped lead to and influence the development of this program was a study that had been conducted during the year 2000 that was designed to develop a Regional Manager Success Profile. The intent in developing this profile was to provide a sharp picture of what superior performance in the regional manager role looked like in order to guide both the future selection of individuals for and the development of individuals already in this position. The development of this profile involved interviews with the president of the North American business, all five division presidents reporting to him, key senior human resource executives, selected others who had a clear perspective on the role and demands of the RM position, and selected "star" performers in the RM position. The content of the interviews focused on identifying

1. How the business had changed in the past five to ten years
2. How these changes had affected "the recipe for success" in the RM role
3. The critical results and competencies that differentiated the "star" performers from the average ones
4. What experiences were felt to be key to the preparation of someone to step successfully into the role and the kinds of problems that had derailed some individuals who had been put into the position

The Regional Manager Success Profile that emerged from this work (and was finalized in early 2001) identified both the key results that the top RMs needed to produce and the critical competencies that they needed to be able to demonstrate in order to excel in the position (see Exhibit 12.1). The availability of this success profile made the design of a customized leadership experience for developing future RMs easier and more effective.

In addition to the success profile that emerged from this process, a variety of other useful information was gathered in the course of this preliminary work that has proved valuable in guiding the ongoing efforts to design training and development initiatives for regional manager leadership. Key elements of this additional information include

- Specific examples of ten critical but common practical leadership challenges that individuals stepping into the RM role might expect to face and that they must be prepared to handle if they are to be effective (for example, inheriting a region that has been steadily losing market share, needing to significantly upgrade the talent or morale level of the regional staff team, needing to strengthen or rebuild trust and credibility with the owner-operators)

- Identification of the kinds of jobs or experiences that an individual might have prior to becoming an RM that would help better prepare him or her for taking on the role

Although some elements of this additional information were incorporated into the leadership development experience that is the primary focus of this chapter, other aspects are just beginning to be used to help shape a broader and more complete set of development programs and experiences that are being designed to better prepare future leaders for success at the regional leadership level throughout McDonald's.

### Objectives of the Leadership Development Experience

The design of the leadership development program for high-potential RM candidates had a number of key objectives. These included

- Help participants take a critical look at themselves and their current management capabilities and develop an individualized personal learning plan that could help them increase their likelihood of future success as RMs

- Provide participants with an action learning assignment that would help them grow in their understanding of the business while contributing to the development of practical ideas to address the significant business issues they worked on

- Provide participants with an opportunity to build relationships with key peers from across the organization with whom they could partner as part of their ongoing development

- Provide significant exposure of the candidates to senior executives in the organization and vice versa

- Demonstrate the potential value and power of action learning as a new model for accelerating the development of leaders and as a way to complement the more classroom-based approaches that were already in use

## ASSESSMENT OF PARTICIPANTS

### The Role of Assessment

It was decided that the Regional Manager Success Profile would be used not only to shape the design of the overall program but also as part of the process of assessing the strengths and development needs of individuals who were participating in the program. Although a number of the individual candidates selected for this program had been through various management assessment experiences at different points in their careers, none of these assessments had been tailored to evaluate the individuals against the more specific demands and requirements associated with success in the RM role. Thus, the RM Success Profile provided a tool that was uniquely tailored to help the individuals better understand their readiness to step into the role and to identify the kinds of development needs they might need to address to enhance their likelihood of effectiveness. As will become apparent later in this chapter, the opportunity to get feedback about one's readiness for promotion into a specific role (rather than just feedback about generic management skills) turned out to be one of the more compelling aspects of this leadership development experience for the participants.

It should be made clear that all fourteen participants who had been identified as high-potential candidates for future advancement to the RM role were assessed *after* they were selected by their division presidents for inclusion in the program. In other words, at this stage, the assessments of individuals against the RM Success Profile were not used as the basis for selection into the high-potential group and this leadership program.

The specific objectives of the assessment of individual participants were to

- Provide individuals with an evaluation of themselves against the RM Success Profile so that they could identify key strengths to build on and key development areas to work on in order to enhance their potential effectiveness in the RM role

- Provide the organization with data on development areas the group might benefit most from having targeted in this and other future leadership development programs

## Process and Approach

The assessment process was conducted by a team of external consultants (Ph.D. psychologists) and took place between the times that participants were told they had been selected for the program and that the program was launched.

The assessment process itself included

1. Having participants complete prework including
   - A self-assessment against the fourteen competencies that comprised the RM Success Profile
   - A brief survey regarding the extent to which they had had the opportunity to already be exposed to, manage, and learn from a set of six learning challenges that were similar to practical on-the-job leadership challenges typically faced by RMs
   - A brief synopsis of their career histories highlighting key jobs and learning experiences on the path toward the RM role

2. Administering an in-depth (three- to four-hour) behavioral-event focused interview designed to evaluate the individuals' career accomplishments and experience against the key elements in the RM Success Profile (for example, results "track-record" as well as competencies demonstrated)

## Insights Emerging from the Assessment Results

Although there was considerable variability across the individuals assessed, it was apparent that as a group the participants would benefit most from a program targeting development in the competency areas of

- Strategic perspective
- Maximizing business performance
- Insightful listening
- Problem solving and innovation
- Mental agility

Further, when the participants were evaluated in terms of the extent of their prior learning as a result of opportunities to deal with the various types of key leadership challenges they would likely face as RMs, it was clear that a number of them had a somewhat limited view of how to lead the business due to

- Having "grown up" primarily in a single region and thus having seen a fairly limited set of business conditions and challenges
- Working for relatively few regional managers, thus limiting the modeling of varied leadership styles and approaches in operating as an RM
- Being accustomed to focusing primarily on executing the plans and tactics developed for them at more senior management levels (rather than having personal responsibility for formulating strategy and vision)

These insights regarding the needs and readiness of individuals targeted for development for the regional manager role were used to shape the leadership program described here and are currently being leveraged to shape training initiatives for the future.

## Initial Feedback and Coaching

Prior to the start of the leadership program, the individual consultants who had conducted the assessments met with each individual participant in a one-on-one session to discuss his or her results. The intent of this meeting was to help participants identify areas of personal learning needed *prior* to the start of the program so that they might be able to begin to take advantage of opportunities to learn or practice new behaviors in the course of the program itself. This feedback session also set the stage for subsequent work on the development of personal development action plans for each participant that was to take place during and after the action learning program itself.

# THE PROGRAM

## Designing the Leadership Development Experience

A number of factors and influences were used to help shape the design decisions for the leadership program. Among these were the results of the initial work done to create the RM Success Profile, the results of the initial assessment of the skill and development levels of participants against elements of the success profile, and an understanding of the kinds of leadership development experiences that these participants had already been part of in the past. These considerations helped identify some specific needs and opportunities and led to the design of a leadership development program intended specifically to

- Provide participants with the opportunity to learn, practice, and demonstrate key competencies identified as in need of development, including

  A broad, strategic conception of the business

  Mental agility and creativity in problem solving

  Listening and collaboration skills

- Expose participants to selected regional manager role models who can expand their perspective about the RM role by sharing some of their key experiences and learnings in the position

- Provide participants with the opportunity to work closely with senior level executives from whom they could learn (about leadership and about the business)

- Give participants an action learning assignment that addressed real issues facing the business overall (and that would complement typical classroom-based training offered)

- Provide participants with an experience that was both organizationally relevant (tied to achieving McDonald's growth objectives) and personally relevant (tied to developing specific competencies needed for success in the RM position to which they aspired)

- Take place in a concentrated period—ninety days with a definite commitment to present results to the president of the business and his team

## Content of the Program

The program consisted of four phases over a period of six to twelve months.

**Phase One.** In Phase One, the participants met initially for three and a half days. Content in this phase included

- Strategic business context for the program and for their development as a group
- Introduction of personal learning journals to be used throughout
- Explanation of the basis for the RM Success Profile and a presentation of the aggregate profile results for the entire group
- Initial individual development planning
- The use of learning partners
- Presentations on the business from "star" RM performers
- Introduction of the group to the two action learning assignments
- Introduction of division president champions who would assist each learning group through the process
- Development of team charters for tackling their action learning assignments
- Presentation of their initial work on their issue to senior management
- Recording of personal learnings from the initial meeting

**Action Learning Assignments.** The action learning assignments were tied to specific business issues or questions that had been identified as high-priority by the senior leadership of the company. The actual business issues or questions selected were, in fact, drawn from a list of key initiatives identified as part of a "Blueprint Plan" developed at the corporate level to drive and support doubling the size of the business in ten years. It was believed that tying the program content to the business strategy in this way would make the learning experience more real and compelling for the participants and the output more valuable to the business.

**Phase Two.** Phase Two consisted of the next ninety days over which the two action learning teams tackled their respective assignments:

*Group One.* Identify opportunities and make recommendations to simplify marketing and operations within all the regions

*Group Two.* Make recommendations for how to transform the critical role of business consultant in the regions in order to support the company's growth objectives

During this phase, the groups met on several occasions to brainstorm and refine ideas, members carried out individual assignments (gathering data, accessing experts throughout the system for interviews), and learning partners connected with each other to stay on track with their individual learning objectives.

**Phase Three.** Phase three involved the entire group of participants re-assembling at corporate in ninety days to present their results and recommendations to senior management.

**Phase Four.** Phase Four involved senior management actually implementing many of the ideas developed by the learning groups, as well as ongoing follow-up and coaching of individual participants.

## Tools, Instruments, and Training Materials

There were a number of support tools, instruments, and training materials that were developed and used throughout the program. Among these were

- RM Success Profile. This profile was developed as a "blueprint for success" for individuals in the RM role. It includes a picture of both the competencies and the results that must be demonstrated and produced by RMs in order to excel in the role. It is provided as Exhibit 12.1.

- Individual participant assessment and development reports developed by the external assessors with and for the individual participants. These reports identified individual strengths and weaknesses relative to the success profile.

- Personal learning journals for each participant that focused on identifying his or her learning needs and objectives, significant learning events and insights, and ongoing progress.

- Action-learning tools, including

  Team tools; for example, Project Map, Team Charter (see Exhibit 12.2), Roles and Responsibilities Chart, Team Metrics (Exhibit 12.3), Team Communications Model, Team Process Check (Exhibit 12.4)

  Project tools; for example, Stakeholders Commitment Chart, Data Collection Methods: Pros and Cons (Exhibit 12.5), Affinity Diagram, Force-Field Analysis (Exhibit 12.6), Flowchart Process Measures, Cause and Effect Diagram, Project Review Checklist (Exhibit 12.7)

  Presentation tools; for example, defining your audience's needs, choreographing the presentation, organizing the presentation content, using visuals effectively.

### Reinforcing and Building on Learning

Although the program was well received by participants, it was felt important to take some specific steps to reinforce the learnings gained. Examples of some of these steps included

- Follow-up memos to the group regarding program outcomes
- Progress reports on the specific participant recommendations that had been implemented
- Feedback provided to the managers of the participants so that they could reinforce ongoing learning
- Follow-up progress checks with individual participants by executive coaches on implementation of development plan ideas

In order to reinforce the participants' learning from the program experience steps were taken to help participants be able to connect their program-specific insights and learning plans with the overall organization's ongoing personal development system and processes:

*Integration with the HR Systems in the Organization*

- Showing participants how the unique job-specific competencies developed as part of the success profile for the RM position linked to the organization's more generic core and leadership competencies that serve as a key component within the overall performance development system
- Encouraging participants to take their specific learning and development goals and plans emerging from this program and "add them to" the development plans that they had put together with their managers earlier in the year
- Providing participants with information on how to use the in-house resources for competency development and link it to the kinds of personal development needs identified in this program
- Offering additional external resources for personal development (for example, coaching) where required for specific development needs

# EVALUATION

## Methods and Measures

Efforts were made to identify and gather both process- and outcome-oriented measure of the program's effectiveness. Examples of the evaluation data collected included

- Questionnaires of participants at the end of each of the four phases of the program

- Invitation of comments and suggestions from all of the senior executives involved with the program or participants
- Data on completion and implementation of individual action plans
- Tracking of participants' promotions and job success
- Follow-up phone calls and surveys to program participants one year after program completion

## Program Outcomes

The evaluation data gathered to date include information on objective outcomes that have occurred with participants, as well as their subjective assessment of program impacts.

**Objective Data on Program Impact.** The recommendations presented by two teams were both adopted and integrated into the Strategic Agenda for the U.S. business in 2002. One focused on simplification at the restaurant level, and the other focused on the redefinition of the business consultant's role.

Ten of fourteen participants have been successfully promoted into key regional leadership positions. Thirty percent of those promoted into these key leadership positions were rated at the top of the performance rating scale after only six months in position in their new jobs. The remaining 70 percent were performing at a strong level.

**Subjective Assessment of Program Impact.** Results of the one-year follow-up survey with program participants indicated that they felt the action-learning experience and the feedback and insights on their own individual effectiveness and development needs have helped them be much more effective in their current roles as a result of their

- Having learned the importance of and practicing better listening skills, particularly when working in groups (for example, allowing others to express their opinions, understanding before reacting)
- Recognizing the value of teams and diversity of thought (for example, one general manager (GM) provided the example of how the learnings from the program helped him assemble his team during the restructure, picking talented individuals to maximize the strengths of his team)
- Looking at the business differently today (for example, with a more strategic perspective, "big picture thinking," focused on building a foundation for the future versus just short-term results) as a result of the program's reinforcing their understanding of the notion of linkage and how the many different aspects of the business need to be considered when making changes

- Enhanced communication with and leveraging of people and idea resources within the broader McDonald's system

- Putting increased emphasis on their efforts to coach and develop others

- Being exposed to different management styles that allowed them to realize the strengths of different approaches

- Becoming more self-aware and beginning to put more emphasis on their own personal development by working on the specific issues and opportunities that were targeted in the feedback from their personal assessments

## Critical Success Factors

Feedback from participants indicated that there were a number of key features of the program and its design that helped make it successful. The participants especially appreciated

- Having the ability to make a significant contribution to the business through working on real business problems and seeing their recommendations implemented by senior management

- Having their own personal success requirements articulated in the context of a leadership model tailored to the RM position to which they aspired (as opposed to a more generic model of leadership effectiveness)

- Getting personal feedback and coaching based on the assessment of their competencies and "readiness" for advancement

- Having the opportunity to network with highly talented peers as well as "content experts" in other areas of the business and build relationships with them

- Having senior managers be available, involved, and engaged in the action learning program

- Having the opportunity to be part of a diverse learning group (for example, different thinking styles, work approaches, ethnicities)

- Having the opportunity to significantly broaden their understanding of the organization and view of the business

## Lessons Learned and Opportunities for Improvement

Although the feedback from and about the program was generally quite positive there were also some specific opportunities for improvement identified. These included

- *Use of learning partners.* Participants indicated that they did not have enough time to interact closely with their learning partner during the course of the program. Although they liked the concept, there just wasn't enough time to really get to know and bond with partners during the program.

• *Assessment results linkage to program.* Although the individualized feedback that participants received relative to the RM Success Profile prior to the program was felt to be very helpful, participants indicated that it could have been better linked to the specific development activities contained in the action learning program three-day kick-off and follow-up sessions.

• *Assessment results linkage to IDPs.* All of the participants expressed that the individual assessment component of the program had increased their self-awareness of strengths and development needs and had worked to make positive behavioral changes, but none of the participants had incorporated the assessment results into their formal individual development plans (which had been put together earlier in the year prior to the program). Part of this was simply due to a lack of time, but more could have been done to facilitate this linkage between program information and the ongoing performance development process within the company.

• *Improving the assessment process.* Although a number of the participants found the personal assessment process to be quite valuable, many felt that its value or impact could have been heightened by gathering and including 360-degree feedback to supplement the data gathered in the interview conducted by individual assessors (this suggestion has since been implemented). In addition, participants felt that there should have been greater clarity from the very start with regard to who in the organization would have access to the results of their assessment data (that is, some understood that their data would be shared with their managers and others understood that it was confidential—for them only).

## Additional Benefits and Impacts Realized After Initial Program Completion

In addition to the successful achievement of the main objectives of the program described above, a number of additional impacts of the program have also been realized within the organization:

• The success of the program set the stage for the establishment of a senior level position devoted specifically to executive development.

• The positive response to the success profile developed specifically for the RM position and used to shape this program set the stage for increased use of a leadership competency model within the organization and for a commitment to develop additional job-specific success profiles to differentiate the effectiveness and potential of individual managers in key roles.

• This program demonstrated the viability and value of the action learning approach to leadership development within McDonald's. As a result, action learning has now become the preferred methodology for developing leaders in the organization and will be used in future development programs for high-potential candidates.

# ENHANCED PROGRAM LAUNCH

In June of 2003, an enhanced leadership development program was launched. The Leadership at McDonald's Program (LAMP) was designed to bring together a global pool of twenty-two high-potential directors viewed as having potential to move into officer level positions for a nine-month long intensive leadership development experience. Key learnings from the McDonald's Leadership Development Experience launched in 2001 (and described above) contributed significantly to the design of this new accelerated development program for McDonald's.

The Leadership at McDonald's Program (LAMP) is an integrated approach to developing high-potential talent. Although it clearly focuses on accelerating the development of individual participants, the program process is also designed to more broadly benefit the organization by driving real business results, shaping culture, and building leadership depth. To achieve these goals the program focuses on

- *Increasing the ability of participants to improve business results in their current roles as well as prepare them for achieving success at the next level.* Similar to the action learning component of the Leadership Development Experience (LDE) that was so well received, LAMP gives participants the opportunity to work in small groups to identify significant business improvement opportunities and develop specific actionable recommendations to be presented to executive management. In LAMP, participants are also expected to develop their improvement recommendations by scanning the external environment and using ideas from sources outside of McDonald's to encourage innovation.

- *Leveraging participants' on-the-job accountabilities as opportunities to learn and develop.* Feedback from the LDE program indicated a need to more closely tie participants' identified development needs to concrete actions included their current Individual Development Plans. LAMP focuses on strengthening the connection between the development needs identified in individual program participants' assessments and readily available opportunities in their current roles to build relevant skills. It also incorporates the direct involvement of participants' bosses into the development planning process during the program.

- *Helping participants gain the insight needed to further develop individual leadership capabilities.* Taking into account the very positive feedback from LDE program participants on the value of being assessed against a specific leadership model tied to success in the role(s) they were aspiring to, the LAMP program provided participants with a look at how they matched up against the LAMP leadership framework designed for officer-level positions. In addition, the insights gained from the assessment process for LAMP were strengthened with the added use of 360-degree feedback and realistic work and business simulations.

- *Broadening participants' focus and expanding their mindset from regional to global.* A clear need identified for most participants in the initial LDE program was to broaden their strategic perspective of the business that was generally limited by the narrow scope of their localized experience. The LAMP program placed strong emphasis on helping participants develop a more global perspective through the use of a two-week executive education program provided by the Thunderbird International Consortia.

- *Providing opportunities to build strong peer networks—externally as well as internally.* The opportunity to build strong peer networks as a result of program participation was recognized as a key benefit of the initial LDE program. The LAMP program not only facilitated the building of stronger internal peer networks for participants but added the opportunity for participants to extend this network building to external peers (from noncompeting global companies) with whom they worked in the Thunderbird executive education program.

As of this writing, the participants are approximately three weeks away from the end of the 2003 program. The program will conclude with the subteams presenting their business improvement recommendations (see summary of the business improvement recommendation process in Exhibit 12.8), a debriefing of the presentation "experience" as well as overall learnings from all aspects of the program, and a team celebration. Program follow-up will include the establishment of key mentoring relationships, sponsorship of the 2004 program participants, and a "reconnecting" experience six months after conclusion of the program.

# SUMMARY

This chapter described the development and implementation of a leadership development program targeted to help prepare selected candidates for advancement into a key leadership position for the McDonald's business (that is, regional manager). The combination of doing preliminary work to identify the specific requirements for success of leaders in this role (versus taking a "generic" approach to leadership) and the use of a more practical and engaging training method (action learning) resulted not only in producing significant benefits for the initial program participants but also in helping to set the stage for influencing the design of current and future leadership initiatives within the company.

Exhibit 12.1. Regional Manager Success Profile

| Results | |
|---|---|
| *Types* | *Metrics* |
| Employee | • Staff and commitment survey results<br>• Understanding of company strategy and future vision<br>• Solid staff expertise<br>• Performance standards and accountability for results<br>• Development of leadership talent for the system |
| Customer | • Customer-count targets<br>• Quality, service, cleanliness, and value standards scores<br>• Customer experience feedback |
| Owner-operator | • Owner-operator (O/O) feedback/confidence<br>• Results-focused O/O teams<br>• Engagement of O/Os with the strategic platform<br>• Operator cash flow targets |
| Structure and process | • Performance on corporate initiatives<br>• Infrastructure and process improvements |
| Financial | • Operating income targets<br>• Positive economic profit (EP) contribution<br>• Net new unit plan targets |
| Competencies | |
| Thinking skills | • Mental agility<br>• Focus and balance<br>• Strategic perspective<br>• Problem solving and innovation |
| People skills | • Self-management<br>• Insightful listening<br>• Impact and influence<br>• Mature assertiveness<br>• Teamwork and collaboration<br>• Communicates effectively<br>• Peer leadership |
| Business understanding | • Marketplace perspective<br>• Maximizes business performance<br>• Financial acumen<br>• Business judgment |

Exhibit 12.2. Team Charter—Sample Format

| Team Leader, Members, and Sponsor (if appropriate) | |
|---|---|
| | |
| **Team Purposes** | **Links to Organization's Context** |
| Task purpose<br>Interpersonal purpose | (How the purpose contributes to specific plans and objectives, addresses gaps in the organization's performance, or addresses specific customer needs) |
| **Process to Be Used** | **Success Measures and Progress Measures** |
| (For example, specific problem-solving methodologies, information technologies, conflict-resolution techniques) | (For example, cycle time, error rates, or costs to be reduced; productivity to be increased; customer satisfaction to be improved; gaps to be closed) |
| **Boundaries of the Team's Work** | **Resource Availability and Constraints** |
| (For example, issues outside of team's scope, beginning and end points of a process to be improved, decision-making authority) | (For example, budget, equipment, training) |
| **Key Milestones** | **Team Member Time Commitments** |
| (For example, formal reviews, deliverable dates, final deadline) | |
| **Team Operating Principles** | |
| | |

Exhibit 12.3.  Team Metrics

| | Subjective Measures | | | Objective Measures | | |
|---|---|---|---|---|---|---|
| Team Metric | | | | | | |
| Description | | | | | | |
| Responsibility | | | | | | |
| How Measured | | | | | | |
| Variance | | | | | | |
| Kick-off | | | | | | |
| Frequency | | | | | | |
| Status | | | | | | |
| Issues | | | | | | |

## Exhibit 12.4. Team Process Check

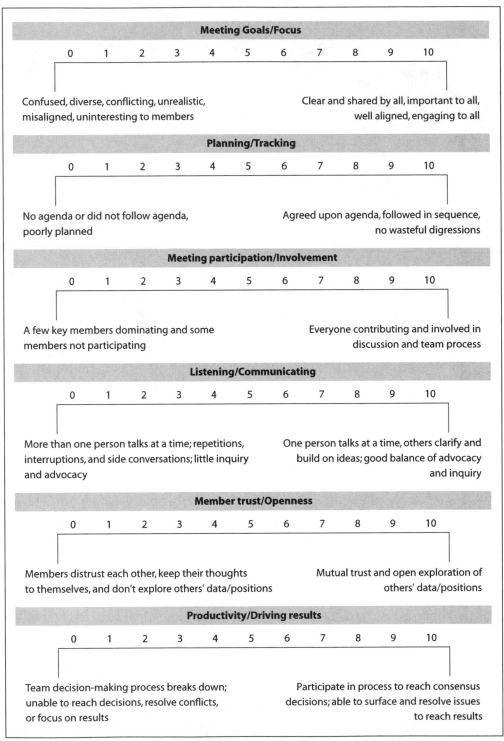

**Meeting Goals/Focus**

| 0 | 1 | 2 | 3 | 4 | 5 | 6 | 7 | 8 | 9 | 10 |

Confused, diverse, conflicting, unrealistic, misaligned, uninteresting to members

Clear and shared by all, important to all, well aligned, engaging to all

**Planning/Tracking**

| 0 | 1 | 2 | 3 | 4 | 5 | 6 | 7 | 8 | 9 | 10 |

No agenda or did not follow agenda, poorly planned

Agreed upon agenda, followed in sequence, no wasteful digressions

**Meeting participation/Involvement**

| 0 | 1 | 2 | 3 | 4 | 5 | 6 | 7 | 8 | 9 | 10 |

A few key members dominating and some members not participating

Everyone contributing and involved in discussion and team process

**Listening/Communicating**

| 0 | 1 | 2 | 3 | 4 | 5 | 6 | 7 | 8 | 9 | 10 |

More than one person talks at a time; repetitions, interruptions, and side conversations; little inquiry and advocacy

One person talks at a time, others clarify and build on ideas; good balance of advocacy and inquiry

**Member trust/Openness**

| 0 | 1 | 2 | 3 | 4 | 5 | 6 | 7 | 8 | 9 | 10 |

Members distrust each other, keep their thoughts to themselves, and don't explore others' data/positions

Mutual trust and open exploration of others' data/positions

**Productivity/Driving results**

| 0 | 1 | 2 | 3 | 4 | 5 | 6 | 7 | 8 | 9 | 10 |

Team decision-making process breaks down; unable to reach decisions, resolve conflicts, or focus on results

Participate in process to reach consensus decisions; able to surface and resolve issues to reach results

Exhibit 12.5. Pros and Cons of Data Collection Methods

|  | Pros | Cons |
|---|---|---|
| One-on-one interviews | • Opportunity to build relationships with those interviewed.<br>• Direct/indirect nonverbal communication will allow you to pick up additional information.<br>• Details can be clarified when necessary. | • Getting access to the people you need to interview may not be easy.<br>• Telephone interviews sometimes catch people off guard and keep them from communicating.<br>• Those not interviewed may feel "discriminated against." |
| Focus groups | • You can get a lot of data in a short time.<br>• Group synergy can lead to deeper inquiry.<br>• Allows you to obtain several points of view. | • Scheduling may be difficult.<br>• There is a risk of "group think" or self-censoring in front of group.<br>• Process may become dominated by strong or vocal leader. |
| Surveys | • You can get a lot of data, inexpensively, from many people.<br>• You can get information from people who may otherwise be inaccessible.<br>• Anonymous answers promote greater openness.<br>• Can be used to alert the organization as part of an intervention. | • Questions cannot be clarified.<br>• You can't identify the exact sources of the responses, so they may be difficult to interpret.<br>• You may not receive open and honest answers to all questions.<br>• Require attention to design and implementation. |

(Continued)

**Exhibit 12.5. Pros and Cons of Data Collection Methods** *(Continued)*

| | Pros | Cons |
|---|---|---|
| Direct observation | • You get first-hand information from what you personally observe.<br>• There is less chance of misunderstanding from someone else's observation.<br>• You can redirect your focus as situation changes. | • You may not have access to the situations that need to be observed.<br>• Direct observation may alter the situation being observed.<br>• It may difficult to observe enough situations to be able to make generalizations. |
| Analysis of existing data | • Saves time, money, and resources.<br>• Data may be more respected from primary researcher.<br>• You may get information that you would not otherwise have access to.<br>• What others don't see as relevant may be vitally important. | • The data may be incomplete, unreliable, or out of date.<br>• The data may be difficult and or time consuming to obtain or understand.<br>• Data obtained may be irrelevant to your research. |

Exhibit 12.6. Force-Field Analysis

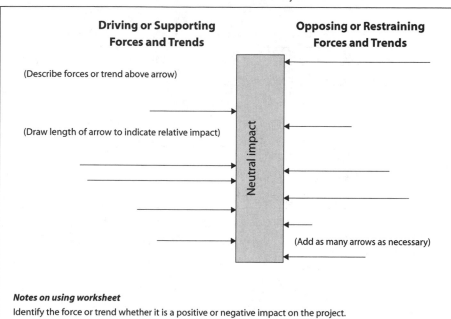

**Notes on using worksheet**

Identify the force or trend whether it is a positive or negative impact on the project.

Label the force or trend on the appropriate side of the central (neutral impact) axis.

Immediately under the label, draw an arrow whose length reflects the team's perception of the relative amount of impact that force or trend is likely to exert on the project's success—short arrows indicate minor impact; longer arrows indicate major impact.

**Exhibit 12.7. Project Review Checklist**

| Task | Applicable | Time Needed | Date Needed | Done |
|------|------------|-------------|-------------|------|
| **What planning needed for the execution of the project:** | | | | |
| • Set project review dates at the start of the project. | ☐ | | | ☐ |
| • Ask project team members to keep the dates sacrosanct on their personal calendars. | ☐ | | | ☐ |
| • Create a template so that each member can report progress on his or her part of the project in a standardized way. | ☐ | | | ☐ |
| • Ensure the project sponsor is aware of the dates. | ☐ | | | ☐ |
| **Before the review:** | | | | |
| • Identify all participants; send announcements. | ☐ | | | ☐ |
| • Specify the goal of the review. | ☐ | | | ☐ |
| • Develop an agenda with times for specific areas if the review is going to last longer than three hours | ☐ | | | ☐ |
| • Prepare pertinent materials and distribute them well in advance | ☐ | | | ☐ |
| • If needed, arrange for logistics support (room, coffee, food, audio-visual support, etc.). | ☐ | | | ☐ |
| **During the review:** | | | | |
| • Welcome participants and make any introductions. | ☐ | | | ☐ |

**Exhibit 12.7.** (*Continued*)

| Task | Applicable | Time Needed | Date Needed | Done |
|------|-----------|-------------|-------------|------|
| • Ask for someone to act as a recorder and take notes unless there is a formal secretary. | ☐ | | | ☐ |
| • Set goals for the review. | ☐ | | | ☐ |
| • Review agenda; modify as needed. | ☐ | | | ☐ |
| • Announce decision-making model. | ☐ | | | ☐ |
| • Describe relevant rules and processes. | ☐ | | | ☐ |
| • Monitor group processes. | ☐ | | | ☐ |
| • Stay focused on the task. | ☐ | | | ☐ |
| • Sum up at the end of discussions. | ☐ | | | ☐ |
| • Ensure the recorder has captured any decisions before moving on. | ☐ | | | ☐ |
| • Watch the logistics and time-keeping. If people have effectively finished their contribution, offer to excuse them if they wish. | ☐ | | | ☐ |
| • Before the end, review decisions reached. | ☐ | | | ☐ |
| • Develop any action plans needed. | ☐ | | | ☐ |
| • Ask participants to evaluate the effectiveness of the review. | ☐ | | | ☐ |
| • Thank participants. | ☐ | | | ☐ |
| • After the review: | | | | |
| • Follow up with minutes as soon as possible. On a fast-moving project they should be issued the same day. | ☐ | | | ☐ |
| • Implement action plan. | ☐ | | | ☐ |

**Exhibit 12.8. Business Improvement Recommendation Process**

## Background

Achieving McDonald's business strategies and goals will require that McDonald's leaders do things differently. Although it is important that our leaders are confident in the company and their own ability, that confidence cannot result in the perception that others can't and aren't doing things better than we are. In fact, in healthy companies, innovation occurs when every leader has a mindset of continuous improvement and is constantly scanning the external environment for better ways of doing business.

Therefore, we are using the Leadership at McDonald's Program (LAMP) as a vehicle to support and reinforce a culture of continuous improvement and innovation within McDonald's. Each LAMP subteam is charged with leveraging their combined LAMP experiences, especially their experience at Thunderbird University, to scan for potential ideas from external sources that, if adopted or adapted appropriately, have the potential to have a significant impact on McDonald's performance.

## Team Deliverable

Four subteams are to search and discover, from any sources external to McDonald's, one significant "business improvement opportunity" that they recommend be seriously considered by the executive councils for possible adoption within McDonald's. The opportunity should be one that supports or accelerates the achievement of our key business strategies.

Each team is to do enough research on their recommendation to be able to present a business case to the chairman's and president's councils and have their proposed action plan for taking the recommendation to the next step of feasibility be adopted and funded, should funding be required.

## Purpose of the Business Improvement Recommendation

- *Organizational leadership.* Reinforce a continuous improvement and innovation mindset and culture within McDonald's. Put a strong focus on the importance of leaders to be constantly seeking to "scan and mine" the external environment for ideas that, if adopted within McDonald's, could have the potential of positively and significantly affecting business results.
- *Team leadership.* Provide each of the four teams a real versus role-play opportunity to learn more about how to be a part of and lead a high-performing team responsible for delivering an important business recommendation to a high-profile audience of senior leaders of the business.

**Exhibit 12.8.** (*Continued*)

- *Personal leadership.* Provide every LAMP participant the opportunity for personal development around innovation, idea development and adaptation, managing change, stakeholder analysis, and executive presentation and influence.

### Ground Rules

1. The core idea must come from somewhere outside of McDonald's.
2. There must be evidence to confirm that the recommendation has worked successfully in another organization(s).
3. There is no need to get approval from a person or any organization inside McDonald's before presenting recommendation.
4. Each team presentation can go no longer than thirty minutes, leaving fifteen minutes for discussion with the council members.
5. Teams have complete freedom within this framework.

### Evaluation of Recommendation by Council Members

- Assess the quality of the thought process and logic that went into the recommendation.
- Evaluate the presentation approach, style, and form in terms of its impact on persuading you toward approving the recommendation.
- Rate the degree to which the team effectively handles questions, challenges, and concerns during the discussion.
- Assess the feasibility of successfully implementing this recommendation and gaining the benefits for the business.

Executive council members will also provide each team with specific, written feedback on what they liked most about the team's recommendation and one or two suggestions they have for how the team could have improved their presentation.

# ABOUT THE CONTRIBUTORS

**James Intagliata** is president and founder of the NorthStar Group, a management consulting firm that specializes in senior-level executive assessment, individual leadership coaching, and competency modeling. Over the past twenty years he has consulted to a diverse group of clients and senior executives in businesses ranging in size and maturity from venture capital–backed start-ups to Fortune 100 companies dealing with dramatic new challenges in their business and marketplace. In addition to his consulting work, he has held faculty positions at the State University of New York at Buffalo and the University of Missouri at Kansas City and taught organizational theory and management at the graduate level. He received his Ph.D. in clinical psychology in 1976 from the State University of New York at Buffalo. His recently published articles include "Leveraging Leadership Competencies to Produce Leadership Brand: Creating Distinctiveness by Focusing on Strategy and Results" (with co-authors Dave Ulrich and Norm Smallwood) in *Human Resources Planning*, Winter, 2000.

**David Small** is currently senior director, U.S. leadership development and succession planning for McDonald's Corporation in Oak Brook, Illinois. In this role he is responsible for talent management and leadership development for McDonald's U.S. business. David has a master's degree in industrial and organizational psychology from the University of Colorado, and has worked in the field of employee selection and assessment systems, performance development, succession planning, and leadership development for over fifteen years. David's professional career includes working for U.S. West and Ameritech/SBC prior to joining McDonald's Corporation in 1995.

# CHAPTER THIRTEEN

# MIT

*Developing the higher-level skills to create and sustain a self-perpetuating learning organization through mental models, systems thinking, personal and organizational visioning, and several other best practice organizational learning exercises and tools that achieved significant results.*

OVERVIEW                                                              310

DIAGNOSIS AND ASSESSMENT OF NEEDS                                     310

MAINTAINING THE SPIRIT AND SETTING THE TONE                          312

INTERVENTION                                                         313

    Program Design Stage                         314
    Overall Competency Models                     315
    Program Implementation                        315
    The Journey Continues                         316
    Training Methodologies and Tools              316
    Leading Indicators of Performance             317
    Behavioral and Attitudinal Changes            318
    Significant Shifts in Organizational Practices 318

INSIGHTS AND REFLECTIONS                                             319

REFERENCES                                                           320

EXHIBITS

    Exhibit 13.1: Status of Strategic Plan Action Items,
      1999 and 2002                        322
    Exhibit 13.2: Systems Diagram                 324
    Exhibit 13.3: Model I: Organizational Learning
      Capabilities                        325
    Exhibit 13.4: Model II: Competency Model
    Operationalizing Organizational Learning      326
    Exhibit 13.5: Agenda for Session I             327
    Exhibit 13.6: Agenda for Session II            327

Exhibit 13.7: Session Follow-up Questionnaire      328
Exhibit 13.8: Training Content: Exercises Used
     in Organizational Learning Sessions      329

ABOUT THE CONTRIBUTORS      333

# OVERVIEW

This case study describes the steps that the Massachusetts Institute of Technology's Department of Facilities is undertaking to transform into a self-perpetuating learning organization. The overarching goal is to create an organization that constructs, operates, serves, and maintains physical space in ways that enhance MIT's mission to advance knowledge and educate students in science, technology, and other areas of scholarship. Also it is a story about a leader's vision and courage to build a leader-full organization and bring together customers and representatives from every corner and level of the department to set its strategic direction.

# DIAGNOSIS AND ASSESSMENT OF NEEDS

Most journeys begin with a single step; however, this journey began with two questions: *Where's the plan, and what are people talking about?* In July 1993, Victoria Sirianni became head of MIT's Department of Facilities. Her first act of official business was to review the department's strategic plan; however, there wasn't one. Also, during her visits from functional unit to functional unit she learned that there were some very unhappy people; more unhappy people than she expected. Prior to accepting the position of chief facilities officer, Vicky, as she prefers to be called, had been employed by the Department of Facilities for twenty years and worked in several capacities within the discipline of space planning. Nevertheless, her finding surprised her. Her new goal was to find the answers to these two questions and do something about them. Thus began the transformation of MIT's single largest administrative department.

Soon after Vicky accepted her new position, but unknown to her at the time, the Institute was beginning to launch business process reengineering efforts in several main operational areas as a means to simplify convoluted work processes and save money. Facilities was selected to be one of the target areas, so to prepare, Vicky encouraged members of the department to learn as much as they could about reengineering.

Although sidetracked by the rumors of impending reengineering for a few months, Vicky asked Laura Lucas, now learning and performance coordinator, to survey everyone within the department and determine the basis for the unhappiness. The questions were direct: *How are we communicating internally, do you feel that your ideas and suggestions are valued, and do you believe that you and your coworkers perform to the highest standard of excellence?* The answers were just as direct: *Our biggest problem presently is that [name deleted]'s autocratic style has led to a breakdown of communications and mistrust between workers and line supervisors, there is nothing that could be said to change this so it won't matter, and everyone should do their fair share of the work.* Whether these responses were from people lashing out at their supervisors and workmates or those reacting to the uncertainty of reengineering, it was easy to conclude that something was wrong. Fortunately, there were many positive comments. For example: *I'm proud to support a fine institution such as MIT, I'm proud that it's in the midst of real change and that we may be able to make this a high-quality energized environment, and Facilities is a friendly place to work.*

Whether the problems were real or perceived they had to be addressed. To this end, Vicky, Laura, and Joe Gifun, currently assistant director of Facilities for infrastructure renewal and special projects, imagined that Facilities employees could take control of the future. Therefore, they pulled together a large number of people representing every aspect of the department, took the information collected by the survey, combined it with information from other initiatives already under way, and used it to write the department's first strategic plan.

The word was sent out asking for people to come forward to participate in writing the plan. Fifty volunteers were distributed into one of four focus groups: communications; empowerment and accountability; leadership, management, and fairness; and recognition. Each team included a mix of unionized service staff, administrators, architects, engineers, computer experts, administrative assistants, and maintenance, grounds, and custodial service supervisors. The goal was to make each focus group as cross-functional as possible. Each group was charged with analyzing the survey responses and determining the strengths, weaknesses, opportunities, and challenges for the particular focus area and to recommend concrete action items. All of the work was compiled into one document and the strategic plan was published and distributed to all members of the department in December 1994.

As one of the outcomes of the strategic plan was the desire and necessity for more training, Facilities launched three departmentwide training efforts: communications, teamwork, and diversity. Also, Facilities built a mechanism to ensure linkage between learning and performance and worked with human resources to determine competencies for each job classification. It was at this stage that Laura restructured Facilities' training department to focus on learning and performance.

The Strategic Leadership Team (SLT) was formed soon after the creation of the strategic plan and was a collective of several formal leaders but mostly informal leaders. The SLT comprised a diverse group of people from all walks of department life and several customers who came together to express their frustrations and ideas about current practices and the future of the Department of Facilities. The SLT also acted as an advisor to Vicky and her directors and as a sounding board for new ideas. Members of the SLT operated under two rules: keep a departmentwide strategic focus and maintain the spirit of the original strategic plan and its amendments.

There were fifty-six action items listed in the strategic plan, and much progress has been made. Exhibit 13.1 shows the status of the fifty-six action items in 1999 and again in 2002. Of particular interest is the action item that is labeled "in progress"; it calls for the implementation of an external and internal communications program. Since 1994 several communications programs and processes have been put into place. Although some have had a moderate level of success, complete success has been elusive. Facilities has yet to determine the balance point between level of service (the information the internal and external customer needs and the form in which it is delivered or presented) and cost. Facilities defines the *internal customer* as the Facilities employee who functions as a customer when requesting services from another team or functional unit, such as technical assistance on a project, training, and building-system repairs. The *external customer* is any member of the MIT community who is not a Facilities employee.

# MAINTAINING THE SPIRIT AND SETTING THE TONE

People say that there needs to be full support "at the top" for successful growth and change in any organization. MIT's Department of Facilities was very lucky to have a leader who was committed to making a difference within the department and had the vision to put the appropriate pieces together to make that happen. The department is a team-centered environment where people can express ideas and work together at resolving issues, formulating policy, and, yes, developing a strategic vision for the department. The department respects independent thinking and believes in the reengineering concept of empowering people to get the job done and done well. To do so, one needs to have the appropriate tools, resources, and the ability to learn from mistakes.

Under Vicky's leadership, the department began to use teamwork as a means to discuss alternatives, make decisions, and resolve issues as they came up. These teams worked both within and across established service areas— operations, utilities, design and construction, capital projects, finance and accounting, administration, systems engineering, and infrastructure—where each service area is led by a director. From 1998 to summer 2002, three standing teams supported Vicky, the directors, the operational leadership team, and the strategic leadership team. The operational leadership team has transformed over time and consists now of functional unit managers; it provides a forum for the managers to discuss operational issues that have an impact on all units and to update each other on current and upcoming activities. The strategic leadership team has transformed as well, and Vicky and the directors have adopted its format, investigatory function, and team-based leadership model.

Over the course of time, Facilities employees experienced the value of teams first-hand; therefore, individual teams would be formed for specific purposes and in many cases without formal permission. These ad hoc teams, whether official or unofficial, became a breeding ground for informal leaders and a tool used by informal leaders to advance an idea. Informal leaders came from all pay categories. They were supervisors, managers, unionized service staff, administrative assistants, support staff, and even directors. In many cases, teams have made departmental decisions and developed and implemented major processes. This practice created an environment of openness and enabled cross-functional discussions to help individuals understand that most issues were important to all, not just to an individual's service area.

The Facilities division maintains an open environment that can constantly refresh itself. Facilities employees understand change and the need to develop a culture that reflects upon itself and continues to enhance the lives of its teams, leaders, and individuals. Formal and informal teams exhibit much pride, engage their members, and produce high-quality work. Teams are the place where Facilities looks for emerging leaders.

## INTERVENTION

Although some previous initiatives had failed and others lived out their useful lives satisfying their intended purposes, one can readily observe that Facilities is a very different organization now. Nevertheless, Facilities, like any organization that desires to thrive in the marketplace, must provide its customers with higher value than their competitors, in this case facility management and maintenance firms. Facilities, like its competitors, must at the very least keep pace with the changing technology in building systems, such as those that monitor and control the interior climate of buildings and fulfill, at least minimally, the expectation of the MIT community to provide more service and deliver it much faster than it has ever been. So the need for learning continues but at a much higher developmental level. The current goal is to help Facilities employees become better thinkers so that they will have the skills to create and sustain a self-perpetuating learning organization. To achieve this goal, Facilities sought the help and experience of Dr. Carol Zulauf, a professor of organizational learning at Suffolk University. Dr. Zulauf, consulting partner, Pat Kennedy Graham, director of administration, and Joe Gifun invested much time in frankly discussing all that has happened, good and bad, within the Department of Facilities over prior years to ascertain its current strengths and weaknesses and recommend a course of action to Vicky. The primary methodology used during the planning discussions was guided brainstorming. Once ideas were recorded, they were clarified if necessary and challenged. The result was to develop a series of learning modules introducing Peter Senge's five disciplines. The first module was introduced to the assistant directors and members of the operational leadership and strategic leadership teams and focused on systems thinking. The second module, personal mastery, was offered to informal leaders, whether or not they were members of a current team, and others who had shown the initiative to lead. Highlights of these programs are presented as follows.

## Program Design Stage

The strategic goals and priorities that were developed and introduced by the operational leadership team encompassed the following:

- Improve customer service
- Enhance and protect MIT's assets
- Design, build, and deliver on the capital projects
- Continuous improvement in core processes
- Meet MIT's commitment to the environment
- Develop individual and organizational capabilities

Dr. Zulauf, working very closely with two of the key people from the Department of Facilities, focused on two subsets within the "develop individual and organizational capabilities" strategic goal: (1) develop, adopt, and implement new HR practices and (2) renew learning and performance effort.

When the consulting partner first started to envision the interventions for this project, using these strategic goals and priorities as her driving force, she had as her overall framework the organizational and individual capabilities as defined by the Balanced Scorecard, developed by Dave Ulrich and others in *Results-Based Leadership*. This framework included, from the organizational perspective, considering the capabilities for learning and innovation, working toward "boundary-less-ness," or in the language of the Department of Facilities, working cross-functionally, and building in accountability. The employee perspective encompasses increasing performance by developing and leveraging employee capabilities and intellectual capital. The results, over time, would include new best practices within Facilities and a positive impact on Facilities' internal and external customer base.

With the focus on developing organizational and employee capabilities as the overall framework for designing the initial learning and performance initiative, the consulting partner then took this overall framework to the level of using organizational learning capabilities to develop a culture of learning for leaders within the Department of Facilities. The design of this leadership development system was linked directly to the strategic goals and priorities initially promulgated by Facilities.

The critical success factors encompassed two guiding principles:

- That the capacity to grow and learn will transform our systems
- That learning is fundamental to leadership

The consulting partner believes in understanding a system before implementing an intervention or envisioning the dynamics of that system. Exhibit 13.2 illustrates those key dynamics.

Having a systems perspective increases the ability to view how an intervention or change will affect the system and what the outcomes and consequences may be. Developing the systems perspective was the cornerstone of the program design and implementation.

## Overall Competency Models

Two significant models have been used to guide the development of the sessions at MIT. One is from Peter Senge, which shows the organizational learning capabilities as the overarching disciplines; the other competency model, developed by Warner Burke, highlights the specific competencies that this consulting partner has directly linked to the disciplines of organizational learning. Model 1 and Model 2 are displayed as Exhibit 13.3 and Exhibit 13.4, respectively.

## Program Implementation

The specific content of this program focused on developing leaders to envision change within Facilities and to embrace the systems perspective in order to have the participants start to see how they are part of the whole system. To quote Kathleen Dannemiller, organizational change expert, "If you see yourself as part of the system, you are on the path to making real change" (Linkage OD Summit, October 2001). The agendas for the first two training sessions are shown as Exhibits 13.5 and 13.6, with the actual training content shown as Exhibit 13.8.

The critical elements of this implementation hinged on the purposeful linkage to the strategic mission of the department through an exercise in which participants started by envisioning their department in five years time, envisioning in detail how it operates in a healthy, productive, sustainable way. A key question for this exercise was: *What was it you and others did back in 2001 to achieve this remarkable transformation?* The participants became engaged and energized as they started to design their future direction. From there, we focused on the influence of systems and systemic change, which got the participants involved in a new way of thinking about their organization and the impact their decisions have on each other.

## The Journey Continues

This first session set the stage for continued work in building a learning organization and developing the future leaders within Facilities. Our second session focused on developing personal mastery with its foundational premise based on this thought:

> *The missing link in leadership development is growing the*
> *person to grow the leader.*
> —Kevin Cashman (1998, p. 18)

Other key thoughts:

- We tend to view leadership as an external event. We see it as something people *do,* instead of an expression of who we *are.*
- It is our being in action.
- Our being says as much about us as a leader as the act of leading itself.
- As we grow, so shall we lead.

The different sections in this personal mastery session concentrated on the participants identifying the creative tension within themselves and their organizations.

## Training Methodologies and Tools

In both sessions, different methodologies and training tools were employed to stimulate maximum participant engagement and learning: causal loop diagramming for the systems thinking session, hands-on exercises, small-group work, video clips, dialogue sessions, guided presentations, and exercises to continue after the formal in-class work.

Session 2 also set the stage for continued development and follow-up by implementing two specific steps to reinforce learning after the program. One incorporated the practice of keeping a journal in the spirit of encouraging the participants to begin the process of recording any key learnings, insights, lessons learned, and "do differentlies" that they have experienced (for definition of "do differently," please see Exhibit 13.8). In addition to writing about these experiences, participants were also encouraged to write about how these insights, lessons learned, and so forth affected or changed their work practices or interactions. A follow-up was undertaken with each participant six to eight weeks after the session to find out how the session influenced participants' interactions and reflections as leaders.

# Leading Indicators of Performance

The performance measurement focuses on the leading indicators of performance. For example, leading indicators of developing leadership and organizational learning capabilities are building new relationships cross-functionally; enhancing customer interactions, both internally and externally to Facilities; increasing the communication flow within the department; and linking our progress and results back to the strategic goals already delineated by MIT's Department of Facilities.

**Feedback and Follow-up from Our Participants.** One participant from the first session on developing leadership capabilities gave feedback stating that, "You did a great job integrating examples from the morning session [which was on delineating strategic goals] into your presentation."

Another participant from the first session said, "The content is very useful as it causes one to be intentional." How the consulting partner is interpreting that comment is that once something becomes part of our conscious thought process, or intentional, then one is on their way to making (behavioral) changes.

For Session 2, we implemented two measures: a written evaluation right after the session and a follow-up questionnaire six to eight weeks later. At the conclusion of the session, participants were asked, on a scale of 1 to 5, with 5 being excellent, please rate the following:

1. Seminar content—relevance, timeliness
2. Facilitator—knowledge of subject, enthusiasm, teaching style, preparation
3. Seminar materials—clarity, appropriateness
4. Seminar exercises—variety, link to subject area
5. Additional comments, thoughts, and ahas

Feedback included such comments as

- Worth a follow-up
- Exercises were excellent
- Keep the momentum going by holding more sessions
- This session will help me plan my future
- This session made me think about things I hadn't thought about before
- I think this is a great class for everyone to go to, also may open a lot of eyes
- Well thought out exercise on how to look deeply at ourselves, goals, visions, and limitations

The questionnaire, shown as Exhibit 13.7, was sent to the participants six to eight weeks after the session.

## Behavioral and Attitudinal Changes

Some very powerful shifts have occurred in how people view and interact with others. Some examples are shared below:

> I do find myself trying to be more authentic in my interactions with others. The question in my mind, *Why should I care?* was transformed to *Why do I care?* As a result, I've been able to give feedback to people who don't directly report to me because I care enough to take the risk.

> The video [on Personal Mastery that was shown in Session 2] touched me at the core. It shook me to ask, *What is my signature?*

It also must be underscored that real change comes about in seemingly subtle ways, yet has a powerful impact on a relationship or how people interact with each other. The following example is another peek into how a shift occurred between two coworkers as a result of the exercise in Session 2 to identify our conscious and shadow beliefs.

> In the breakout session, a coworker and I found some commonality in "trying to be perfect" [which they identified as a shadow for themselves] and not accomplishing more because the product we work on isn't quite as good as it could be. Since the seminar, we've been able to exchange some "not-so-perfect" reports but good enough to suit the needs. When the coworker asked me for the reports, he said, "It doesn't have to be perfect . . ." I knew what he meant.

Also, regarding the Personal Mastery exercise that asked participants to identify their "Word-in-a-Box," one participant said,

> Since the class, I have become mindful of my "word in the box" as well as the things that I need to change in order to incorporate "my word" into a variety of environments.

One last, yet again very powerful comment from one of the participants who wants to create a culture of learning, creativity, and growth within this organization:

> I want to create an organization that anticipates learning opportunities and constantly asks the questions, *Why and why not?*

## Significant Shifts in Organizational Practices

The Department of Facilities does not have the mechanisms in place at this time to quantitatively determine the return on investment on learning and organizational change efforts. Nevertheless, the following comparisons may help the reader understand the magnitude of the change that has occurred following the implementation of the strategic plan (see Exhibit 13.1 for the strategic plan).

## INSIGHTS AND REFLECTIONS

Facilities has taken many steps along the road to becoming a learning organization; however, what needs to be done to make certain that the journey results in success? Employ Senge's discipline of personal mastery, specifically creative tension, and focus on the gap between current reality and vision. Within this gap are the things that need to be implemented, the issues that need to be resolved, and the questions that need to be answered. For example:

• How does Facilities build an organization that learns from its experiences and records these experiences in a way that is accessible to all employees? Some functional units have adopted the practice of conducting after-action reviews following select events, such as annual commencement exercises or difficult projects. Participants find the after-action review process beneficial, so a goal is to teach more people to perform them. The Department of Facilities maintains a central archive of all construction documents; however, it needs to find the means to capture learnings and information about nonconstruction-related studies, projects, and events. At this time, these records are kept by individuals and are not readily accessible to others unless the inquirer knows or learns that a specific individual has the information.

• Employees need to have the means and training to communicate effectively between all levels of the organization. Facilities employees have access to many communications and customer service courses whether they are conducted by the Facilities Learning and Performance Center or HR's Organizational and Employee Development instructors; however, higher levels of interpersonal and presentation skills are necessary for the future. Therefore, more training is necessary.

• Capitalize on the power of cross-functional teams. Although Facilities has experienced great success with cross-functional teams, more people need to learn the skills required to be good team members.

• Link learning to performance at all levels. The discussion of learning goals and achievements is encouraged in annual performance appraisal meetings; however, the practice needs to be more widespread. Implement the steps necessary to help employees become stewards of a $3 billion physical asset. To help everyone make decisions that enhance the learning, research, and business aspects of the Institute and seek out and rectify problems before they are able to adversely affect MIT's building systems and mission. Facilities employees must possess the skills to work more effectively and efficiently with complex processes, demanding clients, rapidly increasing technologically sophisticated systems, and increasingly stringent regulations. Members of the MIT community and MIT's physical assets, its buildings and grounds, benefit from highly skilled facilities personnel. The Learning and Performance Center is implementing more technical skills training along with many courses in diversity, management, computers, leadership, and safety.

• How does Facilities measure the value of its service in terms of the internal and external customer? At the completion of every service request by Repair and Maintenance, the functional unit responsible for all of the repairs to existing building structures and systems, and Design and Construction Services, the functional unit responsible for all renovations, the internal or external customer is asked to provide feedback on the quality of the service. Returned evaluations are reviewed and changes implemented if necessary. Learning and Performance measures the value of its training in the workplace with an evaluation form that is distributed at the conclusion of every course and by way of dialogue sessions one to two months following the conclusion of select courses. The form asks questions about the specific course and for suggestions regarding new courses, and the dialogue focuses on the application of new skills and knowledge. Very few historical statistical data are available; therefore, longitudinal studies are not possible at this time. Facilities is beginning to collect data and expand measurement capabilities to other functional units.

At this early stage of its development, Facilities' learning organization effort is fragile and requires unflagging vigilance, much maintenance, and continuous, consistent, and strong leadership. The primary elements for growth are already in place: the realization by many employees that to be successful in the long-term, Facilities must become a learning organization; a visionary chief facilities officer; a few enlightened leaders; and a cadre of informal leaders to sustain this growth and lead, influence, and motivate the rest of the organization throughout the many changes and transformations that will be occurring. Facilities' journey is clearly under way.

*The journey of a thousand miles starts from beneath your feet.*
—Lao Tzu, *Tao Te Ching*, Book Two, Chapter 64

# REFERENCES

Burke, W. W. (2001). Competency Model. *OD Practitioner, 33*(3), 15.

Cashman, K. (1998). *Leadership from the Inside Out.* Provo, Utah: Executive Excellence Publishing.

Dannemiller, K. (Oct. 2001). "Whole Scale Change." Paper presented at Linkage Organization Development Summit, Chicago, Ill.

Lao Tzu (4th century B.C./1963). *Tao Te Ching,* D. C. Lau (trans.). Baltimore, Md.: Penguin.

Senge, P. (1990). *The Fifth Discipline: The Art and Practice of the Learning Organization.* New York: Doubleday.

Ulrich, D., Zenger, J., and Smallwood, N. (1999). *Results-Based Leadership.* Boston, Mass.: Harvard Business School Press.

**Exhibit 13.1. Status of Strategic Plan Action Items, 1999 and 2002**

|  | Number of Action Items | |
|---|---|---|
|  | *1999* | *2002* |
| Complete | 29 | 45 |
| Partially complete | 16 | 10 |
| In progress | 5 | 1 |
| No action | 6 | 0 |

*Note:* "Partially complete" refers to an action item with several deliverables where at least one but not all of the deliverables are complete; whereas, "in progress" refers to an action item with several deliverables where none are complete.

| *Prior to Strategic Plan* | *Following Strategic Plan* |
|---|---|
| Training centrally documented for 27 percent of employees | Training documented for all employees |
| Fourteen courses were offered annually to unionized service staff | Forty-five individual courses were offered to all employees in 1998, one year following the formation of the Learning and Performance Team. Currently Learning and Performance offers a similar number of courses; however, many of the original courses have been updated or replaced with those addressing current needs. |
| Thirty computers plus thirty terminals were in use | Four hundred computers are in use |
| Only select individuals received computer training | All employees receive training in electronic mail and web fundamentals |
| Training was generally focused on technical issues | Learning is aligned to strategic goals |
| Annual performance reviews for administrative staff were conducted informally and inconsistently | The annual performance review process for administrative staff is formal and consistently applied |
| Administrative assistants did not receive annual performance reviews | Administrative assistants receive annual performance evaluations |

Exhibit 13.1. (*Continued*)

| | |
|---|---|
| Unionized service staff did not receive annual performance reviews | Unionized service staff participate in an annual performance feedback session with their coach |
| Recognition for good work was dependent upon a customer sending praise to the employee by the way of a letter. The letter would be placed in the employee's file | Employees recognize each other for doing good work. All cash rewards are tied to strategic goals. Praise from customers is welcome, but most recognition originates from within Facilities. |
| No customer involvement in strategic decisions | Customers participate in the decisions that could affect the strategic direction of Facilities |
| The receipt of a repair request is not acknowledged | An acknowledgment for the receipt and completion of each repair request is sent to the customer automatically |
| Select employees communicate with customers | All employees communicate with customers |

### Exhibit 13.2. Systems Diagram

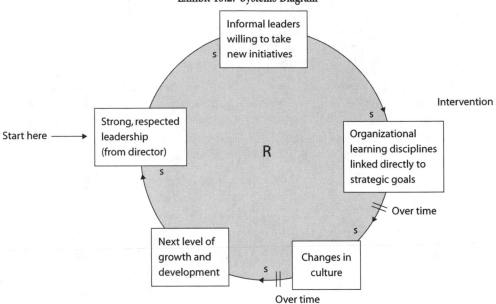

To read the systems diagram:

The strong, respected leadership consistently demonstrated by the chief facilities officer, Vicky Sirianni, has influenced informal leaders to take the initiative to implement new processes and practices, which then leads up to the intervention: having the organizational learning disciplines directly linked to the strategic goals of the department. This is not a one-time intervention. On-going initiatives have been and currently are being developed. Over time, the objectives of these initiatives are to lead to (a) changes in culture by having new practices and ways of interacting and (b) employees continually learning and striving for the next levels of growth.

*Note:* The "s" indicates increases in growth or the direction of influence in a positive direction.

Exhibit 13.3. Model I: Organizational Learning Capabilities

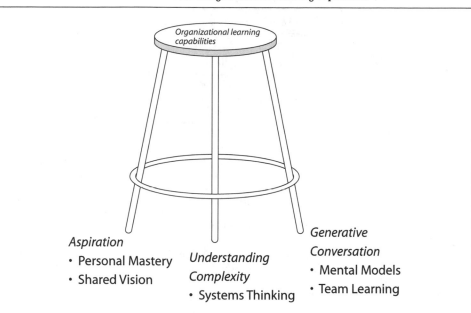

Aspiration
- Personal Mastery
- Shared Vision

Understanding Complexity
- Systems Thinking

Generative Conversation
- Mental Models
- Team Learning

*Personal Mastery* is the discipline of personal growth and learning. It is the ability to create the results in your life that you truly seek.

*Shared Vision* binds people together by their common aspirations. Shared vision is vital for the learning organization because it provides the focus and energy for learning (Senge, 1990, p. 206).

*Systems Thinking* allows us to see the interconnectedness and interdependencies in any given situation. It is a holistic way of thinking and looking at the world.

*Mental Models* are the pictures we have in our minds of how the world works. They are our assumptions and belief systems.

*Team Learning* is about alignment of goals, roles, learning together for the greater good. It is a collective discipline.

*Source:* P. Senge (1990). Reprinted with permission.

**Exhibit 13.4. Model II: Competency Model Operationalizing Organizational Learning**

| Key Competencies | |
|---|---|
| *Develops the Ability to:* | *Link to Organizational Learning Capabilities:* |
| Tolerate ambiguity | Systems thinking |
| Influence | Team learning |
| Confront difficult issues (through inquiry)* | Team learning |
| Support and nurture others | Team learning |
| Listen well and empathize | Team learning, mental models |
| Recognize one's own feelings, intuitions quickly | Personal mastery, team learning |
| Conceptualize | Systems thinking |
| Discover and mobilize human energy | Team learning, personal mastery |
| Create learning opportunities | Entirety of organizational learning |
| Sense of mission (and vision)* | Personal mastery, shared vision |
| Maintain sense of humor | Result of environment that honors and supports fun and learning together |

*Model adapted by Consulting Partner, 2001–2002.

*Source:* Copyright © 1982 W. Burke. Reprinted with permission.

## Exhibit 13.5. Agenda for Session I

*The Development of Leadership Capabilities: Its Link to Individual and Organizational Capabilities*

I. Successful Change Exercise

- Two Purposes:

  1. Link this morning's session on strategic goals to individual and organizational growth
  2. Provide a basis for our focus on organizational learning and effectiveness

II. Discussion: Leadership, Learning, Performance

- Capacity to Grow → Learn → Transform Our Systems
- Organizational Learning Capabilities
- Learning and Performance

III. The Influence of Systems and Systemic Change

- Four Response Modes
- Identifying the Interconnecting Influences—Discussion and Small-Group Application

IV. Leadership Dialogue: Key Learnings and Leadership Story

## Exhibit 13.6. Agenda for Session II

*Developing Personal Mastery and Vision*

I. The Foundational Premises for This Session

II. Persona and Character Models of Personal and Leadership Development

III. Qualities Guiding Character and Persona

IV. Personal Mastery

V. The Inner Journey Itself
   A. Conscious Beliefs
   B. Shadow Beliefs

VI. Two Forces of Personal Mastery

VII. The Linkage of Personal Mastery to the Other Disciplines

VIII. Developing Personal Vision

IX. Personal Mastery Exercise

X. Your Organizational Vision

XI. Ongoing Personal Mastery Exercise: Do Differently

### Exhibit 13.7. Session Follow-up Questionnaire

Developing Personal Mastery and Vision: Follow-up questions from our session on July 11, 2002

We wanted to check in to see how our session has had an influence on your interactions and reflections as a leader. Thank you for taking the time to think about these questions.

1. How have you seen your view of leadership change since our session? Have you had any shifts in thought, action, or how you perceive things? (For example, think of persona-character, conscious-shadow beliefs that we talked about.)

2. Have you started to think about developing a personal or organizational vision? Please elaborate . . .

3. What did you learn in our session that you would be able (or have already been able) to use?

4. Was there an "aha" for you? If so, what was it?

5. Have you been able to do a "Do Differently?" What changes did you or others experience as a result of the "Do Differently?"

6. What would you like to see as the focus for any subsequent sessions?

**Exhibit 13.8. Training Content: Exercises Used in Organizational Learning Sessions**

**Session I**

### The Development of Leadership Capabilities:
### Its Link to Individual and Organizational Capabilities

### Exercise I—Successful Change Exercise

Understanding and Managing Change

1. We have all experienced a successful change, whether with an organization, a community, a church, or even in our family. Describe an experience you've been a part of that achieved a powerful change in a productive way. What happened? What made it successful?

2. Take yourself forward in time. It is 2005 and your organization/department is operating in a healthy, productive, and sustainable way. What is going on? How is it different? What was it you and others did back in 2001 to achieve this remarkable transformation?

### Exercise II—Application Exercise: Your Own Specific Example

In teams, choose an example from your own environment that you'd like to diagram using the systems thinking tools. With your team members, have one person be the owner of the problem. The other team members will act as facilitators and consultants in helping the "client" diagram the problem. Use the following steps and diagrams as tools to guide you.

| Systems Thinking Template | Completed | |
|---|---|---|
| Step 1: Stating the Problem | Yes | No |
| Step 2: Telling the Story | Yes | No |
| Step 3: Identifying the Key Variables | Yes | No |
| Step 4: Visualizing the Problem | Yes | No |
| Step 5: Creating the Loops | Yes | No |
| Step 6: Evaluating the Whole Process | Yes | No |

Step 1: State the problem.

Step 2: Tell it as a story.

Step 3: Identify the key variables.

Step 4: Visualize the problem using a behavior over time (BOT) graph.

Step 5: Create the loop.

Step 6: Evaluate the whole process, key insights.

(*Continued*)

**Exhibit 13.8. Training Content: Exercises Used in Organizational Learning Sessions** (*Continued*)

**Session II**

### Developing Personal Mastery and Vision

### Exercise I—Personal Mastery Exercise

This exercise will help you define your personal vision: what you want to create for yourself and the world around you. This is one positive way to channel the stress in your life to more rewarding and fulfilling endeavors.

#### *Your Own Personal Vision: Steps in the Process*

**Step 1: Knowing what you want your life to be**

Create your life plan first by knowing why you are here, often called your mission. Summarize your mission with using one word—your word-in-the-box. In other words, what "one word" guides you . . . that you want to strive for.

Your word-in-the-box could be service, excellence, teamwork, peace, happiness, or anything else . . .

Here's your very own place for your word-in-the-box:

**Step 2: Going deeper with our word-in-the box**

Think about your word-in-the box and what that word means to you and your life's mission or purpose. Picture that word in three different environments:

- At Home/Your Social Life
- At Work
- Within Yourself

What would you need to change in order to bring forth/incorporate your word even more in each of these three environments?

_____

_____

_____

_____

Exhibit 13.8. (*Continued*)

**Step 3: Creating a Result** (Begin with the end in mind)

Imagine achieving a result in your life that you deeply desire. Begin with the question, "What do I really want?" Describe the experience you have imagined by asking these questions: What does it look like? How does it make me feel? (proud, significant, successful, other feelings . . .)

_____

_____

_____

_____

**Step 4: Describing Your Personal Vision**

You will now want to focus on and get clear about the results you want to see in your life. Here are some questions to help you in this area:

- What do you want to be doing in three years time that you are not doing today?

_____

_____

_____

_____

- What critical skills or "learnings" will you have developed in that time?

_____

_____

_____

_____

- What do you want to contribute (or leave behind) as your legacy?

_____

_____

_____

_____

- What are some concrete, practical steps that you can take to continue to develop your personal vision?

_____

_____

_____

_____

(*Continued*)

**Exhibit 13.8. Training Content: Exercises Used in Organizational Learning Sessions** (*Continued*)

### Exercise II—Development of an Organizational Vision

Take yourself forward in time. It is 2005 and your organization/department is operating in a healthy, productive, and sustainable way.

–What is going on?

–How is it different?

–Why are we going there?

–How are we going to get there?

–What was it you and others did back in 2002 to achieve this remarkable transformation?

–What creative tensions need to be resolved in order for this change to happen?

*Note:* This exercise was expanded upon from Session I and highlighted again in Session II to reflect changes in thinking and to capture new participants.

### Exercise III—Ongoing Personal Mastery Exercise: Do Differently

In order to start to initiate any kind of change, it is necessary to first identify something that you want to change or do differently in your life. You can start with a goal that you've been wanting to initiate, work on some "irritation" or challenge that you've been experiencing, or just do something in a different way to stretch your creativity.

This exercise involves three steps.

**Step 1: Make some change . . . do something differently . . . start on some goal.** Describe that experience:

_____

_____

_____

_____

**Step 2: Describe any insights you had from your "do differently."**

_____

_____

_____

_____

**Step 3: Can you now transfer those insights to a sustained, on-going practice?**

_____

_____

_____

_____

*Source:* Copyright © Zulauf & Associates, 2001–2002. Reprinted with permission.

*References: The Journal of Personal and Professional Success,* Vol. 2, Issue 4, and *The Fifth Discipline Fieldbook.*

# ABOUT THE CONTRIBUTORS

**Joseph Gifun,** PE, is assistant director of facilities for infrastructure and special projects in the Massachusetts Institute of Technology's Department of Facilities, where he has worked in various capacities over the past eighteen years. During the past nine years, Joe's focus has shifted from engineering to business process design and organizational learning. He participated in the creation of the Department of Facilities' strategic plan and led the design and implementation of the department's repair and maintenance reengineering effort and co-managed the resultant process. He developed and implemented MIT's infrastructure renewal program and led it from its inception. Joe is a registered professional engineer in the Commonwealth of Massachusetts and he holds a Bachelor of Science degree in civil engineering from Lowell Technological Institute and a Master's degree in adult and organizational learning from Suffolk University.

**Patricia Kennedy Graham** is director of administration for the Massachusetts Institute of Technology's Department of Facilities. In that capacity, Pat has responsibility for the human resource, learning and performance, and IT teams that support the entire department. Additionally, she participates as a member of the operational leadership team, the strategic leadership team, and the director's team for the department. Pat worked at MIT's Lincoln Laboratory, a federally funded research and development center, as associate group leader. Pat left Lincoln Laboratory to be the director of administration for the Boston office of Deloitte & Touche. Prior to returning to MIT to work in the Department of Facilities, she was managing director at Surgency, Inc., a management consulting firm specializing in best business practices and e-business transformation consulting. Pat received her Bachelor of Arts degree from Boston College and Master's degree in administration from Boston University.

**Dr. Carol Ann Zulauf** is associate professor of adult and organizational learning at Suffolk University in Boston. She also has her own consulting practice, specializing in leadership, team development, and systems thinking. Her clients span high-tech, federal and state government, health care, education, and consumer product organizations. Her prior work experience includes being a senior training instructor for Motorola, Inc. Dr. Zulauf has many publications to her credit, including her newly published book, *The Big Picture: A Systems Thinking Story for Managers* (Linkage Press, 2001). She is also a frequent presenter at regional, national, and international conferences.

CHAPTER FOURTEEN

# Motorola

*This case study describes Motorola's success in quickly acquiring, developing, and leveraging the world-class leadership talent it needed to turn around the company's performance and accelerate its return to prominence in the world market through talent management, recruitment and selection procedures, career planning and development, linkage of performance to rewards, assistance in transition, and clear standards for leadership.*

| | |
|---|---|
| OVERVIEW | 335 |
| THE DEMAND SIDE | 335 |
| THE SUPPLY SIDE | 336 |
| LEADERSHIP SUPPLY IS A CORE BUSINESS PRINCIPLE | 337 |
| THE NEW MOTOROLA LEADERSHIP SUPPLY PROCESS | 337 |
| Recruit and Select | 337 |
| Performance Management | 338 |
| TALENT MANAGEMENT | 338 |
| Career Planning and Development | 338 |
| Rewards | 338 |
| TRANSITION ASSISTANCE | 338 |
| PERFORMANCE MANAGEMENT IS KEY | 339 |
| Leadership Standards | 339 |
| Motorola's Performance Management Process | 340 |
| Link to Rewards | 341 |
| SO WHAT? | 342 |
| LESSONS LEARNED AND "DO DIFFERENTLIES" | 342 |
| REFERENCES | 344 |
| ABOUT THE CONTRIBUTORS | 344 |

# OVERVIEW

Why would the CEO of a Fortune 50 company with more than 100,000 employees worldwide dedicate one-third of his time to the creation and implementation of a leadership development system? *Because companies with the best leaders win.*

Beginning in 2000, Motorola undertook significant restructuring of its businesses in response to financial downturn brought about by (among other things) the dot-com crash and the concurrent telecom industry meltdown. As leadership teams were redistributed across new organization structures, it became increasingly clear to decision makers that the internal cadre of leadership talent was not sufficient to meet the challenges facing the new organization.

In essence, the leadership situation facing Motorola was an economic one—a question of supply and demand. The new organization structure created demand not only for more leaders, but also for a different kind of leader who could transform the company and sharpen Motorola's competitive edge. But the internal leadership supply chain was not producing sufficient talent to meet this new demand; to compound matters, a war for talent had erupted in the external market, further reducing supply.

# THE DEMAND SIDE

*Demand for more leaders.* As part of the restructuring, Motorola undertook an exercise to estimate the number of additional general managers and functional vice presidents that would be needed to achieve the company's five-year growth targets. The gap between the number of leaders needed over five years and the number of leaders available was substantial. The situation looked even worse once anticipated retirements, open positions, and underperformers were taken into account. The message was clear: the company needed more leaders to grow but simply did not have enough "ready now" leaders in the pipeline to do so.

*Demand for a different kind of leader.* Historically, Motorola's strategy was to invent exciting new technologies and then create new markets around them. The company prospered as it executed this strategy in an era of economic growth with virtually no competitive threat in its principal markets. The late 1990s, however, introduced a new reality when competitors began to bring new products and technologies to market more quickly than Motorola, and subsequently won market share in spaces Motorola once owned almost exclusively. It was apparent that Motorola's traditional style of leadership was not up to the job of transforming the company to take on the competition by becoming more customer-focused, solutions-oriented, quick to adapt to changes in markets and technologies, and collaborative across business units. So beyond having too few leaders, Motorola also was short of leaders experienced in driving change and rebuilding the business.

*The war for talent.* In McKinsey & Company's 1998 landmark study, *The War for Talent,* Ed Michaels concluded that going forward, companies' competitive edge would lie almost exclusively in the quality of its leadership: "Capital is accessible for good ideas and good projects. Strategies are transparent; even if you've got a smart strategy, others simply copy it. And the half-life of technology is growing shorter all the time. . . . In that kind of environment, all that matters is talent." In a few short words, the McKinsey study summed up the environment in which Motorola found itself and underscored the importance of dramatically transforming the leadership supply chain to produce the kind of leaders required to sharpen the company's competitive edge.

# THE SUPPLY SIDE

*Internal talent supply.* During the period of tremendous growth Motorola experienced in the early- to mid-1990s, scant attention was given to developing the next generation of leaders. More pressing was manufacturing and shipping product to meet seemingly insatiable customer demand. As a result, a large contingent of next-generation leadership talent never fully developed fundamental management and leadership skills. Later, as Motorola restructured in response to the market downturn, reduction of the workforce by nearly one-third further limited the size of the internal leadership pipeline and the available mix of leadership skills.

*External talent supply.* At the same time Motorola was experiencing a dramatic increase in leadership demand, so was the rest of the world. The dot-com craze and concurrent rapid expansion of the global economy enticed numbers of business school graduates and experienced leaders alike away from traditional corporate roles to Internet start-up companies, thus reducing the external supply of available talent. With leadership demand outstripping supply, a fluid, free agent market emerged of technical, professional, and management talent who sold their services to the highest bidder and were quick to move on when a better deal was offered elsewhere. Even as the world economy slowed, the free agent market persisted, possibly because employees feel less loyal to their employers, who through downsizing, cost cutting, and "doing more with less" have demonstrated less loyalty to employees. So even though more talent may be available during economic slowdown, competition for *quality* leadership talent remains intense.

*Changing demographics.* From a purely statistical standpoint, the demographic shift in the U.S. population from the Baby Boom generation, the oldest of whom are rapidly approaching retirement, to the Baby Bust generation portends an even smaller pool of leadership talent in the coming years. The McKinsey study stated it quite succinctly: "In 15 years, there will be 15 percent fewer Americans in the thirty-five- to forty-five-year-old range than there are now. At the same time the U.S. economy is likely to grow at 3–4 percent per year. . . . That sets the stage for a talent war."

## LEADERSHIP SUPPLY IS A CORE BUSINESS PRINCIPLE

Framing the leadership issue as a matter of insufficient supply for projected demand was key to creating awareness that attracting, developing, and retaining leadership talent is an essential core business process. To understand why the supply side of the equation was not functioning effectively, Motorola benchmarked best practices in financially successful companies. When a composite map of best practice leadership supply processes was overlaid on a map of Motorola's "as-is" leadership supply practices, gaps and weaknesses requiring attention were clearly illuminated. As a result, the CEO called for a new leadership supply process to be created and implemented quickly, as the market would not wait for the company to catch up.

From the outset, it was determined that the new leadership supply process would be designed "for leaders by leaders." Active involvement of the company's leaders created buy-in for the organizational and cultural change that naturally would accompany this significant shift away from traditional practices. It also increased the likelihood that the deliverables of the redesign effort would work and would pass the "user acceptance" test.

## THE NEW MOTOROLA LEADERSHIP SUPPLY PROCESS

The new Motorola leadership supply process comprises six major components: recruit and select, talent management, career planning and development, transition assistance, performance management, and rewards. The components were designed to work interdependently to produce the quantity and quality of leadership talent required to win. All are founded on Motorola's standards of leadership behavior, and the entire process is supported by an integrated, web-based information system referred to as Talent Web.

### Recruit and Select

The recruit and select process is a proactive approach to managing leadership supply relative to demand. Business strategy is translated into leadership needs, which are compared to the make-up of the available internal supply and actions taken to close any gaps through accelerated development of internal talent or acquisition of talent from the external market.

### Performance Management

The performance management process aligns employees' performance expectations, results, behaviors, and career plans with the organization's business goals. It consists of quarterly dialogues that help employees maximize their contributions to the business and attain job satisfaction, beginning with goal setting at the start of the year, performance monitoring throughout the year, and then performance evaluation at the end of the year. As will be discussed later in this chapter, performance management is the central component of the leadership supply process.

## TALENT MANAGEMENT

Great companies manage their talent as aggressively as they do their P&Ls. At Motorola, talent management is an ongoing process of moving, developing, and rewarding top talent and reassigning or transitioning out of the company underperforming talent. The highlight of the process is a series of semi-annual, formal meetings with the chief executive officer to discuss how talent is being leveraged in the organization. Action plans are agreed upon, and progress to plan reviewed in the next set of meetings.

### Career Planning and Development

Career planning and development focuses both on performance development for the current role and career development for future roles. The intent is to create an environment in which developmental activity is perceived as a good thing—a visible investment in talent and the future of the organization. Development options are several, including, for example, mentoring, executive coaching, expansion of job scope, transfer to a new job offering specific development opportunities, special projects, in-class or Internet-based coursework, lateral job rotations, assignment in an "office of" or "assistant" role, and international assignments.

### Rewards

Executive rewards play a key role in driving Motorola's change to a performance-based culture. Differential investment—rewarding executives commensurate with their overall contribution to the success of the company—sends a clear message to employees that *results* and *leadership behavior* are what count.

## TRANSITION ASSISTANCE

The transition assistance process was created to provide a formalized, systematic way to either re-deploy or remove from the leadership pipeline individuals who are not progressing satisfactorily. Such a mechanism is necessary to ensure that sufficient resources are available to acquire, develop, motivate, and maintain a steady flow of top talent into leadership roles.

# PERFORMANCE MANAGEMENT IS KEY

Economic success is closely tied to a strong performance ethic in an organization. This was a conclusion drawn in a 2001 McKinsey & Company (McKinsey, 2001) survey of senior executives in high-performing companies. High-performing companies align operations and practices to an attractive end state and set aggressive, well-understood goals for achieving it. Organization members feel a sense of ownership for achieving the end state, are given frequent and accurate performance feedback, and experience *rewards and consequences* commensurate with performance.

The McKinsey results reinforced the findings of Motorola's benchmarking study that an objective performance management process, based on specific leadership and performance criteria, was key to creating the performance-based culture required to reshape the company's future.

## Leadership Standards

Early on, Motorola recognized that change would only begin when the company's leadership was clear on what they were to do and how. Consequently, a new set of leadership standards was articulated to define the kind of leader needed to achieve the organizational and cultural change critical to turning around Motorola's business performance.

In-depth interviews were conducted with Motorola executives and thorough reviews of the academic and popular literatures were compiled to develop a framework of the leadership competencies and behaviors required to transform Motorola to a customer-focused and performance-based corporation. The outcome of this work was Motorola's "4e's + Always 1" leadership standards:

- Envision. Identifies meaningful and innovative change that produces profitable growth. Comes up with the vision, strategies, and viable plan that achieve it.

- Energize. Excites employees, customer, and partners around winning ideas. Brings extraordinarily high personal energy to everything. Creates an environment where everyone has a passion to excel and an opportunity to contribute.

- Edge. Cuts to the essence of what is important. Makes bold, timely decisions. Insists that the organization outperform expectations. Brings a healthy dissatisfaction with the way things are. Makes tough calls when the business or individuals are not performing.

- Execute. Achieve results significantly better and faster than our competitors by employing innovative, proven, and rigorous management practices. Personally meets commitments and keeps promises.

- And always, Ethics and character. Conducts business ethically always and everywhere. Treats all people and all cultures with respect and dignity. Keeps one's personal ambitions and emotional reactions from interfering.

Motorola's CEO also articulated a five-point plan for achieving business results in which improved leadership effectiveness topped the list.

## Motorola's Performance Management Process

Motorola's performance management process is an ongoing cycle of setting personal goals that align with the business's scorecard objectives, then observing and discussing performance issues, development plans, job match, and career plans throughout the year. The process culminates with year-end assessment of leadership behavior and business results, calibrated across leadership ranks, which in turn informs differential investment decisions (for example, incentive plan payout, executive education opportunities, assignment to special CEO project teams) based on relative contribution to the company's performance. Outcomes of assessment and calibration of relative performance feed into goal setting for the next year, and the cycle repeats.

**Planning Dialogue.** The planning dialogue occurs at the start of the year, and its purpose is to create mutual understanding of performance expectations between employees and their managers. The discussion focuses on defining *results* goals aligned with the business or function scorecard, and *leadership* goals focused on behavior most critical for attaining expected results. Once goals are defined, the discussion turns to establishing professional development and career plans that will enable employees to achieve their immediate performance and future career goals.

**Checkpoint Dialogues.** The purpose of checkpoint dialogues held in the second and third quarters is to review progress to goals. Key to these discussions is performance feedback from key work partners and matrix managers. Checkpoint dialogues provide the opportunity for employees and their managers to assess progress to goals and development plans, discuss goal modifications to support changing circumstances, create action plans to address barriers to success, and check for understanding and agreement.

**Assessment of Results and Behaviors.** At year-end, two performance assessments are made. First, leadership effectiveness is evaluated via a web-based multirater assessment based on the "4e's + Always 1" leadership standards and administered to executives, their managers, and their subordinates. Rater input is combined statistically to produce an overall *leadership behavior* score. Second, performance to *results* goals is evaluated and jointly agreed upon by the employee and manager, using metrics established during the planning dialogue.

**Calibration.** Following year-end performance assessment, managers participate in a calibration process—supported by the web-based information system—to share rationale for performance evaluations and come to agreement on the relative performance of the employees reporting to them.

Managers view their direct reports' *results* and *leadership behavior* scores plotted graphically (with results plotted on the horizontal axis and behaviors plotted on the vertical axis). Discussion follows of each person's individual and relative contribution based on results, leadership behaviors, and other legitimate business factors (such as job complexity, stretch in goals, technical skills, special expertise, breadth of experience). The end result is a collectively determined relative ranking of employees into most effective, solidly effective, and least effective groupings.

**Summary Dialogue.** Following calibration, managers and employees complete the summary dialogue to review individual performance through year-end, discuss calibration outcomes, refine development plans, and begin planning for the coming year. Aiding the discussion is a comprehensive feedback report derived from the multirater assessment that not only displays ratings and comments but also suggests development actions from *For Your Improvement* (Lombardo & Eichinger, 2000) for areas requiring improvement. These suggestions are very useful in guiding development of performance goals, creating development plans, and discussing career plans.

## Link to Rewards

Executive rewards play a key role in driving Motorola's change to a performance-based culture. Differential investment—rewarding executives commensurate with their overall contribution to the success of the company as determined during calibration—sends a clear message to employees that *results* and *leadership behavior* are what count. Leaders considered most effective have produced breakaway results and have demonstrated exemplary leadership behavior. They are rewarded with challenging job assignments, promotional and developmental opportunities, and significant monetary awards. Somewhat less, yet still considerable, investment is made in solidly effective leaders—those who "deliver the goods" consistently and demonstrate leadership behavior. They are compensated competitively and provided opportunities for continued learning and development. Modest investment is made in least effective talent to find a way to improve performance through job reassignment, performance improvement plans, referral to the company's employee assistance program, or as a last resort, separation with dignity.

# SO WHAT?

By the end of its third full year of implementation, the leadership supply process was producing observable change. In those years, new leadership talents were placed in all but three of the roles reporting to the CEO; one-third of the new senior staff had been brought in from outside the company; and a balance of technical and general management skills among the staff had been achieved. By year-end 2003, Motorola had placed over seventy new leaders in its top one hundred jobs, including a new CEO, COO, CFO, CTO, and six sector presidents.

Probably the most telling story, however, is Motorola's improved business performance in a very tough economic environment. Based on the company's fourth quarter, 2003 financial report:

- Earnings per share were $0.38 (excluding special charges), up from −$1.78 at year-end 2001
- The company had reported profitability for seven consecutive quarters
- Operating margin was 4.3 percent, up from −6.0 percent for 2001
- The company had reported twelve consecutive quarters of positive cash flow
- Net debt was $100 million, down from $7 billion in 2000
- Net debt to net debt + equity ratio was 0.3 percent, the lowest in twenty years

# LESSONS LEARNED AND "DO DIFFERENTLIES"

Reflection over the past three years of development and implementation yields insights into what worked well, and what didn't work so well. Both provide perspective for others contemplating the leadership supply issue.

*What Worked Well?*

- Strong sponsorship by a key executive during the redesign phase led to CEO ownership of the process.
- Business leaders were actively involved in the redesign process. Human resources did not own the redesign, but instead worked with and through business leaders who led the redesign teams.

- Hiring an outside consultant to complete the benchmarking study gave Motorola access to information about leadership programs in other companies without expending scarce internal resources to collect and consolidate this information.

- Web-enabling the process was key to achieving consistency of application throughout the company. It also minimized ongoing administration because the web-based tools compile and report without the need for human intervention.

- The Office of Leadership, the new central organization created to manage the leadership supply process, was purposefully kept very small. With web-based tools and implementation carried out by resources within the individual business units, the Office of Leadership was staffed by fewer than ten people, minimizing cost to the organization and avoiding the trap of creating a centralized bureaucracy.

- The CEO *mandated* that executives comply with the new leadership supply process, particularly with respect to assigning rewards commensurate with personal and organizational performance. Although unpopular, the mandate served to jump-start the process, short-circuit resistance to change, and quickly gain acceptance as the value of the process became evident.

- Establishing semi-annual talent management reviews between sector president and CEO created a rhythmic cadence to the process, reinforced the expectation that development and deployment of leadership talent was to be managed as aggressively as P&Ls, and ensured continued ownership of executive leadership talent and the leadership supply process by the CEO.

### "Do Differentlies"

- The broader human resources organization was not kept up-to-date during the redesign phase. As a consequence, implementation was hampered by the need to assuage feelings of ill will from having been excluded from "the action," convince HR associates of the need for change, and enlist them as change agents as the process was rolled out.

- An external *management consulting* firm was brought in to build, integrate, and pilot HR processes, tools, and procedures. Given the success achieved through partnership with an external consultant in the redesign phase, this approach seemed reasonable. Unfortunately, the consulting team was not up to the challenge and the project lost momentum until an internal team was assembled to take over and complete it. In retrospect, the build and implementation phases should have been led by an internal team from the outset, with consultants brought in as needed to work on discrete, specific components requiring expertise not available within Motorola.

- The web-based infrastructure supporting the process was developed internally, saddling Motorola with the cost of ongoing maintenance and system improvements. Had the sophisticated HR systems that exist today been available then, the better option would have been to customize commercially available software to meet Motorola's specific needs.

# REFERENCES

Lombardo, M. M., & Eichinger, R. W. (Eds.). (2000). *For your improvement* (3rd ed.). Minneapolis, Minnesota: Lominger Limited, Inc.

McKinsey & Company. (1998). "The war for talent." *The McKinsey Quarterly,* No. 3.

McKinsey & Company. (September 2001). "Performance ethic: out-executing the competition." *Organization and Leadership Practice.* Charlotte, South Carolina: McKinsey & Company.

# ABOUT THE CONTRIBUTORS

**Kelly Brookhouse,** in her role as director, leadership, learning, and performance at Motorola from 1999 to 2003, played a central role in conceptualizing and directing Motorola's leadership supply core process redesign effort, including design and development of the procedures, tools, support materials, and integrated information systems required to translate the leadership supply process from vision to reality. Prior to joining Motorola in 1997, Kelly was senior vice president of Aon Consulting's start-up preemployment testing outsourcing group established in 1994. Her career began as a human resource consultant with HRStrategies, during which time she designed, validated, and implemented preemployment testing, developmental assessment, and performance management programs for numerous Fortune 100 companies, including Motorola. Kelly obtained her doctorate in industrial and organizational psychology in 1987 and is a member of the American Psychological Society and the Society for Industrial and Organizational Psychology. Kelly currently is director, leadership development at Capital One Financial Services, Inc.

**Jamie M. Lane,** vice president, leadership, learning, and performance, Motorola, Inc., has been with Motorola since 1998 and was actively involved in the leadership supply core process redesign efforts. Jamie's current role is vice president of leadership, learning, and performance for one of Motorola's business units. During 2001 and 2002, Jamie was responsible for performance management, the TalentWeb, the leadership standards, and organization effectiveness for Motorola. Prior to that role, Jamie was responsible for training and development for Motorola employees, where she led a team of over 300 professionals through nine business-focused learning teams and four global regions. Prior to joining Motorola, Jamie spent two years as a director in organization development and training at McDonald's Corporation. Prior to joining McDonald's in 1996, Jamie spent eighteen years with a major professional services and consulting organization. Jamie has an M.S. from Benedictine University in organization behavior with an emphasis in organization development and international management. She has a bachelor's degree in accounting and is a Certified Public Accountant. Jamie is a member of the Development, Education and Training Council of the Conference Board, the Executive Development Network, ASTD, and the American Society of Certified Public Accountants (AICPA). She was on the board of trustees for National Technological University.

CHAPTER FIFTEEN

# Praxair

*An organizational change model for aligning leadership strategy with business strategy in order to drive marketplace differentiation with a heavy emphasis on assessment tools such as customer focus conferences, management practices such as employee surveys, customer scorecards, performance management processes, a series of conferences and follow-up practices, and a commitment to evaluation.*

| | |
|---|---|
| OVERVIEW | 347 |
| THE OLD GAME IN THE PACKAGED GAS MARKET | 347 |
| THE NEW RULES | 348 |
| DIAGNOSIS: DELIVERING ON THE PROMISE | 349 |
| Early Problems | 349 |
| TWO TYPES OF DESIRED OUTCOMES | 350 |
| ASSESSMENT: HIGH INVOLVEMENT BUILDS HIGH COMMITMENT | 350 |
| Assessment Tools | 351 |
| Assessment Steps | 351 |
| Assessment Findings | 352 |
| Exhibit 15.1: Assessment Steps | 353 |
| DESIGN: AN ITERATIVE PROCESS | 354 |
| Management Practices Are Central to the Change in Leadership Culture | 354 |
| Visible Senior Management Support | 355 |
| Critical Success Factors in the Design of PDI's New Leadership Strategy | 356 |
| IMPLEMENTATION: ALIGNING LEADERSHIP STRATEGY WITH BUSINESS STRATEGY | 357 |
| ONGOING SUPPORT AND DEVELOPMENT: A SYSTEMS APPROACH | 358 |
| EVALUATION: ARE WE ON THE RIGHT PATH? | 359 |

LESSONS RELEARNED                                                    360

NOTES                                                               361

    Exhibit 15.2: PDI's Leadership Philosophy Map                   362

ABOUT THE CONTRIBUTORS                                              364

# OVERVIEW

Is it really possible to be an A company in a C industry, especially when starting as a C player? In the late 1980s and early 1990s Praxair's then parent company decided to exit the low-margin, high-cost packaged gases (cylinder) segment of the industrial gas industry. But in 1994 different market conditions, and a stronger balance sheet, following Praxair's spin-off as an independent company warranted reentering this $8 billion market, where sales of packaged gases and consumable hardgoods, primarily to the metal fabrication industry, constitute 70 percent of the total revenue. Despite its long association with the industry, Praxair reentered the market as a C player, aggressively acquiring over one hundred small, regional distributors in the United States and Canada to gain market share, as well as to secure a position in a business with good fundamentals. In the early stages of this acquisition period it was unclear what the end-game strategy would actually be. After several years acquisitions were suspended in early 1998 until the longer-term strategic intent could be decided and the acquired companies made more profitable.

In time the managers of Praxair Distribution Inc., (PDI) the division responsible for Praxair's packaged gas business in the United States and Canada, came to realize that a fresh approach to this traditional, low-tech industry was required if business results were to be improved. The goal was nothing less than emerging as the clear industry leader, with 6–8 percent sales growth and 15 percent net income growth annually, and sequentially improving ROC to above reinvestment levels. These aggressive goals could not be realized without applying new rules to an old game.

# THE OLD GAME IN THE PACKAGED GAS MARKET

Traditionally, regional packaged gas distributors bought their gases (oxygen, nitrogen, argon, acetylene, helium, carbon dioxide, and various specialty gases) in bulk from major gas manufacturers, repackaged them into high-pressure cylinders, and distributed them to welding shops, industrial sites, hospitals, and manufacturing centers. Hardgoods, in the form of welding rods and wire, cutting tips, helmets, gloves, and welding machines, typically made up 40 percent of the revenue to these same end-use customers.

A traditional regional distributor employed eighty to 120 people in functions such as sales, cylinder filling and handling, route delivery, retail store sales, warehousing, and administrative support. Annual sales for these regional companies ranged from $2 million to $25 million, but the average was $8 to 10 million. Pay scales, benefits packages, and employee training were often less than competitive, resulting in turnover exceeding 30 percent a year. Management practices were typical of those found in entrepreneurial, family-owned and operated businesses. Although much larger, PDI was managed in much the same way.

# THE NEW RULES

PDI's sales in 1992 totaled $250 million but by 1998 were over $900 million, reflecting an aggressive acquisition strategy. Return on capital, however, had fallen from 9.1 to 6.5 percent by 1998, when acquisitions were stopped. PDI's leaders realized that a fresh approach to the traditional, low-tech industry was required if business results were to be any different.

In effect, PDI embarked on a well-known business model, but one fraught with difficulties. Known as a "strategic rollup," PDI's business model could be summarized as

- Take a highly fragmented industry
- Buy up hundreds of owner-operated businesses
- Create a business that can reap economies of scale
- Build national brands
- Leverage best practices across all aspects of marketing and operations
- Hire better talent than small businesses could previously afford[1]

In a few words, the new business model was to "be big and act small." The challenge would be to maintain the nimbleness of a small business while leveraging the economies of scale and market clout of a large enterprise.

If the 1995–1998 period was the acquisition phase, 1999–2000 was the fix-it phase. During this period the emphasis was on creating a clear, consistent vision and strategy, replacing nearly 65 percent of the senior management staff who lacked the skills or the desire to execute the new strategy, and implementing disciplined processes in sales, operations, and distribution across all fifteen Canadian and U.S. divisions. Integration and alignment was the focus of the turnaround efforts during this time period.

Beginning in 2001, the focus shifted to realizing the potential of the new business model by launching a business strategy grounded on differentiation. New national product and service offerings were introduced during this period based on exclusive distribution rights and private label hardgoods. Growth of the business and eventual leadership of the industry depended on successful implementation of these new rules.

One other rule needed to be broken—the traditional management practices that had been standard industry orthodoxy for more than fifty years. The final challenge was to determine whether a new leadership strategy could contribute to the overall success of the business strategy. Could the way people are managed contribute to marketplace leadership?

# DIAGNOSIS: DELIVERING ON THE PROMISE

The problem with a rollup business model is that it is especially difficult to execute. The promise of market leadership is hard to deliver. In general, rollup strategies most often get stuck at the second stage of creating an institution that can truly deliver value beyond that achievable by small, regional businesses. In the mid-1990s, PDI found itself facing a number of the problems typical of strategic rollups.

## Early Problems

Problems encountered early on included

- A loss of marketshare; new customer gains were more than offset by customer losses

- Declining ROC as synergies proved more elusive than originally expected

- Diverse cultures within acquired companies resisted changes in operating procedures and new management practices

- Employee surveys for two years in a row indicated that PDI was less customer-focused than intended and difficult to do business with, owing in part to a variety of incompatible information technology systems

- Management skills of many frontline managers were not sufficient to achieve differentiation through new customer contact behaviors

- Frontline supervisors did not understand their role in business-improvement initiatives

- Substantially different business and market conditions existed in the United States and Canada, compounding efforts to capture synergies

- Acquisitions had been made in low-growth, rust-belt manufacturing regions in the United States

To address these problems, Praxair appointed a new management team in 2000 headed by Wayne Yakich, previously PDI's VP of sales and operations, and chartered his new team with delivering on the promise of the new business model.

## TWO TYPES OF DESIRED OUTCOMES

The Yakich team communicated a clear vision, explained the strategy required to execute the business model, and set forth a new set of core values. Among the emphases of the new values was a realization that "this is a people business." Previously, this concept had been given lip service, but was not taken seriously. It became the cornerstone for an entirely new leadership strategy, one that would enable employees to become part of the differentiation equation in the marketplace. Now the leadership strategy would be as widely implemented as the business strategy and enable nearly 3,000 customer contact employees to truly differentiate themselves from those of all competitors.

Therefore senior managers championed the work to develop a new leadership strategy just as seriously as they drove the business strategy. In both cases differentiation was the goal. The new management team had to transform a loose confederation of businesses with different cultures, different operating procedures, different values, and different ways of managing employees into a market leader that combines the speed advantages of being small with the scale advantages of being large.

In order to execute both the business strategy and the leadership strategy, two skill sets were required. The first consists of traditional business skills—determining what the marketplace wants and how to deliver it. The second consists of leadership skills used to mobilize people so that they have an understanding of the requirements for market success and how to deliver on them.[2] Although the ultimate business goal for PDI's new senior management team was successful implementation of the business strategy, their ultimate leadership goal was a new leadership culture, generally understood as the sum of the habits of leaders. In other words, leaders must begin treating employees differently if employees were to treat customers differently.

## ASSESSMENT: HIGH INVOLVEMENT BUILDS HIGH COMMITMENT

Generally speaking, employees don't support solutions when they don't understand the original problem and when they aren't involved in both the *assessment* and the *design* of a business improvement intervention. This maxim of organizational change is frequently overlooked. Assessment should not be done in the dark. If the assessment activities engage the group targeted for change, resistance is reduced and support for the change is much greater.

A second maxim of organizational change is that the assessment and design phases should model the new values that underlie the change initiative—in this case, a valuing of the contribution people can make to bottom-line business success.

With these principles in mind, Yakich chartered a three-person change team to develop assessment tools for use with PDI's top 175 managers, including all senior managers, fifteen division general managers (DGMs) and all of their direct reports. The change team, comprising the director of HR, the manager of training and development, and an external consultant, recommended a four-step leadership strategy design process[3] to engage these 175 managers in assessing the current state of the leadership practices and the changes required if PDI employees were to become a sustainable source of competitive advantage.

Listed below are the assessment tools, the steps followed in the assessment process, and the assessment findings. The assessment process was deliberately conducted to prepare the organization for future changes by engaging more than five hundred employees—175 leaders in the top three levels of management and over 325 employees—across all fifteen regional businesses.

## Assessment Tools

The assessment tools were the following:

- An employee survey solicited feedback on the extent to which the business strategy and leadership strategies were effective.

- A tool was used for comparing the current leadership strategy with the one required to differentiate employees in the marketplace.

- An assessment tool called a Leadership Philosophy Map[4] was used to define the core assumptions behind the portrait of a new manager.

- A leadership cultural assessment tool for use with senior managers and division general managers (DGMs) clarified the change in leadership culture required to support the newly emerging leadership strategy.[5]

- Customer focus conferences[6] conducted in each of the fifteen divisions brought representative customers together with customer contact employees. The purpose of these conferences was to clarify the customer contact behaviors, in terms of both attitudes and actions, that would differentiate PDI employees from all other competitors.

## Assessment Steps

The assessment was conducted in the following four steps:

1. All senior managers participated in a six-hour session to apply the leadership strategy design tool to crystallize their own thinking about needed changes.

2. Division general managers conducted four-hour sessions with twelve to fifteen managers from the next level of field managers, during which the leadership strategy design tool identified gaps in the current and desired leadership behaviors. This step also resulted in one Leadership Philosophy Map from each session.

3. The 15 DGMs and senior PDI leaders then analyzed the input from all the sessions to determine common themes and assess the gap between the current leadership strategy and the one required to differentiate employees. At this time, the group realized that they did not really have a clear picture of the customer contact behaviors required to make PDI employees distinctive. Rather than settling for a best guess, they authorized a series of one-day, voluntary customer focus conferences so that exemplary employees and customers, working together, could develop the attitudes and actions that would set PDI apart from all other suppliers. All fifteen divisions opted for the customer focus conferences when they realized how energizing they were for employees and how well received they were by participating customers.

4. Fifteen customer focus conferences were held, each engaging twenty to twenty-five employees and two to three customer representatives who shared their views on what customer contact behaviors would set PDI employees apart from those of other suppliers. The output from these conferences was a set of differentiating attitudes and actions identified for each of the different customer contact groups (sales, drivers, inside sales, counter sales, technicians, and so forth). These attitudes and actions were consolidated into a master set for use companywide with each group of customer contact employees.[7]

## Assessment Findings

The assessment phase lasted over fifteen months. But by the time it was completed, there was widespread agreement on the shortcomings of the current leadership strategy and how to improve it. Resistance during the implementation phase was virtually nonexistent. Nearly every leader in the top three levels of management understood why his or her current ways of managing employees was deficient. And they all were willing to implement the action plans that they themselves adopted, including prioritized management training, revised performance review procedures, and new performance-based compensation schemes—all changes not normally supported by line managers. Below is a summary of the major findings of the assessment phase.

The assessment phase was far more than a few surveys or focus groups. It was an intensive set of actions, engaging more than five hundred employees and simultaneously laying the foundation for implementation actions endorsed by those whose behaviors were expected to change.

### Exhibit 15.1. Assessment Steps

| Assessment Step | Assessment Findings |
|---|---|
| 1. Senior management leadership strategy design session | • The leadership culture is in drastic need of change. DGMs and their direct reports must be engaged in a process to determine the current leadership strategy and how better to manage employees |
| 2. DGMs conducted four-hour leadership strategy design sessions | • 175 managers are in surprising agreement that the leadership strategy will not lead to differentiating customer contact behaviors<br>• The industry orthodoxies on the management of people were alive and well in PDI<br>• The new portrait of a successful PDI manager must contain a different people-management component<br>• The leadership values must be changed and incorporated into key management practices<br>• Field managers were skeptical of senior managers' commitment to stay the course on the new leadership strategy |
| 3. DGMs and senior team consolidate input from all leadership strategy design sessions | • The new leadership philosophy map summarizes the required portrait of all managers in PDI<br>• The new portrait makes it clear that current supervisors have not been trained in requisite management skills<br>• Nearly all of the 175 managers have a strong desire to improve their managerial skills<br>• The differentiating attitudes and actions are too general at this stage to be useful. Therefore, employees and customers must be engaged to add greater specificity |
| 4. Customer focus conferences to determine differentiating customer contact behaviors | • Customers confirm the critical role of customer contact employees in differentiating PDI from other suppliers<br>• Employees are surprised that their opinions count and are being taken seriously<br>• Employees leave feeling highly engaged and willing to change their own behaviors. The message that employee opinion matters ripples throughout the company<br>• Employees feel frustrated that some managers tolerate weak to mediocre customer contact behaviors<br>• Specific attitudes and actions are developed for the different groups of employees who contact customers<br>• Barriers to improved customer focus are identified and local action plans adopted |

# DESIGN: AN ITERATIVE PROCESS

Organizational change of the magnitude undertaken by PDI is often likened to changing the tires on a car that is traveling at 70 miles per hour. The metaphor is quite apt. No change plan, no matter how well designed, can possibly anticipate all the bumps and curves in the road. Consequently, PDI followed an iterative design process. Each step of the change was designed, implemented, and then evaluated. The next step was designed based on the outcomes of the previous one. Along the way, business performance, budget constrictions, and market dynamics, to name just a few of the "bumps" in the road, had to be considered in designing the next steps. For instance, no one anticipated needing customer focus conferences to help clarify customer contact behaviors. They were designed as a result of an unforeseen outcome from the previous step— that line managers did not know how employees could distinguish themselves in the eyes of customers. That being said, the PDI change team followed two fundamental principles, a focus on new or revised management practices and visible senior management support.

## Management Practices Are Central to the Change in Leadership Culture

The first three steps of PDI's leadership strategy design process were actually assessment steps. The true design work took place when the management practices were aligned with the new leadership values. Values mean nothing if they aren't reflected in how managers actually behave. Therefore, the PDI change team asked senior managers and field managers to prioritize the management practices to be changed first. The intent was to identify the management practices that would have the most impact early in the change process. The priority management practices were (1) skills training for managers and (2) realignment of the profit-sharing plan to incorporate division performance as part of the formula.

Other management practices to be redesigned included:

- *Employee survey*—to include questions about the new leadership strategy and the consistent practice of the new customer contact behaviors.

- *Customer scorecards*—to provide feedback from customers on the attitudes and actions for each group of employees who routinely talk to customers. The feedback is managed by employee groups who take ownership for the results and formulate ways to improve their own customer contact behaviors. Managers are consulted when policy questions are involved or when actions may have an impact on other functional areas.

- *PDI playbook*—a desktop reference guide for all employees containing pertinent company information, including PDI's vision, values, goals, business strategies, and department-specific guidelines for what to do and what not to do to help PDI reach its performance goals.

- *Praxair performance management process*—the annual performance review process, including training and development actions, for exempt and nonexempt employees.

- *Leadership commitment day*—a designated day to reinforce throughout all management ranks the importance of implementing the PDI leadership strategy and of living the leadership values.

- *DGM of the future assessment*—an assessment process for DGMs to use in thinking about their own development needs as well as subordinates with the potential to become DGMs. Self-assessments are discussed with PDI senior managers, resulting in future development objectives.

## Visible Senior Management Support

The critical role of senior managers in the success of a change process has long been acknowledged. Senior management support is absolutely essential to making changes in leadership culture. The commitment of Yakich and the entire senior team proved pivotal in the early days of the design and implementation. The PDI change team took advantage of all business meetings, company publications, conferences, and teleconferences to communicate the message that change in PDI's leadership culture was a vital link to success in the marketplace. Listed below are just a few of the communication opportunities designed into the change initiatives.

- *DGM meetings.* Held twice a year, the meetings provided an update on the leadership strategy work and laid out plans for next steps of the implementation process.

- *Annual business conferences.* The annual meetings of sales managers, operations managers, and functional staff groups provided a forum to communicate expectations for changing how employees are managed in order to support new employee behaviors with customers.

- *Monthly growth commitment teleconferences.* Teleconferences provided direct contact between sales reps and senior managers on the status of marketing and sales plan implementation. They also afforded opportunities for Yakich and his senior team to model new leadership values.

- *Quarterly town meeting teleconferences.* Senior managers spoke directly with employees about business results and progress in the implementation of the leadership strategy.

- *Division leadership conferences.* Senior managers and the human resource change team conducted leadership conferences in each of the fifteen divisions, and in the functional staff groups, to underscore the linkage between the business and leadership strategies and the role of each manager in their implementation.

- *In-house publications.* The quarterly newspaper, *TOPICS,* provided an excellent opportunity to highlight success stories, expectations for managers, and the critical link between the business strategy and the leadership strategy.

## Critical Success Factors in the Design of PDI's New Leadership Strategy

The following factors proved to be critical in the successful implementation of PDI's new leadership strategy. Some critical success factors are structural, some relational, and some are procedural.

- *Broad involvement in the assessment phase.* Engaging the group targeted for change in the assessment and design phases enabled the incorporation of their thinking in the design but also began building a readiness for change.

- *DGM participation.* Asking DGMs to conduct four-hour leadership strategy design sessions proved critically important in helping these managers understand the new leadership strategy while advocating its importance.

- *Customer focus conferences.* Perhaps the design element with the most impact, the customer focus conferences engaged customers and employees in a dialogue that echoed throughout the company.

- *Senior management support.* In meetings, publications, teleconferences and one-on-one discussions, senior management conveyed that the new leadership strategy was for real.

- *Local champions.* Customer focus champions were designated in each division to assist in the implementation of customer focus conferences. This local resource was an invaluable design element to the overall success of the new leadership strategy, because the champions provided feedback and support for local implementation. They served as an extension of the change team, as did field human resource managers, who fulfilled a critical role in the training and implementation phase.

- *The change team make-up.* The change team comprised the HR director, the manager of training, and an external consultant, and possessed a complementary mix of expertise, experience, and knowledge of the organization's people.

- *Link to the business strategy.* At all times the work on the leadership strategy was linked back to the business strategy. This provided a constant reality check for the change team and those involved in implementation.

- *Momentum.* The change team quickly realized that an essential element in all design and implementation components is momentum. If it is lost, managers begin to think that the change agenda no longer matters. Maintaining momentum is especially critical in the early stages.

# IMPLEMENTATION: ALIGNING LEADERSHIP STRATEGY WITH BUSINESS STRATEGY

In PDI's effort to transform its leadership strategy, the implementation phase was quite straightforward. By the time the implementation phase was reached, there was enthusiastic support for the pending changes. Most of the changes were in the form of new management practices, as mentioned earlier. Another core implementation activity was the training of nearly five hundred frontline managers and supervisors. They had not been exposed to either the business strategy or the leadership strategy during the assessment and design phases.

As the focus of implementation shifted to these frontline managers, the DGMs once again played a critical role. Using presentation materials developed by the change team, the DGMs and their local human resource managers presented an overview of the business strategy and a more extensive explanation of the leadership strategy. Frontline managers were also introduced to the new attitudes and actions for their customer contact employees. The focus of these sessions was the critical role frontline managers play in achieving marketplace success.

Another feature of the implementation phase was the launching of a six-module supervisory skill-training program. Performance coaching, conflict management, and communications modules were scheduled for all PDI field managers over a period of fifteen to eighteen months. This was the first training of its kind offered to many of these managers. Taught by human resource managers, this training reinforced the message that PDI was serious about instituting a new leadership strategy.

A third element of implementation was the gathering of baseline data on the extent to which PDI managers were currently following the new leadership philosophy and values embedded in the leadership strategy. These data were collected at national conferences of sales and operations managers and during the fifteen division leadership conferences. The data serve as a means of tracking the progress in implementing the new leadership strategy.

One unexpected event during a DGM meeting proved quite beneficial in the long run despite being disconcerting at the time. The DGMs voiced candid concerns about how well the senior team actually followed the new leadership philosophy and values. Their feedback essentially expressed frustration that the "walk" of senior managers didn't match their "talk." This discussion served to reinforce the importance of the leadership strategy and to heighten the awareness among senior managers that they, too, must change. In addition to agreements reached during this meeting, subsequent sessions among senior managers led to additional changes in their own actions. What could have been a crisis point for the implementation of PDI's new leadership strategy turned out to be a recommitment to its strategic importance.

# ONGOING SUPPORT AND DEVELOPMENT: A SYSTEMS APPROACH

PDI realized that behavior change could best be promoted through a systems approach. Without such an approach the new behaviors were not likely to become part of the new leadership culture. The revisions to the many management practices discussed earlier constituted much of the systems work. As these new ways of managing people were implemented, managers realized that PDI was serious about leading differently.

For instance, the revised performance management system will eventually result in all PDI managers receiving feedback on the extent to which they are driving the new leadership strategy in their work groups. And their performance ratings will be linked to their compensation. Likewise, the revised employee survey will provide managers with feedback on how thoroughly their division has embraced the new leadership strategy. Leadership Commitment Day, a new management practice, will further demonstrate that PDI expects managers to lead in such a way that PDI employees distinguish themselves from those of competitors.

New management practices will continuously be introduced to reinforce the new behaviors and values inherent in PDI's leadership strategy. A Perspectives Conference is being launched, for example, for new college hires to help them understand PDI's leadership strategy and its link to winning in the marketplace.

But in addition to new and revised management practices, PDI managers are being provided individual coaching, skills training, and periodic feedback on their progress. PDI employees will receive feedback from customers via the customer scorecards. Ongoing skills training, coaching from their managers, and the annual performance discussions are other sources of support.

In summary, a systems approach not only means that current management practices are linked to the business and leadership strategies, but also that all new initiatives are likewise linked. PDI found that establishing this linkage is the best means of reminding managers and employees that expectations for changed behaviors are real, and that failure to change has consequences.

# EVALUATION: ARE WE ON THE RIGHT PATH?

In the early stages of a change process it is difficult to determine whether your efforts are producing the desired results. Unfortunately, concrete evidence tends to come in the form of lagging indicators. At this early stage, the positive impact on business performance has at least covered project costs. In the early going, the best that one can hope for is that leading indicators signal promising results. The leading indicators to which PDI looked were key stakeholders.

More than thirty-five customers, for instance, said during the customer focus conferences that if PDI employees were to implement the differentiating customer contact behaviors, they would consider PDI to be true business partners, something they want but rarely see among suppliers. The customer scorecards will soon be yielding data from customers as part of the leading indicators of success. An early indicator of business impact is reflected in the following comment from a customer:

> Good Morning, I have received several comments regarding your drivers. They are helpful, professional, courteous, neat, and respectful of our staff. This is a refreshing change from the service we have been receiving from our other two suppliers. This also extends to the employees I have talked to on the telephone at your service depots. It is nice to hear "How can we help you" rather than a whole explanation of how cylinders and tanks are filled and why we can't do it. A job well done. This type of service and professionalism will ensure a continued relationship with [our company] and Praxair.

Approximately seven hundred managers and more than two thousand employees have been exposed to either the new leadership strategy or the results of the customer focus conferences or both. The early indicators in the form of anecdotal evidence tell PDI that it is on the right path. Stories are surfacing throughout the United States and Canada of employees following the new attitudes and actions to the delight of customers. Managers are reporting delight at seeing their employees take initiative to address long-standing operations issues.

PDI suppliers have provided another early indication that PDI is on the right path. A major hardgoods supplier to the industrial gas industry has seen the impact of PDI's new business strategy in the marketplace and realizes that the leadership strategy has played a part. Inquiries are beginning to come in about how the leadership strategy was developed and whether it could be adapted for use in the supplier's own business. In a similar vein more than one customer who participated in the customer focus conferences has inquired how they might run a conference for their own customers. And the PDI distributor network has expressed similar interest.

Although it is difficult to quantify the impact, improving business results are clearly related to employee and managerial actions. Sales are running below planned growth, due to the recession in the North American manufacturing economy. But operating profit is on or close to plan. Employees are showing evidence of understanding the business realities and are committed to doing their part to control costs, reduce customer turnover, and win new business.

Going forward, PDI will monitor progress through a variety of measures:

*Future Measures for Monitoring Success*

- Tracking progress against the baseline data gathered at the beginning of implementation
- Monitoring employee survey results
- Tracking the adoption of new customer contact behaviors via customer scorecards
- Following the turnover rate among employees, which is expected to drop as a result of changed management practices
- Monitoring the rate of customer churn, which is expected to slow as new customer contact behaviors build stronger ties to customers
- Measuring the new customer win rate, also expected to improve as new product and service offerings, coupled with differentiating actions and attitudes, create a more compelling offering

# LESSONS RELEARNED

Someone once observed that "experience is recognizing the same mistake when you make it again." PDI's experience with large-scale change has proven again some familiar truths for managing change. What is noteworthy about PDI's change initiative is how it is engaging its people as a source of sustainable competitive advantage. Market advantage gained through technology, product functionality, geographic presence, or financial positioning is easily matched by competitors in ever-decreasing cycle times. The one competitive advantage that is difficult to duplicate is that gained through people. Wayne Yakich and his team of senior managers realized that the packaged gas business is a people business. In order to turn around a stalled strategic rollup plan, he needed the commitment of all 750 managers and 3500 + employees at 435 locations. Rather than making the same mistake as his predecessors, Yakich opted for a different approach. He knew that a business strategy based on different products and services, while desirable, could eventually be duplicated, but that a leadership strategy that differentiated employees could complement the business strategy and quite possibly add a sustainable advantage that would translate into market leadership.

# NOTES

1. Kocourek, Paul F., Chung, Steven Y., and McKenna, Matthew G. *Strategic Rollups: Overhauling the Multi-Merger Machine* (Strategy Publication Issue 19). New York: Booz Allen Hamilton. Available at http://www.strategy-business.com/export/export.php?article_id = 16858

2. See "Executive vs. Leaders: Is There a Difference," Rich Rardin, *Manchester Review,* Spring/Summer, 1999.

3. Four-step leadership strategy design tool. Step 1: Identify those customer contact behaviors that would truly differentiate PDI employees from all others suppliers. Step 2: Identify current and desired leadership philosophy within PDI using the leadership philosophy map. Step 3: Make explicit the new leadership values that are implicit in the desired leadership philosophy. Step 4: Redesign current management practices to reflect the new leadership values. These management practices, when implemented, will give substance to the new values, which in turn will reflect the new leadership philosophy, which when followed will reinforce the new customer contact behaviors.

4. PDI's leadership philosophy map reflects the current leadership philosophy among managers as well as their desired one (see Exhibit 15.2). The definitions to each of the four parts follow:

   Mental Model—the culturally accepted understanding of the leader's role

   Motive—the driving force behind the leader's actions

   Manner—the way in which employees are treated

   Methods—the overall characterization of the processes or procedures leaders use

5. Leadership culture assessment model and tool adapted from Roger Harrison and Herb Stokes, *Diagnosing Organizational Culture* (San Francisco: Jossey-Bass, 1992).

6. Process steps for conducting customer focus conferences:

*Preconference*

- Launch employee participant nomination process: three to four people from each of four to five customer contact groups
- Invite local customers to participate
- Prepare local meeting space and related logistics

*Conference Design*

- Welcome, introductions, and ground rules
- Customer presentations

Exhibit 15.2. PDI's Leadership Philosophy Map

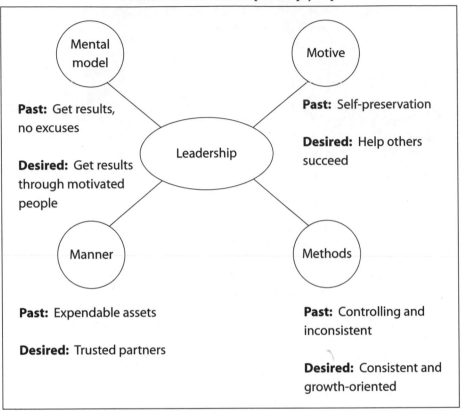

- Employee small groups to review their own customer contact behaviors; prepare presentation to customers
- Dialogue between customers and employees; employees revisit attitudes and actions and recommend five each
- Lunch
- Employee small groups discuss and report barriers to being more customer focused
- Employees report actions needed from managers to enhance customer focus
- Employees report on ways to train colleagues in new attitudes and actions and on how to monitor successful implementation

*Postconference*
- Explain conference outcomes to all employees
- Design training on new customer contact behaviors
- Budget and conduct training
- Create and begin using customer scorecards for feedback on effectiveness

7. Here's a sample of attitudes and actions for one role group, counter sales:

*Counter Sales: Attitudes and Actions*

- Attitude: safety first

  Demonstrates a safety-first attitude

  Advises customers on safe handling of products

  Helps load product safely into customer's vehicle

  The store is free from tripping and other safety hazards

- Attitude: "can-do" problem solver

  Displays and uses flyers, Solution Guides, and other resources

  Probes, listens, understands customer needs, and offers best solution

  Demonstrates knowledge of our products and business

  Answers questions and explains related products and services

  Someone from Praxair has called to see whether all is well after I have made a significant purchase (for example, a welding machine)

- Attitude: responsive and reliable

  Provides accurate and reliable information

  Fills orders quickly and accurately

  Returns phone calls promptly

  Follows up on orders

  Stocks items I frequently use

- Attitude: honesty

  Tells the truth, does not hide mistakes

  Finds out correct answers when not sure

  Keeps commitments to get back to customers

- Attitude: professional and positive

  Acknowledges customer even when tied up with someone else

  Greets customer by name, smiles, makes eye contact

  Comes out from behind the counter, shakes hands, and gives name

  Treats all customers as though it was their first visit

  Keeps store clean and appealing

  Helps customers take product to vehicle

  Takes pride in personal appearance

- Attitude: team player

  I get high-quality service at all Praxair stores

  Offers to share technical expertise

  Draws on other Praxair resources to solve my problem

# ABOUT THE CONTRIBUTORS

**John Graboski** is director, human resources, at Praxair Distribution, Inc. He has worked in the corporate world for twenty-five years, in marketing and sales, as well as HR, in three very different industries (telecommunications, health care insurance, and industrial gases). Still a marketing guy at heart, he looks at his role as one of helping employees sell not only the company's products but also themselves successfully to customers. He lives with his wife, Ginny, and two teenage daughters, Caitlin and Lexi, in Cheshire, Connecticut.

**Ruth Neil** is manager, training and development, at Praxair Distribution, Inc. She has a thirty-four-year track record in organizational change initiatives, especially through training and development, employee relations, and employee communications interventions. Her focus has been on grassroots implementation of strategic change leading to service excellence in organizations and to increased employee competence and commitment.

**Rich Rardin** is president of BenchStrength Development, LLC. He helps organizations develop leadership strategies that align with and drive their business strategies in order to achieve marketplace objectives. A skilled facilitator, Rich empowers teams, as well as individual executive leaders, to overcome barriers to organizational change objectives while living out their core values. He has worked in leadership and organization development with a variety of Fortune 500 and nonprofit companies for over twenty-five years. He has presented his proprietary executive coaching model at human resource conferences worldwide. Rich and his family reside in Newtown, Connecticut.

# CHAPTER SIXTEEN

# St. Luke's Hospital and Health Network

*This case study describes how this hospital and health network implemented a leadership development program that achieved breakthrough results in patient satisfaction, improved quality of care, overall service, efficiency, and top status in the industry through a series of quality improvement initiatives, behavioral change programs, and an emphasis on a five-point leadership model that is focused on results.*

| | |
|---|---|
| OVERVIEW | 366 |
| HISTORY | 366 |
| INTRODUCTION | 367 |
| DIAGNOSIS | 368 |
| DESIGN | 369 |
| DEVELOPMENT | 369 |
| IMPLEMENTATION | 372 |
| KEY TO (CONTINUED) SUCCESS | 375 |
| FORUM EVALUATION | 375 |
| ORGANIZATIONAL RESULTS | 376 |
| LEADERSHIP COMMITTEE OUTCOMES | 382 |
| ENDNOTES | 383 |
| Exhibit 16.1: Strategic Plan Goals and Objectives | 384 |
| Exhibit 16.2: Management Philosophy, Vision for Patient Satisfaction, PCRAFT Core Values, Service Excellence Standards of Performance, and Performance Improvement Plan | 386 |
| Exhibit 16.3: Leadership Steering Committee Mission, Vision, Goals, and Member Roles | 388 |
| Exhibit 16.4: The Five Points of the Star Model | 389 |
| Exhibit 16.5: Sample Forum Evaluation | 390 |

Exhibit 16.6: 2000–January 2004: St. Luke's Hospital and
Health Network Major Accomplishments by Five Points
of the Star Model                                                     391
Exhibit 16.7: Press Ganey Report                                      392
Exhibit 16.8: Accountability Grid for Best "People Point
of the Star," Fall 2003: Linking Education to Changing Behavior       393
Exhibit 16.9: Management Performance Evaluation                       394

ABOUT THE CONTRIBUTORS                                                400

# OVERVIEW

This case study illustrates the unique methodology taken by St. Luke's Hospital and Health Network in assisting its managers become stronger leaders. Led by the leadership steering committee, a deliberate approach with a creative delivery strategy has been used for nearly three years in efforts to continuously develop the leadership skills and abilities of the over 260 managers in the health network.

The strategy stems from a five-point model that embodies the foundation principles that are required for managers and leaders to realize the St. Luke's mission and vision. The implementation of these principles is primarily realized through the delivery of regular leadership forums. This casual learning environment is where managers can frequently interact, ask questions, and challenge themselves by learning from other colleagues in different clinical, fiscal, and operational environments. These forums, and subsequent associated events, provides additional outlets where managers can use new methodologies and ideas to better maximize their resources in accordance with the Five Points of the Star model.

While this program is in its infancy, St. Luke's has already realized the benefits in areas of fiscal, clinical, operational, managerial, and human resource performance.

# HISTORY

St. Luke's Hospital and Health Network has a rich history of providing quality health care to generations of families. Since it was chartered in 1872, St. Luke's has grown from a community hospital to the region's most nationally honored integrated health care network; it comprises tertiary, nonprofit hospitals, more than 1,400 physicians, and numerous other related health organizations. The network provides direct services to people in the Lehigh Valley, surrounding counties, and, in some cases, neighboring states. The network includes more than 800 licensed beds, 72 medical specialties, more than 5,500 employees, and 40,000 annual patient admissions and is the second largest employer in Lehigh County. As it has evolved, St. Luke's has always stayed at the forefront of medical technology. Today St. Luke's is known for its nationally recognized heart and ICU care, its preeminence as a teaching institution, the excellence of its physician, nursing, and other clinical staff, and its superior customer service. In its 130 years, St. Luke's has stayed true to its mission to provide excellent care.

# INTRODUCTION

At St. Luke's, the board of trustees provides the stimulus, vision, and resources to develop and successfully implement an effective strategic plan. The plan provides an overall foundation within which the network and its entities operate and form their own strategic plans. The goals and objectives of the plan also align targets and interests of the network's constituents, whose success is interdependent (see Exhibit 16.1).

As noted in the excerpts from the strategic plan, St. Luke's has a strong foundation and a clear commitment to its people as evident in its mission, vision, and guiding principles. In addition, St. Luke's builds upon that foundation through the management philosophy, vision for patient satisfaction, PCRAFT (pride, caring, respect, accountability, flexibility, teamwork) core values, service excellence standards of performance, and performance improvement plan (see Exhibit 16.2 for all elements listed above).

St. Luke's mission, vision, and guiding principles are communicated throughout the network in varied written and verbal ways—such as framed, hanging copies of the mission, vision, values, and management philosophy; the mnemonic PCRAFT visually presented in creative ways; the Wall of Fame; the employee handbook; the standards of performance booklet; customer service and management tips; *Essentials* (the annual mandatory education newsletter); the network web site (www.slhhn.org)—stated as part of new employee orientation, and reinforced in educational programs and at employee meetings.

Richard A. Anderson, president and CEO of St. Luke's Hospital and Health Network, is often heard to say, "St. Luke's is more than bricks and mortar . . . it is people." Through its people, the network is steadfast in its commitment to a mission of healing, realized through a sustained effort to create a lasting culture of service excellence. The administration throughout the network, led by Mr. Anderson, embraces some basic concepts that foster a culture of service excellence. Those concepts include

1. Employee satisfaction yields patient satisfaction yields a successful business (Build your people . . . they build your business)

2. Employee satisfaction begins and ends with effective leaders who provide

   - Vision
   - Clear expectations regarding care and service
   - Development and education
   - Effective communication
   - Role modeling
   - Constructive feedback
   - Recognition

3. Effective leaders can and need to be developed

4. Leadership development and education is based on educating to change behavior

Evidence of this is reflected in the interviewing (and hiring) practices, job descriptions, performance evaluations, and ongoing assessment of competence. Employee involvement is actively and perpetually encouraged at St. Luke's. Many workplace processes and systems exist to reinforce that involvement.

# DIAGNOSIS

*Leadership "owns" the responsibility to create, support, and sustain an environment that values St. Luke's employees, physicians, and volunteers.*
—Richard Anderson, president & CEO, St. Luke's Hospital and Health Network

In late 2000, senior administration began to realize that the health care environment was becoming increasingly challenging to all hospitals in the United States. From reimbursement to privacy, a wide array of large issues consistently presented itself to the senior administrators across the health care landscape. Being cognizant of these early challenges, St. Luke's was assertive in already implementing plans to handle the operational, clinical, and fiscal challenges of its immediate environment. However, management uncovered that although it had action plans to take on all challenges in these three areas, it was not taking the same assertive approach to meeting the needs of its managers. St. Luke's was not fully providing its own team with the ability to grow and expand their management and leadership skills in parallel with the environmental challenges that surrounded them.

In embracing the concepts noted above, the St. Luke's Hospital and Health Network Administration recognized the need to provide consistent, effective leadership development across the network. In order to accomplish that end, a leadership steering committee, chaired by Robert P. Zimmel, senior vice president of human resources for the network, was formed in June 2001. The leadership steering committee includes representation from the different network entities and, by design, teams people with varied backgrounds, communication styles, and skill sets. The mission, vision, goals, and member roles of the committee were initially established and remain as guides to all that is planned and implemented by the committee (see Exhibit 16.3). Completion of the initial foundation work allowed the leadership steering committee to move into the process of design.

# DESIGN

The beginning steps to this change effort began by looking around, getting "out of our woods," if you will, and seeking out other models of leadership in health care. The leadership steering committee performed the obvious literature search; however, not many substantial and successful models were found.

Following the research assessment, members of the leadership steering committee visited several sites that were considered qualitative performance indicators. The target group was specific hospitals highly ranked in numerous categories of the Press Ganey survey. While the visits were helpful and some knowledge was gained, committee members also left these sites with a strong belief that St. Luke's was on the right track with many of its existing practices. A key learning for this leadership group was the recognition that these organizations were intentional in their leadership development. They designed set times throughout the year when they brought leaders together to educate. These set times seemed to serve as the "milestone" days when growth opportunities would be deployed to employees.

# DEVELOPMENT

Prior to forming the committee that currently exists, a few charting members of the leadership steering committee traveled to St. Charles, Illinois to attend a seminar hosted by Delnor Hospital. It was there that the leadership steering committee was introduced to philosophies and methodologies of Quint Studer. From Quint Studer and other industry leaders, the mantra, "As you grow your leaders, you grow your organization" was introduced to the St. Luke's team. In addition to Studer's influential philosophies, the St. Luke's team was introduced to Studer's "Five Pillars of Success." From these pillars, the leadership steering committee designed the Five Points of the Star model. (A star has significant meaning to the organization, as an eight-point star is included in the St. Luke's logo.) The Five Points of the Star were identified as people, quality, service, cost, and growth (see Exhibit 16.4). Each point also has indicators that are used to ensure that the vision of each point is being achieved.

The vision of the *people point* was defined as having all leaders, staff and volunteers in St. Luke's Hospital and Health Network feel valued and recognized from all levels within the Network. The indicators for this point are

- Having a strong customer service orientation throughout the system
- Implementing a process for professional development
- Retaining quality staff
- Acknowledging staff longevity and dedication
- Recognizing our volunteers
- Reducing employee turnover
- Letting employees know that they are the advocates for the success of the entire network and that their contribution, regardless of the department or function, is valuable and critical to the success of the institution

The *quality point* was designed to gauge the qualitative successes of the organization against benchmark data gathered for hospitals of similar size. St. Luke's continuously strives to reduce turnaround times, improve environmental quality, decrease length of stays, become the employer of choice in the local area, be nationally recognized for clinical outcomes, and ultimately become the organization of choice. Finally, in addition to the aspirations of the leadership steering committee, the hospital itself wanted to be ranked as a top hospital by industry experts for providing quality care and services.

The *service point* sets clear guidelines of what is expected of each employee and volunteer. The network has partnered with Press Ganey to gauge patient satisfaction. St. Luke's works to wow the patient community with friendliness. The institution recognizes its accomplishments and takes accountability for any shortcomings. Every quarter managers are expected to evaluate their scores and determine whether and where improvement is needed. Departments excelling against their national peers are celebrated at each monthly management meeting.

The *cost point* is by far the most difficult point St. Luke's has had to communicate over the past years. Although maintaining a positive bottom line is clearly the vision, the greater challenge is leveraging employee resources appropriately to maximize efficiency. The administrative leadership monitors the management by establishing competitive employee wages, negotiating with vendors, taking steps to decrease operating costs, and maintaining adequate staffing levels.

Finally, the *growth point* was designed with the vision to thrust St. Luke's in the marketplace as the largest health network in Pennsylvania. This would become evident by the total number of patients, visits, and admissions.

St. Luke's would increase revenue, volume, and market share across all entities of the network. Looking into the future, St. Luke's Hospital and Health Network wishes to serve the needs of other patients in both new communities and bordering states.

As a mechanism to illustrate the importance of the Five Points of the Star model while continuing to develop network leaders, a series of forums was conducted. The forums were designed to educate and stimulate learning with a desired outcome of changing behaviors. Forums were presented on a regular basis, with each session primarily focusing on one point of the star model. Originally, the intent was to have quarterly forums, but after considering the demands placed on the steering committee to produce the forums and the time constraints on the leaders to attend the sessions, the number of forums was reduced to three per year. Each forum was based on the idea of incorporating outside lecturers and presenters, coupled by internal administrators or leaders who could implement the concepts presented by the guests while relating them to St. Luke's Hospital and Health Network. The net result of each forum was that managers became knowledgeable not just of present practice but also of other highly regarded practices away from the network. Managers had the opportunity to evaluate and, if applicable, implement new ideas into everyday practice.

The implementation of these regular forums constituted another change to the St. Luke's culture. No longer could policies and procedures alone direct the network's leaders. Rather, the leaders had to think, plan, and respond differently to a dynamically changing health care environment while working in successfully growing organization.

The forums always focused on the Five Points of the Star model and provided educational and informational content to help develop the skills of the network leadership. The manner in which the forums were conducted fostered a casual atmosphere that was entertaining yet informative. Presenters at these sessions were coached to entertain and interact and avoid a lecture-type format. Attending leaders were encouraged to socialize and network with their colleagues. The leaders often stepped out of their more conservative roles and participated in learning exercises or even presented in a humorous fashion. This quickly revealed the diverse talent that made up the leadership team and made for a more enjoyable time. All of the forums were held away from the workplace to provide a brief separation from the job and focus the attention on the learning.

Another key element to the success of the leadership forums was and remains the consistent interjections of fun. Although fun in the workplace may not be valuable to other corporate cultures, St. Luke's Hospital and Health Network considers this value vital to its culture. During forum planning, all members brainstorm methods of delivering valuable learning in an environment that is both comfortable and enjoyable to guests. This attitude stems from the senior administration that exercises this methodology on an everyday basis. Management meetings commonly have a comfortable tone. In addition, St. Luke's provides various programs during the year to appreciate the efforts and time of its entire staff. As important, St. Luke's is committed to celebrating success and recognizing its staff throughout the year. Although there are various events, the greatest of them all is the St. Luke's Hospital and Health Network Annual Picnic. This day-long festival is an event that attracts over three thousand attendees. It also includes organized team competitions for employees and their families.

Producing three quality forums a year for 260 managers has been a major undertaking. Fortunately, the leadership steering committee was experienced at project work and implementing major changes. The steering committee decided to split the responsibilities up into six subgroups, thus making the process of producing a forum more manageable. The steering committee members selected a subgroup in which to participate and became responsible for coordinating that part of the forum. The committee expanded some of the subgroup work by inviting other managers to assist with the tasks. The subgroups would report back to the steering committee for updates, feedback, and, at times, constructive criticism.

The leadership steering committee would decide on which point of the star to focus and provide a general framework for the forum, along with one or two keynote speakers. A subgroup then worked on the content of the forum by selecting specific topics for the presenters and prepping them on the desired direction and style. Another subgroup provided the decorations to support the theme and created the ambiance of the forum. A third subgroup provided the logistical needs and coordinated the location, the audio-visual equipment, and the food menu. A fourth subgroup communicated weeks in advance to invite leaders to attend, providing periodic reminders that were cleverly done and effective in reaching everyone. Two other subgroups were formed to provide an evaluation process and the ability to link previous, present, and future forums. The evaluation tool was important not only to hear feedback but also to assess the effectiveness of the leadership steering committee's intent to educate, inform, and change behaviors. The linkage component was critical to continually tie the forums all back together as a process and not allow each forum to be an independent event that was forgotten at the end of the day.

# IMPLEMENTATION

The actual presentation of the leadership forums has been specifically designed to embody the goals of the organization as a whole through the Five Points of the Star model. In specific reference to employee satisfaction, the leadership forum was dedicated to providing multiple programs per year that both educate and challenge the over 260 St. Luke's managers. Although each forum has a different focus, the structure is relatively the same. The morning portion is dedicated to the guest lecturer (or presenter), who provides a presentation based on his or her experiences away from St. Luke's that have parallel values and applicability. Many of the speakers share commonalities in personality and approach in that they provide valuable learning while being charismatic, energized, and audience-grabbing in delivery. The afternoon session involves the presentation of network administrators and staff, who take some of the concepts presented by the guest, and relate them to everyday challenges and opportunities within the network. The leadership steering committee maintains the same delivery standards for its own staff as it does for featured guests. It regularly works with and even reviews the presentations to ensure that the audience will both learn and enjoy from them. The successful outcome is seen in qualitative feedback received from St. Luke's staff indicating that these forums have made a difference in the way they operate both as individual managers and as members of teams or committees.

As the leadership forums approach their third full year of implementation, it is valuable to trace back to their original development. The journey, as well as the theme of stars for our leadership events, began on September 18, 2001, with the "Journey to the Stars," a kick-off event for the management team. The scene was intentionally dramatic, with star-glittered sunglasses for all managers, *Star-Trek* theme music, a star-studded glowing ceiling, and an agenda emphasizing personal growth and development. The journey was "destined" to transform managers to leaders.

The following three forums primarily focused on people, including the introduction (and understanding) of the Myers Briggs Type Inventory (MBTI) and campus-specific (hospital) satisfaction survey results (Press Ganey). Leadership core competencies, developed in a group management approach, were introduced to managers in a forum focused on the *people* point of the star. Additional topics that were part of that forum included using the MBTI to assist in both staff communications and conflict resolution. This forum illustrated to staff that MBTI could be used to facilitate more effective conversations with various personalities.

Subsequent leadership forums focused on three other points of the star: *service, quality,* and *growth.* Service featured two highly successful local company leaders who shared their blueprints for service. Dr. James Bagian, of the Department of Veteran Affairs, presented quality in health care through examples from his experiences as both a NASA astronaut and in implementing process improvements of the Veterans Administration. Dr. Bagian reinforced principles and topics that were essential for attaining positive outcomes from qualitative excellence. In particular, he highlighted

- Health care is of the train-and-blame mentality; eliminate the "Who is at fault?" questions as an initial response.

- When assessing your quality program, your starting point is your safety program. Reason: safety systems keep you focused on the people, the product being manufactured, and the system through which the service or product is delivered. Keeping this focus ultimately determines the quality outcome.

- Do a very good needs analysis in the beginning. Work on the areas that need improvement, don't just gather statistics around things going wrong. This is a problem-solving, proactive approach.

- Clearly define the things you want to measure, how you will measure them (what tools you will use), and what you will do with the data to help improve the system.

- Don't point the finger of blame if something fails. Treat failure as a teachable moment, use the opportunity to learn from it and instruct those involved in the problem. Create an environment of learning when mistakes happen.

- Create quality review teams that are made up of people from different disciplines.

St. Luke's senior vice president of finance discussed the *growth* point of the star. Financial growth at all campuses and as a network was highlighted. The senior vice president of network development cleverly presented St. Luke's network strategic plan. Based on the game show *Jeopardy,* the senior vice president of network development and colleagues reenacted the game in a humorous fashion. While educating the network of particular growth facts and strategies, mock answers were also given as a means to joke about fictional ideas and take the occasional sarcastic "jab" at present senior administration across the network. This format was well received regarding the quantitative feedback and general comments received on postforum surveys. The third speaker of the growth forum, the CEO from St. Luke's Quakertown, made a humorous but educational presentation called "Building a Great Place to Work." While highlighting programs that did work, through multiple slides and pictures he mocked programs that were not as successful.

Although leadership forums were grand stage events, they were only held three times per year. The leadership steering committee recognized both the need and demand of its employees by having regular stimuli for its managers. Therefore, the Book Club was established across the network. The foundation principle of Book Club is to provide the managers a book that offers opportunities to learn different practices and methodologies for being leaders and employees. The concept implemented in the network was to deploy the book to all leaders, and have regular Book Club meetings designed to create small think tanks. Key books that have been implemented include *Good to Great*[1] and *The Power of Full Engagement.*[2]

The net result of these book readings has been managers having the opportunity to learn and reflect in a nonwork setting. General group feedback has indicated that managers enjoy these books and in some way take something from each one in everyday action.

As a means to assist managers in understanding their respective character traits, the Myers Briggs Type Inventory was rolled out at St. Luke's Hospital and Health Network in fall 2001. The management team was invited to participate in taking the MBTI in September 2001. The initial education session, which gave the leadership group the grounding it needed in understanding MBTI type, occurred in October 2001. This was the beginning point of the St. Luke's journey of becoming an MBTI organization. The development of a resource that listed the MBTI type of a manager was another educational step that was necessary to St. Luke's Hospital and Health Network culture.

Whereas some cultures show individual employee MBTI by displaying it on a pin or on their door, St. Luke's did not feel comfortable with that method. For the St. Luke's work culture, the most practical answer was to develop the Type Directory. This directory is a guide that lists managers' MBTI type and phone number. Unlike other concepts such as signs on office doors or nametag depictions, the Type Directory was intended to meet the needs of all employees across the network. Unlike a in one-hospital atmosphere, managers in the network often interact with other managers and administrators from other hospitals within the network. The Type Directory allows all individuals to interact more easily. The presence and importance of MBTI is seen in the second generation of this directory, which was released in spring 2003. At that time, even more managers had discovered their MBTI type and agreed on the importance of sharing it with others across the network. Its importance is considered so great that it has been placed on the Intranet, providing online information to all network managers.

## KEY TO (CONTINUED) SUCCESS

As the leadership forums have continued to be successful in both design and implementation, a core component of its successful rollout has been the ongoing support from senior management. The leadership steering committee made conscious decisions to involve senior leadership from the kick-off meeting to presentations involving senior leaders' particular expertise regarding points of the star. At each leadership forum, Richard Anderson welcomes leaders and provides insightful comments to the leaders present regarding their importance to the network and the time they spend learning at each of the forums. The commitment of senior leadership's presence at each of the leadership forums continues to be vital to the success of the forums.

# FORUM EVALUATION

The effort to educate the leadership steering committee was not grounded in an *assumption* of what people needed. The committee wanted to learn from people what they needed; this feedback has continued. Surveying the group and meeting their needs is not only a "concierge" mentality—a total commitment to customer service in all facets of service delivery—but it also is consistent with our early message to the leadership team, "We want to hear from you!" At the various leadership forums, signs have been created that announce, "We heard you" and identify the changes made to the forum since the last meeting. All such changes were driven by attention to the group's feedback.

The leadership steering committee continues to utilize the feedback gained from forum evaluations (see example in Exhibit 16.5) and analyzes it via a process improvement approach. The effectiveness of the program is measured based on identified objectives defined in the evaluation tool. Comments and suggestions from the evaluation process have been used to determine future program content. This information has also helped identify leadership initiatives. Interest in participation on leadership task forces is assessed via the evaluation process. Managers from all network entities have volunteered to participate in these endeavors. Projects include

- Revision of the management performance evaluation to reflect the Five Points of the Star model (people, quality, service, cost, and growth)
- Ongoing linkage accountability grids

Leadership development is based on educating to change behavior. Service has been an area of significant development in the St. Luke's Hospital and Health Network. Many examples of behavioral change in this area have been noted:

- As stated previously, the management evaluation was revised to reflect leadership development accountability standards.
- The St. Luke's Hospital and Health Network Performance Standards were disseminated in a booklet as part of the Leadership Development series. The goal of the booklet was to provide minimum expected behavior and performance standards across the network. These standards are now part of the staff performance evaluation process.
- Numerous letters have been received by senior administration denoting the positive customer service environment.

As a result of reported behavioral change, the senior administrative team from Presbyterian Medical Center of the University of Pennsylvania Health System conducted a site visit to experience and learn about our various customer service endeavors.

# ORGANIZATIONAL RESULTS

Over the past few years, the leadership of the St. Luke's administration has resulted in the institution's realization of greater success on all Five Points of the Star model (see Exhibit 16.6). Although the organization as a whole has realized achievement, individual departmental leadership of administrators and managers have been the backbone of this success. Individual initiatives led by one leader or a team of leaders have benefited not just their own respective departments, but also other departments across their individual facility. Each successful project has resulted from the original project champions' reviewing their department and comparing it with the ideal principles of the Five Points of the Star model. By identifying opportunities, tangible benefits have been realized through the successful completion of multiple initiatives.

Listed below are four examples that illustrate how leaders have used the Five Points of the Star to recognize initiatives within their departments where improvement could be made to realize better outcomes.

---

### CASE #1: Point of Star—Quality

Title: "A Multidisciplinary Approach to Decreasing Central/Umbilical Line Associated Bacteremia in the NICU"

Project team leaders: Ellen Novatnack, Steven Schweon, and Charlotte Becker

The project goal was to decrease the central/umbilical line associated bacteremia rate in the <1000 gram neonate to below the twenty-fifth percentile when benchmarked against the Centers for Disease Control and Prevention (CDC) National Nosocomial Infection Surveillance (NNIS) System. Interventions would have an impact on all NICU birth weight categories.

Infants in the NICU are at greater risk for health care associated (nosocomial) infections due to their compromised immune status, low birth weight, and the complex invasive diagnostic and therapeutic treatment regimens that they are exposed to. Central/umbilical line associated bacteremia rates in the <1000 gram birth weight category in the NICU were above the ninetieth percentile for twenty-four months when benchmarked against NNIS. Device (central and umbilical line) utilization ratios were below the twenty-fifth percentile when compared to NNIS. Therefore, it was concluded that the high infection rates might be related more to infection control issues than to device use.

The strategy for improvement was based on implementing and reinforcing infection control interventions to reduce the frequency of infection by utilizing a comprehensive, multidisciplinary approach. Representatives from Infection Control and Prevention, NICU, and Support Services collaborated to identify problems, make recommendations, provide staff education, reinforce preventive measures, implement changes, and revise policies and procedures.

Specific examples of the multiple interventions include revising policies on tubing changes, enforcing proper hand hygiene technique, changing the antimicrobial handwashing agent to one that was kinder and gentler to the skin, enforcing glove use when appropriate in conducting environmental rounds, observing staff providing care, introducing a waterless alcohol hand rub as an alternative to soap and water and placing it at every cubicle, enforcing current policy and procedures, dating peripheral IV insertion sites, stopping the practice of precutting tegaderm and band aids, eliminating drawer stock of gauze so sterile gauze is used, wiping down all shared equipment after each patient use, enforcing the nail policy and limiting jewelry.

Support Services also made changes. Respiratory Therapy interventions included emptying the vent water traps into the trash can, covering tubing when alternating between CPAP and nasal cannulas, and storing ambu bags in a clean plastic bag at the bedside. Environmental Services consolidated cleaning products. Radiology began cleaning and disinfecting ultrasound probes between patients and covering all radiology plates with clean plastic bags for each patient.

After two years of elevated infection rates and implementing strategies, the data indicated that four months of a decreasing rate and then six consecutive months of no infections had occurred, a rate that falls below the NNIS tenth percentile. Based on the performance improvement project, the actions taken in the NICU resulted in a decrease in central/umbilical line associated bacteremia rates in the <1000 gram neonate.

The NICU staff gained a heightened awareness that infection control preventive activities reduce infection rates. Hospital administration learned what could be accomplished through a successful infection control program. The Joint Commission of Accredited Healthcare Organizations (JCAHO) surveyor (May 2001) was impressed with the multidisciplinary approach and favorable results. The deputy director of the Healthcare Outcomes Branch at the CDC sent a letter recommending our efforts and congratulating us on our success.

A spot check was performed in the NICU from March 1 to May 31, 2003, by conducting targeted surveillance using the previously established guidelines. The rate of central/umbilical line associated bacteremia in the <gram neonate was 0 infections per 1,000 line days, which falls below the NNIS tenth percentile, demonstrating sustained positive results over time.

---

### CASE #2: Point of Star—Service

Title: "Incorporating Family Centered Care in Pediatric Nursing Practice"
Project team leader: Charlotte Becker
In 2001, nursing staff reviewed the Press Ganey results for the last three surveys (2000–2001) and learned that the department was not scoring as high as managers expected. Following the review, the plan was to develop new approaches and physical changes within the Pediatric Unit to improve family-centered care.

The pediatric team chose to focus on providing family-centered care. New approaches when caring for multicultural, nontraditional family units needed to be addressed. An open-minded, flexible, and patient-centered approach was introduced and emphasized with the pediatric staff members. There were physical changes within the pediatric unit that needed to be addressed.

The network first began by providing concierge customer service education. These sessions consisted of two hours of education to

- Discuss why customer satisfaction is so important
- Provide basic skills for effective communication
- Provide tools to enable the employee to embody the role of a concierge

Unit-based education was focused on education from the Family-Centered Care Conference.

The Needs Assessment was completed using baseline Press Ganey reports from July 1, 2002, to June 30, 2003. The items the pediatric team chose to work on were

- Pleasantness of room decorations
- Accommodations and comfort for visitors
- Staff sensitivity to inconvenience
- Staff attitude toward visitors
- Room temperature

The staff held brainstorming sessions to generate ideas from the survey results. They also focused on the additional, written, negative comments on the survey forms.

To address various areas of concern, the following actions were implemented for each respective factor.

Pleasantness of the room's decorations:

- Pictures were taken of all pediatric patients (with parent's consent) and hung for display. "Thank You" cards were also displayed. (9/02)
- All children had a private room. (9/02)
- A dinosaur food truck was purchased for the pediatric trays. (10/02)
- A refrigerator and microwave were added to the parents' lounge for families to use. (9/02)
- Water fountains were replaced with an ice machine and water dispensing unit. (10/02)
- Portable video games systems were donated and placed in moveable carts for patients' use. (11/02)
- Meals were provided free of charge for breastfeeding mothers.

Accommodations and comfort of visitors:

- Coffee, tea, hot chocolate, crackers, and cookies were placed at the nursing station each morning. (10/02)
- Eight hundred VCR tapes, video systems, and games were donated. (Collected as an Eagle Scout project, for patient use.) (10/02)
- AOL access was added to the portable laptop donated by our Ladies Auxiliary for visiting family members. (1/02)
- Newborns needing additional hospital stay were transferred to pediatrics. Mothers who were discharged could stay with their newborns while their baby was being treated.

Room temperature:

- All individual heating systems in each room were cleaned and upgraded.
- Individual room thermostats were added with signage explaining how to adjust the temperature.
- Individual fans were provided as requested.
- Window darkening coating was placed on the interior of the windows.
- The return (fresh) air flow was increased to the pediatric unit. In addition, the ventilation unit was replaced. (10/03)

Staff sensitivity to inconvenience and staff attitude toward visitors:

- Families were provided 20 percent cafeteria discount cards. (9/01)
- Parents choosing to stay with their child were given hygiene supplies. (9/00)
- A VCR was placed in every child's room with appropriate controls. (11/02)
- "Please Do Not Disturb" signs were placed in the unit. (1/02)
- All units had distributed welcome pamphlets (and signs were updated). (5/03)
- Snack, soda, and juice vending machines were made available in an area conveniently adjacent to the pediatric floor.

The changes that were instituted were measured by the results of the Press Ganey Report results from July 1, 2003, to September 30, 2003 (see Exhibit 16.7). An increase in scores was shown in all five areas of the needs assessment.

---

**CASE #3: Point of Star—Cost and Quality**
Title: "Guidelines for the Use of Interventional Cardiology Medications in the Cardiac Catheterization Lab—A Multidisciplinary Approach"
Project team leader: Howard C. Cook
Utilizing the principles of value analysis and evidence-based medicine, a program was developed highlighting guidelines for the use of glycoprotein IIb/IIIa inhibitors (abciximab [ReoPro], eptifibatide [Integrilin]), and the direct thrombin inhibitor bivalirudin (Angiomax) in interventional cardiology procedures. The goal of this project was to assure optimum patient outcomes and maximum financial efficiency. It was recognized that abciximab was utilized in approximately 60 percent of all cases involving these agents. This agent was also the most expensive of the three agents usually employed. A thorough review of the medical literature was undertaken to see whether there were specific indications or patient types who benefited most form the use of abciximab. For all others, the preferred agent would be eptifibatide (or bivalirudin, if the clinical situation was appropriate). At the same time, a national survey of top cardiac hospitals (based on Solucient data) was conducted to see whether they had established criteria for the use of these products. Once all data were reviewed, a proposal was presented to the cardiology steering committee for approval. At that time, criteria were fine-tuned and the project was approved. Educational signage was displayed in all procedure rooms, indicating situations in which abciximab would be preferred and requesting the use of eptifibatide (or bivalirudin) in all other patients. Target drug usage data, as well as

concomitant interventional medications used, were documented to determine compliance to approved criteria. Physicians who consistently used abciximab outside of approved criteria were contacted and the program was reviewed. There was a consistent reduction in the number of cases that fell outside of established criteria as the program continued. Success of the project was measured by evaluating the cost per case of interventional procedures in which the target drugs were used. Since its beginning in April 2003, the estimated annual savings to the institution is in excess of $250,000. There have been no reports of adverse drug events as a result of the therapeutic preferences of this program to date.

### CASE #4: Point of Star–People

Title: "Creating a Best Place to Work"

Project team leader: Joe Pinto, director, service improvement

St. Luke's wished to be recognized nationally in clinical outcomes, cost-effective care, and patient satisfaction. To achieve this recognition, the director of service improvement looked to Press Ganey to provide a large medium in which St. Luke's could compete against over 1,600 hospitals across the country. Using the Press Ganey survey as well as its research resources, St. Luke's was able to identify the questions that were highly correlated with employee friendliness and courtesy. As part of the analysis, St. Luke's examined the questions that were highly correlated with the likelihood of patients to recommend the hospital to others. Following the assessment, a plan was devised based on the principle that happy employees correlate to satisfied customers, which in turn leads to patients that will recommend St. Luke's to other people.

Following the research and assessment of the future goal, the first step in the implementation process began by creating a customer service program. This program was mandated and was designed to illustrate the necessary steps to implement appropriate customer service behaviors and standards of performance. Key areas ranged from conflict resolution to service recovery and etiquette. The second step was creating the employee recognition and reward committee. This committee of staff members is charged with awarding the PCRAFT (pride, caring, respect, accountability, flexibility, teamwork) award to twelve hospital employees per year (see Exhibit 16.2). These employees are required to consistently exhibit the values of the organization, and documented examples have to be included in their respective nomination form. The third key step in the strategy process was the implementation of awards for departments' patient satisfaction scores. The objective of the departmental quarterly recognition program was to reward and recognize employees, managers, and departments for outstanding achievement related to patient satisfaction. To achieve recognition, a department must receive one of the following:

- Highest percentile ranking on the survey
- Overall mean score that is highest above the hospital mean score
- Highest percentile ranking consistently (three quarters or more)
- Largest improvement in overall mean score

Following a win of this award, the department managers receive up to $100 to be used on the department, accompanied by recognition from the COO and at monthly management meetings. The final component of the overall strategy focuses on individual achievement via the "High-5" recognition. A staff member who has his or her name appear in patient letters, Press Ganey comments, over the phone, in patient letters, or through Project Bravo recognitions—a St. Luke's program that recognizes employees for positive customer service—more than five times receives a High-5 Award. The recognized employee receives a gift certificate to either a restaurant or other outside facility, a letter from the COO, a pin with the slogan "above and beyond," and their name displayed on the Employee Wall of Fame.

The results of this comprehensive strategy are based on Press Ganey scores and other major achievements. In 2003 marked achievements in Press Ganey scoring included the following:

- The Environmental Services Department scored within the ninetieth percentile for four consecutive survey periods in the measure of room cleanliness and staff courtesy.
- The nursing staff ranked above the eightieth percentile in nurses' attitude.
- Organizational achievements included a ranking over the eightieth percentile in overall cheerfulness, eighty-fourth percentile in staff sensitivity to the inconvenience of being in a hospital setting, and eighty-third percentile in attitude toward visitors.

Although the Press Ganey scores alone provided tangible proof of success, just as valuable was being named in the "Best Places to Work Foundation for Pennsylvania." In the Top 100 Best Places, St. Luke's ranked twenty-eighth in the large-size category (employee number greater than 250). The award is based on a written summary of practices, as well as an anonymous employee survey of randomly selected employees. The employee survey represents 75 percent of the total grade.

## LEADERSHIP COMMITTEE OUTCOMES

As leadership forum programming continued to evolve, the steering committee established a linkage committee. The linkage committee membership was representative of the entities within the network. The primary goal of the linkage committee was to link education to changing behavior. To exercise this goal, accountability grids were created following each leadership forum. The accountability grids (Exhibit 16.8) contained expectations for senior and middle management leaders with defined timelines as appropriate. The expectations contained within each accountability grid related to the education provided at the leadership forum.

Several works, born out of the leadership forum, have contributed significantly to the organization's definition of leadership skills. One of these works is the leadership core competencies, which was the result of work accomplishments by the entire leadership team. Seven key competencies were identified:

- Motivator
- Team builder
- Goal orientation
- Communicator
- Commitment to service
- Organized, prioritizing
- Resourceful

Each of these competencies has specific behavioral identifiers that further define each competency. The management performance evaluation was redesigned by an ad hoc group of managers who participated in the leadership forum. This group designed a new management evaluation tool that incorporated the core leadership competencies (Exhibit 16.9).

An additional work that originated out of the leadership steering committee was the development of a booklet on service excellence standards of performance. This booklet clearly defines, in a behavioral way, the standards set for "concierge service delivery" on the part of all members of the hospital team. All new employees are required to attend concierge training as part of the orientation to the hospital.

# ENDNOTES

1. Collins, J. (2001). *Good to great.* New York: HarperCollins.
2. Loehr, J., & Schwartz, T. (2003). *The power of full engagement.* New York: Simon & Schuster.

**Exhibit 16.1. Strategic Plan Goals and Objectives**

*Mission Statement.* The mission of St. Luke's Hospital and Health Network is to provide compassionate, excellent quality and cost-effective health care to residents of the communities we serve regardless of their ability to pay.

The entities constituting the St. Luke's Hospital and Health Network will accomplish this mission by

- Making the patient our highest priority
- Promoting health and continuously improving care provided to heal the sick and injured
- Coordinating and integrating services into a seamless system of care
- Improving the level of customer service provided throughout the network
- Ensuring all health care services are relevant to the needs of the community
- Striving to maximize the satisfaction of our employees, patients, medical staff, and volunteers
- Training allied health professionals, nursing and medical students, and residents in a variety of specialties and to attract them to practice within the network's service area

*Vision Statement.* The entities of St. Luke's Hospital and Health Network will be nationally recognized for excellence in clinical outcomes, cost-effective care, and patient satisfaction.

This vision will be achieved by

- Continuously improving patient, employee, volunteer, and physician satisfaction
- Benchmarking clinical outcomes and improving the processes that lead to optimal care
- Managing the resources of the network to minimize costs
- Partnering with physicians and other providers, recognizing our success is dependent on cooperation and common goals
- Continuously updating our view of "reality" consistent with a rapid change in the environment, technology, and the practice of medicine

**Exhibit 16.1.** (*Continued*)

---

*Principles.* The following principles will be the foundation of the goals, management, and future development of the network.

- Each network entity has a responsibility to operate financially at break-even or better on a stand-alone basis over the long term. Our entities should focus on their core services and divest of nonprofitable services that are not essential to our mission.
- Day-to-day management of operations must be performed locally. It should be based on a continuously simplified management structure that promotes effectiveness, efficiency, and accountability for its integrity. However, decentralized management still requires various degrees of network oversight to coordinate the allocation of resources and informed decision making.
- The development of any network is an evolutionary process that depends on members' sharing a sense of purpose, belonging, and a commitment to collective success. There needs to be an ongoing commitment to integration, leading to a seamless system of care.
- To establish and sustain the St. Luke's "brand" of quality and customer service, it is necessary to establish network-wide standards that are measured against national benchmarks. However, each entity must decide how best to implement them in a cost-effective and responsible fashion.
- Regular and effective communication is a prerequisite for integration, satisfaction, and ownership among the network's stakeholders.
- Employees are one of our most important assets.
- Medical care should be delivered at the local level as a first choice and within the resources of the network whenever appropriate.
- All persons included in the network are accountable to the community to adhere to the network's mission and vision and ultimately to improve the health status of the community.

---

**Exhibit 16.2. Management Philosophy, Vision for Patient Satisfaction, PCRAFT Core Values, Service Excellence Standards of Performance, and Performance Improvement Plan**

The management philosophy, vision for patient satisfaction, and PCRAFT core values are, as follows:

Management Philosophy for St. Luke's Hospital

*Introduction*

- We believe that quality patient care will best be provided in an environment supported by a positive management philosophy.

*Objectives*

- To demonstrate by behavior and attitude that employees, physicians, and volunteers are St. Luke's most valuable resource
- To create a positive work environment through timely and effective communication and involvement of employees, physicians, and volunteers

*Management Principles*

1. Promote open, timely, and effective communication throughout the organization
2. Promote an environment that recognizes individual differences and encourages individuals to treat one another with respect and dignity
3. Foster an environment in which creativity and professional and personal growth are encouraged
4. Encourage decision making at the department level
5. Create clear goals, performance expectations, standards of accountability, and provide timely feedback to the people with whom we work; each employee is expected to

   - Cultivate a caring atmosphere in our hospital
   - Place the needs of the patients first
   - Interact positively with physicians, visitors, fellow employees and volunteers
   - Solve problems
   - Follow through on commitments
   - Continually improve hospital systems, emphasizing quality
   - Be fair and consistent in all dealings
   - Conduct all business dealings in an ethical manner
   - Be fiscally responsible

Exhibit 16.2. (*Continued*)

- Treat everyone as responsible adults
- Recognize there are consequences for all behaviors, both positive and negative

6. Provide a safe working environment
7. Provide a compensation and benefit program that enables St. Luke's to recruit, develop, and retain qualified, loyal, and experienced employees

*Vision for Patient Satisfaction*

- St. Luke's Hospital and Health Network wants to set the industry standard for achieving and sustaining the highest level of patient satisfaction for our patients and their family members in every encounter.

*Core Values*

- At St. Luke's Hospital and Health Network, our people are the source of our strength; their commitment and involvement determine our future success. To achieve our vision, we are guided by our values. Great focus is placed on our values. The mnemonic **PCRAFT** was developed to help staff remember and more readily "live" the values. St. Luke's Values are as follows:

**P**ride—We take pride in our accomplishments and our organization.

**C**aring—We show consideration for others and their feelings. We treat others, as we want to be treated.

**R**espect—We recognize the value, diversity, and importance of each other, those we serve, and the organization.

**A**ccountability—We are responsible to make decisions and solve problems in a timely and effective manner.

**F**lexibility—We adapt to the changing needs and expectations of those we serve.

**T**eamwork—We work together to improve quality.

**Exhibit 16.3. Leadership Steering Committee Mission, Vision, Goals, and Member Roles**

The mission, vision, goals, and member roles for the leadership steering committee include

*Mission*

- To fully develop the excellence within each leader

*Vision*

- To become the *best* leaders in health care . . . to be teachable again and always

*Goals*

- Educate to change behavior
- Move from managers to leaders
- Harness the creative energy of our network and focus it in the same direction
- Create a service, action-oriented culture based on consistency, relationships, and accountability
- Build trust
- Reduce rework, redundancy, and duplication
- Set up a built-to-last culture
- Establish a focus on Five Points of the Star—service, people, quality, growth and cost—enabling us to align and connect back to our mission, vision, values, and goals

*Member Roles*

- In order to organize the work of the committee, ad hoc groups were established and still exist to support the different actions needed to ensure success of our endeavors; these Ad Hoc groups include

  Curriculum, content

  Communication

  Ambience, atmosphere

  Logistics

  Linkage

  Evaluation, measurement

**Exhibit 16.4.  The Five Points of the Star Model**

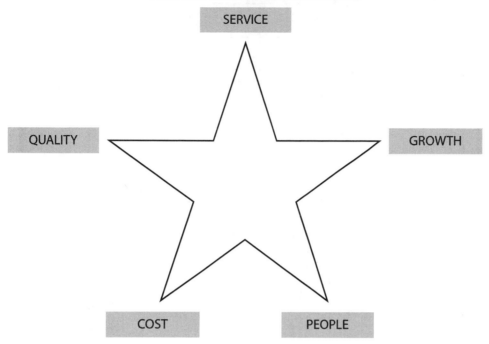

## Exhibit 16.5. Sample Forum Evaluation

*Example:* This is an example of the Forum Evaluation results from the Leadership Forum held on March 8, 2003 at Lehigh University in Bethlehem, Pennsylvania.

**LEADERSHIP FORUM**
**March 20, 2003**
**Lehigh University**

There were 182 completed evaluation forms returned from the meeting.

| | Strongly Disagree | | Disagree | | Neutral | | Agree | | Strongly Agree | | Total No. Ans. |
|---|---|---|---|---|---|---|---|---|---|---|---|
| | (No. of | (%) Ans.) | (No. of | (%) Ans.) | (No. of | (%) Ans.) | (No. of | (%) Ans.) | (No. of | (%) Ans.) | |
| 1. The program today has helped me to better understand our growth as a network. | 0 | 0% | 0 | 0% | 5 | 3% | 66 | 36% | 98 | 54% | 169 |
| 2. Evan Jones was effective in explaining the financial aspects of our strategic growth. | 2 | 1% | 2 | 1% | 3 | 2% | 54 | 30% | 121 | 66% | 182 |
| 3. Bob Martin's presentation heightened my awareness of our strategic initiatives across the network. | 0 | 0% | 5 | 3% | 13 | 7% | 68 | 37% | 96 | 53% | 182 |
| 4. Brooke Huston's presentation helped me to understand how to build a Great Place to Work at St. Luke's. | 0 | 0% | 2 | 1% | 13 | 7% | 104 | 57% | 60 | 33% | 179 |

*Note:* This is an example of the forum evaluation results from the leadership forum held on March 8, 2003 at Lehigh University in Bethlehem, Pennsylvania.

**Exhibit 16.6. 2000–January 2004: St. Luke's Hospital and Health Network Major Accomplishments by Five Points of the Star Model**

*People*

- 100 Best Places to Work in Pennsylvania
- Employee turnover rate of 12.8 percent at St. Luke's Bethlehem (awaiting trended information—no national benchmark)
- RN turnover for Medical/Surgical and Critical Care areas was 14.15 percent in FY 2003. This is down from 16.98 percent in FY 2002.

*Note:* This data is only for St. Luke's Hospital, and not the entire network.

*Quality*

- *U.S. News & World Report,* America's Best Hospitals, Cardiology and Open Heart Surgery 1999, 2000, 2001, 2002, 2003
- 100 Top Hospitals: Benchmark for Success 1997, 2001
- 100 Top Cardiovascular Hospitals: Benchmarks for Success 1999, 2001, 2002, 2003
- 100 Top ICU Hospitals: Benchmarks for Success 2000

*Service*

- St. Luke's Hospital and Health Network participates in Press Ganey. All hospitals in the network are ranked among national leaders in various individual areas of performance and service.
- Unit and departmental plans for customer service improvement

*Cost*

- Average length of stay (ALOS) has decreased from 5.07 days in FY 2000 to 4.34 days in FY 2003.

*Note:* Excluding newborns and TCU

- Operating margin has increased from 0.6 in FY 2000 to 1.5 in FY 2003

*Note:* For the St. Luke's Hospital only the operating margin has increased from 2.2 in FY 2000 to 3.0 in FY 2003.

*Growth*

- Admissions for the network were 33,742 in FY 2003. This is up from 29,564 in FY 2000.

*Note:* Excluding newborns and TCU

- Outpatient visits have increased from 392,770 in FY 2000 to 530,033 in FY 2003
- Emergency room (ER) visits have increased from 73,731 in FY 2000 to 93,075 in FY 2003.
- Total clinic visits have increased from 67,124 in FY 2000 to 88,026 in FY 2003
- Achieved Level I Trauma Center Accreditation based on volume growth and quality care
- Most birth in the region in FY 2003

### Exhibit 16.7. Press Ganey Report

| Question-PEDS | Mean Score 7/1/02– 9/30/02 | N 7/1/02– 9/30/02 | Mean Score 7/1/03– 9/30/03 | N 7/1/03– 9/30/03 | Mean Score Change |
|---|---|---|---|---|---|
| Pleasantness of room décor | 85.5 | 19 | 82.6 | 23 | (2.9) |
| Room temperature | 72.4 | 19 | 81.5 | 23 | 9.1 |
| Accommodations and comfort for visitors | 82.4 | 17 | 85.7 | 21 | 3.3 |
| Staff attitude towards visitors | 85.7 | 14 | 92.9 | 21 | 7.2 |
| Staff sensitivity to inconvenience | 87.5 | 16 | 93.8 | 20 | 6.3 |

Exhibit 16.8.  Accountability Grid for Best "People Point of the Star," Fall 2003:
Linking Education to Changing Behavior

| Who | What | Completed by | Completed Yes or No |
|---|---|---|---|
| Senior leadership and management | As a manager, review the daily structure of your work day. Take a personal assessment in terms of work-life balance issues to make the most of your hours at work each day. Set a goal to feel that you accomplish something each day in both work and personal life. | Ongoing | |
| Senior leadership and management | Choose and implement in your personal journey of work-life balance one of the items presented by Ellen Galinsky at the end of her presentation. (Goal is to list the top ten that she presented . . . left an e-mail message with Bob W. to see if we could get this from her.) | Ongoing | |
| Senior leadership | Provide an environment that promotes an individualized work-life balance journey for direct reports. This includes initiating a conversation with each direct report with the goal of developing an individualized work-life balance plan. | Ongoing | |

Exhibit 16.9. Management Performance Evaluation

# St. Luke's Hospital and Health Network

Name _____

Department and Job Title _____

Entity _____

Evaluator _____    Evaluation Period_____

Date _____

## MANAGEMENT JOB PERFORMANCE EVALUATION

### Instructions to Determine Level of Performance Rating

1. Use a point system to differentiate between the performance levels.

| Performance Rating Levels | |
|---|---|
| *Point Factor* | *Definition* |
| 4 | Performance is exceptional as evidenced by consistent achievement of the maximum results attainable. |
| 3 | Performance is consistently above expected standards as evidenced by specific achievements. |
| 2 | Performance meets expected standards. |
| 1 | Performance fails to meet expected standards. Improvement is required. |

Ratings of .5 (i.e., 1.5, 2.5, 3.5) are permissible in situations where improvement has been noted since the last evaluation but is not consistent enough to move to the next rating factor.

2. Assign a performance rating (1–4 points) to each of the core competencies. If all competencies were rated "extraordinary" (4 points), the appraisal would have a perfect score of 28 points.

**Exhibit 16.9.** (*Continued*)

3. Upon completion of the evaluation, summarize the rating and score for each core competency on the scoring summary. The individual score is the total of the competencies.

4. The total point score translates to the following levels of performance:

| Total Points | Performance Level |
|---|---|
| 8 but less than 13 points | Needs improvement |
| 13 but less than 21 points | Good |
| 21 but less than 29 points | Very good |
| 29–32 points | Extraordinary |

Comments are not required for ratings of "good" or "very good." Comments are required for core competencies rated as "needs improvement" or "extraordinary."

## MANAGEMENT CORE COMPETENCIES

*Commitment to Service*                                          Rating: _____

- Committed to excellence in customer service
- Effectively models the network mission, vision, values and customer service behaviors
- Assures staff compliance to the organizations' mission, vision, values, and customer service behaviors
- Ensures timely responses to inquiries, complaints, and concerns from all customers
- Anticipates problems and is willing to take risks to meet and exceed the needs of the customer
- Consistently responds to and supports change that improves overall service to the customer

Comments/Opportunities for Improvement: _____

*Communication Skills*                                          Rating: _____

- Is committed to excellence in service by ensuring timely and effective responses to inquiries, complaints, and requests from all customers
- Ability to communicate visions effectively
- Demonstrates active listening skills
- Effectively communicates ideas both orally and in writing
- Effectively presents ideas or information at meetings

(*Continued*)

**Exhibit 16.9. Management Performance Evaluation (*Continued*)**

- Maintains confidentiality of information, as appropriate
- Demonstrates open and approachable communication style
- Provides constructive feedback to all customers
- Positively promotes St. Luke's Health Network at all times
- Communicates openly, candidly, and sincerely

Comments/Opportunities for Improvement: _____

*Motivational Skills*                                    Rating: _____

- Motivates, inspires, and challenges staff to excel in their performance
- Builds team spirit, energy, excitement, and enthusiasm
- Proactively responds to and supports change
- Promotes fun in the workplace
- Recognizes and rewards effective performance
- Encourages participation and empowers staff
- Serves as a role model for others to "think out of the box"
- Acts as a mentor, teacher, and coach to others

Comments/Opportunities for Improvement: _____

*Organizational Skills*                                  Rating: _____

- Effectively delegates activities, responsibilities
- Uses effective time management skills
- Sets clear expectations
- Mentors others to develop effective organizational skills
- Clearly identifies priorities of network and communicates these priorities
  to staff
- Uses appropriate methods for collecting and reporting data
- Verifies licensure and certification of staff
- Completes projects in a timely manner

Comments/Opportunities for Improvement: _____

*Team Building Skills*                                   Rating: _____

- Develops and implements employee retention and recruitment strategies that
  enhance the team
- Promotes open communication, assists to resolve conflict, and makes decisions
  considering the impact on others
- Builds team spirit and acts as a coach through mentoring, listening, and
  leading by example

Exhibit 16.9. (*Continued*)

- Encourages team decision making
- Effectively manages people, resources, and time to achieve team goals
- Recognizes special contributions and achievements and encourages professional growth

Comments/Opportunities for Improvement: _____

*Resourcefulness* *Rating:* _____

- Seeks out new information and technologies to improve performance.
- Identifies and implements ways to reduce costs and streamline efforts
- Adjusts to changing work needs and demands. Helps others respond quickly. Helps remove barriers to effectiveness
- Effectively maintains compliance with budget (justifies variance, as needed)
- Utilizes network resources for help or guidance
- Recognizes diversity in group as an avenue to expand vision

Comments/Opportunities for Improvement: _____

*Performance Improvement Management Skills* *Rating:* _____

- Develops appropriate department PI plan
- Demonstrates data-evidenced examples of successful PI activities
- Provides ongoing education and involvement of staff in PI as evidenced in department staff meeting minutes
- Attends required PI management training
- Provides focused PI reports to the PI council and management team.

Comments/Opportunities for Improvement: _____

*Goal Orientation* *Rating:* _____

- Works effectively to achieve individual, team and organizational goals
- Effectively plans and maintains compliance with budgets
- Makes decisions considering the impact on others
- Effectively manages people, resources in time to achieve results
- Fosters continuous learning, takes risks, helps others to overcome obstacles and understand that "mistakes and problems" provide opportunities for learning
- Balances long-term and short-term objectives and goals
- Effectively works within a group (contributes to the success for achievement of identified goals)

(*Continued*)

### Exhibit 16.9. Management Performance Evaluation (*Continued*)

- Compliance with internal and external regulatory requirements (i.e., Hospital Policies, JCAHO, HCFA, Department of Health)
- Articulates an organizational vision and its influence on departmental goals
- Promotes a supportive atmosphere and makes decisions considering the impact on others

Comments/Opportunities for Improvement: _____

*Future Goals, Developmental Plan,*                              *Achievement Dates*
*Objectives, Projects* _____

Should be related to management evaluation factors. Must be specific, qualifiable, and include an established time frame _____

|  |  |
|---|---|
|  |  |
|  |  |
|  |  |
|  |  |
|  |  |
|  |  |
|  |  |
|  |  |

Exhibit 16.9. (*Continued*)

### SCORING SUMMARY

| *Core Competencies:* | *Rating* |
|---|---|

Commitment to service . . . . . . . . . . . . . . . . . . . . . . . . . .

Communication skills . . . . . . . . . . . . . . . . . . . . . . . . . . .

Motivational skills . . . . . . . . . . . . . . . . . . . . . . . . . . . .

Organizational skills . . . . . . . . . . . . . . . . . . . . . . . . . . .

Team building skills . . . . . . . . . . . . . . . . . . . . . . . . . . .

Resourcefulness . . . . . . . . . . . . . . . . . . . . . . . . . . . . . .

Performance improvement management skills . . . . . . . . .

Goal orientation . . . . . . . . . . . . . . . . . . . . . . . . . . . . .

Total _____

| *Competency Assessment* | *Met* | *Unmet* |
|---|---|---|
| • Completed timely *performance evaluation* for staff | ☐ | ☐ |
| • Completed annual *competence assessment* for staff | ☐ | ☐ |
| • Attended mandatory management training and development programs | ☐ | ☐ |
| • Demonstrates understanding and application of safe working conditions in the areas of employee, patient, and environmental safety and follows appropriate reporting requirements in these areas of safety. | ☐ | ☐ |

**EVALUATOR'S COMMENTS:**

**EMPLOYEE'S COMMENTS:**

Employee's Signature: _____  Date: _____

Evaluator's Signature: _____  Date: _____

Department Head Signature: _____  Date: _____

Administrative Signature: _____  Date: _____

# ABOUT THE CONTRIBUTORS

**Andrew Starr** is the director of clinical operations for St. Luke's Hospital. His primary responsibilities are managing the clinical and business aspects for multiple departments in the perioperative service line. Prior to his present position, Andrew was a performance management engineer for Premier, Inc. His responsibilities included department based projects that have resulted in cost savings, revenue enhancement, and productivity enhancement in both clinical and nonclinical areas. Andrew also worked in the health/managed care/life sciences practice of Cap Gemini Ernst & Young. During his two years at CGEY, Andrew was involved with projects associated with business transformation and health care package implementation. Andrew also has prior clinical experience as a dialysis technician. His educational repertoire includes both a master's degree in business administration and master's degree in health services administration from Xavier University. He also has a bachelor's degree in biology from the State University of New York (SUNY) at Oswego.

**Robert Zimmel** is the senior vice president for human resources for St. Luke's Hospital and Health Network. He is responsible for all the human resource functions for the network. Bob has been with St. Luke's for nineteen years and has served in various HR roles throughout his career. He is currently a member of the President's Council and serves as the chairperson of the leadership steering committee for the leadership initiative for the network. Bob received his B.S. in business from the Indiana University of Pennsylvania and an M.A. in personnel services and higher education from the Indiana University of Pennsylvania as well.

**Janice Bauer** is the assistant vice president of patient care services. Over the past two years, Jan has served as a leader to multiple units, including the Emergency Department, CCU, ICU, and Trauma Department. Jan has been part of the organization since 1979 and has served in a variety of positions. Jan's successful growth has included achievement in past positions such as nursing supervisor, nurse manager, administrative director of emergency services, and administrative director of trauma.

**Margaret Hayn** is the assistant vice president of acute care and maternal child health. Prior to taking on this role, Margaret was the director of woman's and children's service line and continence management program. Prior to these roles, Margaret also served in a variety of leadership roles during a fifteen-year tenure at St. Luke's Hospital. Margaret has been involved in nursing for nearly thirty years. Her distinguished academic record includes a master's degree in nursing and in family practice. She also holds a bachelor's of nursing from

Columbia University. Margaret is published in numerous journals and has served as a guest speaker and lecturer in many academic and hospital forums.

**Carol Kuplen** is the vice president, senior nurse executive for St. Luke's Hospital and Health Network. Carol's primary responsibility includes providing administrative oversight of nursing services for a five-hospital, nonprofit, integrated health care network. Other responsibilities include developing and implementing nursing leadership philosophy, identifying outcome expectations, leading recruitment and retention initiatives, and facilitating the redesign of nursing care delivery systems. Prior to her present position, Carol successfully served in other capacities within St. Luke's, including director of the Cancer Network. Mrs. Kuplen has also worked in various positions at other prestigious hospitals, including Georgetown University Medical Center and Geisinger Wyoming Valley Medical Center. Her educational repertoire includes M.S. in nursing from the University of Pennsylvania and a B.S in nursing from Georgetown University.

**Bob Weigand** is the director of management training and development for St. Luke's Hospital and Health Network. He is responsible for designing, developing, implementing, and evaluating leadership development programs throughout the network. Weigand incorporates experiential learning into his training curriculum. He has published articles and contributed to three books on the topic of training evaluation. Weigand is certified in the Myers Briggs Type Inventory. He currently is on the faculty of several local colleges, where he teaches part time. Weigand was previously employed at the Reading Hospital, where his work included working with family practice residents on communication skills. He received his B.A. in psychology from Ricker College in Houlton, Maine, and a master's in psychology from Assumption College in Worcester, Massachusetts.

**Debra Klepeiss** currently functions in the role of senior hospital director, operations and service management at St. Luke's Allentown Campus. She has been employed by St. Luke's Hospital and Health Network for twenty-eight years. Over that time span Debra has been in many different roles, encompassing staff nursing, nursing management, human resources management, performance improvement, accreditation and compliance, organizational development, education, leadership development, service improvement, and patient satisfaction. Klepeiss is a RN and has a human resources certificate, and a B.A. in business management.

**Lisa Dutterer** has been the vice president for ambulatory and ancillary services for St. Luke's Hospital Allentown Campus since January 2001. Lisa is responsible for all the outpatient services at the campus in addition to the allied health services that support the care of the inpatient. Prior to her current position, she was administrative director for the inpatient and outpatient rehabilitation services at the hospital of the University of Pennsylvania Medical Center and Presbyterian Medical Center. Lisa's career in health care started as a licensed physical therapist at Germantown Hospital in Philadelphia. She received her B.A. in biology from Bridgewater College in 1988 and an M.S. in physical therapy from Arcadia University in 1991.

**Sherry Rex** is the director of human resources at St. Luke's Quakertown Hospital. Prior to joining St. Luke's, she served as the manager of benefits and compensation at *The Morning Call,* a subsidiary of Tribune Publishing. She was also the payroll manager for the CoOpportunity Center, a shared services center for Times Mirror, the prior parent company of *The Morning Call.* Sherry also served as the human resources and operations manager for the Bon-Ton Department Stores. Following her graduation from college, she completed the executive training program for Boscov's Department Stores. Sherry is a graduate of Widener University, where she earned a bachelor's degree in arts and sciences.

**John Hrubenek** is director of property management, St. Luke's Hospital and Health Network. Prior to that position he was the director of support services. He holds a bachelor's degree in economics and business from Lafayette College and a master's in business administration from Lehigh University.

**Donna Sabol** is the assistant vice president of network performance improvement for St. Luke's Hospital and Health Network. Prior to her present position, Donna served in various positions within the health network, including director of organizational development. Donna has been associated with St. Luke's for twenty years. She is an RN and holds an M.S. in nursing from DeSales University and a B.S. in nursing from Wilkes University.

Additional thanks to Francine Botek, Gary Guidetti, Ellen Novatnack, Steven Schweon, Charlotte Becker, Howard Cook, and Joe Pinto.

# CHAPTER SEVENTEEN

# StorageTek

*Aiming for a high-performance culture led StorageTek to develop a transformation plan that balanced traditional operational management with the innovation required to be competitive in the information technology industry. A key element of the plan is successfully coordinating initiatives already embedded in the organization and supplementing those initiatives with new thinking.*

| | |
|---|---|
| OVERVIEW | 404 |
| INTRODUCTION | 404 |
| A New Chairman Confronts the Issues | 406 |
| DEFINE THE CHALLENGE | 406 |
| Figure 17.1: Phases of Transformation | 407 |
| Define the Goal | 408 |
| Figure 17.2: Definition of High-Performance Culture | 408 |
| Figure 17.3: Alignment to Build a High-Performance Culture | 409 |
| Create a Sense of Urgency | 410 |
| Lessons Learned | 411 |
| WORK THROUGH CHANGE | 411 |
| Focus on Results and Defining Expectations | 412 |
| Table 17.1: Performance Measurement (Spring 2002) | 413 |
| Improve Management Competency | 414 |
| Grow Organizational Capabilities | 415 |
| Figure 17.4: Transforming on Three Levels | 416 |
| Lessons Learned | 417 |
| ATTAIN AND SUSTAIN IMPROVEMENT | 418 |
| Figure 17.5: StorageTek Timeline of Organization Transformation | 419 |
| STORAGETEK: THE HIGH-PERFORMANCE ORGANIZATION | 420 |
| Exhibit 17.1: Summary of Lessons Learned | 421 |

REFERENCES                                                    422

ABOUT THE CONTRIBUTOR                                          422

# OVERVIEW

This change management case study describes the approach used by StorageTek to develop and implement a transformational plan to establish the company as a high-performance leader in the information technology (IT) industry. After a series of ups and downs in its thirty-four year history, StorageTek® (Storage Technology Corp., NYSE:STK), during the later years of the 1990s and into the early years of 2000, was once again in a state of unbalance between operational management and the innovation required to be competitive. Steps were taken to turn the company around, but there was little improvement. StorageTek leadership recognized the need for a systematic plan to transform the company into a high-performance organization.

The transformation plan outlined the steps to be taken in three stages. Using best-practices research, StorageTek defined the high-performance organization and the leadership model required to implement the plan. Both focused on results in a competent and open, trusting environment. The second stage required working through the change by creating a focus on results, defining individual expectations, improving management competencies, and growing organizational capabilities. Specific to this stage were improvements to performance management systems, communications, customer relationships, and many other areas. The third stage of attaining and sustaining improvement is under way.

In light of the economic downturn worldwide, the challenge was to continue to follow the transformation plan. Lessons learned are applicable to other organizations beginning a major transformation or analyzing and implementing corrections to the current path.

# INTRODUCTION

Four IBM engineers with a dream of building better and less expensive tape drives for data storage founded StorageTek in Boulder, Colorado, in 1969. Today, StorageTek is a $2 billion worldwide company with headquarters in Louisville, Colorado, and an innovator and global leader in virtual storage solutions for tape automation, disk storage systems, and storage networking. The StorageTek headquarters is about halfway between Denver and Boulder, Colorado, on a 450-acre campus in the shadow of the Rocky Mountains. Of the approximately

7,200 employees worldwide, about 2,200 are based in Colorado. Among other benefits available to headquarters employees, there is on-site daycare, a medical center and pharmacy, and a wellness center, including a three-mile outdoor jogging trail.

"Jesse Aweida, founder of StorageTechnology [now StorageTek] [1969] and CEO until 1984, was convinced that a high level of operational management and 'just enough' innovation would keep the company ahead of IBM" (Richard Foster and Sarah Kaplan, *Creative Destruction,* Doubleday, 2001, p. 90). From 1969 to 1981, the company experienced great success and rapid growth with the first product shipped in 1970, just fourteen months after start-up. That was followed by the introduction of magnetic disk in 1973. By 1981, the company had grown to 13,000 employees and $603 million in revenue.

The balance between operational management and innovation was difficult to maintain, and StorageTek filed for Chapter 11 bankruptcy protection in 1984. Emerging from bankruptcy in 1987, StorageTek once again had a keen sense of its customer value proposition and business focus. By 1990, the company reached $1 billion in revenue, and in 1992 the stock reached a record high of $78 per share. In the mid-1990s, the cultural focus was on creating a foundation for a company that was built to last. StorageTek formalized its core purpose and core values (see sidebar). Unfortunately, by 2001, StorageTek was once again struggling. There was no revenue growth in 2000 and 2001 and market share was eroding—StorageTek was left behind during the technology boom of the late 1990s and early 2000. Once again, the balance between operational management and "just enough" innovation had been lost.

---

*Core Purpose*
To expand the world's access to information and knowledge.

*Core Values*
Share ownership for the relentless pursuit of results
Provide superior customer partnerships
Innovate and renew
Operate with honesty and integrity
Above all else, value self and others

---

Over thirty-five years, StorageTek developed a unique corporate culture. Like all corporate cultures, there were aspects that were very healthy and others that clearly got in the way of the goals of innovation, competitiveness, and balance. In the community, in the industry, and within the employee population, the company had a legacy of uneven performance and of hiring employees in good times and firing them in bad. The company was known for starting lots and finishing little, and for rewarding "fire fighting" rather than permanent fixes. A consensus and relationship-driven culture meant that decision making was slow and, even when decisions were made, they could be appealed and reversed. One executive labeled it "the right of infinite appeal!" There was much to be proud of, however. In employee satisfaction surveys, employees reported that they felt valued and respected, and respected their colleagues. Employees believed their work added value to the company. Finally, employees said they had the flexibility to manage work-life balance.

## A New Chairman Confronts the Issues

Patrick J. Martin joined StorageTek in July 2000 as chairman, president, and CEO. Pat was patient as he listened to customers, stockholders, and employees and learned about StorageTek and the storage industry in which the company competed. He studied the strategy of the company. He met talented employees and loyal customers. Still, employee turnover approached 25 percent in 2000 as employees took their skills to more successful competitors. The research and development budget was among the highest in the industry but generated few new products or technological innovations. The company had an infrastructure that was too large, products that were consistently late to market, and arduous processes that made the company slow and difficult with which to do business.

As true as during its earlier times, StorageTek needed to return to a balance between operational management and innovation. Several interventions were tried. The executive team turned over twelve of its fourteen key members in 2001. The CEO "taught" basic ROI (return on investment) via all-employee worldwide briefings using satellite downlinks. Managers had too many goals, tasks, and initiatives upon which to focus, making achievement impossible. A period of "blaming" occurred. A "surprise" mid-year performance review was handled poorly in an environment in which performance management turned out to be "optional." There was little improvement.

# DEFINE THE CHALLENGE

Transforming StorageTek into an industry leader where employees could grow their careers, confident customers could solve their IT challenges, and shareholders could receive a premium for their investment required a long-term plan. For a company with a reputation for starting a lot and finishing little, it was important to set a transformation plan that could be sustained over time with as little bureaucracy as possible.

A scan of the company identified myriad different initiatives—all thoughtful, but disconnected from each other. The desire for a high-performance culture was evident, yet the components and disciplines of such a culture had not been defined for StorageTek. The first two components of transformation—strategic clarity and leadership alignment—were lacking. Several foundation pieces were in place—core values defined by employees in 1996, a change model that balanced the quality of the technical strategy with the quality of the cultural strategy, and a fledgling quality system built as a first step toward Six Sigma. It was important to build on those existing foundation pieces to avoid the perception of another "flavor of the month," so prevalent within the StorageTek culture.

The arrival of a new CEO had offered the opportunity for change. Three months of planning by the organization development team (OD team) led to the development of a long-term transformation plan.

| Stage | Goals | Actions | Tools and Techniques |
|---|---|---|---|
| Define the challenge | Create a sense of urgency<br><br>Define the goal | Leadership conference<br><br>Executive team building<br><br>Defined high-performance organization<br><br>Worldwide employee kick-offs | Learning Map 1<br>BMS model and training<br>*One Vision, One Voice* publication |
| Work through change | Create a foundation of results—focus<br><br>Define individual expectations<br><br>Improve management competency<br><br>Grow organization capabilities | Executive team building<br><br>Performance and development goals for all employees<br><br>Review HR practices for consistency<br><br>Succession planning<br><br>Founded affinity groups | Performance management<br><br>Goal alignment tools<br><br>Leadership required courses and curriculum<br><br>Learning Map 2– strategy update<br><br>Closer to the customer |
| Attain and sustain improvement | Sustain results—focus<br><br>Build sustainable future | Add workforce planning process<br><br>Include "people strategy" in strategic planning | Employee survey<br><br>Engineering excellence curriculum<br><br>Technical talent pool development |

**Figure 17.1** Phases of Transformation.

The first phase of the transformation plan was to define the challenge. There were two goals:

- Define the goal
- Create a sense of urgency

## Define the Goal

The first step was to define the high-performance culture that StorageTek intended to build. The OD team conducted a review of literature and the transformations of other companies, both successful and not. "War for Talent," *The McKinsey Quarterly,* 1998, Number 3, and "The War for Talent 2000," revised July 2001 along with a number of other sources, were particularly useful. Concurrently, the OD team defined a leadership model based on a review of current practice and literature. *Results-Based Leadership* by David Ulrich, Jack Zenger and Norm Smallwood was selected because of the focus on achieving results as well as possessing the competencies of leadership.

The desired StorageTek high-performance culture was defined in three parts:

1. "Performance ethic is the relentless desire to satisfy customers and earn their loyalty, allowing us to out-perform our competitors. A compelling core purpose, vision, and values; ambitious stretch goals focused on results; and performance feedback based on clear expectations support a performance ethic." This is measured by achievement of annual goals.

**Figure 17.2** Definition of High-Performance Culture.

2. "An open, trusting environment enjoys open and candid communication within the company; it requires everyone at every level of the organization to do what we say we will do; and provides growth for individuals and the organization through learning, knowledge sharing, and experience." Open and trusting environment is measured by the annual worldwide employee satisfaction survey.

3. "An effective and growing organization practices six capabilities of shared mindset, speed, accountability, collaboration, learning and talent" (from *Results-Based Leadership* by Ulrich, Zenger, and Smallwood, 1999, p. 40). An effective and growing organization is measured by metrics, such as customer loyalty, revenue growth, market share improvement, and employee turnover rates.

Measures already in place were selected to indicate progress in each of the three parts of the StorageTek high-performance culture. Total shareholder return was selected to measure overall achievement; for StorageTek, shareholder return was characteristically below the industry average.

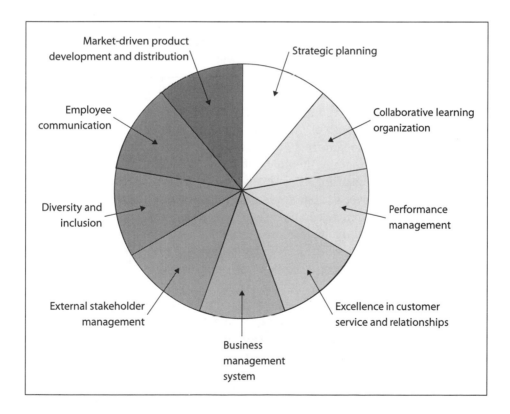

**Figure 17.3** Alignment to Build a High-Performance Culture.

Any complex organization has multiple initiatives and StorageTek was no exception. Incorporated into the model of high-performance culture were the components that must be in alignment with the definition to avoid conflicting messages to employees, customers, and shareholders. For StorageTek, these components included strategic planning, customer and shareholder relationship management, market-driven product and services development, leadership development, quality, employee communications, and human resource practices.

The equation, "Effective Leadership = Results × Competencies" was adopted from *Results-Based Leadership* (Ulrich, Zenger, and Smallwood, 1999). Work began with the executive team in June 2001 to define the leadership blueprint for StorageTek. Work focused on strategic clarity and leadership alignment, including defining the customer value proposition, business focus, and growth strategy.

## Create a Sense of Urgency

Defining a successful future for StorageTek was just one part of defining the challenge. There was also a need to create a sense of urgency among all employees. In August 2001, 170 leaders representing the worldwide scope of the company were invited to participate in a three-day leadership conference. With the theme of "Navigating to New Horizons," Martin, the StorageTek CEO, discussed the state of the business and the competitive environment. While creating a sense of urgency, he also expressed confidence in the future if the company, its leaders, and employees changed.

To further create a sense of urgency, a researcher reported on information from customers who bought from StorageTek as well as those who chose to do business elsewhere, making the voice of the customer real to all attendees. Partnering with RootLearning, a company specializing in transforming strategic direction to employee dialogue, a learning map called "Current Reality: The Flood of Information" engaged all leadership conference attendees in an interactive, cross-functional dialogue about StorageTek's competitive environment. Information on the history of the storage industry, customer business problems, and competitor characteristics and market share were included in the map.

A motivational speaker at the leadership conference delivered the message that "for you to change, I must change," and a group of StorageTek manufacturing employees described how they were tired of waiting for management to make the necessary changes and took action for themselves. Upon arriving at the conference, each attendee received a musical instrument made by indigenous peoples from around the world. Each portion of the conference had a musical piece representing that particular content. For example, executives beat a Navajo ceremonial tom-tom to represent strategy; at the end of the conference, all the pieces were combined to create a symphony of change.

The ceremonial tom-tom also represented the "cadence of change" required to deliver a high-performance culture. The resolve to change and implement changes must be stronger than the resistance to change in order for the changes to be real and permanent.

Late in the fall 2001, Current Reality: The Flood of Information learning map was rolled out worldwide to all employees. Groups of eight to twelve employees gathered at a time to learn about the competitive environment in which StorageTek operates. In January 2002, follow-up by executive team members for all employees in the form of geographical kick-offs continued teaching and reinforcing the key messages begun at the leadership conference. An employee communications newsletter again described the high-performance culture that was our goal and how the many initiatives throughout the company were connected to that goal.

### Lessons Learned

There were three lessons learned from the initial phase of transformational change:

1. Define where the company is going—provide the result of the program with measurement that translates into business objectives.

2. Use as much as possible of what already exists in the organization. This provides a sense of stability for many employees, avoids the temptation to label work done previously as a waste or poor quality, and lessens the "flavor of the month" cynicism.

3. Develop a cadence of change—similar to the base beat of the drum—to maintain employee awareness of the needed changes and provide linkages to various programs and initiatives.

## WORK THROUGH CHANGE

In reality, the first stage of change never ends. However, little progress is achieved if the organization focuses only on defining the challenges. For StorageTek, the second stage, working through change, included the following goals:

- Create a focus on results.
- Define individual expectations.
- Improve management competency.
- Grow organization capabilities.

## Focus on Results and Defining Expectations

Not everything worked perfectly the first time. At the August 2001 leadership conference, a second RootLearning map, "Strategy: Navigating to New Horizons," was introduced to define the StorageTek strategy. It was clear from the feedback that this map did not yet convey a clear message about StorageTek's strategy ready for consumption by all employees. To provide the strategic clarity required for every employee to "buy into" the transformation plan, the map needed to clearly state the StorageTek strategy and provide the bridge for employees to link their individual work to the strategy.

In reworking the learning map, the executive management team members took special care to review the content of the map and clarify key points. The map was piloted with groups of employees in Colorado and France to be certain the strategy was clear before it was translated into eight languages. Again, facilitators worldwide led groups of eight to twelve employees in dialogues about the strategy and the link to employees' own work. As with the first map, the more cross-functional the make-up of these employee groups, the more powerful the learning.

Despite changes to the performance management tools in the three previous years, focus groups of employees and managers told us they believed the performance management system at StorageTek was an optional one. Numerous employees reported having no goals or performance reviews. Managers reported confusion about expectations and offered that they suffered no consequences for taking short-cuts in performance management. Unfortunately, many managers applied the "peanut butter" approach and gave all employees a similar rating and merit increase rather than differentiate high performers from low. It was no wonder that there was a lack of clarity around expectations and results to be achieved! Three efforts began in the fall of 2001 for implementation January 1, 2002, to solve these problems.

The first effort was to align goals worldwide and assure that every employee knew what was expected and how he or she would be measured. The StorageTek Quality department developed a Web-based tool that provided every employee visibility to all goals through department level. The Quality department audited goals, providing feedback on improvement. Goals were then tied to individual performance goals in the StorageTek performance management system. Each month, there is a thorough reporting of goal achievement to the executive team. Resources and priorities are discussed as necessary to meet goals.

The second effort was the redesign of the performance management system to support the StorageTek definition of a high-performance culture. The tool is Web-based and provides for employee assessment in three parts. The underlying philosophy implies each employee must perform to or exceed expectations in all three areas to enable StorageTek to achieve a high-performance culture. First is the focus on results through assessment of achievement of performance goals. The second is an assessment of how well the employee is keeping skills and knowledge levels current and achieving set development goals. The third is a 360-degree assessment of twenty-six behaviors that indicate an individual is acting in accordance with the core values and organizational capabilities. The manager and employee jointly select those asked to provide the feedback; feedback can come from peers, subordinates, customers, partners, and vendors. (Subsequent analyses of data led to limiting the number of behaviors to sixteen that statistically correlated to performance.)

The performance review discussion takes place between the employee and manager, and is an open and honest discussion of performance in all three areas based on self and manager assessment, along with feedback from others. The performance review is completed early in the first quarter of each year for the previous calendar year, with a midyear performance checkpoint conducted in summer to assure that an employee is on track to achieve annual goals. Managers are required to meet a distribution curve of ratings at the functional or business unit head level at each review.

Employees who do not receive a "meets expectations" or higher rating are counseled on how to improve their performance through a plan of action. An employee who continues to fall below a "meets expectations" rating leaves the

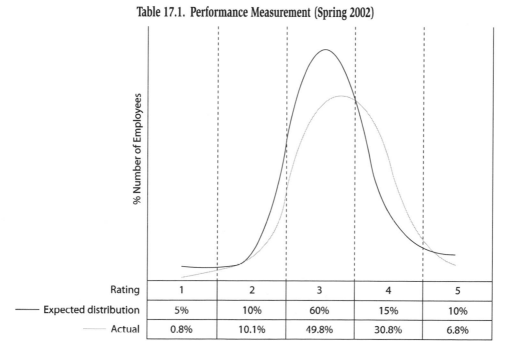

Table 17.1. Performance Measurement (Spring 2002)

| Rating | 1 | 2 | 3 | 4 | 5 |
|---|---|---|---|---|---|
| —— Expected distribution | 5% | 10% | 60% | 15% | 10% |
| ········ Actual | 0.8% | 10.1% | 49.8% | 30.8% | 6.8% |

company. Likewise, employees who exceed expectations receive larger merit increases and receive special development attention.

The expected distribution curve was not met the first time (spring 2002) and managers were sent back to revise their ratings. Although not a popular move, requiring managers to meet the distribution curve sent the message that StorageTek was serious about performance. The expected distribution curve was met with many fewer adjustments for the midyear performance check (summer 2002). Subsequently, few adjustments were needed to meet the curve.

The third effort was a review and electronic sign-off of StorageTek's code of business conduct. Months before the media began reporting on various corporate misstatements of earnings, StorageTek translated its code of business conduct into eight languages and asked each employee to read and sign that he or she understood what was expected in terms of lawful and ethical business conduct. Working together, the Office of Corporate Counsel and human resources followed up with employees on questions and concerns. Every employee is expected to act in accordance with this code of conduct.

## Improve Management Competency

At the August 2001 leadership conference, work began on creating a leadership brand. The intent of a leadership brand is to succinctly communicate to leaders what is expected of them and how these expectations relate to achieving the strategic objectives of the company. Following the conference, agreement was reached on the following leadership brand:

> StorageTek leaders act with speed, simplicity and accountability so that we bring value to every customer interaction. We will become the number one total storage solution provider by effectively delivering high-quality products and services, resulting in sustainable shareholder value.

StorageTek's leadership brand stated a common set of expectations for all managers, which was introduced and reinforced through a leadership and management curriculum with required courses. The curriculum is built to address the needs of various levels of management—new manager, program or project manager, first level manager, and executive.

"What gets measured, gets results" applies to leadership development, too. Historically, there appeared to be little opportunity for employees to grow their career through the management levels. For every external hire at director and above levels during 2002, there was just one internal promotion into those same levels. StorageTek set a goal of achieving a 3:1 ratio of internal promotions to external hires at the director level and above by 2006. Development is a long-term investment in talent. Succession planning has placed attention on internal candidates for these positions, which include vice presidents, directors, and country managers. Development focuses on the experiences needed to perform well at these executive levels through the use of an experience interview tool. The resulting development plan includes both learning and assignments needed to acquire the necessary skills.

To assure a pipeline of talent, candidates with high potential have been identified around the world and are provided with development plans and specific development opportunities. Further, an aggressive college-recruiting program has brought over sixty recent college graduates (undergraduate and advanced degrees) into the company. An eighteen-month evolving-leaders development program assures that these new employees receive specialized development. Development includes community service projects to assure the balance defining the StorageTek culture.

## Grow Organizational Capabilities

*Organizational Capabilities*

*Shared mindset*—We speak with one voice (about strategy, vision, core values, and performance ethic).

*Talent*—We attract, retain, and develop employees with the skills to make the company successful.

*Collaboration*—We share information broadly across the organization, which emphasizes cross-functional teamwork and learning rather than competition among groups.

*Speed*—We demonstrate the capacity for change, agility, flexibility, and reduced cycle time with an emphasis on simple, repeatable, efficient processes. Decision making is fast. Unproductive work is eliminated.

*Accountability*—We complete our work with rigor and consistency, meeting scheduled commitments and following through on plans and programs to deliver what's promised. Every employee is held accountable for behavior and results.

*Learning*—We generate new ideas and share those ideas across the company.

The organizational capabilities are shared mindset, talent, collaboration, speed, accountability, and learning. Growing and practicing these capabilities in a way unique to StorageTek is a key component of the high-performance organization because it allows StorageTek to differentiate itself from its competitors. With the belief that growing organizational capabilities is first a management responsibility, the capabilities were introduced at the 2001 leadership conference. Soon thereafter, the capabilities were intertwined through the language of the second RootLearning map, "Strategy: Navigating to New Horizons," embedded in the Leading for Results workshop and performance management system, and used to link various initiatives within the organization.

Knowing the audience and varying the messages to meet the audience's needs is important to assure understanding at all levels of the organization. For example, strategic clarity work at the executive level included interaction through workshops with Norm Smallwood and work on clarifying roles and responsibilities. For managers and directors, there was involvement in creating and participating in the learning maps. For employees, kick-offs and learning map participation provide opportunities for strategic clarity.

The Business Management System (BMS) was introduced as the overarching quality model. Starting with defining the customer and continuing with defining

| | Strategic clarity | Leadership/Management skills | Performance management including goals | BMS (quality) | Close to the customer | Diversity and Inclusion | Communications | Rewards and recognition | Market-driven technology leadership |
|---|---|---|---|---|---|---|---|---|---|
| EMT | RBL Work Roles and Responsibilities | Leadership Conference Succession | Goals | Monthly Reporting | E2E | Hiring Goals Affinity Group Sponsorship | Executive Visability | MBO's Stock Incentives | |
| Directors and managers | Creating and Participating in Learning Maps | Curriculum Executive Finance Succession | Goals Implemented | Process Improvement Monthly Reporting | E2E CSmart Goals C2it Game | Hiring Goals Affinity Groups | Round Tables Staff Meetings | MBO's Stock Incentives | Engineering Excellence |
| Employees | Kick-Offs Learning Maps 1 and 2 | | Goals Behaviors Development | Knowledge Process Improvement | C2it Game CSMART Goals | Affinity Groups | Focus [On] Voice Staff Meetings | R&R Program | Engineering Excellence Traning/Development Dual Salary Ladder |

**Figure 17.4** Transforming on Three Levels.

vision, goals, resources, measures, and improvements, every employee completed training led by his or her manager and focused on his or her department. Combined with the goal-setting and follow-up process described earlier and ISO audits every six months, there is a direct link to shared mindset and accountability capabilities. The introduction of meeting guidelines provided a focus on speed, accountability, and collaboration. The latest step to Six Sigma with the introduction of Black Belt training and projects positions StorageTek well to focus on the operational excellence needed to balance a successful company.

*Closer to the customer* is the descriptor for all the customer initiatives within StorageTek. With the belief that external results come from internal actions, there is a strong focus on the employee, as well as traditional customer initiatives. For example, a board game developed by StorageTek and provided in eight languages invites employees to play a game in which decisions must be made to meet customer expectations; winning or losing "hearts" and money is based on the decisions made. A CD provides directions and includes executives telling famous customer relationship stories, as well as some of their own. Shared mindset, learning, and collaboration are the capabilities affected.

Employee communications have been redesigned to provide clear and concise information to employees. Changes were made to the "look and feel," frequency, and content to deliver information employees deemed of greatest value. Executive visibility programs, including round tables, give employees more opportunities to meet with executives informally. E-mail is the primary method of communication. A weekly employee electronic newsletter, with geographically sectioned information, provides overall messaging and information. During the week, messages of importance are targeted to various groups of employees worldwide on a need-to-know basis. An electronically distributed, print-ready, bi-monthly newsmagazine is used to provide greater understanding of StorageTek information. Recently introduced is a hierarchy of messaging to help employees prioritize e-mail messages, and a letter from the StorageTek CEO on timely topics. Shared mindset, speed, and collaboration are the organization capabilities of focus.

## Lessons Learned

Five lessons were learned from the "work through change" stage:

1. Although the initiatives are corporatewide, for the maximum benefit the actions should be focused on individual requirements at three levels of employees: executives, managers, and employees. The initiatives are the same but the practices and implementation are flexed to the needs of each group.

2. All employees must be held accountable for achieving results. Looking for others to blame is one sign of an immature organization.

3. Assess what the organization can absorb and be willing to be flexible. There is never just one way to accomplish a goal, so look for alternatives when the first choice isn't working.

4. Be willing to take the 80 percent solution; nothing is ever perfect.

5. Keep up the cadence of change—just like the steady bass drum beat of the ceremonial tom-tom.

## ATTAIN AND SUSTAIN IMPROVEMENT

As 2004 began, StorageTek initiated the third stage of change. The goals of this stage are

- Continue results focus
- Build sustainable future foundation

Continuing the focus on results and alignment to a high-performance culture will involve adding other initiatives while continuing to focus on and deliver results in the areas already introduced. In some cases, there are small changes to keep programs and practices contemporary, such as reducing the performance management behavioral measurements to sixteen from twenty-six, as described earlier.

The results of the October 2002 all-employee satisfaction survey showed a decrease in employee satisfaction from 2001. All categories were significantly lower, with the most dramatic decrease in the Top Leadership category. These results were not unexpected but they were disheartening. Employees were not happy about significant changes made in the organization, including business decisions to move assembly from headquarters to Puerto Rico and outsource the operation of the internal information technology department. Resources were scarce as StorageTek controlled costs during difficult economic times. Going forward, there will need to be continued focus on strategic clarity with thorough explanations of business decisions and their impact on the business overall. To put a greater focus on employee satisfaction at a departmental level, each manager was required to have a 2003 performance goal on employee satisfaction, specifically addressing issues in the department. There was good news when the October 2003 survey indicated that overall employee satisfaction had increased slightly. The addition of the Dennison survey in 2003 provided managers greater understanding of the levers of change and sustainability for their departments.

Future initiatives at StorageTek will focus on aligning human resource practices such as rewards and recognition with a high-performance organization. The addition of workforce planning and a "people strategy" to the strategic planning process continue the focus on results. Other plans include taking advantage of an already-in-place dual salary ladder to build a technical talent pool, and a more robust engineering excellence recognition program to honor creativity and innovation beyond the current patents, papers, and presentations program.

Maintaining the right balance of operational management and innovation will be key to building a sustainable future. StorageTek must meet the challenge of overcoming its legacy of ups and downs by establishing a track record of results

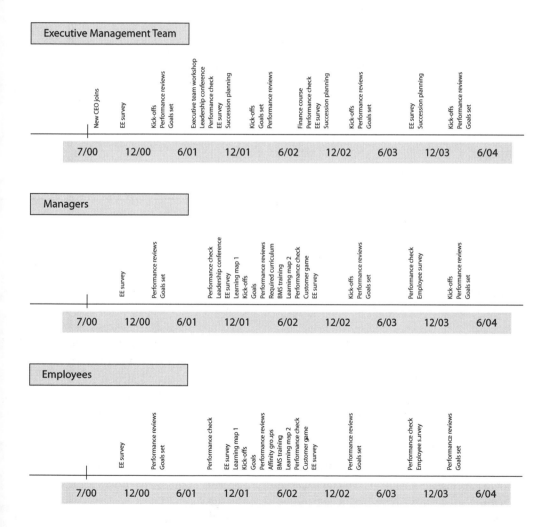

**Figure 17.5** StorageTek Timeline of Organization Transformation.

that customers, shareholders, and employees can count on. To do that, all employees must

1. Be accountable for achieving results
2. Act with speed in meeting customer requirements
3. Behave consistently with a shared mindset resulting in believability to the customer
4. Collaborate and learn together to drive out redundancy
5. Develop and share talents so that StorageTek is a great place for highly skilled employees to spend their careers

The right balance also means remaining a company focused on its employees and maintaining a culture where employees feel valued and respected, believe their work provides meaning, and can achieve work-life balance.

## STORAGETEK: THE HIGH-PERFORMANCE ORGANIZATION

During 2001 and 2002, the United States and much of the world was in an economic slump. Information technology spending was down significantly and the price of data storage technology was eroding. Through the first half of 2002, revenue was flat and market share was static at best.

Then third quarter 2002 results indicated a glimmer of hope that StorageTek might have made the turn after all. Reported results included a slight growth in revenue, an increase in market share, and double-digit growth in services. With a pipeline of orders for fourth quarter, new products introduced, and a slight hint of optimism, perhaps StorageTek had begun to achieve the real and lasting results desired. The fourth quarter and 2002 full year financial results were very positive. "This was our best quarter for revenue in the past two years and has resulted in StorageTek gaining market share in tape, disk, networking and storage services," said Pat Martin, chairman, president, and chief executive officer. Results for 2003 continued to show success with revenue growth and strong earnings. The "cadence of change" delivered the desired results of a high-performance organization. The challenge ahead is to stay the course in maintaining the balance between traditional operational management and innovation.

As a high-performance organization, StorageTek wants to be respected in the communities in which its employees work and live, recognized by people who want to do business with it, selected as an employer of choice, and known for operating guidelines including integrity and core values. Achieving these goals will mean that StorageTek will enjoy a perceived value evidenced by stock price and an increase in highly talented employees. Total shareholder return should increase as a result.

Exhibit 17.1. Summary of Lessons Learned

| Transformation Phase | Lessons Learned |
|---|---|
| Define the challenge | Define where the company is going—provide the result of the program with measurement that translates into business objectives |
| | Use as much as possible of what already exists in the organization |
| | Develop a cadence of change to maintain employee awareness |
| Work through change | Focus actions on individualized requirements on three levels |
| | Hold all employees accountable for achieving results |
| | Assess organizational readiness for change and stay flexible |
| | Take the 80 percent solution |
| | Maintain the cadence of change |
| Attain and sustain improvement | Stay the course |
| | Adjust and improve as needed |

# REFERENCES

Foster, R., and Kaplan, S. *Creative Destruction.* New York: Doubleday, 2001, p. 90.

Ulrich, D., Zenger, J., and Smallwood, N. *Results-Based Leadership.* Cambridge, Mass.: Harvard Business School Press, 1999.

"War for Talent." *The McKinsey Quarterly,* 1998, Number 3.

"The War for Talent 2000." *The McKinsey Quarterly,* July 2001.

# ABOUT THE CONTRIBUTOR

**Susan Curtis** is StorageTek's leadership coach. Curtis joined StorageTek in 1998. In her former role as director of leadership and change management, she was responsible for leadership development, including succession planning, employee communications, professional development, training, and change management. Before joining StorageTek, Curtis held several organizational development, leadership development, and training management positions with Johns Manville, Rockwell International, and EG&G. She taught at the community college level for a number of years in Florida and designed the curriculum for the Community College of Aurora (Colorado) at its founding. Curtis is a founder of Women'sLink, an intercorporate leadership development and networking program that links midlevel corporate women with senior-level women. Curtis also contributed expertise to the design of Web-based culture assessment and career development tools. These tools and Women's Link are currently available to members of the Women's Vision Foundation. Finally, she was a member of the Goodwill Industries of Denver board of directors for six years, including one year as chair. Curtis earned bachelor's and master's degrees from Iowa State University and a Ph.D. in curriculum and instruction, post-secondary education from the University of Florida.

# CHAPTER EIGHTEEN

# Windber Medical Center

*A patient-centered care model for creating a healing environment that leads to shorter lengths of stay, lower infection rates, and reduced mortality rates through a healing culture that embraces mind, body and spirit.*

OVERVIEW 424

INTRODUCTION: PATIENT EMPOWERMENT 425

DIAGNOSIS: THE DECISION TO CHANGE 425

ORGANIZATIONAL CHALLENGE 426

Reasons for Change 427
Change Objectives 427

APPROACH 428

ASSESSMENT: THE MAN SHOW 428

Physicians 429
Employees 430

FEEDBACK USE 430

DESIGN: PLANETREE PHILOSOPHY 431

INTERVENTION: FUNDAMENTAL CHANGES 431

THE PLANETREE TEAMS 432

LOOKING BACK 432

The Change Circle 433
It Gets Worse Before It Gets Better 433
I'm from the Government and I'm Here to Help 434
Getting Back on Track 434
Quantifying the Results: Exhibits 435
Exhibit 18.1: Average Length of Stay 435
Exhibit 18.2: Nosocomial Infection Rate 436

Exhibit 18.3: Mortality Comparison by Hospital                436
Moving Ahead Again                                           437

LESSONS LEARNED                                              437

ABOUT THE CONTRIBUTOR                                        438

# OVERVIEW

This change management case study explores and details the transition of a small, urban hospital from a traditional, acute care facility to a Planetree hospital. Plantree hospitals are accredited by the Planetree organization, whose mission is "to serve as a catalyst in the development and implementation of new models of health care, which cultivate the healing of mind, body, and spirit; are patient-centered, value-based, and holistic; and integrate the best of Western scientific medicine with time-honored healing practices" (from Planetree website: www.planetree.org).

The philosophy of Windber Medical Center was developed and nurtured in the Industrial Revolution. The change from this paternalistic, parent-to-child environment to one in which patients have choice and participate in their care in surroundings that embrace holistic, patient-centered care is not new, but it is revolutionary.

This little hospital, located just a few miles from the site where United Flight 93 went down on September 11 and less than ten miles from the Quecreek mine where the nine coal miners were rescued is nearly one hundred years old. Windber Hospital was started by a coal mining company, the Berwind White Coal Company, to take care of its workers. When Western Pennsylvania coal went out of style due to high pollution levels, the hospital and the town also fell out of favor.

Under the leadership of a new president, the organization took on the challenge of recreating itself by enlisting physicians and employees to return as patient advocates and also returning to the caring, nurturing roots of health care.

Using already existing care models and the power of love, the organization began a change journey that would forever alter its culture into a unified approach that makes patient-centered care its top priority. The hospital, which has gone on to gain national attention, has created a research institute and garnered over $30 million in grants during the past four years. Because of Planetree, it has established itself as a prime example of a model hospital for the future.

The lessons learned by the Windber Medical Center are important for any organization undergoing a major change initiative in which success of the entire organization depends on the outcome of the effort.

# INTRODUCTION: PATIENT EMPOWERMENT

When a patient walks into the typical hospital, the overwhelming, confusing signage, the smell of antiseptics, the curt and often unforgiving attitude of the employees, and the awesome power of the physicians are usually clear indicators that they should leave their dignity at the door.

Following the introduction of the Baby Boom generation to the United States, much has changed both good and bad. We have changed the way the world deals with fashion, protest, drugs, credit card debt, and investing. Not all of those lessons have been positive, but they have forever changed the way our country approaches war, marriage, and health. As we Baby Boomers transition into our Baby Geezer years, our expectations of how the aging process will work, how we will deal with illness, and how we will cope with end-of-life issues have already begun to change.

With nearly a thousand competitive tertiary care hospital beds available only seven short miles away from Windber Medical Center, the change management mission was clear: *Do not create what people would like. Create, instead, what people will love in a hospital environment that embraces holistic care.*

This challenge did not involve simple cosmetic changes. It involved moving an entire workforce on through the Industrial Revolution into the Age of Intelligence. It meant changing sixty years of care giving and iron clad control in a way that embraced patients and their families through empowerment.

These change management efforts required a total commitment from every employee, manager, and caregiver. Many of the individuals involved in the organization did not want to believe in this philosophy because it took the ultimate power away from them. So the question became, *Could leadership create a patient-centered care philosophy and survive?*

# DIAGNOSIS: THE DECISION TO CHANGE

In 1996, the three-hundred-employee Windber Hospital was merged into the Conemaugh Health System, but like many "follow the leader" mergers in that era, this affiliation brought few meaningful changes to the system. The really significant opportunity that did develop was to change the leadership. The new president of the organization was recruited from very nontraditional ranks. With a background in education, the arts, and tourism before entering health care management, his philosophy was not traditional. It included bringing the best in health care and patient empowerment to the organization. His most often asked question was, "Why do you do it like that?"

During the previous decade a philosophy of care had emerged that addressed a type of environment that put the patient in the center of the care mission,

Planetree. Rather than the typical, system-first emphasis, this philosophy put the patient first. Planetree embraces the concept that the mind and body are intricately interrelated and that healing must address the needs of the mind and spirit as well as the body. All facets of the Planetree model—open communication, patient choices, family-friend involvement, music, art, massage, architecture, use of complementary therapies, and others—work to uphold this concept.

Because the hospital had a palliative care unit for its hospice, it was relatively easy to convince the board that the need existed to be kind, caring, compassionate, loving, and nurturing to patients. That six-bed unit had eighty volunteers, 123 clergy volunteers, and embraced the family in every way. So trips were made to other Planetree hospitals.

Of the 150 physicians on staff at the time, only a few openly endorsed this program. Generally, the attitude embraced by the physicians was one of *wait and see*. The employees who embraced the program were already seen as kind, caring individuals, but in spite of the lack of overt endorsement for this approach to care, the board and president went forward with their decision to bring change to the little hospital on the hill.

A new building was designed to bring a wellness center to the organization, and in January 2000, that building was completed. It had been designed to house rehabilitation, a heart disease reversal program, and integrative health. The Integrative Health Center was for traditional therapies as well as complementary and alternative therapies. Included in the programs were yoga, stress management, Tai-Chi, Ai-Chi, Reiki, Spiritual Counseling, Aroma Therapy, Massage, Infant Massage, Music Therapy, and Acupuncture.

## ORGANIZATIONAL CHALLENGE

During the first two weeks of his employment, the president of the newly renamed Windber Medical Center quickly realized that the organization needed deep and almost unlimited change in a culture that was deeply engrained in a world that had clearly ceased to exist.

So he had his assistant schedule approximately 270 appointments for him, one every ten minutes from 7:30 in the morning until well after normal shift change hours each day for two weeks. He met with every employee in the facility, introduced himself, and then listened as they expressed their concerns, their beliefs, and their dreams to him. In less than ten working days, he knew the culture.

He then attempted to recreate the same process with his medical staff. That mission was much less successful. In fact, it was nearly impossible. The power of the organization was clearly nestled in that group of individuals. Of the 150-plus physicians on staff, approximately sixteen held the organization in their control.

Of that sixteen, five were from the Far East, and four were born and raised in the Windber area. This group formed the nucleus of what would create five years of struggle. These physicians controlled patient flow and the care philosophy, but they were independent physicians who could take their patients anywhere they selected and could also close the facility overnight if they changed their allegiance.

## Reasons for Change

The president was not making these decisions completely out of personal fondness for change. One month after taking over in his position, the accounting firm of Ernst and Young (E&Y) presented him with the first chapter of a strategic plan that predicted the demise of Windber Medical Center in less than five years. This was due to competition, changes in insurance reimbursements, and increased penetration of managed care products in the market.

Congress also enacted the Balanced Budget Amendment Act, which would forever change the way hospitals, especially nonteaching and nonrural hospitals, would be paid by Medicare and Medicaid. The full impact of that act was not known in 1997, but it proved to be much more detrimental than any of the other E&Y predictions. The change in reimbursements to small, urban hospitals would plunge many of them into bankruptcy over the next few years, and Windber was no exception.

**Stakeholder Expectations.** The public and local communities and politicians desperately needed the facility to remain open. In 1997, in an area noted for the second highest outmigration of population of anywhere except East St. Louis, Missouri, Windber desperately needed the $8 million payroll provided by its largest employer. Clearly, *patient first* was the key to the future of this hospital in rural Pennsylvania.

## Change Objectives

In a number of town meetings, the president explained his vision of the Planetree philosophy to the entire medical center. The senior management team verbally committed to the following transformation process:

- Make patient-centered care the number-one priority of the organization
- Commit to providing a loving, nurturing environment to the patients and their families
- Address all patient and patient family issues quickly and efficiently
- Become recognized locally, regionally, and nationally for this new type of commitment to care in which the patients' dignity is not compromised

To be sure that everyone was aware of these expectations, the president conducted nearly a dozen hour-long meetings over a five-day period. Once again he met with every employee possible. These meetings were repeated every few months for nearly three years. Patient-centered care was the point of these meetings.

# APPROACH

Working with individuals who had been employed at Windber Medical Center for fifteen or more years proved to provide an environment that was not only resistant to change but completely opposed to change. It became evident when the president attempted to demonstrate his commitment to this new philosophy by initiating steps to create the Planetree look. As the walls were transformed from Pepto Bismol pink to new shades of gold and yellow, the employees began to react as if their world was collapsing. This was a clear indicator that outside help was needed in this transformation.

Several approaches were embraced by management:

- Four employees were chosen from the four areas of employment, all staff-level employees, to go to the Disney Institute for training. Their expenses were paid, and upon their return they began to tell what they had learned to all of the employees of the hospital.

- A management consultant trained in conflict management was employed to train all of the employees in Emotional Quotient training. Each employee was tested in order to determine his or her personality profile. They then tested their family members and shared with their peers. This training progressed to enable employees to learn how to deal with each personality type.

- Heads of other departments were given gift certificates and encouraged to go to resorts, hotels, and restaurants to observe new models of care.

These new models were not without critics. At least a third of the managers resented the idea of giving up their power over the patients and their families. Many nurses who were directly connected to the older physicians also resisted these changes. It took nearly three years to change the employee evaluation system to allow these thirty-two individuals, approximately 10 percent of the workforce, to be removed.

# ASSESSMENT: THE MAN SHOW

Although health care would seem to be a sacred guardian of human life that treats each individual with compassion, love, and care, it is, in fact, based upon the military model. Many physicians approach their patients as unenlightened.

Many administrators do the same with their subordinates, as do many caregivers. It is a world often driven by power and money.

When hospitals were reimbursed for the total number of days a patient was hospitalized, those days were numerous. WMC's first patient was hospitalized for seven years and eight months. When reimbursement methodology changed, hospitals started "drive-by deliveries" for pregnant moms.

A preliminary diagnosis of the organization clearly demonstrated where the power was. It was with the physicians and their minions. Those senior managers who believed in the power of the medical staff clearly sided with them on every decision.

In order to overwhelm the resistance, the president, a former marketing executive, began to seek and obtain overwhelming endorsements from the media in the area. Numerous television, radio, and print endorsements were forthcoming for even taking on this enormous task of attempting to change this very conservative system back to it roots.

This effort resulted in a partial power shift. The board and administration were clearly pursuing a popular path with the patients and media, and resistant members of the medical staff were forced to *go underground* in the form of passive aggressive resistance. Another unexpected negative from this attention emanated from senior leadership at the health system. So the question became, *Could leadership create a patient-centered care philosophy and survive?*

All of the vice presidents were removed and replaced twice over a three-year period until the right combination of warm, caring, empowering individuals were put in place; interesting enough, they were all women.

Hence, the Man Show began to take on an all-new look, and a nurturing, loving environment began to take hold.

## Physicians

The obvious key to the success of this program was to find physicians who had a deep moral belief in patient empowerment. There were three very religious individuals who emerged as leaders in our efforts. Each represented a different specialty, and each had commonsense influence over the other physicians on staff. These docs helped keep things on an even keel in meetings where confrontation was the core intent of many of those threatened by this new philosophy.

Issues over noninvasive complementary techniques like massage and spiritual touch came to the forefront of these medical staff meetings. Open medical records, unlimited visiting hours, unlimited access to psychologists, clergy, family members, and even pets were often topics that engendered heated discussions from the *bulls,* or the bullies.

The other phenomena that developed were resistance to all forms of general change. Where a public work-out center might have been embraced in the traditional world of old Windber medicine, in the new order it was resisted. Musicians in the halls were seen to be invasive, as was massage for the patients, employees, and physicians. The physicians were the most difficult and most important change agents. At times they acted as desperate victims as the core of their power was diminished.

### Employees

Another key to the process was the employee. Change at the staff level was critical. Employees were rewarded for being *caught* caring. They were empowered to *make things right* when patients or their family members were upset. They were encouraged to go the extra mile when necessary. For the first two years this worked beautifully.

As the bottom fell out of health care due to the shortage of registered nurses and the impact of the Balanced Budget Amendment, however, those employees who were motivated not to change began using the Planetree philosophy as a lever to *get even* with administration.

Any time the employees, specifically nurses and laboratory technologists, were upset about pay raises or working conditions, they were less attentive to the patients, and told the patients and their families that they were overworked and underpaid. Both of these statements were true.

The manner in which management corrected this problem involved surrounding the patients with volunteers and complementary care givers. A typical patient would be seen by a massage therapist, aroma therapist, behavioral psychologist, clergy, volunteers with art carts, and, when desired, pets for pet therapy.

## FEEDBACK USE

Planetree teams were put together to teach, train, and gather feedback from the employees. After the first two years of change, meaningful growth, and strong profits, during which time the employees enjoyed significant increases in salary, morale was at an all time high.

During the following two years the finances were the driving force behind the primary unrest. These Planetree teams served an integral part of the curative process for advancing the philosophy.

Each meeting started with a venting session intended to allow the employees in attendance the opportunity to express themselves. After each session the team would prepare anonymous debriefing reports to be read by senior leadership. This feedback began to bring light to the subject of the employee's concerns.

The Planetree team made sure that all participants had access to the summary pages as well. The president discussed the findings with employees during his regular employee meetings. Due to these findings, employee satisfaction surveys, Lunch with the President, individual meetings, and newsletters were all forthcoming.

In spite of all of these ongoing efforts, nothing changed until a windfall came to the hospital through a settlement with an insurance provider that enabled the hospital to give 30 percent raises to key caregivers. The reality here is that happy, well-paid employees were critical to the success of Planetree.

# DESIGN: PLANETREE PHILOSOPHY

The core of the Planetree philosophy is as old as human healing and caring. It involves the holistic care that nurtures the mind, body, and spirit. It embraces the creation of an environment that recognizes a healing process that does not emanate purely from drugs or surgeries. It is a truth that has been known for thousands of years but has been overpowered during the past fifty years by modern medicines.

Planetree embraces a philosophy that includes the creation of a healing environment through architecture, natural light, plants, music, aroma therapy, the presence and encouragement of loved ones, and the nurturing provided by clergy and psychologists.

Each day bread is baked in the hallways, popcorn is popped in the lobby, music is played, and massage is offered to patients as they wait, to the employees at their workstations, and to the physicians in the hallways and in their offices. More important, the patients are empowered to ask, participate, and know.

It is all about the belief that healing can occur in many ways.

# INTERVENTION: FUNDAMENTAL CHANGES

The work of the Planetree teams, the senior leadership, the board and staff was all-inclusive and continues to this day. Each aspect of this change culture was carefully planned, executed, and managed.

- Formal on-the-job training and classroom training from internal Planetree leaders, consultants from Planetree staff, and outside consultants
- Annual refresher course for all employees
- Employee training course for all new hires
- Establishment of an anonymous telephone hotline for employees to identify any feelings of wrong doing toward them
- Celebration of major accomplishments with parties, ice cream sundaes, dinner certificates, awards, trips to baseball games, and cash; recognition in written communication and gifts from senior managers

- Empowerment of employees with the authority to care for patients' needs up to $300 in costs per incident
- A portion of the employee compensation is tied to performance

*Success Factors*

1. The extensive training by professionals and peers
2. Mention of Planetree in every communication to employees made it the single focus of the mission of the organization
3. Employee recognition by senior leadership
4. The president's *walk the talk* approach
5. The humanistic approach to the removal of employees who would never be able to provide Planetree care
6. Recognition by local, regional, and national press for the unique patient-centered care, trademarked Windbercare, provided by the employees and volunteers at Windber Medical Center

Together, these factors helped overcome the internal resistance and program obstacles.

# THE PLANETREE TEAMS

The value of the Planetree teams cannot be discounted. It was because of their ongoing work and dedication that progress occurred. These employees worked dozens of hours on their own time at special meetings on and off campus to ensure that the Planetree sessions were meaningful.

Because the sessions were peer to peer, they were much more effective.

All employees were required to attend sessions where sensitivity training occurred. Role-playing of employees as patients was an important part of the programs.

A SWAT team made up of social workers, psychologists, and clergy provides on-the-job help. This crisis intervention team was an important aspect of providing support for employees when crisis situations arise.

# LOOKING BACK

The transition of a small, 102-bed, urban hospital located in a community of less than four thousand people to national prominence was neither easy nor safe. The president of the organization was challenged numerous times by physicians, system executives, and employees. It was a passion for change that allowed the dream to become a reality. None of the goals could have been accomplished without hard work and commitment from the entire staff.

## The Change Circle

The textbooks talk about unfreezing, changing, and refreezing a culture. In this case the refreezing of the culture is a never-ending task. The change circle for moving a traditional hospital to the Planetree model takes years. As the reputation of the organization continued to grow, new physicians and employees attracted to the holistic, caring culture came seeking employment at the facility. The addition of these special caregivers enabled the culture to change more dramatically and completely. It also began to balance the power of the medical staff.

The organization was a typical Industrial Revolution model. Employees clocked in each day minutes before they were to be at their position within the hospital. They went to their workstations, and the day revolved around the physicians' and employees' schedules.

In many cases, the staff did not recognize the patient as a customer. The patient was an inconvenience. Their presence was an interruption.

In order to see the need for change, studies depicting the future demise of the organization were made available at employee meetings. These studies were not used as *gospel* but only as a warning signal that the organization had five years to make a significant change.

The importance of making the patient the center of care was a difficult job. It was totally foreign to the culture of much of health care. Although the employees of Windber Medical Center and especially those of the palliative care unit were exceptionally caring individuals, the general rule of thumb was that the rules were the rules. Patients were scheduled at the convenience of the physician and the technician. This required the changes previously outlined.

## It Gets Worse Before It Gets Better

The overall atmosphere of the organization was one of waiting for the wave to pass over. In fact, each aspect of the Planetree philosophy was undermined, ignored, and blatantly pushed aside while the employees waited for their fifth president to be fired or their sixth manager to be promoted or dismissed. It was the revolving door theory. If you ignore it, they will go away. When it became obvious that the change agents and the philosophy were, for the most part, going to stay, then positive reinforcement could begin to take hold.

It was also a we-they relationship with the physicians and employees. One physician had all of the nurses on his group e-mail and used that e-mail to undermine the senior leaders on a regular basis. So those employees would cling to their protective physician for power as they ignored management.

## I'm from the Government and I'm Here to Help

As the program moved forward and received the positive attention of local politicians, federal, state, and local grants began to pour into the organization for special programs, research projects, and capital additions.

Instead of pleasing the employees, making them happy and secure, these grants caused jealously between the departments that received them and those that did not. As new buildings came on line, the employees located in the older buildings were resentful and openly hostile. As new employees came on board, the long-time employees were disruptive and, many times, unkind toward them.

It was a very interesting evolution that did not and could not work out until salaries, remodeling, and attention occurred housewide, five years into the transition.

## Getting Back on Track

After several years of training, growth through increased census and patient numbers, grants, and national recognition, Planetree began to take hold as a way of life at Windber Medical Center. There are still physicians who do not want to allow patient empowerment, there are still not always care teams in place, there are days when patients don't smell the bread, see the volunteers, or see the special complementary medicine specialists, but 95 percent of the time, things are as they should be.

Because we wanted everyone to feel as though they were in the best five star hotel, a spa, and a healing garden, we hired a hotel manager to run our house-keeping, dietary, and maintenance departments and provide room service, fresh flowers, bread, live music, artwork, and fountains and invite loved ones to stay with their sick relatives. We have unlimited visiting hours. We also provide pajama bottoms and bathrobes. More like their home or better. A healing environment.

In our birthing suites, we have midwives in room deliveries and use such complementary therapies as birthing balls, aromatherapy, music and massage therapy, infant massage, Jacuzzi tubs, and hand-held massagers. We also have double beds for the families to use after the baby is born. Mother, father, and baby occupy the same room. These birthing suites also contain computer hookups to the Internet, live music, and TV-VCR, and we bake fresh bread daily and offer tea and coffee.

As part of our commitment to the community, we have added a "Center for Life." This is the senior center for senior citizens. Seniors come each day and have access to our gym, our doctors, and trained staff. In this center, older citizens have access to social services and preventative health options.

The medical center has a palliative care unit for our hospice for pain control, respite for the family, and end-of-life care. We can accommodate a family of four in each patient room.

The Joyce Murtha Breast Care Center is a model of breast care for women. It contains all state-of-the-art equipment for digital mammography, breast biopsy, osteoporosis, and 3D ultrasound, and even has a cosmetologist to assist women who are going through chemotherapy treatments.

## Quantifying the Results: Exhibits

After several years of patient-centered care, some curious anomalies began to appear. Our patients had the lowest mortality rate for adjusted acuity, they had an extremely low length of stay, and our infection rate was well below the national average. (See Exhibits 18.1–18.3.)

### Exhibit 18.1. Average Length of Stay

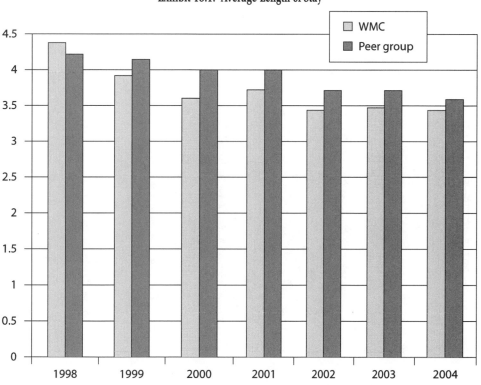

*Source:* The Hospital Council of Western Pennsylvania. Reprinted with permission.

**Exhibit 18.2. Nosocomial Infection Rate**

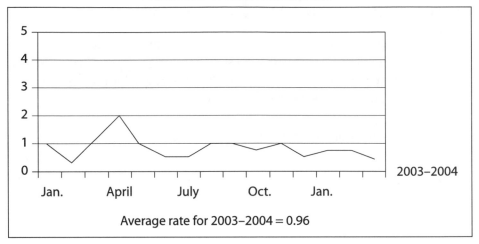

*Source:* The Hospital Council of Western Pennsylvania. Reprinted with permission.

**Exhibit 18.3. Mortality Comparison by Hospital**

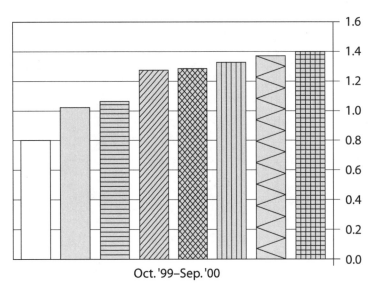

Risk-adjusted index is statistically significant at a confidence level of 95%.

*Source:* The Hospital Council of Western Pennsylvania. Reprinted with permission.

### Moving Ahead Again

The Planetree philosophy is the future of health care. It embraces all aspects of holistic care.

- We value Planetree as the medical center's number-one priority
- Patient-centered care is the center of the philosophy

Windber, PA—David Klementik, Chairman of Windber Medical Center's Board of Trustees, was named today by the prestigious publication *Modern Healthcare* as Trustee of the Year for hospitals and health systems with fewer than 250 beds or annual revenue of less than $75 Million.

During a recent visit to Windber Medical Center, former Health and Human Services Secretary Donna Shalala summed up the WindberCare vision brilliantly, saying: "Close your eyes if you want to see health care in the future. Then open them, and see the extraordinary facility here at Windber. This is the future of health care, it focuses on prevention and research. Keeping people healthy and focusing on the end of life" (Modern Healthcare Magazine, January 22, 2001).

*Modern Maturity* selected Windber Medical Center as one of the top 15 Hospitals with Heart in the United States.

Its president was chosen as Outstanding Rural Health Leader of the year for Pennsylvania in 2001.

## LESSONS LEARNED

Lesson #1—Work with the physicians first, last, and always.

Lesson #2—Make sure that the right senior leadership is in place early and often.

Lesson #3—Establish an effective employee screening and evaluation system. Some people never can or will be Planetree.

Lesson #4—Be sure that the employees are taken care of first, last, and always. Happy employees make happy patients.

Lesson #5—Recognition of team players by senior leadership on a regular basis is important and powerful.

Lesson #6—Don't give up.

# ABOUT THE CONTRIBUTOR

**F. Nicholas Jacobs** currently is president of Windber Medical Center and the Windber Research Institute. He has been with the Conemaugh Health System since August 1993 and before that was vice-president for administrative services at Mercy Medical Center for five years. Mr. Jacobs holds a master's degree from Indiana University of Pennsylvania and Carnegie Mellon University, plus a health care certification from Harvard University and the Grantsmanship Center. He is a Fellow in the American College of Health Care Executives and was awarded the Community Rural Health Leader of the Year in 2001 by the Pennsylvania Rural Health Association. In addition, Mr. Jacobs served as an adjunct instructor for St. Francis University and has been a guest lecturer at Ohio State University, the Graduate School of Indiana University of Pennsylvania, Carnegie Mellon University, and other regional, state, and national conferences and workshops.

# CHAPTER NINETEEN

# Conclusion

## *Practitioner Trends and Findings*

*To provide additional context for the practices presented in this book, we asked contributors to complete a survey to gain a more comprehensive view of their organizational change and leadership development program. The survey comprised of five themed sections: (1) business diagnosis (including the type of initiative, business revenues, and costs and revenues associated with the initiative), (2) resistance to change, (3) design and implementation, (4) evaluating the initiative, and (5) summary.*

*Though each organization differs with respect to area of expertise, amount of yearly revenues, and types of initiatives undertaken, each shares a similar goal of creating more successful and results-oriented organizations by way of organizational change and leadership development.*

COMPANY AND INITIATIVE BACKGROUND 440

BUSINESS DIAGNOSIS AND ASSESSMENT 440

Table 19.1: Top Five Reasons Organizations Made
the Business Case for the Initiative, in Order of Frequency 441
Table 19.2: Assessment Methods by Frequency of Use 442

RESISTANCE TO CHANGE 442

Table 19.3: Types of Resistance Encountered, in Order
of Percentage Frequency Encountered 443

REDUCING RESISTANCE 443

Table 19.4: Top Champions of Change in the Companies
Initiative, in Order of Percentage Frequency 444
Table 19.5: Top Critical Success Behaviors of Senior Leadership
for the Initiative, in Order of Percentage Frequency 444
Table 19.6: Challenges in Gaining Consensus During and for
Best Practice Organizations' Initiatives, in Order of Frequency 445

DESIGN AND IMPLEMENTATION                                    445

Table 19.7: Content That Was Most Emphasized
    in Training Initiatives, in Order of Frequency of Use    446
Table 19.8: Specific Content Most Emphasized within
    Training Interventions, in Order of Percentage Frequency  447
Table 19.9: Key Factors for Leadership Development
    and Change, in Order of Frequency of Use                 447
Table 19.10: Other Key Factors Indicated by Best
    Practice Organizations                                   448

EVALUATING THE OD/HRD INITIATIVE                            448

Table 19.11: Evaluation Method Usage                         450
Table 19.12: Positive Results of Initiatives, in Order
    of Percentage Frequency                                  450

SUMMARY                                                      450

NOTES                                                        451

# COMPANY AND INITIATIVE BACKGROUND

The organizations appearing in this book vary in the number of employees, revenues, and industries. Industries represented throughout this book are aerospace, consulting services, consumer products, electronics, financial services, higher education, hospitality and restaurants, information technology, manufacturing, and telecommunications. Respondents come from different divisions, including commercial services, corporate, facilities, human resources, manufacturing, and science and technology, among others.

# BUSINESS DIAGNOSIS AND ASSESSMENT

*The greatest compliment that was ever paid me was when one asked me
what I thought, and attended to my answer.*
—Henry David Thoreau[1]

Prior to embarking on any initiative to change some aspect of organizational culture, each organization engaged in diagnosis, using a customized needs assessment to further determine the most prudent course of action. The initial step of assessing guarantees that initiatives and interventions are well thought out and planned. Needs assessment provided organizations, its leaders,

Table 19.1. Top Five Reasons Organizations Made the Business
Case for the Initiative, in Order of Frequency

| Business Case | Frequency |
| --- | --- |
| Productivity needs | 1 |
| Competitive pressures | 2 |
| Consumer needs | 3 |
| Growth | 4 |
| Corporate vision | 5 |

employees, and customers the opportunity to uncover specific issues and perspectives on change.

Diagnosis for our best practice organizations considered the increasing numbers of competitors from a growing global marketplace, fluctuating economic conditions, and the rise and fall of industries. Another challenge organizations are facing is the realization and acknowledgement of the importance of customers in their decision-making processes and potentially a more important stakeholder—the employee.

Best practice organizations used a variety of methods to measure the need for their initiatives. These methods ranged from observation of work practices and employee behavior to more concrete and less subjective measures such as surveys, focus groups, and performance appraisals. The later methods helped reduce the number of alternate hypotheses that were made by the program designers and also served to reinforce the perceptions of senior management and program designers' use of observation techniques. Surveying and appraisals took the form of several instruments in the assessment phase, including 360-degree assessment, multirater assessment instruments, and various individual assessment instruments.

The diagnosis and assessment phase of the best practice leadership development and change programs proved to be an excellent method of gaining support and marketing the initiative. By better understanding the learning and change needs of participants, organizations became more knowledgeable and more able to adapt to the changing needs and demands of its participants and employees. The results of the assessment instruments often formed the basis of the training programs and other specific company change initiatives.

Assessment methods in the "Other" category ranged in depth of diagnostic techniques from financial performance to quality indicators to employee turnover to and customer feedback to comments from board members.

Table 19.2. Assessment Methods by Frequency of Use

| Assessment Methods | Frequency of Use |
|---|---|
| Observation | 1 |
| Surveys | 2 |
| Interviews | 3 |
| Focus groups | 4 |
| Meetings | 5 |
| Performance appraisals | 6 |
| Other | 7 |
| Survey box/opinions | 8 |

# RESISTANCE TO CHANGE

*You have to have confidence in your ability, and then be tough*
*enough to follow through.*
—Rosalynn Carter[2]

In thinking about the forces of change—technology, economics, competition, social and cultural, and the changing workforce, including diversity and skills levels—it seems that every organization is in a constant state of change. One of the most challenging obstacles to overcome in any organizational transformation effort is the resistance encountered during change. Resistance can be due to any combination of factors, including psychological, technological, or cultural fears, security or economic concerns, or fear of the unknown, to name a few. Of those who responded, the most prevalent obstacles to implementing the initiative were difficulty in gaining consensus from disparate parties (40 percent of respondents) and maintaining that managers are accountable for following through with action items (33 percent of respondents). Survey data also showed that 27 percent responded to having difficulty with each of the following items: implementing change in different regions of the world, achieving project sponsorship, assisting employees in applying new technologies and applications, and others, including continued learning and sustaining the focus on the initiative. All organizations reported some type of resistance.

**Table 19.3. Types of Resistance Encountered, in Order of Percentage Frequency Encountered**

| Types of Resistance | Frequency |
| --- | --- |
| Fear of change, the unknown, and loss of control | 1 |
| Time constraints | 2 |
| Negative reaction to "soft skills" training | 3 |
| Negative reaction to failed prior initiatives | 4 |
| Sense of mistrust | 5 |

# REDUCING RESISTANCE

*You cannot shake hands with a clenched fist.*
—Indira Gandhi, 1982[3]

Although resistance is often viewed as negative, it was often viewed positively by our best practice organizations to help to guide the design and development of the leadership development and change initiatives. Employees presenting opposing viewpoints, or what some call "pushback," were instead perceived as a sound-board and sometimes as a "balancing system" for the organization. Of course, a critical mass of supporters are necessary for any change initiative. The challengers to the system, however, have proven to be important in balancing systems that are too synchronous or closed in their decision-making processes. Challengers serve to clarify and bring more awareness of the initiative to the organization. It was proven through our best practice contributors that challengers are healthy to the system in this way. Employees need to be reassured that positive change is not something to fear but instead something to be embraced for the organization. As described by Richard Beckhard in his model for resistance

First steps (F) × (multiplied by) Vision (V) × Dissatisfaction (D)
> (is greater than or overcomes) Resistance (R)

It is therefore important to have stable and visible senior leadership that is supportive of the changes taking place, a clear picture of what is going to be accomplished as a whole system, step-by-step approaches to achieve change, and a clear understanding throughout the organization of the dissatisfaction, so that the entire organization is aware of what needs to be changed for the greater good.

Table 19.4. Top Champions of Change in the Companies Initiative, in Order
of Percentage Frequency

| Change Agents | Frequency (%) |
| --- | --- |
| President and chief officers | 73 |
| Senior executives | 60 |
| OD, HRD, training, strategy, implementation team | 33 |
| Entire organization | 13 |
| Driven jointly by managers | 7 |

Table 19.5. Top Critical Success Behaviors of Senior Leadership for the
Initiative, in Order of Percentage Frequency

| Behavior | Frequency (%) |
| --- | --- |
| Allocates funds for the initiative | 93 |
| Models behavior consistent with strategy | 73 |
| Integrates initiative into strategic plan | 60 |
| Facilitates education or training | 47 |
| Participates in education and training | 73 |
| Articulates case for change | 67 |
| Ties compensation to initiative | 27 |

Because of the need for consistency in senior leadership support, we asked
our contributing organizations which ways organizational leaders showed support for the initiative. Results indicated that leadership makes significant
attempts and gestures to model behavior, quell fears, and work with funding
sources.

The organizations within this book clearly make the choice to treat people
with dignity, understanding, and respect while balancing organizational needs
and objectives. And they are aware that the truth of one individual is not necessarily "the Truth but simply one person's wisdom. Organizations in this book
clearly understand that employees are adult learners with various and diverse
positions, needs, interests, learning styles, personality styles, levels of intellectual development, and thinking styles (see Table 19.6).

Table 19.6. Challenges in Gaining Consensus During and for Best Practice
Organizations' Initiatives, in Order of Frequency

| *Organizational Understanding* | *Ranking of Frequency of Understanding* |
| --- | --- |
| Diverse interests, positions, and needs | 1 |
| Diverse thinking styles | 2 |
| Different levels of intellectual development | 3 |
| Different personality styles | 4 |
| Different communication skill-levels and styles | 5 |
| Diverse learning styles | 6 |

# DESIGN AND IMPLEMENTATION

*Imagination continually frustrates tradition, that is its function.*
—John Pfeiffer

Organizations are beginning to recognize the need to integrate their initiatives into the existing culture and environment of the company. There is also a greater awareness seen in this best practices book than others of the human factors involved in championing or enabling change. From considering the employee as customer to being more aware of client input into internal systems, there appears to be a new emphasis on people-centered initiatives. The mention of work-life balance as an important initiative for implementing change reflects the development of appreciation for employees. In addition, the overwhelming support for leadership development programs may reveal the importance of demonstrating a willingness to develop effective managers rather than allow poor management to negatively affect productivity, employee morale, and retention.

Some interesting remarks in the "Other" category also related to effective communication included raising and resolving issues; faster decision making; increased alignment; commitment to shared purpose; courage; motivation; knowledge of organizational structure, operations, products, and services; and *Sensei* (ability to teach and transfer knowledge to others).

Following the proven wisdom that there must be buy-in and commitment from senior leaders, the majority of organizations indicated presidents, chief officers, and other senior executives as top champions of change. What is relatively new is the entire organization or "whole system" as a champion of change. These data acknowledge that it is not just top-level management, but all employees who play an important role in enabling change.

**Table 19.7.  Content That Was Most Emphasized in Training Initiatives, in Order of Frequency of Use**

| | |
|---|---|
| Teaming, teamwork | 1 |
| Customer service | 2 |
| Ethics and integrity | 3 |
| Giving and receiving feedback | 4 |
| Results-based decision making | 5 |
| Coaching | 6 |
| Business acumen | 7 |
| Emotional intelligence | 8 |
| Innovation | 9 |
| Systems thinking | 10 |
| Building networks and alliances | 11 |
| Diversity (race, ethnicity, thinking styles, or all forms) | 12 |
| Financial acumen | 13 |
| Productivity | 14 |
| Sales | 15 |
| Other | 16 |
| Stress management | 17 |
| Consensus building | 18 |
| Diversity (specifically race or ethnicity) | 19 |

Ethics and integrity were indicated by nearly half of the organizations as being an area of emphasis in training programs. Data around the need for ethics and integrity training has remained consistent throughout all of our best practice research. Results-based decision making as training content indicates a new level of accountability in making decisions. Coaching, emotional intelligence, and giving and receiving feedback all seem to demonstrate the desire to relate and communicate more effectively with others for more enabled and functional workplaces and teamwork, as well as faster decision making and an emphasis on profitability, sales, and improvement of relationships in the workplace for increased retention.

The top methods for the implementation of leadership development and change varied from results-driven practices for learning and transferring learning on-the-job to the kind of interactions and experiences of leaders throughout all levels of the organization. Our best practice companies indicated a diverse

Table 19.8. Specific Content Most Emphasized within Training
Interventions, in Order of Percentage Frequency

| Content | Frequency (%) |
|---|---|
| Teaming, teamwork | 73 |
| Giving and receiving feedback | 53 |
| Results-based decision making | 47 |
| Ethics and integrity | 47 |
| Customer service | 47 |
| Coaching | 47 |
| Innovation | 33 |
| Business acumen | 33 |
| Emotional intelligence | 27 |

Table 19.9. Key Factors for Leadership Development and Change, in Order of Frequency of Use

| Key Factor | Frequency of Use |
|---|---|
| Action(able) learning | 1 |
| Exposure to senior executives | 2 |
| Increasing awareness | 3 |
| Experiential learning | 4 |
| 360-degree feedback | 5 |
| Working from core individual values and vision | 6 |
| Commitment to corporate vision and strategy | 7 |
| Simulation-based learning | 8 |
| Group interventions | 9 |
| Visioning sessions | 10 |
| Internal case studies | 11 |
| Modeling | 12 |
| Whole-scale interventions | 13 |
| Scenario planning | 14 |
| Cross-functional rotations | 15 |
| Assessment centers | 16 |
| Organizational or corporate indicator models | 17 |
| Other | 18 |

**Table 19.10. Other Key Factors Indicated by Best Practice Organizations**

- Eight-week follow-up on action plans
- Leadership development training, employee behavior standards, measuring the important things, accountability at all levels, communications at all levels
- Shared ownership of ideas, trust individual and group expression and improvisation
- Dedicated internal coaches to participants
- Cross-functional strategic leadership teams
- Use of informal opinion leaders identified through survey and targeted behaviors for change
- Personal growth and behavior/learning plan and written contract; postprogram reassessment nine to twelve months following participation
- Development of a leadership strategy that is aligned with and helps drive the business strategy
- Building of effective networks and thinking without boundaries

set of implementation tactics that included whole-scale interventions, simulation-based learning, and experiential learning that form the foundation for effective learning. By far, action learning led the way in the most popular form of learning, because of its emphasis and ease of measurement.

Key factors in the "Other" category included such practices as storytelling and sustaining a leadership change culture through consistent communication and common language for positive cultural change throughout the organization.

When asked what other remarkable key features that organizations leveraged for the success of their leadership development and change program, our best practice organizations indicated several practices worthy of noting:

# EVALUATING THE OD/HRD INITIATIVE

*It is never too late to become what you might have been.*
—George Eliot[4]

Although the evaluation stage is arguably one of the most important components of the leadership development and change process, it is often not given the attention it deserves. Beckhard and Harris (1977) defined evaluation as "a set of planned, information-gathering, and analytical activities undertaken to provide those responsible for the management of change with a satisfactory assessment of the effects and/or progress of the change effort."[5] Nearly all companies use various systems to evaluate the effectiveness of the OD initiative.

However, the subject of measurement can vary from one company to another, as well as the methods in which evaluation can be taken.

Organizations that participated in this best practice book used five methods of implementing evaluations. The first evaluation method used in our study was behavioral change evaluation. This method measures the gap between specific behaviors before and after the intervention. Although intervention can improve desired dimension, it can also help in eliminating undesired behavior. Therefore, the gap can be positive or negative. The method is well implemented in the frame of routine performance appraisal processes, whereas previous evaluation can be used as a base line for comparison. The main contribution of this method is by its ability to measure visible behaviors, which have a direct relationship to performance. The second type of evaluation was organization assessments, surveys, and tracking. This method can be conducted during the intervention (a formative base) or immediately after the completion of the intervention (summative base). The format of this method is based on paper or computer tools that collect information against specific questions. Although not found in our study, evaluation can also be conducted in a longitudinal base. Longitudinal evaluations are conducted after a specific time has passed after the completion of the intervention. This method can add to the measure of a time perspective.[6]

The third evaluation method used was return on investment (ROI) calculations. Although not always manageable to calculate, several of the companies were able to measure the results against the cost of investment in their initiatives. When conducted, this method serves as a meaningful tool that has the benefit of connecting the initiative to the business lexicon. The fourth evaluation method was results evaluations. This method measures the effect of training on achieving organizational goals. It is most effective when the initiative aims to achieve specific and measurable goals. The fifth method is based on feedback sessions. This method can be structured around specific questions or as an open discussion. It has the advantage of receiving direct and immediate feedback. In our study, feedback sessions were conducted on both a formative and summative basis.

The table below presents the ranking of usage of each of the five evaluation methods by best practice organizations in the study.

The survey results also indicated that although the frequency of evaluation is varied according to the unique characteristics of every initiative, most initiatives were measured at least twice a year.

This best practice book was built on the premise that organizations achieve measurable results from their initiatives. We asked our best practice organizations to indicate what kinds of positive results their initiatives had. Results in this category were clearly in the areas of organization effectiveness and achievement of business strategy and objectives. These objectives varied from cost

**Table 19.11. Evaluation Method Usage**

| Evaluation Method Usage | Ranking |
|---|---|
| Behavioral change evaluation | 1 |
| Organization assessments, surveys, tracking | 2 |
| ROI calculations | 3 |
| Results evaluation | 4 |
| Feedback sessions | 5 |

**Table 19.12. Positive Results of Initiatives, in Order of Percentage Frequency**

| Positive Results | Frequency (%) |
|---|---|
| Organizational effectiveness (e.g., communication, consensus building, project planning) | 87 |
| Strategic imperatives fulfilled | 73 |
| Team performance | 67 |
| Cost savings | 53 |
| Customer satisfaction | 33 |
| Financial results | 27 |
| Shareholder value | 7 |

savings to gaining consensus on a project that led to tangible business results to customer satisfaction to financial results and even to shareholder value.

# SUMMARY

*Only those who dare to fail greatly, can ever achieve greatly.*
—Robert F. Kennedy[7]

The summary results underscored the critical importance of senior management support. These data did not disregard the crucial role of participants in designing the program itself, thus supporting the need for employees at all levels of the organization to be active and equal partners and players in leadership development and change. All of our data suggest that the more involvement, understanding, and respect given to the diverse needs and styles of employees at all levels, the lower the resistance to change. In addition, there seems to be increased value derived from building on existing systems and involving all levels of employees in the development of new processes, both of which help truly integrate change initiatives into the organization's culture.

The top-ranking critical success factors included

1. Support and participation of senior management

2. Connecting development and the initiative with the strategic plan

3. Involvement of participants in design

4. Integration with other divisional processes, practices, or systems

5. Pilot program before launch

6. Continuous evaluation

7. Leveraging of internal capacity

Having employees become more involved in the development of the initiatives directly addresses some of the most significant challenges, such as fear of the unknown, aversion to loss of control, and of course aversion to change. Building on existing successful systems helps reduce the sense of mistrust that comes from "initiatives of the month."

There is no doubt that these best practice organizations both endured struggles and enjoyed rewards, but what is even more certain is that they will continue to strive toward increasing organizational effectiveness through innovative, results-oriented, and integrated multilayered leadership development and change initiatives. Louis Carter, his co-editors David Ulrich and Marshall Goldsmith, and the Best Practices Institute look forward to continuing their work with the world's best organizations, which are passionate about positive change and leadership development.

# NOTES

1. H. D. Thoreau. *Civil Disobedience, Solitude: And Life Without Principle.* Minneapolis, Minn.: Prometheus Books, 1998.

2. R. Carter (b. 1928). United States First Lady, wife of Jimmy Carter.

3. I. Gandhi, quoted by *Christian Science Monitor,* May 17, 1982.

4. George Eliot was the pseudonym of novelist, translator, and religious writer Mary Ann Evans (1819–1880).

5. R. Beckhard and R. Harris. *Organizational Transitions.* Reading, Mass.: Addison-Wesley, 1977, p. 86.

6. W. J. Rothwell, R. Sullivan, and G. N. McLean. *Practicing Organization Development: A Guide for Consultants.* San Francisco: Jossey-Bass, 1995, p. 313.

7. R. F. Kennedy, "Day of Affirmation Address," University of Capetown, South Africa, June 6, 1966.

# ABOUT THE BEST PRACTICES INSTITUTE

The Best Practices Institute (BPI) and Best Practice Publications were founded by Louis Carter in New York City just after September 11, 2001, while Carter was a graduate student at Columbia University. BPI was formed to bring the best-thought leadership and research in the field of organization and social change to leaders of governments, social systems, nonprofit organizations, and for-profit organizations in an increasingly complex and chaotic world. In order to achieve this goal, Carter—with the help of a team of five interns from Columbia University's MBA and Social/Organizational Psychology program—recruited a panel of twenty-three experts in the field of leadership and organization development and eighteen best practice organizations to form the basis of the Change Champion's Model for meaningful change and to complete the research behind this book.

Carter's Change Champion's Model is based on the assumption that only through a deep and profound exploration and understanding of one's own and others' life experiences and perspectives is true positive social, personal, and organizational change accomplished. Carter's book with Best Practice Publications and the Best Practices Institute, entitled *The Change Champion's Fieldguide*, received praise from sources in the People's Republic of China, India, and America. Vijay Govindarajan, professor of international business and director of the Center for Global Leadership at the Tuck School of Business at Dartmouth College, endorsed the book by saying, *"The Change Champion's Fieldguide will become one of the most quoted, referenced, and used business books in the first decade of the 2000s."* Professor Li Jianfeng, Ph.D., of the

Renmin University School of Business and Cisun Academy of Management in Beijing translated the book into Mandarin and Cantonese and published the book through Huaxia Publishing House (Beijing) for distribution throughout all provinces of China. Dr. Debi Saini, professor of leadership at the Management Development Institute in Gurgaon, India, is currently bringing the book and its teachings to the Indian market.

Louis Carter's Best Practices Institute and Change Champion thought leaders include David Cooperrider, Jerry Sternin, David Ulrich, Mary Eggers, Marshall Goldsmith, Dr. John Sullivan, Ryan Matthews, Stu Noble, William Rothwell, and Larry Susskind. The Change Champion's Model and several BPI workshops have been presented by Louis Carter in Singapore, Bangkok, Beijing, and at American universities and corporations.

For more information on the Best Practices Institute and Best Practice Publications, visit http://www.bpinstitute.net or contact Louis Carter directly at lcarter@bpinstitute.net.

Louis Carter, CEO
Best Practices Institute, LLC
25 Crescent Street
Suite 531
Waltham, Massachusetts 02453
http://www.bpinstitute.net
http://www.bestpracticepublications.com
customer support: lcarter@bpinstitute.net
888-895-8949
For international calls, please see our Website for details.

# ABOUT THE EDITORS

*L*ouis Carter is founder and president of the Best Practices Institute, an organization that provides best practices to organizations and individuals throughout the world. Carter also serves as vice president of research at Linkage, Inc.

Carter has written, edited, or directed more than six books, numerous leading research projects, and learning or development programs on leadership and change, including *The Change Champion's Fieldguide.* His three new books, *Best Practices in Leadership Development and Organization Change: How the Best Companies Ensure Meaningful Change and Sustainable Leadership, America's Best Led Hospitals,* and *Best Practices in Leading the Global Workforce* will be released in 2005.

Carter has lectured domestically and abroad for organizations ranging from Tsinghua University School of Economics and Management in Beijing to Texas A&M University to the American Society for Training and Development to Universal Network Intelligence in Singapore and Bangkok. A passionate advocate for values-based leadership, Carter's articles, books, and work have been featured in *Investors Business Daily, Business Watch* magazine, SGQE, ASTD, and several other trade and professional journals. He has been described as "a real futurist in the human resources arena continuing to challenge and educate practitioners on new methodologies—on the cutting-edged leadership" by Lou Manzi, vice president of global recruitment at GlaxoSmithKline.

Carter is a graduate of Columbia University's Graduate Program in Social and Organizational Psychology. His work has been featured in business and professional texts and publications as well as at leadership conferences and courses around the world.

*David Ulrich* is currently president of the Canada Montreal Mission for the Church of Jesus Christ of Latter-day Saints while on a three-year sabbatical (until July 2005) as a professor of business from the University of Michigan. He studies how organizations build capabilities and intangibles of speed, learning, accountability, talent, and leadership through leveraging human resources. He has published over one hundred articles and book chapters and twelve books. He was the editor of *Human Resource Management Journal* from 1990 to 1999. He is on the board of directors for Herman Miller, a Fellow in the National Academy of Human Resources, and cofounder of the Michigan Human Resource Partnership. He has received numerous honors for his professional contributions. He has consulted and done research with over half of the Fortune 200.

*Marshall Goldsmith* (Marshall@A4SL.com) is a world authority in helping successful leaders achieve positive, measurable change in behavior. The American Management Association has named Marshall as one of fifty great thinkers and leaders who have influenced the field of management over the past eighty years. His work has been featured in a *Harvard Business Review* interview, *Business Strategy Review* cover story (from the London Business School), and *New Yorker* profile. His work has received national recognition from almost every professional organization in his field. Marshall has been asked to work with over seventy major CEOs and their management teams. He conducts workshops for executives, high-potential leaders, and HR professionals. His Ph.D. is from UCLA. He is on the faculty of executive education programs at Dartmouth, Michigan, and Cambridge (U.K.) Universities. Marshall is a founding director of A4SL—The Alliance for Strategic Leadership, a founder of the Russell Reynolds executive advisors network, and a partner with Hewitt Associates in providing global executive coaching, and he has served as a member of the board of the Peter Drucker Foundation. Aside from his corporate work, Marshall donates substantial time to nonprofit organizations, such as the International and American Red Cross, where he was a "National Volunteer of the Year."

Marshall's eighteen books include *The Leader of the Future* (a *Business Week* best-seller), *Coaching for Leadership.* (Choice award winner, Outstanding Academic Business Book), *Global Leadership: The Next Generation,* and *Human Resources in the 21st Century.*

# INDEX

**A**

Accelerated Performance for Executives (APEX) program, 1–19. *See also* Agilent Technologies, Inc.

Accountability: of Agilent's coaching program, 4, 6–7; at Delnor Hospital, 52–53, 61, 64; at Emmis Communications, 87, 94–97; at Hewlett-Packard, 184, 185; in Intel's Leadership Development Forum, 219; at Lockheed Martin, 241, 245; at St. Luke's Hospital, 376, 382, 393; at StorageTek, 415, 417

Accountability grids, 69, 376, 382, 383

Ackerman, R., 29, 40

Acquisition growth: culture and change management for, 80–83, 86–87; exercise for managing, 157; negative effects of, 86–87

ACT (apologize, correct, and take action), 52

Action learning, *xxiii*; in First Consulting Group's leadership development program, 130; in GE Capital's leadership development program, 167; in Hewlett-Packard's leadership development program, 184; in Mattel's Project Platypus process, 262–281; at McDonald's, 285, 289–290, 292–295; tools for, 290

Action planning, 217, 220, 221, 232

Active matrix liquid crystal display (AMLCD), 31–32

Adoption curve, 254–255

Adult learners, employees as, 444–445

Aerospace industry case studies. *See* Honeywell Aerospace; Lockheed Martin

After-action review, 40, 319

Agilent Technologies, Inc.: Accelerated Performance for Executives (APEX) program, *xxvi*, 1–19; assessment at, *xxii*, 3–4, 8, 15; background on, 2; Business Leader Inventory of, 3, 15; case study, 1–19; coaching at, *xxiii*, *xxvi*, 1–19; early coaching efforts at, 2–3; evaluation at, *xxvii–xxviii*, 10–13, 16–17; Global Leader Profile of, 3–4, 5, 8, 15; implementation at, 8–10; Leadership Development Showcase of, 7; lessons learned at, 13–14; on-the-job support at, *xxvi*; overview of, *xvii*, 2; program design of, 4–7; Semiconductor Products Group (SPG) of, 3; top leadership support at, *xx*, 14

Agility, 30

Agruso, V., 88, 89, 95

Air Research, 196

*Akron Beacon Journal*, 279

Alignment scene, 271–276

All-sports radio, 81

Alliance for Strategic Leadership Coaching & Consulting (A4SL C&C), 3, 6–7, 8–9, 10, 18

AlliedSignal, 196, 198; Honeywell merger with, 198, 199

Alternative health therapies, 426, 429
"America's Best Hospitals," 391
Andersen Consulting, 165, 179
Anderson, B., 248, 249, 250
Anderson, D., 3, 18
Anderson, R. A., 367, 368, 375
Anecdotal evaluation, 251–252
Annual business conferences, 355
Annual Emmis Managers Meeting, 84, 85, 93
Annual excellence awards, 56
Archetypes, 269
*Archetypes and Strange Attractors* (Van Eenwyk), 274
Argyris, C., 162, 167, 179
Assessment: in Agilent's APEX coaching program, 3–4, 8, 15; in Corning's innovation change initiative, 24; in Emmis Communications' culture change process, 85–86; in First Consulting Group's leadership development program, 126–128, 133, 135; in GE Capital's leadership development program, 168–170; at Hewlett-Packard, 182–183; at Honeywell, 203–204; implementation and, *xxvi*; in Intel's Leadership Development Forum, 220, 225, 226; in McDonald's leadership development program, 285–288, 294; methods and instruments of, 127–128, 133, 169–170, 351, 441–442; at MIT, 310–312; in Motorola's leadership supply system, 340–341; organization effectiveness models and, *xix–xx*; phase of, *xxii, xxvi*, 440–442; at Praxair, 350–353; in St. Luke's Hospital leadership development program, 373, 374–375; at StorageTek, 412–413; trends and themes in, 440–442; at Windber Medical Center, 428–431. *See also* Evaluation; Measurement
Assessment Plus, 4, 18–19
Atkins Kacher LIFO, 127, 133
Atkinson, J., *xxix*
Attitudinal change, in MIT's organizational learning initiative, 318
Autobiography, leadership, 216, 220, 221, 233–236
Awards: at Delnor Hospital, for excellence, 56, 61; at Emmis Communications, 84, 93–94; of Intel's Leadership Development Forum, 220, 225, 227; at St. Luke's Hospital, 381
Aweida, J., 405

**B**

Baby Boom generation, 336, 425
Baby Bust generation, 336–337
Bagian, J., 373
Balanced Budget Amendment Act, 427, 430

Balanced Scorecard, *xxvi*, 314; at Emmis Communications, 94–95, 97, 108; at MIT, 314
*Balancing Act, The* (Patterson et al.), 260–261
Baldrige (Malcolm) model, integration of Six Sigma with, 198–199
Baptist Hospital, Pensacola, 46
Barker, J., 216
Barker, K., 54
Barnholt, N., 2
Barrier analysis: for Delnor Hospital's customer service improvement, 49–50; for First Consulting Group's leadership development program, 125–126
Baseball team, 82
Bass, B. M., 162, 179
Bauer, J., 400
Becker, C., 377, 378
Beckhard, R., 443, 448, 451
Behavior standards, for patient service, 49, 59–60, 376
Behavioral change, *xix, xxii*; accountability for, 245; alignment of, with business model, 197, 201–202; alignment of, with values, 166–167, 173, 354–355; coaching for, 5, 10–13; correlation of, to business performance improvement, 252–253, 259; critical behaviors for, 244, 254, 256; demonstration of, 187, 188; evaluation of, 449; key factors for, 447; leadership forums for, 371, 393; at Lockheed Martin, 239–261; making the case for, 240–241, 242; in MIT's organizational learning initiative, 318; opinion leaders for, 246, 247–252, 254, 257; senior leaders' modeling of, 358; at St. Luke's Hospital, 376, 393; top-down approach to, 245–246
Behavioral event focused interview, 287
Behavioral measurements, *xxvii*, 449
Behavioral needs profile, 127
Benchmarking. *See* External benchmarking
Benchmarks for Success, 391
BenchStrength Development, LLC, 364
Bennis, W., 121, 123, 126, 128, 129, 138, 216, 218, 237
Berwind White Coal Company, 424
Best of the Best (BoB) award, 56, 71
"Best Places to Work Foundation for Pennsylvania," 382, 391
Best Practice forums, 172
Best Practices Institute (BPI), research study, *xv*; case study organizations in, *xv, xvi–xvii*, 440; major findings of, *xvi–xxi*, 439–451
Best Practices Institute (BPI), Step-by-Step System to Organization and Human Resources Development, *xvi, xxi–xxviii*

Biometric feedback, 54–55, 70
Birthing suites, 434
Black Belts, Six Sigma, 199, 201, 204, 206–207, 208, 210–211, 417
Blaming, 406, 417
Blyme, C., 279
Bob Costas Show, 82
Bongarten, R., 83, 84
Bonsignore, M., 199, 202
Book Club, 374
Booth Company, 215, 237
Bossidy, L., *xxi*, 196, 197, 199, 202
Brainstorming: in Mattel's Project Platypus, 272–273; in MIT's organizational learning initiative, 314
Brand stories, 269–279
Break-out work sessions, 133, 137
Breakthrough invention, 30
Bridge-building, cross-organizational, 38–39
Brookhouse, K., 344
Burke, W. W., *xx*, 315, 320
Burnett, S., 194
Business Improvement Recommendation Process, 306–307
Business Leader Inventory, 3, 15
Business Management System (BMS), 416–417
Business Model Exercise, 152–156
Business services industry case study. *See* First Consulting Group
Business Y model, 107–108

C
Cadence of change, 411, 418
Calibration scores, of leadership performance, 341
Call-backs, 51–52
Campbell, D. P., 162, 179
Camping trip, 222–223
Capabilities, organizational, 409, 415–417
Capra, F., 264–265, 276, 280
Career history assessment, 286
Career planning and development, 338
Career Systems International, 223, 237
Carter, L., *xv*
Carter, R., 442, 451
Case study approach: in First Consulting Group's leadership development program, 132, 133, 135–136, 137, 139–140, 152–159; in GE Capital's leadership development program, 170–171; in Intel's Leadership Development Forum, 223; Organization Analysis (OA) model of, 170–171
Cashman, K., 217–218, 237, 316, 320
Celebrations, *xxvi*, 372, 431

Centers for Disease Control, National Nosocomial Infection Surveillance (NNIS) System, 377–378
Centers of Excellence, 37, 39
Centralization: of Corning's research and development function, 23; of Emmis Communications, 86
Challenge, talent and, 210
Challenging the process, 222
Chamberlain, Colonel, 168
Champion training, 199
Champions, 40, 261; customer focus, 356; in Six Sigma, 199, 200, 208; types of, by organizational position, 444; whole systems as, 445
Change agents, 40; leaders-as-teachers as, 241, 246–247, 251–252, 254; opinion leaders as, 246, 247–252, 254, 257; physicians as, 430
Change Champions, 261
Change circle, 433
Change diffusion, 248, 254–255
Change initiatives: evaluation issues in, 251, 252, 448–450; modification of, to fit business model, 201–202; multiple, 406–407, 410; for organizational learning, 309–321; overzealous implementation of, 200–202, 204; resistance to, 243, 245–251, 433, 442–443, 451; results of, 449, 450; seatback, 196–197; top-down approach to, 245–246; value creation purpose of, 204–205
Change-management or catalyst programs, *xxv. See also* Corning; Emmis Communications; Honeywell; Lockheed Martin; Massachusetts Institute of Technology; StorageTek; Windber Medical Center
Chaos theory, 274–276
Check-ins, coaching, *xxvi*, 5, 6
Checkpoint dialogues, 340
Chemcor, 31
Chemicals industry case study. *See* Praxair
Chung, S. Y., 361
Clark, K. E., 162, 179
Clark, M. B., 162, 179
Clarke, B., 216
Clawson, J., 166, 168, 179
Coaches: in Agilent's APEX program, 6–7, 8, 9, 14; for cultural change, 46–47; internal *versus* external, 169; learning, in Corning's innovation process, 39–40, 42
Coaching, *xvi*; Agilent's APEX program of, 1–19; assessment and, *xxii*, 3–4, 15; content, 8; evaluation of, 10–13, 16–17; fees for, 6; in First Consulting Group's leadership development program, 130, 140; follow-up to, 10, 12–13, 14, 16–17; in GE Capital's leadership

Coaching (*Continued*)
development program, 169, 170, 172; global coach pool for, 6–7, 9; high-performance *versus* remedial, 14; internal marketing of, 7; lessons learned about, 13–14; in McDonald's leadership development program, 287–288; on-the-job support in, *xxvi*; options for, 5–6; participant qualification and selection for, *xxiii*, 6, 8–9, 14; program designs for, *xxii–xxiii*, 4–7; results guarantee for, 6–7; team, 9, 137–138, 170, 172

Coalition building, for change initiatives, 202

Code of business conduct, 414

Cohen, E., 163, 179, 260

Coherence and chaos, 274–276

Collaboration: for knowledge sharing and innovation, 38–40, 41; Mattel's Project Platypus process of, 262–281; as StorageTek organizational capability, 415

Collective ingenuity, 28

Collective self-examination, 28

Collegial culture, 128–129

Collins, J., 383

Commitment, top leadership. *See* Top leadership support

Commitment to excellence, 48–49, 60

Communication: at Delnor Hospital, 59; at Emmis Communications, 92–94, 99, 105–107; exercise in, 158; at Lockheed Martin, 244; in Mattel's Project Platypus, 277–279; at Praxair, 355–356; at St. Luke's Hospital, 367; at StorageTek, 409, 417; at Windber Medical Center, 426–428, 432. *See also* Internal marketing

Communications industry case studies. *See* Corning; Motorola

Communities of practice, 37, 39

Community service projects, 415

Compaq, 182, 183, 190

Competency models, *xix–xx*; culture linkage to, 110–115; at Emmis Communications, 94, 95, 109–116; for First Consulting Group's leadership development, 127, 128, 130–132; at GE Capital, 164–165; Kouzes and Posner model of, 218; for McDonald's regional managers, 284, 287, 297; for MIT's organizational learning initiative, 315, 325, 326; for Motorola's leadership supply process, 339–340; at St. Luke's Hospital, 382–383, 395–398. *See also* Leadership behavioral profiles

Complementary therapies, 426, 429

Computer hardware industry case studies. *See* Hewlett Packard; StorageTek

Concierge service delivery, 375, 383

Conemaugh Health System, 425. *See also* Windber Medical Center

Conference calls, 106, 107, 137

Conflict, in living systems, 275

Conflict management, at Windber Medical Center, 428

Conflicts of interest, with consolidation, 87

Conger, J. A., 167, 172, 179

Connolly, M., 193

Consolidation, 87. *See also* Acquisition growth

Consultants, *xxviii–xxix*; for Delnor Hospital culture change program, 46–47; for Emmis Communications culture change program, 88; external combined with internal, 184, 185; for Hewlett-Packard's leadership development program, 184; for Intel's Leadership Development Forum, 221; leadership competency frameworks and, 165; for McDonald's leadership development assessment, 286, 287–288; for MIT's organizational learning intervention, 313–314, 315; for Motorola's leadership supply process, 337, 343–344; for Windber Medical Center's transformation initiative, 428

Consulting industry case study. *See* First Consulting Group

Consulting industry realities, 122–123

Consumer products industry case study. *See* Mattel

Continuous improvement: of Corning's innovation process, 41–42; Malcolm Baldrige model of, 198–199; Six Sigma and, 198–199. *See also* Six Sigma

Conversant Solutions, LLC, 182

Cook, H. C., 380

Cooperrider, D. L., 167, 179

Corning Competes, *xxv*, 30

Corning Incorporated: assessment at, 24; background on, 22; best practices for innovation at, 34–36; case study, 20–42; change objectives of, *xviii–xvix*, 23–24; continuous improvement at, 42–43; critical success factors for, 27–28; diagnosis phase at, 22–24; EAGLE2000TM program of, 22, 31–33; evaluation of, 36; five-stage StageGate model of innovation used by, 25–26, 28, 36, 41; as high-tech company, 29–33; implementation at, 29–36; innovation/change-catalyst program of, *xxv*, 20–42; learning machine of, 36–40; lessons learned at, 40–41; on-the-job support at, 33–36; overview of, *xvii*, 21; program design at, 25–29

Cost improvement, at St. Luke's Hospital, 370, 380, 391

Cote, D., 196

Cowan, P., 160

Craig, C., 27, 29, 30, 39, 40

Cray, C., 21

"Creating a Best Place to Work," 381–382

Creation workshops, 272

Creative culture speakers, 269

*Creative Destruction* (Foster and Kaplan), 405

Critical behaviors, for behavior change at Lockheed Martin, 244, 254, 256

Critical success factors: for change initiatives, 444; in Corning's innovation change management initiative, 27–28; in First Consulting Group's leadership development program, 130–132; in Intel's Leadership Development Forum, 230; in McDonald's leadership development program, 293; in Praxair's leadership strategy initiative, 356–357; top-ranking, 451; in Windber Medical Center's transformation, 432

Cross-functional/cross-disciplinary integration: for culture change at StorageTek, 412; for innovation, 25–26, 27–28, 29, 30, 33, 38, 40–41; for knowledge sharing, 38–39, 41; for leadership development program, 128–129; for organizational learning at MIT, 311, 312–313, 314, 319

Crossland, R., 216

Crucial conversations, 244, 247, 253, 256

*Crucial Conversations* (Patterson et al.), 260–261

Culture, organizational: alignment of leadership development with, 166–167; of change, 30; collegial, 128–129; commitment to, xvii–xix, 48–49, 60; competency linkage to, 110–115; country cultures *versus,* 173; employer-of-choice, 79–119; of entitlement, 86, 87; fun in, 371–372; high-performance, definition of, 408–410; leadership role in, 162; of learning, 38–39, 315, 318; of ownership, 52–53, 61; of participation, 185; of resistance, 243–251, 433; of service excellence, 49–52

Culture change programs, *xix*; with acquisition growth, 80–83, 86–87; alignment in, 89–92; approaches in, 88; coaches for, 46–47; communication and promotion of, 92–94, 105–107, 205–207; at Delnor Hospital, 43–78; at Emmis Communications, 79–119; employee training in, 95–96; for firm brand and employee satisfaction, 79–119; for high-performance, 403–422; impact of, on business

performance, 252–253, 259; leaders-as-teachers for, 241, 246–247, 251–252, 254; lessons learned in, 60–61, 99–100; at Lockheed Martin, 239–261; opinion leaders for, 246, 247–252, 254, 257; for service excellence, 43–78; at St. Luke's Hospital, 371–372; at StorageTek, 403–422; stress management for, 54–55, 61; at Windber Medical Center, 423–438

Cummings, R., 83

"Current Reality: The Flood of Information" learning map, *xxv*, 410–411

Curtis, S., 422

Customer contact behaviors assessment, 351, 352, 353

Customer focus conferences, 351, 352, 353, 356, 359, 361–363

Customer scorecards, 354, 358

Customer service improvement: at StorageTek, 416–417. See also Employee satisfaction improvement; Patient satisfaction improvement; Service enhancement

Customer service teams, 49–50, 51, 62

Customers: change initiatives and, 204–205; employees as, 89, 312; understanding, 34, 41

**D**

Damage control, 99

Dannemiller, K., 315, 321

Dashboard of indicators, 58, 73

Data Collection Methods: Pros and Cons, 290, 301–302

Deal, T. E., 166, 179

Debt-leverage issues, 87

Decentralization, 23, 86

Decision-making improvement, 446; with Hewlett-Packard's leadership development program, 190; with Honeywell's Six Sigma initiative, 208–209

Deering, L., 45–46, 47, 49–52, 56, 59–60, 78

Defense industry case study. *See* Lockheed Martin

Defense industry realities, 240, 241–242

Delnor Hospital: accountability building at, 52–53, 61, 64; alignment of behaviors with goals and values at, 59–60, 75–77; background on, 45–46; case study, 43–78; commitment to excellence at, 48–49, 60; communication at, 59; employee satisfaction at, 56–57, 58–59, 61, 72; five pillars of, 47, 58; leadership development at, 53–55, 61, 65–69; lessons learned at, 60–61; measurement at, 50, 53, 57–59, 61, 64, 73–74; nine

Delnor Hospital: (*Continued*)
  principles of, 44–45, 47, 48–60; on-the-job
  support at, *xxvii*; overview of, *xvii*, 44–45;
  reward and recognition at, 50, 55–56, 58, 61;
  St. Luke's Hospital and, 369; top-down
  commitment at, 46–48, 60
Demographic change, 336–337
Deneka, C. "S.", 33, 40
Dennison survey, 418
Diagnosis, business: for Corning, 22–24; for
  Emmis Communications, 86–88; for First
  Consulting Group's leadership development
  program, 122–126; futuring *versus*, 167; for
  GE Capital, 162; for Hewlett-Packard,
  182–183; for MIT, 310–312; for Motorola,
  335–337; phase of, *xxi–xxii*, 440–442; for
  Praxair, 349–350; for St. Luke's Hospital,
  368–369; trends and themes in, 440–442; for
  Windber Medical Center, 425–426, 427
Dialogues: to discuss emotional issues, 199;
  for leadership development, 340, 341; to
  overcome resistance, 244, 247, 248–249,
  253, 256
Differential investment in talent, 341–342
Differentiation strategy, alignment of
  leadership strategy with, 346–364, 412
Diffusion of innovations, 248, 254–255
*Diffusion of Innovations* (Rogers), 260
Discontinuous improvement, 30
Disney Institute, 428
Diversity Channel, 93
Division leadership conferences, 355–356
"Do differentlies": in MIT's organizational
  learning initiative, 316, 332; in Motorola's
  leadership supply system, 343–344
Domalick, K., 50
Dowling, J., 89
Druyan, D., 242
Dual-path results model, 89, 102
Dutterer, L., 401–402
Dynamic Leadership, 181–194. *See also*
  Hewlett-Packard
Dyrek, Deborah, 51

E

E-consultancies, 122–123
E-mail, company, 106, 107
E-vendors, 122–123
EAGLE[2000TM], 22, 30–33
Early adopters, 254, 255
Eckert, R., 263, 277
Economic downturn, *xxviii*, 14, 84, 336,
  404, 420
Edge competency, 339

Education case study. *See* Massachusetts
  Institute of Technology (MIT)
Effective Communication Exercise, 158
Eichinger, R. W., 341, 344
Electronics industry case studies. *See* Agilent
  Technologies, Inc.; Intel; StorageTek
Eleven Commandments, 82, 83, 86, 94, 96, 101
Eliot, G., 448, 451
"Ello," *xxv*, 279
Emmi Awards, 84, 93–94
Emmis Attribute Model, 109
Emmis Communications: accountability at, 87,
  94–97; acquisition growth of, 80–83, 86–87;
  Annual Report, 94, 107; assessment phase at,
  85–86; background on, 81–83; Balanced
  Scorecard of, 95–96, 97, 108; case study,
  79–119; change drivers for, 87; change
  initiative promotion at, 92–94, 105–107;
  change objectives of, *xvii–xviii*, 88; companywide communication at, 92–94, 99, 105–107;
  competency models of, 94, 95, 109–116;
  cultural foundations of, 82, 86, 87; culture and
  change management at, 79–119; diagnosis
  phase at, 86–88; Eleven Commandments of,
  82, 83, 86, 94, 96, 101; employer-of-choice
  qualities of, 83–85, 97–98; employment brand
  of, 83–85; evaluation phase at, *xxvii*, 97–98;
  executive alignment at, 89–91, 99; firm
  brand of, 80, 88, 90, 92, 94; implementation
  phase at, 89–97; innovation at, 90, 96–97;
  leadership brand of, 92, 117; leadership
  development at, 84, 89–92; lessons learned at,
  99–100; on-the-job support at, *xxvi*; overview
  of, *xvii*, 80–81; performance management at,
  87, 94–97, 109–118; program design for,
  88–89; recognition at, 84, 93–94, 118
*Emmis Weekly Update*, 105
Emmissary, 93, 105
Emotional balance, 54–55, 61
Emotional issues: with change initiatives, 199;
  creativity and, 271; in Mattel's Project
  Platypus, 271, 274; venting, at Windber
  Medical Center, 430
Emotional Quotient training, 428
Employee assistance program, 84
Employee benefit and welfare programs, 84
Employee commitment index score, 98
Employee morale, 87
Employee policies, 84
Employee satisfaction improvement: customer
  satisfaction and, 56–57, 61, 368; at Delnor
  Hospital, 45–46, 56–57, 58–59, 61, 72;
  at Emmis Communications, 79–119; at
  St. Luke's Hospital, 368, 372, 381–382, 391;

at StorageTek, 418; at Windber Medical Center, 430–431

Employee stock ownership, 84

Employee Survey Reaction Plan, 85

Employee training, at Emmis Communications, 95–96

Employee Wall of Fame, 381

Employer-of-choice initiatives: at Delnor Hospital, 57; at Emmis Communications, 79–119; at St. Luke's Hospital, 381–382, 391

Enabling others to act, 223–224

Encouraging the heart, 223

*Encouraging the Heart: A Leader's Guide to Rewarding and Recognizing Others* (Kouzes and Posner), 223, 237

Energize competency, 339

Enron, 166

Entitlement culture, 86, 87

Entrepreneurial behavior, internal, 28

Envision competency, 339

Ergonomics, 38

Ernst & Young (E&Y), 427

ESAP (Emmis Sales Assault Plan), 83

Ethics, 340, 446

Evaluation: of Agilent's APEX coaching program, 10–13, 16–17; anecdotal, 251–252; of Corning's innovation change process, 36; of Emmis Communications' change initiative, 97–98; of First Consulting Group's leadership development program, 138–140; of GE Capital's leadership development program, 172–173; of Hewlett-Packard's leadership development program, 187–190, 192; of Intel's Leadership Development Forum, 225–229; of large-scale change efforts, 251, 252; of Lockheed Martin's Workforce Vitality initiative, 251–253, 256–257, 258, 259; of McDonald's leadership development program, 291–295; methods of, *xxvii–xxviii*, 291–292, 449–450; of MIT's organizational learning initiative, 317–319; phase of, *xxvii–xxviii*, 448–450; of Praxair's leadership strategy initiative, 359–360; of St. Luke's Hospital's leadership forums, 375–376, 390–391; trends and themes in, 448–450; of Windber Medical Center's transformation effort, 432–437. *See also* Assessment; Measurement

Evolution scene, 276–278

Excellence, service: commitment to, 48–49, 60; concepts that foster, 367–368

Execute competency, 340

Executive team commitment: at Emmis Communications, 86, 89–91, 99; at First

Consulting Group, 128–129, 134. *See also* Top leadership support

Executive visibility programs, 417

Expectations: alignment of, in Six Sigma case study, 200–202; for Intel's Leadership Development Forum, 217; setting, for Emmis Communications' change initiative, 99–100

Experts, outside, *xxiv. See also* Consultants

Expression, in Mattel's Project Platypus, 269–271

External benchmarking: in First Consulting Group's leadership development program, 127, 128, 130, 133, 138; on hospital quality, 370; in Intel's Leadership Development Forum, 225; for Motorola's leadership supply process, 337, 343

**F**

F-16 Fighter Jets, 240, 241–242, 246, 248

Face-to-Face sessions, 271, 274, 276, 277–278

Facilitators: of First Consulting Group's leadership development program, 134, 136–137; of Hewlett-Packard's leadership development program, 185

Facilities design, 38

Factory-specific leadership development program, 213–238. *See also* Intel

FAST workshops, 89–91, 103–104

FCC regulations, 87

Field beta tests, 99

Finance industry case study. *See* GE Capital

Financial analysis, post-program: of Hewlett-Packard's leadership development program, 189–190; of Motorola's leadership supply system, 342

Finkelstein, S., 162, 179

Fiorina, C., 182, 184

Fireside chats, 169

Firm brand, of Emmis Communications, 80, 88, 90, 92, 94

FIRO-B, 127, 133

First Consulting Group (FCG): assessment at, *xx, xxii*, 126–128, 133, 135; background on, 121–123; barriers analysis of, 125–126; case study, 120–160; change objectives of, *xviii*, 123–124, 141; critical success factors for, 130–132; diagnosis phase at, 122–126; evaluation phase at, 138–140; implementation phase at, *xxiv*, 134–135; Leadership First program of, *xxiv*, 120–160; lessons learned at, 135–137; on-the-job support at, *xxvi–xxvii*, 121; out-of-classroom follow-up at, 137–138; overview of, *xvii*, 121–123; participant selection at, 125–126, 129, 135,

First Consulting Group (FCG): (*Continued*) 142–144; professional compensation and development system (PCADs) of, 126–127, 138, 140; program design phase at, 128–134, 141; risk-reward analysis of, 124–125; situational approach of, 132–134, 135–136, 139–140, 152–159; situational assessment for, 123; 360-degree assessment at, 127, 129, 133, 145–149; top leadership support at, *xx*, 128–129, 134–135

Fisher-Price, 263

Five Disciplines Model of Peter Senge, 314, 315

Five Pillars of Success, 369

Five-Point Star Model, 367; accomplishments by, 391; cost point of, 370, 380, 391; examples of employment of, 377–382; growth point of, 370–371, 374, 391; illustration of, 389; leadership forums on, 371–376; origins of, 369; people point of, 370, 373, 381–382, 391; quality point of, 370, 377–378, 380, 391; service point of, 370, 373–374, 378–380, 391

Five-Practices Leadership Model of Kouzes and Posner, 218, 220, 222

5 L Model of Developmental Coaching, 223

Flat panel glass, 31–33

Flexibility: in coaching program, 4, 6; in cultural change management, 61; in innovation process, 40

Flexible critical mass, 25

*Flight of the Buffalo*, 225, 238

Follow-up: in Agilent's APEX coaching program, 10, 12–13, 14, 16–17; in First Consulting Group's leadership development program, 137–138; in GE Capital's leadership development program, 170, 172–173; in Hewlett-Packard's leadership development program, 184, 186, 191; in McDonald's leadership development program, 291–292; in MIT's organizational learning initiative, 316; in St. Luke's Hospital's leadership development program, 382–383, 393; in StorageTek's culture change program, 418–420. *See also* On-the-job support

*For Your Improvement* (Lombardo & Eichinger), 341

Force-Field Analysis, 290, 303

Ford, R., 251

Fort Hill Company, 189, 194

"Fortune 100 Best Companies to Work For," 97

Foster, R., 405, 422

"4e's + Always 1" leadership standards, 339–340, 341

Freezing, 433

*Friday5s, xxv*, 186, 188, 193, 194

Fulcrum, for behavioral change at Lockheed Martin, 240–241, 244

Fun, 371–372

Fusion process, 31–33

Futuring, 167

**G**

Gandhi, I., 443, 451

Gap assessment, 126, 127, 337, 449

Garrett Turbine Engines, 196

GE: Honeywell and, 200, 202; Six Sigma at, 198

GE Capital: action learning at, *xxiii*, 167; assessment at, *xxii*, 168–170; background on, 162; case study, 161–180; competency model of, *xix*, 164–165; diagnosis at, *xxi*, 162; evaluation at, *xxvii*, 172–173; follow-up at, 170, 172–173; implementation at, 167–172; leadership development conceptual framework of, 166–167; leadership development of, 166–167; leadership development methods of, *xxiii*, 167–172; overview of, *xvii*, 162; program design for, 163–167; results at, 172–173; top leadership support at, *xx*, 163–164

Gift giving, 273–274

Gifun, J., 311, 313–314, 333

Gladwell, M., 260

Global Leadership Profile, 3–4, 5, 8, 15

Global mindset, 296

Global scope: of Agilent's APEX coaching program, 4, 14; of Hewlett-Packard's leadership development program, 185–186

Goal alignment: in Delnor Hospital's service excellence initiative, 60, 75–76; in StorageTek's culture change initiative, 412

Goldsmith, M., 170, 172, 179, 186, 193, 451

*Good to Great*, 374

Graboski, J., 364

Graham, G., 55

Graham, P. K., 313–314, 333

*Great Ideas Contest*, 96

Green Belts, Six Sigma, 208, 211

Greenleaf, R. K., 271, 280

Grenny, J., 260–261

Gross, T., 216, 237

Group management approaches, 136–137, 373

Growth commitment teleconferences, 355

Growth improvement initiative, of health network, 370–371, 374, 391

"Guidelines for the Use of Interventional Cardiology Medications in the Cardiac Catheterization Lab," 380

GuideMe, 186

**H**

Halm, D., 238

Hambrick, D. C., 162, 179

Hamill, S., 273, 280

Hancock, D., 240–249, 250–251

Harris, R., 448

Harrison, R., 361

*Harvard Business Review*, 133, 216

Hayn, M., 400–401

HBO, 82

Health care industry case studies. *See* Delnor Hospital; St. Luke's Hospital and Health Network; Windber Medical Center

Health care industry realities, 368, 425, 427, 428–429, 430, 433

HeartMath Freeze Frame technique, 54–55, 70

HeartMath LLC, 54–55

Hewlett, B., 182

Hewlett-Packard (HP): Agilent Technologies, Inc., and, 2, 3; assessment at, 182–183; case study, 181–194; change objectives of, *xix*; coaching at, 3; Compaq merger of, 182, 183, 190; development methods of, *xxiii*; diagnosis at, *xxii*, 182–183; Dynamic Leadership program of, *xix*, 181–194; evaluation at, 187–190, 192; implementation at, *xxv*, 185–186; on-the-job support at, 184, 186, 191; overview of, *xvii*, 182; program design at, 183–185

*Hidden Connections, The* (Capra), 276

"High-5" award, 381

High-performance culture improvement, 403–422. *See also* StorageTek

High-potential leaders, McDonald's Leadership at McDonald's Program for, 295–296

Hofestede, G., 173, 179

Holistic health care, 431, 433, 437. *See also* Patient-centered care model

Holy Cross Hospital, Chicago, 46

Homework assignments, 133, 134, 159

Honeywell Aerospace: AlliedSignal merger with, 198, 199; assessment at, 203–204; background on, 196; case study, 195–212; change journey of, 198–202; change objectives of, *xix*, 200–202, 207–208; Engines, Systems, and Services division of, 202–210; GE and, 200, 202; implementation at, 210–212; Malcolm Baldrige model at, 198–199; overview of, *xvii*, 196; results at, 211–212; Six Sigma at, *xix*, *xxi*, 195–212; success criteria for, 205–207; top leadership support at, *xxi*, 200–202, 205–208; top talent approach of, 209–210; United Technologies and, 200; vision of, 205–209

Honeywell International, Inc., 195–212

Hospice care center, 426, 435

Hospital case studies. *See* Delnor Hospital; St. Luke's Hospital; Windber Medical Center

Houghton, A. (Alanson), 22

Houghton, A. (Arthur), 22

Houghton, A., Jr., 22

Houghton, A., Sr., 22

Houghton, C., 22

Houghton, J. R., 21, 23, 24, 29, 30, 31, 40, 41

Howard, D., 28

Hrubenek, J., 402

Human resource development methods, *xv–xvi*

Human resource (HR) systems: high-performance culture alignment with, 418–419; leadership development integration with, 291, 343. *See also* Rewards and reward systems

Human Synergistics, 168

**I**

IBM, 404, 405

Ideas into Dollars, 34, 35, 38

Immersion programs, *xxiii*, 136

Immersion scene, 267–269

Implementation: of Agilent's APEX coaching program, 8–10; assessment and, *xxvi*; of Corning's innovation change process, 29–36; elements of, *xxiv–xxvi*; of Emmis Communications' change effort, 89–97, 99–100; of First Consulting Group's leadership development program, 134–135; of GE Capital's leadership development program, 167–172; of Hewlett-Packard's leadership development program, 185–186; of Honeywell's Six Sigma initiative, 210–212; of Intel's Leadership Development Forum, 219–225; of Lockheed Martin's Workforce Vitality initiative, 244–251; of McDonald's leadership development program, 289–290; of MIT's organizational learning initiative, 315–316, 327–328; phase of, *xxiv–xxvi*, 445–448; of Praxair's leadership strategy initiative, 357–358; of St. Luke's Hospital leadership development program, 372–375; of StorageTek's culture change program, 407, 411–418; trends and themes in, 445–448; of Windber Medical Center's transformation, 431–432

*Improvisation for the Theater* (Spolin), 272, 273

Improvisational theater, 269–279

In-house leadership institution, 53–55

Inclusion phase, 269

"Incorporating Family Centered Care in Pediatric Nursing Practice," 378–380

Incremental improvement, 30

*Indianapolis Monthly,* 81

Individual Development Plans, for McDonald's leadership development program, 295

Industrial gas company case study. *See* Praxair

Industrial gas industry realities, 347–348

Industrial Research Institute, 29, 30

Industrial Revolution model of health care, 424, 425, 433

*Industry Week,* Plant of the Year award, 253

Information technology industry case studies. *See* Agilent Technologies, Inc.; Intel; Motorola; StorageTek

Information technology industry realities, 420, 422

Innovation, *xvi;* balancing operational management with, at StorageTek, 405, 419–420; chaos and, 275–276; continuous improvement and, 41–42; Corning's change management initiative for, 20–42; cross-functional integration for, 26, 27–28, 29, 30, 33, 40–41; diffusion of, 248, 254–255; at Emmis Communications, 90, 96–97; five-stage StageGate model of, 25–26, 28, 36, 41; knowledge management and, 36–40; learning and, 36–40; Mattel's Project Platypus process for, 262–281; methods for encouraging, *xxiv–xxv,* 34–36; people and, 263–264; Total Quality Management integration with, 22–24, 27, 29, 36–37

Innovation effectiveness, 33–34, 41–42

Innovation People!, 27–28

Innovation pipeline, 33, 34

Innovation project management, 33, 34, 36

Innovative Learning Methods, 218

Intagliata, J., 91, 95, 308

Intel: assessment at, *xxii,* 220, 225, 226; background on, 215–217; case study, 213–238; coaching at, *xxii, xxiii, xxvi;* evaluation and results at, *xxvii,* 225–229; Fab 12s Organization Development Team (ODT) of, *xxvii,* 213–238; implementation at, 219–225; Leadership Development Forum (LDF) of, *xxvii,* 213–238; leadership development purpose and objectives at, 215–217; lessons learned at, 229–230; on-the-job support at, *xxvi;* overview of, *xvii,* 214–215; program design at, 217–219, 221, 229; session-by-session program example for, 221–225; WOW! Projects at, *xxvii,* 220, 221, 222, 227–228, 231

Intel Manufacturing Excellence Conference (IMEC), 214–215

Interaction: for knowledge sharing, 38, 41; for overcoming resistance, 246–247

Interconnectedness, team, 278–279

Internal marketing: of Agilent's APEX coaching program, 7; of Emmis Communications' change initiative, 92–94, 105–107; of First Consulting Group's leadership development program, 134–135, 139; of Honeywell's Six Sigma implementation, 205–207; of Windber Medical Center's change initiative, 426–428. *See also* Communication

Involvement. *See* Participation

Irritants, customer, 49–50

ISO audits, 417

Iterative design process, 354–357

**J**

Jacobs, N. F., *xx,* 438

Jeopardy, 374

Job protection, 87

Joint Commission of Accredited Healthcare Organizations (JCAHO), 378

Joint Strike Fighter (JSF) contract competition, 240, 242, 246, 252, 253–254

Joint ventures, in consulting industry, 122–123

Joyce Murtha Breast Care Center, 435

**K**

Kaplan, S., 405, 422

Keilty, Goldsmith & Company, 3, 18. *See also* Alliance for Strategic Leadership Coaching & Consulting (A4SL C&C)

Kennedy, A. A., 166, 179

Kennedy, R. F., 450, 451

*Killer Angels* (Shaara), 168

Kirk, B., 34

Kirkpatrick, D. L., 187, 193

Kittoe, M., 50, 58

Klementik, D., 437

Klepeiss, D., 401

Knowledge re-use quotient, 38, 41

Knowledge sharing and management: in Corning's innovation process, 36–40, 41; in Delnor Hospital's leadership development program, 54; at Emmis Communications, 96–97; at MIT, 319

Knowledge speakers, 267

Knowledge (technology) warehouse, 38

Kocourek, P. F., 361

Kotter, J., 215, 216

Kouzes, J., 216, 217, 218, 220, 222, 237

Kozlowski, T., 28
Kraft Foods, 263
Kuehler, D., 265, 266, 281
Kuplen, C., 401

**L**
Laggards, 254
Lagging indicators, 359
Lane, J. M., 344–345
Language, common: for culture change management, 99; for innovation, 25, 33; in Mattel's Project Platypus, 269–271
Lao Tzu, 320, 321
Leaders: informal, as influencers, 247–249; as teachers, 241, 246–247, 251–252, 254
Leadership: management *versus*, 215–216; role of, in culture modeling and reinforcement, 162
*Leadership, an Art of Possibility*, 224, 238
Leadership Action Plan (LAP), 220, 232
Leadership Autobiography, 216, 220, 221, 233–236
Leadership behavioral profiles, *xxii*; of Agilent, 3–4, 5, 15; of First Consulting Group, 127, 128, 130–132. *See also* Competency models
Leadership brand: of Emmis Communications, 92, 117; of StorageTek, 414–415
Leadership Breakthrough Award (LBA), 220, 225
Leadership Commitment Day, 355, 358
Leadership cultural assessment tool, 351
Leadership development, *xvi*; Agilent's APEX coaching case study of, 1–19; consulting firms and, *xxviii–xxix*; content of, 446, 447; at Delnor Hospital, 50, 53–55, 56, 61, 65–69; design elements for, 132–134; at Emmis Communications, 84, 89–92; at factory level, 213–238; First Consulting Group case study of, 120–160; GE Capital case study of, 161–180; global, 4, 14, 173, 185–186; Hewlett-Packard case study of, 181–194; integration of, with HR systems, 291, 343; Intel case study of, 213–238; leaders' participation in design of, 128–129, 134, 162, 163–165; at McDonald's, 282–308; methods of, 446–447; at Motorola, 334–345; pre-work for, 167–168, 174, 286; return on investment on, *xxviii*, 190, 191, 341–342; sample exercises for, 152–158; self-development approach to, 215–216, 217–218, 229; Six Sigma and, 202–210; at St. Luke's Hospital, 365–402; at StorageTek, 414–415; strategic objectives and, *xviii*; tools for, 290

Leadership Development Forum (LDF), 213–238. *See also* Intel
*Leadership Engine, The* (Cohen and Tichy), 260
Leadership First, 120–160. *See also* First Consulting Group (FCG)
Leadership forums, St. Luke's Hospital, 367, 371–377, 382–383. *See also* St. Luke's Hospital
Leadership Impact (LI) Survey, *xxii*, 168, 169
Leadership Philosophy Map, 351, 352, 353, 361, 362
Leadership Practices Inventory (LPI), 221, 222, 237
Leadership standards: Motorola's, 337, 339–340, 341; St. Luke's Hospital's, 376
Leadership strategy alignment initiative, 346–364. *See also* Praxair Distribution Inc. (PDI)
Leadership strategy design tool, 361
Leadership supply process: leadership demand and, 335–336; Motorola's development of, 334–345
Leading for Results workshops, 91–92, 99, 416–417
Leading indicators, 359
Lean Experts, Six Sigma, 199, 210, 211
Lean Masters, Six Sigma, 210
Learning: in Corning's innovation process, 36–40; leadership and, 216; linking, to performance, 319–320; organizational, 309–321, 415; team, 325
Learning challenges, exposure to, 285, 286
Learning coaches, 39–40, 42
Learning Company, 263
Learning contracts, 134, 138, 139, 150–151
Learning culture, enhancing, in Corning case study, 38–39
Learning groups, 219
Learning journals, 184, 289, 290, 316
Learning machine, 36–40
Learning maps, *xxv*, 410–411, 412, 415
Learning organization, self-perpetuating: development of, at MIT, 309–321; training methodologies and tools for, 316
Learning partners, 289, 293–294
Lehigh Valley, Pennsylvania, 367
Leibig, E., 25
Leisure industry case study. *See* McDonald's Corporation
Lessons learned: in Agilent's APEX coaching program, 13–14; in Corning's innovation change initiative, 40–41; in Delnor Hospital's service excellence program, 60–61; in Emmis

Lessons learned: (*Continued*)
Communications' change initiative, 99–100; in First Consulting Group's leadership development program, 135–137; in Intel's Leadership Development Forum, 229–230; in Lockheed Martin Workforce Vitality initiative, 253–254; in Mattel's Project Platypus, 269, 271, 273, 274, 278; in McDonald's leadership development program, 293–294; in MIT's organizational learning initiative, 319–320; in Motorola's leadership supply process, 342–343; in Praxair's leadership strategy change initiative, 360–361; in StorageTek's culture change initiative, 411, 417–418, 421; in Windber Medical Center's transformation initiative, 437

Leverage, for behavior change at Lockheed Martin, 241, 254

Linkage OD Summit, 315

Livermore, C. A., 45, 46, 47–48, 49, 52, 53, 54, 56, 57, 59, 60, 78

Living stage, 266–267

Living systems, 264–265, 267; chaos and cohesion in, 274–276; conflict in, 275; inclusion phase of, 269

Lockheed Martin Tactical Aircraft Systems (LMTAS): background on, 241–242; best practices of, 253–254; case study, 239–261; change objectives of, *xviii*, 240–242; evaluation at, *xxvii*, 251–253, 256–257, 258, 259; implementation at, *xxiv*, 244–251; leaders-as-teachers at, 241, 246–247, 251–252, 254; leadership support at, 240–241, 245–247; opinion leaders at, 246, 247–252, 254, 257; overview of, *xvii*, 240–241; resistance at, 243–251; Six Sigma at, 243, 244, 249; Workforce Vitality initiative of, 245–259

Loehr, J., 383

Lombardo, M. M., 341, 344

Loranger, S., 203

*Los Angeles Magazine*, 81

Lucas, L., 310–311

Lucent Technology, 182

Lynch, R., 94

**M**

MacAvoy, T., 21, 22, 23, 24, 25, 26, 27, 40

Magazine division, of Emmis Communications, 81

Malicious compliance, 91

Management, leadership *versus*, 215–216

Management performance evaluation, at St. Luke's Hospital, 383, 394–399

Management practices redesign, 354–355, 358–359

Managerial style profile, 127

Managing Acquisitions and Mergers Exercise, 157

Managing Through People, 215

Managing-up, 59

Manufacturing function integration, in innovation process, 26, 27–28, 29, 31–33, 38, 39, 40, 41

Manufacturing industry case studies. *See* Honeywell Aerospace; Intel

Marketing function integration, in innovation process, 26, 27–28, 33, 40, 41

Martin, P. J., 406, 410, 420

Masa, C., 56

Massachusetts Institute of Technology (MIT), Department of Facilities: assessment at, 310–312; behavioral, cultural, and perceptual change at, *xix*; case study, 309–321; change-catalyst program of, *xxv*, 309–321; change objectives of, *xviii*, 310–312, 314; competency models of, 315, 325, 326; evaluation and results at, 317–318; lessons learned at, 319–320; on-the-job support at, *xxvi–xxvii*, 316; organizational learning models of, *xx*, 314; overview of, *xvii*, 310–312; personal mastery module of, 314, 316, 318, 327–328, 330–332; program design at, 314–315; strategic plan of, 311–312, 322–323; top management support at, 312–313; training methodologies and tools of, 316

Masters, Six Sigma, 204, 208, 210, 211

MatrixWorks Inc., 279

Mattel, Project Platypus, *xix*, *xxiv–xxv*, *xxvi*, 262–281; alignment scenes in, 271–276; background and overview of, *xvii*, 263, 268; case study, 262–281; communication in, 277–279; elements of, 266–267, 268; evolution scene in, 276–278; expression scene in, 269–271; Face-to-Face sessions in, 271, 274, 276, 277–278; immersion scene in, 267–269; on-the-job support at, *xxvi*; philosophical underpinnings of, 264–265; process of, 267–279; results and impact of, 279–280; theater model of, 266–279; the wall in, 267, 270, 272, 273, 275, 276, 278

McClelland, M., 57

McDonald's Corporation: action learning at, *xxii*, 285, 289–290, 292–295; assessment at, *xxii*, 285–288, 294; Business Improvement Recommendation Process of, 306–307; case study, 282–308; change objectives of, *xviii*; coaching at, *xxiii*, 287–288; competency model of, 284, 287, 297; critical success factors at, 293; developmental objectives of, 285, 287, 288, 295; developmental tools of, 290; evaluation at, *xxvii*, 291–295; follow-up at, *xxvi*, 291; implementation at, 289–299; Leadership at McDonald's Program (LAMP) of, 295–296; Leadership Development Experience of, 283–295, 296–307; leadership development program impact at, 292–293, 294–295; lessons learned at, 293–294; overview of, *xvii*, 283–285; program design at, 288; regional manager (RM) development at, 282–307

McKenna, M. G., 361

McKinsey & Company, 336, 337, 339, 344, 408, 422

McLean, G. N., 451

McMillan, R., 260

Measurement: at Delnor Hospital, 50, 53, 57–59, 61, 64, 73–74; at Emmis Communications, 94–95, 108–118; of leadership effectiveness, 340–341; of leadership strategy change initiative, 359–360; at McDonald's, 291–292; of patient satisfaction, 50, 53, 58, 64, 74; at StorageTek, 409; at Windber Medical Center, 435–436. *See also* Assessment; Evaluation

Media endorsements, for change, 429, 432

Media industry case study. *See* Emmis Communications

Media industry realities, 87

Medicaid, 427

Medicare, 427

Melohn, T., 223, 237

Mental models, 325

Mentoring, in First Consulting Group's leadership development program, 130, 134, 137

Meredith, M., 279, 280

Merit compensation program, 94

Michaels, E., 336

Micro-management, 278

Military model, 428–430

Miller, J., 21, 33, 40

Mission statement: for Delnor Hospital, 48; for St. Luke's Hospital, 384

Modeling the way, 225

*Modern Healthcare*, 437

*Modern Maturity*, 437

Momentum, 357

Monthly excellence awards, 56

Morning meetings, 37

Motorola: assessment at, *xxii*, 340–341; case study, 334–345; change objectives of, *xviii*, 335–337; diagnosis at, 335–337; financial results at, 342; "4e's + Always 1" leadership standards of, 337, 339–340, 341; leadership supply process of, 334–345; lessons learned at, 342–343; on-the-job support at, *xxvi–xxvii*; overview of, *xvii*, 335; performance management at, *xix–xx*, *xxvi–xxvii*, 338, 339–342; Six Sigma at, 198; talent demand and supply issues of, 335–337

Mountaineering theme, for coaching program, 5–6

"Multidisciplinary Approach to Decreasing Central/Umbilical Line Associated Bacteremia in the NICU," 377–378

Murphy, 58

Myers Briggs Type Indicator (MBTI), *xxii*, 168, 169–170, 373, 374–375

**N**

National Medal of Technology, 22

Needs assessment, 440–441. *See also* Assessment; Diagnosis, business

Neil, R., 364

Nelson, J. S., 119

Ninth House Network Innovation, 222, 237

Nolet, D., 31

*Nordstrom Way* (Spector), 93

North American Tool and Die, 223

NorthStar Group, 91, 308

Nosocomial infection prevention, 377–378, 436

Novatnack, E., 377

NPR Radio, 273

**O**

Objectives, strategic: aligning behavior standards to, 59–60, 201–202; aligning leadership strategy with, 346–364; commitment to, *xvii–xix*; consulting firms' objectives *versus*, *xxix*; of Corning change initiative, 23–24; of Emmis Communications' change initiative, 88; of First Consulting Group's leadership development program, 123–124, 141; of Honeywell's Six Sigma program, 200–202, 207–208; of Lockheed Martin, 240–242; of MIT, 310–312, 314; of Motorola, 335–337; of Praxair, 349, 350; of St. Luke's Hospital, 384–385; of StorageTek's culture change, 406–411; of Windber Medical Center's transformation, 427–428

OD Source Consulting, Inc., 119

O'Leary, R. A., 42

On-the-job learning, at McDonald's, 295

On-the-job support: in Corning's innovation change management process, 33–36; in First Consulting Group's leadership

On-the-job support: (*Continued*)
development program, 137–138; in Hewlett-Packard's leadership development program, 186, 191; phase of, *xxvi–xxvii*; in Praxair's leadership strategy initiative, 358–359. *See also* Follow-up

Opinion leaders, 246, 247–252, 254, 257

Oral histories, 38

Organization Analysis (OA) model, 170–171

Organization change models, *xix–xx*; for aligning leadership strategy with business strategy, at Praxair, 346–364; customization of, 61; for Delnor Hospital, 47–48, 61; for MIT's organizational learning initiative, 315, 325–326

Organization development (OD) and change: common elements of, *xvii–xix*; consulting firms and, *xxviii–xxix*; investment in, *xxviii*; methods of, *xv–xvi*; trends and themes in, 439–451

Organization development–human resources development (OD–HRD) initiative, *xxvi*

Organizational capabilities development, 409, 415–417

Organizational learning: capabilities for, 325; competency model for, 326; at Corning, 36–40; MIT's initiative for, 309–321; at StorageTek, 415

Orientation, to Intel's Leadership Development Forum, 221–222

Osborne, J., 203, 204, 205, 206, 210, 212

Outstanding Rural Health Leader award, 437

Ownership: environment of, 52–53, 61; of leadership development program, 134

P

Packaged gas industry, 347–349. *See also* Praxair

Packard, D., 182

Parker, G., 58

Participant reactions: to HP's leadership development program, 187, 189, 193; to Intel's leadership development program, 226–227, 228–229; to MIT's organizational learning initiative, 317–318; program improvement based on, 365–376, 390; to St. Luke's Hospital's leadership forums, 375–376, 390

Participant selection: for Agilent's APEX coaching program, *xxiii*, 6, 8–9, 14; for First Consulting Group's leadership development program, 125–126, 129, 135, 142–144; for Intel's Leadership Development Forum, 218; for Mattel's Project Platypus, 266

Participation: in First Consulting Group's leadership development design, 128–129, 134; in GE Capital's leadership development design, 162, 163–165; in Hewlett-Packard's leadership development design, 185; importance of, 450–451; in MIT's renewal planning, 311; in Motorola's leadership supply process, 337, 342; in organizational change, 350, 445; in Praxair's assessment and design phases, 350, 356; requirements for, in Intel's Leadership Development Forum, 217; in St. Luke's Hospital leadership forum design, 375–376, 390

Partners, in Mattel's Project Platypus, 276–277

Partnerships, in consulting industry, 122–123

Past history, leveraging, *xxiii*, 411, 451; in Corning's innovation change initiative, 24, 25, 28, 38, 40, 41

Patient call-backs, 51–52

Patient-centered care model, 423–438; elements of, 427, 431; patient empowerment and, 425, 431; physician and staff resistance to, 426–427, 428–430, 432–433. *See also* Windber Medical Center

Patient satisfaction improvement: culture based on, 49–52; customer service teams for, 49–50, 51, 62; at Delnor Hospital, 43–78; employee behavior standards for, 59–60; employee satisfaction and, 56–57, 61, 368; measurement of, 50, 53, 58, 64, 74; at St. Luke's Hospital, 370, 373–374, 376, 378–380, 383, 387, 391

Patterson, K., 260

Peak performance analysis, 167, 168, 169–170, 175

Pearce, T., 216

Peer networks, 296

Perceptual change, *xix*; in MIT's organizational learning initiative, 318

"Perfect Enough" principle, 184

Performance ethic, 408

Performance management, *xvi*; at Emmis Communications, 87, 94–97, 109–118; learning linkage to, 319–320; at Motorola, 338, 339–342; on-the-job support and, *xxvi–xxvii*; at Praxair, 355, 358; at St. Luke's Hospital, 383, 394–399; at StorageTek, 412–414

Performance scorecard, for Delnor Hospital, 64

Personal engagement, 244

Personal mastery, 314, 316, 318, 325, 327–328; exercises for, 318, 327, 328, 330–332

Perspectives Conference, 358

Peters, L., 261

Peters, T., 216, 222

Pfeiffer, J., 445

Physician culture change, 426–427, 428–430, 432–433

Physician satisfaction, 50, 58–59

Picnics, 372

Pinto, J., 381

Planetree hospital model, 424–437. *See also* Patient-centered care model; Windber Medical Center

Planning dialogue, 340

Playbook, 354–355

Politics, internal, 100

Portfolio management, 28, 33, 34

Posner, B., 216, 217, 218, 220, 222, 237

Post-course management system, *xxv*

Postmodernism, *xxiv–xxv*, 264, 266

*Power of Full Engagement, The*, 374

Practices, current, leveraging, *xxiii*, 411, 451

Praxair Distribution Inc. (PDI): acquisition stage of, 347–348; alignment of leadership strategy with business strategy at, 346–364; assessment at, *xxii, xxvi*, 350–353; case study, 346–364; critical success factors for, 356–357; diagnosis of, 349–350; differentiation strategy of, 349, 350, 352; evaluation at, 359–360; implementation at, *xxvi*, 357–358; iterative design process of, 354–357; lessons learned at, 360–361; on-the-job support at, *xxvi–xxvii*, 358–359; organizational change initiative of, 346–364; overview of, *xvii*, 347–349; rollup strategy of, 348–350; strategic objectives of, 349, 350; top leadership support at, *xx–xxi*, 355–356

Pre-work, leadership development, 168–169, 174, 286

Presbyterian Medical Center, 375

Presentation tools, 290

Press Ganey, 58, 369, 370, 373, 378, 379, 380, 381, 382, 392

Price, M. Q., 261

Process engineering, 38, 39

Product costing, 277

Product life cycles, 182

Product testing, 277

Program design: of Agilent's APEX coaching program, 4–7; of Corning's innovation change process, 25–29; elements of, *xxii–xxiv*, 141; of Emmis Communications' change effort, 88–89; of First Consulting Group's leadership development program, 128–134, 141; of GE Capital's leadership development program, 163–167; of Hewlett-Packard's leadership development program, 183–185; of Intel's Leadership Development Forum, 217–219, 221, 229; iterative, 354–357;

just-in-time, 218; of McDonald's leadership development program, 288; of MIT's organizational learning initiative, 314–315; phase of, *xxii–xxiv*, 445–448; of Praxair's change initiative, 354–357; redesign of, 221, 229, 230, 375–376, 390; of St. Luke's Hospital leadership development program, 369–372; team for, 128; trends and themes in, 445–448; of Windber Medical Center's patient-centered care initiative, 431

Project Bravo awards, 381

Project Platypus. *See* Mattel, Project Platypus

Project Review Checklist, 290, 304–305

Project tools, action learning, 290, 301–305

Property swapping, 87

Prototype building, 277

Purpose, organizational: connection to, *xxiii–xxiv*; innovation program connection to, 40

Pushback, 443

**Q**

Quality improvement: at St. Luke's Hospital, 370, 377–378, 380, 391; at StorageTek, 416–417. *See also* Employee satisfaction improvement; Patient satisfaction improvement; Total Quality Management

**R**

Radio corporation. *See* Emmis Communications

Radio Ink, 82

Rapid prototyping, 184, 222

Rardin, R., 364

Rate-change enablers, 36–37

Readings, for leadership development program, 133

"Real work," *xv–xvi*

Recognition: at Delnor Hospital, 50, 55–56, 58, 61; at Emmis Communications, 84, 93–94, 118; for service excellence, 50, 58; at Windber Medical Center, 431, 432. *See also* Awards

Recruitment: at Motorola, 337; at StorageTek, 415

Reengineering, business process, 30, 38, 39

Refreezing, 433

Regional manager (RM) development, 282–307

Regional Manager Success Profile, 284, 285–288, 290, 294, 297

"Reinvent HP" campaign, *xxii*, 182–183, 185

Relationship building: in First Consulting Group's leadership development program, 134; in Mattel's Project Platypus, 271,

Relationship building: (*Continued*) 277–278; in McDonald's leadership development program, 285, 296

Remedial coaching, 14

Research and development (R&D) change initiative, 20–42. *See also* Corning

Research reviews, 37

Resistance: behaviors of, 244; at Emmis Communications, 91; emotional basis of, 199; involvement and, 350, 450–451; at Lockheed Martin, 243–251; model of, 443; to patient-centered care, at Windber Medical Center, 426–427, 428–430, 432–433; reducing, 443–445; to Six Sigma, 197, 199, 243, 244; trends and themes in, 442–443; types of, 443

Resource Associates, 133

Restaurant case study. *See* McDonald's Corporation

Restructuring, 30

Results-Based Leadership (RBL), 81, 89–91, 93, 94–95; at Emmis Communications, 81, 89–91, 93, 94–95, 103–104; FAST workshops of, 89–91, 103–104; Leading for Results workshops of, 91–92, 99; at StorageTek, 408, 409, 410, 412–414, 418–420, 422

*Results-Based Leadership* (Ulrich, Zenger, and Smallwood), 90, 314, 408, 409, 410, 422

Results guarantee, of coaching firm, 6–7

Return on investment (ROI): of Hewlett-Packard's leadership development program, 190, 191; for leadership development and organization change initiatives, *xxviii*, 449

Revolving door theory, 433

Rewards and reward systems: at Delnor Hospital, 50, 55–56, 58, 61; at Emmis Communications, 94, 117–118; at First Consulting Group, 125; for high performance, 418–419; linkage of, to behavior change, 245; linkage of, to leadership performance, 341–342; at Lockheed Martin, 245, 249; at Motorola, 338, 341–342; for patient care at Windber Medical Center, 430, 432; for service excellence, 50, 58; at StorageTek, 418–419; at Windber Medical Center, 432

Rex, S., 402

Rhoads, R., 31

Rhythmic Top, 40, 81

Rianoshek, R., 193

Riesbeck, J., 26

Risk management, 33

Risk-reward analysis, 124–125

Roadmapping, 28, 33, 34

Rock climbing, 222–223

Rogers, E., 248, 254–255, 260

Rollup strategy, 348–350

RootLearning, 410, 412, 415

Ross, I., 263, 265, 266, 280–281

Rothwell, W. J., 451

Rounding, hospital, 51

Rudolph, S., 238

S

Sabol, D., 402

St. Luke's Hospital and Health Network: assessment at, 373, 374–375; background on, 366–368; case study, 365–402; competency model of, 382–383, 395–398; core concepts of, *xxiii–xxiv*, 367–368; core principles of, 385; core values of (PCRAFT), 367, 381, 387; diagnosis of, 368–369; evaluation at, 375–376, 390, 391; Five-Point Star model of, 367, 369–376, 377–382, 389, 391; implementation at, 372–375; leadership development program of, 365–402; leadership forums of, 367, 371–376, 382–383; leadership linkage committee of, 382–383, 393; leadership steering committee of, 369, 372, 373, 375, 376, 382, 388; management performance evaluation at, 383, 394–399; management philosophy for, 386–387; organizational results at, 376–377, 391; overview of, *xvii*, 366; program design at, 369–372; strategic plan of, 367, 384–385; top leadership support at, 375

Sartre, J.-P., 266, 280

*Sartre on Theater*, 266

Schwartz, T., 383

Schweon, S., 377

Scripting, nurse, 50–51, 63

Seatback initiatives, 196–197

Seattle Mariners, 82

Selection, at Motorola, 337

Self-assessment: in First Consulting Group's leadership development program, 127, 133; in Intel's Leadership Development Forum, 220, 225, 226; in McDonald's leadership development program, 286; in Praxair's leadership strategy initiative, 355

Self-development approach, to leadership development, 215–216, 217–218, 229

Self-discovery speakers, 267–268

Self-nomination, for leadership development program, 129, 135, 143–144

Self-reflection: in GE Capital's leadership development program, 166–167, 168; in Intel's Leadership Development Forum, 216, 220, 224, 229, 233–236

SEMATECH, 225, 227, 238

Senge, P., *xx*, 167, 179, 314, 315, 321, 325

Senior center, 434

Sense of urgency. *See* Urgency, sense of

September 11, 2001, 83, 84

*Servant Leadership* (Greenleaf), 271

Service enhancement, *xvi*; commitment to excellence for, 48–49, 60, 367–368; core concepts for, *xxiii–xxiv*, 367–368; cultural change for, 49–52; at Delnor Hospital, 43–78; at Emmis Communications, 89, 90; at St. Luke's Hospital, 370, 373–374, 376, 378–380, 383, 391; at StorageTek, 416–417. *See also* Patient satisfaction improvement

Service recovery, 52

Sever, E., 29

Severance package, 84

Shaara, M., 168

Shalala, D., 437

Shared memory, 25, 28, 38

Shared mindset, 415, 417

Shared vision, 325

Sharkey, L., 179–180

Shingo Prize, 253

Short-cycle learning machine, 37

Shortcuts, in change model, 99–100

Silva, R. A., 18

Simulation exercise, 224

Sirianni, V., 310–311, 312–313, 314

Situational approach, *xxiv*; in First Consulting Group's leadership development program to leadership development, 132–134, 135–136, 139–140, 152–159; in GE Capital's leadership development program, 169, 170–171; in Intel's Leadership Development Forum, 219

Situational assessment, of First Consulting Group, 123

Six Sigma: at Honeywell, *xix, xxi*, 195–212; at Lockheed Martin, 243, 244, 249; modification of, to fit business objectives, 201–202; Organization Analysis (OA) model and, 170; results of, 211–212; revitalization of, for leadership improvement, 202–210; at StorageTek, 417; success criteria for, 205–207; top firms with, 198; top talent and, 209–210; whole-scale implementation of, 210–212

Slow rolling, 243

Small, D., 308

Smallwood, N., 89–90, 93, 321, 408, 409, 410, 422

SMART goal development, 95

Smith, H., 46

Smith, J., 238

Smulyan, J., 80, 81, 82–83, 84, 87, 89, 91, 93, 97, 98, 106

Spector, R., 93

Speed, as StorageTek organizational capability, 415

Sperduto & Associates, 57, 72

Sperry Flight Systems, 196

Spolin, V., 272, 273, 280

StageGate model of innovation, 25–26, 28, 36, 41

Stakeholders, of change initiatives, 202

Star Model. *See* Five-Point Star Model

Star Trek, 373

Starr, A., 400

Step-by-Step System to Organization and Human Resources Development, *xvi, xxi–xxviii*

Step change, 30

Stewards and stewardship, 276, 278

Stock compensation program, 85, 94

Stokes, H., 361

StorageTek: assessment at, *xxii*, 412–413; attain-and-sustain-improvement phase at, 407, 418–420; background on, 404–406; case study, 403–422; challenge definition phase at, 406–411; change objectives of, *xix*, 406–411; core purpose and values of, 405; culture change program of, *xxv*, 403–422; culture of, 405–406; current practices usage of, *xxiii*, 411; financial results at, 420; goal definition at, 408–410, 411; IBM and, 404, 405; lessons learned at, 411, 417–418; overview of, *xvii*, 404; Six Sigma at, 417; transformation phases of, 406–407; transformation timeline of, 419; work-through-change phase at, 407, 411–418

Stories and storytelling, *xxiii, xxiv*, 28, 38, 167; elements of, 269–270; in Mattel's Project Platypus, 269–279

Storyboards, 221

Strange attractors, 274–276

Strategic plan: for Delnor Hospital, 48; for MIT, 311–312, 322–323; for St. Luke's Hospital, 367, 384–385

"Strategy: Navigating to New Horizons" learning map, 412, 415

Stress management, 54–55, 61

Studer, Q., 46–47, 48, 49, 53, 55, 369

Studer Group, 46, 53

Succession planning, at StorageTek, 414–415. *See also* Leadership development; Leadership supply process

Sullivan, R., 451

Summary dialogue, 341

Supervisory skill-training program, 357

Supplier feedback, 359–360

Surveys, coaching, 8, 10, 16–17

Surveys, evaluation, *xxvii–xxviii*; of Agilent's APEX coaching program, 10, 16–17; of Lockheed Martin's Workforce Vitality initiative, 252–253, 253, 255–256, 258, 259

Surveys, satisfaction: of employee satisfaction, 85, 97–98, 418; of patient and physician satisfaction, 58, 73, 74

Switzler, A., 260

System theory and approach, *xxiv–xxv*; in Mattel's Project Platypus, 264–265; in MIT's organizational learning initiative, 315, 324; in Praxair's leadership strategy initiative, 358–359

Systems thinking, 167, 325

**T**

Talent: demand side of, 335–336; differential investment in, 341–342; management of, 338, 343; Motorola's leadership supply process for, 334–345; as StorageTek organizational capability, 415; supply side of, 336–337; war for, 336, 337, 408

Talent Web, 337

*Tao Te Ching*, 320

Teachable points of view, 163, 169

Teachers, leaders as, 241, 246–247, 251–252, 254

Team Charter, 290, 298

Team Metrics, 290, 299

Team Process Check, 290, 300

Technical tutorials, 37

Technology function, cross-functional integration with, 25–26, 27–28, 29, 30, 33, 40–41

Technology sector realities, 182–183, 335

Technology solutions provider. *See* First Consulting Group

Telecommunications industry case study. *See* Motorola

Telecommunications industry realities, 31, 335, 336

Television corporation. *See* Emmis Communications

Testimonials, for Intel's Leadership Development Forum, 226–227, 228–229

*Texas Monthly*, 81

Theater model, 266–279

Think tank, 96

Thoe, G., 83

Thompson, J., 266–267

Thoreau, H. D., 440, 451

3D Learning, LLC, 238

360-degree feedback: for assessment, *xxii*; in coaching, 8, 9, 10, 16–17; for evaluation,

*xxvii*; in First Consulting Group's leadership development program, 127, 129, 133, 138, 145–149; follow-up, 8, 10, 16–17, 138, 172; in GE Capital's leadership development program, 168–169, 172; at Intel, 215; sample report form for, 145–149; in StorageTek's culture change program, 413

Thunderbird International Consortia, 296

Tichy, N., 163, 169, 179, 260

Time management, of leadership development program, 136

Time to market, 28, 29

*Tipping Point, The* (Gladwell), 260

Tom Peters Company, 222, 237

Top leadership support, *xx–xxi*, 445; for Agilent's APEX coaching program, 14; alignment of, with management expectations, 200–202; at Corning, 40, 41; at Delnor Hospital, 46–48, 60; at Emmis Communications, 86, 89–92, 99; at First Consulting Group, 128–129, 134–135; at GE Capital, 163–164; at Hewlett-Packard, 185; at Honeywell, 200–202, 205–208; at Intel, 230; at Lockheed Martin, 240–241, 245–247, 254; at MIT, 312–313; at Motorola, 342, 343; at Praxair, 355–356; for reducing resistance, 443–444; at St. Luke's Hospital, 375; ways of showing, 444; at Windber Medical Center, 426. *See also* Executive team commitment

TOPICS, 356

Total Quality Management (TQM): integration of innovation change initiative with, 23–24, 27, 29, 36–37; Six Sigma and, 197

Town meetings, 199, 355

Toy company case study. *See* Mattel

*Toy Report and Toy Wishes*, 279

Training programs: in Corning's innovation change initiative, 27–28; in Emmis Communications culture change initiative, 95–96; in Windber Medical Center's change initiative, 428. *See also* Leadership development

Transition assistance process, 338–339

Travel restrictions, 9, 123, 185

Trust and trust building: in Intel's Leadership Development Forum, 222–223; with Lockheed Martin's opinion leaders, 250–251; in Mattel's Project Platypus, 271, 274, 277–278; in StorageTek culture change program, 409

Trustee of the Year award, 437

Turnover, employee satisfaction improvement and, 57, 97

Type Directory, 375

**U**

Ulrich, D., 314, 321, 408, 409, 410, 422, 451
Underhill, B., 3, 18
Unfreezing, 433
*Unified Team Video, The*, 224, 237
U.K. Royal Air Force and Navy, 242
U.S. Air Force, 242
U.S. Congress, 427
U.S. Department of Defense, 240
U.S. Marines, 242
U.S. Navy, 242
*U.S. News and World Report*, 391
U.S. Veterans Administration, 373
United Technologies, 199–200
University of Pennsylvania Health System, 375
Urgency, sense of, *xxi, xxv*; at Lockheed
    Martin, 244; for Six Sigma implementation at
    Honeywell, 198; at StorageTek, 410–411
User-friendliness, of coaching program, 4

**V**

Value creation, change initiatives and, 204–205
Values: aligning assessment and design phases
    with, 351; aligning behavior standards with,
    59–60; aligning leadership behavior change
    with, 166–167, 173, 354–355; of Delnor
    Hospital, 48, 59–60; of Emmis Communica-
    tions, 82, 101; at GE Capital, 166; of Praxair,
    350, 351; of St. Luke's Hospital, 367, 381,
    387; of StorageTek, 405
Van Eenwyk, J. R., 274, 280
Venture Up, 222–223, 237
Video case study, 223
Vision: for Honeywell's Six Sigma program,
    205–209; in Mattel's Project Platypus, 267
Vision statement: for Delnor Hospital, 48; for
    Honeywell Aerospace, 205; for St. Luke's
    Hospital, 384
Visionary exercises, *xxv*; in Intel's Leadership
    Development Forum, 221–222; in MIT's orga-
    nizational learning initiative, 315–316,
    330–332
VitalSmarts, Inc., 260
Vortex Simulation, 224, 238
Vulnerability, 271

**W**

Walker, K., 18–19
*Wall Street Journal*, 21

*War for Talent, The* (McKinsey), 336, 337,
    408, 422
Web-based systems: follow-through manage-
    ment, 186, 191; leadership supply, 337,
    340–341, 343, 344; multirater assessment,
    340–341; performance management system,
    412–413
Weigand, B., 401
Welch, J., 200
Wellness center, 426
WENS-FM, 81, 97
Westwood International, 212
"What If?" stories, 270
Wheatley, M., 263–264
White water, 240
Wick, C., 194
Williams, M., 93
Willyerd, K., 261
Windber Medical Center: assessment at,
    428–431; behavioral, cultural, and perceptual
    change at, *xix*; case study, 423–438; change
    objectives of, 427–428; core concepts of, *xxiv*,
    431; critical success factors for, 432; diagno-
    sis of, 425–426, 427; evaluation and results
    at, 432–437; grant politics of, 434; imple-
    mentation at, 431–432; lessons learned at,
    437; organizational challenges of, 426–428;
    overview of, *xvii*, 424, 425; Planetree,
    patient-centered care model at, 423–438;
    Planetree teams at, 432; program design at,
    431; top leadership support at, *xx*, 426
Word-in-a-Box exercise, 318, 330
Work/action plan, 90 day, 77
Work-life balance, 54–55, 61, 445
Work problem studies, 133, 136, 139–140,
    152–159
Workforce reductions, 84
Workforce Vitality initiative, 245–259
Workout process, 164–165
WOW! Projects, *xxvii*, 220, 221, 222, 227–228,
    231
Wright, T. L., 54, 55, 78

**Z**

Zander, B., 216, 225, 238
Zenger, J., 321, 408, 409, 410, 422
Zimmel, R. P., 369, 400
Zlevor, G., 212
Zulauf, C., 313–314, 333

# Pfeiffer Publications Guide

This guide is designed to familiarize you with the various types of Pfeiffer publications. The formats section describes the various types of products that we publish; the methodologies section describes the many different ways that content might be provided within a product. We also provide a list of the topic areas in which we publish.

## FORMATS

In addition to its extensive book-publishing program, Pfeiffer offers content in an array of formats, from fieldbooks for the practitioner to complete, ready-to-use training packages that support group learning.

**FIELDBOOK** Designed to provide information and guidance to practitioners in the midst of action. Most fieldbooks are companions to another, sometimes earlier, work, from which its ideas are derived; the fieldbook makes practical what was theoretical in the original text. Fieldbooks can certainly be read from cover to cover. More likely, though, you'll find yourself bouncing around following a particular theme, or dipping in as the mood, and the situation, dictates.

**HANDBOOK** A contributed volume of work on a single topic, comprising an eclectic mix of ideas, case studies, and best practices sourced by practitioners and experts in the field.

An editor or team of editors usually is appointed to seek out contributors and to evaluate content for relevance to the topic. Think of a handbook not as a ready-to-eat meal, but as a cookbook of ingredients that enables you to create the most fitting experience for the occasion.

**RESOURCE** Materials designed to support group learning. They come in many forms: a complete, ready-to-use exercise (such as a game); a comprehensive resource on one topic (such as conflict management) containing a variety of methods and approaches; or a collection of like-minded activities (such as icebreakers) on multiple subjects and situations.

**TRAINING PACKAGE** An entire, ready-to-use learning program that focuses on a particular topic or skill. All packages comprise a guide for the facilitator/trainer and a workbook for the participants. Some packages are supported with additional media—

such as video—or learning aids, instruments, or other devices to help participants understand concepts or practice and develop skills.

- *Facilitator/trainer's guide* Contains an introduction to the program, advice on how to organize and facilitate the learning event, and step-by-step instructor notes. The guide also contains copies of presentation materials—handouts, presentations, and overhead designs, for example—used in the program.

- *Participant's workbook* Contains exercises and reading materials that support the learning goal and serves as a valuable reference and support guide for participants in the weeks and months that follow the learning event. Typically, each participant will require his or her own workbook.

**ELECTRONIC** CD-ROMs and web-based products transform static Pfeiffer content into dynamic, interactive experiences. Designed to take advantage of the searchability, automation, and ease-of-use that technology provides, our e-products bring convenience and immediate accessibility to your workspace.

## METHODOLOGIES

**CASE STUDY** A presentation, in narrative form, of an actual event that has occurred inside an organization. Case studies are not prescriptive, nor are they used to prove a point; they are designed to develop critical analysis and decision-making skills. A case study has a specific time frame, specifies a sequence of events, is narrative in structure, and contains a plot structure—an issue (what should be/have been done?). Use case studies when the goal is to enable participants to apply previously learned theories to the circumstances in the case, decide what is pertinent, identify the real issues, decide what should have been done, and develop a plan of action.

**ENERGIZER** A short activity that develops readiness for the next session or learning event. Energizers are most commonly used after a break or lunch to stimulate or refocus the group. Many involve some form of physical activity, so they are a useful way to counter post-lunch lethargy. Other uses include transitioning from one topic to another, where "mental" distancing is important.

**EXPERIENTIAL LEARNING ACTIVITY (ELA)** A facilitator-led intervention that moves participants through the learning cycle from experience to application (also known as a Structured Experience). ELAs are carefully thought-out designs in which there is a definite learning purpose and intended outcome. Each step—everything that participants do during the activity—facilitates the accomplishment of the stated goal. Each ELA includes complete instructions for facilitating the intervention and a clear statement of goals, suggested group size and timing, materials required, an explanation of the process, and, where appropriate, possible variations to the activity. (For more detail on Experiential Learning Activities, see the Introduction to the *Reference Guide to Handbooks and Annuals*, 1999 edition, Pfeiffer, San Francisco.)

**GAME** A group activity that has the purpose of fostering team sprit and togetherness in addition to the achievement of a pre-stated goal. Usually contrived—undertaking a desert expedition, for example—this type of learning method offers an engaging means for participants to demonstrate and practice business and interpersonal skills. Games are effective for team-building and personal development mainly because the goal is subordinate to the process—the means through which participants reach decisions, collaborate, communicate, and generate trust and understanding. Games often engage teams in "friendly" competition.

**ICEBREAKER** A (usually) short activity designed to help participants overcome initial anxiety in a training session and/or to acquaint the participants with one another. An icebreaker can be a fun activity or can be tied to specific topics or training goals. While a useful tool in itself, the icebreaker comes into its own in situations where tension or resistance exists within a group.

**INSTRUMENT** A device used to assess, appraise, evaluate, describe, classify, and summarize various aspects of human behavior. The term used to describe an instrument depends primarily on its format and purpose. These terms include survey, questionnaire, inventory, diagnostic, survey, and poll. Some uses of instruments include providing instrumental feedback to group members, studying here-and-now processes or functioning within a group, manipulating group composition, and evaluating outcomes of training and other interventions.

Instruments are popular in the training and HR field because, in general, more growth can occur if an individual is provided with a method for focusing specifically on his or her own behavior. Instruments also are used to obtain information that will serve as a basis for change and to assist in workforce planning efforts.

Paper-and-pencil tests still dominate the instrument landscape with a typical package comprising a facilitator's guide, which offers advice on administering the instrument and interpreting the collected data, and an initial set of instruments. Additional instruments are available separately. Pfeiffer, though, is investing heavily in e-instruments. Electronic instrumentation provides effortless distribution and, for larger groups particularly, offers advantages over paper-and-pencil tests in the time it takes to analyze data and provide feedback.

**LECTURETTE** A short talk that provides an explanation of a principle, model, or process that is pertinent to the participants' current learning needs. A lecturette is intended to establish a common language bond between the trainer and the participants by providing a mutual frame of reference. Use a lecturette as an introduction to a group activity or event, as an interjection during an event, or as a handout.

**MODEL** A graphic depiction of a system or process and the relationship among its elements. Models provide a frame of reference and something more tangible, and more easily remembered, than a verbal explanation. They also give participants something to "go on," enabling them to track their own progress as they experience the dynamics, processes, and relationships being depicted in the model.

**ROLE PLAY** A technique in which people assume a role in a situation/scenario: a customer service rep in an angry-customer exchange, for example. The way in which the role is approached is then discussed and feedback is offered. The role play is often repeated using a different approach and/or incorporating changes made based on feedback received. In other words, role playing is a spontaneous interaction involving realistic behavior under artificial (and safe) conditions.

**SIMULATION** A methodology for understanding the interrelationships among components of a system or process. Simulations differ from games in that they test or use a model that depicts or mirrors some aspect of reality in form, if not necessarily in content. Learning occurs by studying the effects of change on one or more factors of the model. Simulations are commonly used to test hypotheses about what happens in a system—often referred to as "what if?" analysis—or to examine best-case/worst-case scenarios.

**THEORY** A presentation of an idea from a conjectural perspective. Theories are useful because they encourage us to examine behavior and phenomena through a different lens.

## TOPICS

The twin goals of providing effective and practical solutions for workforce training and organization development and meeting the educational needs of training and human resource professionals shape Pfeiffer's publishing program. Core topics include the following:

Leadership & Management

Communication & Presentation

Coaching & Mentoring

Training & Development

E-Learning

Teams & Collaboration

OD & Strategic Planning

Human Resources

Consulting

# What will you find on pfeiffer.com?

- The best in workplace performance solutions for training and HR professionals

- Downloadable training tools, exercises, and content

- Web-exclusive offers

- Training tips, articles, and news

- Seamless on-line ordering

- Author guidelines, information on becoming a Pfeiffer Affiliate, and much more

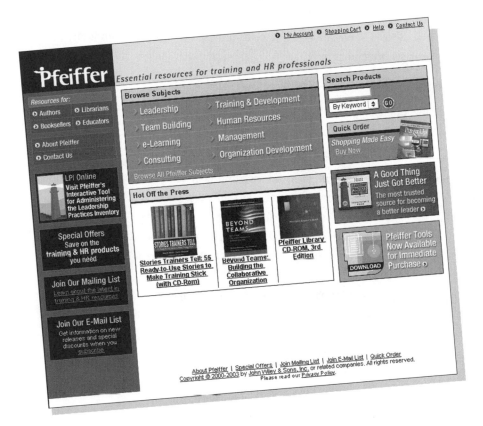

## Discover more at www.pfeiffer.com

# Customer Care

Have a question, comment, or suggestion? Contact us! We value your feedback and we want to hear from you.

For questions about this or other Pfeiffer products, you may contact us by:

E-mail: **customer@wiley.com**

Mail: **Customer Care Wiley/Pfeiffer**
**10475 Crosspoint Blvd.**
**Indianapolis, IN 46256**

Phone: **(US) 800-274-4434** (Outside the US: 317-572-3985)

Fax: **(US) 800-569-0443** (Outside the US: 317-572-4002)

To order additional copies of this title or to browse other Pfeiffer products, visit us online at **www.pfeiffer.com**.

For **Technical Support** questions call **(800) 274-4434.**

For authors guidelines, log on to www.pfeiffer.com and click on "Resources for Authors."

If you are . . .

A **college bookstore, a professor, an instructor, or work in higher education** and you'd like to place an order or request an exam copy, please contact jbreview@wiley.com.

A **general retail bookseller** and you'd like to establish an account or speak to a local sales representative, contact Melissa Grecco at 201-748-6267 or mgrecco@wiley.com.

An **exclusively on-line bookseller**, contact Amy Blanchard at 530-756-9456 or ablanchard @wiley.com or Jennifer Johnson at 206-568-3883 or jjohnson@wiley.com, both of our Online Sales department.

A **librarian or library representative**, contact John Chambers in our Library Sales department at 201-748-6291 or jchamber@wiley.com.

A **reseller, training company/consultant, or corporate trainer**, contact Charles Regan in our Special Sales department at 201-748-6553 or cregan@wiley.com.

A **specialty retail distributor** (includes specialty gift stores, museum shops, and corporate bulk sales), contact Kim Hendrickson in our Special Sales department at 201-748-6037 or khendric@wiley.com.

Purchasing for the **Federal government**, contact Ron Cunningham in our Special Sales department at 317-572-3053 or rcunning@wiley.com.

Purchasing for a **State or Local government**, contact Charles Regan in our Special Sales department at 201-748-6553 or cregan@wiley.com.